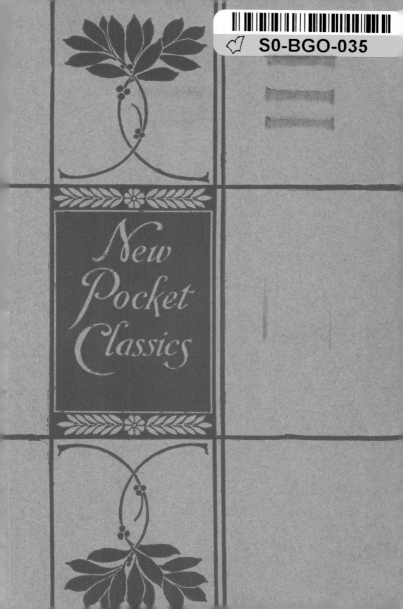

New
Pocket
Classics

New Pocket Classics

Essays — Yesterday and Today

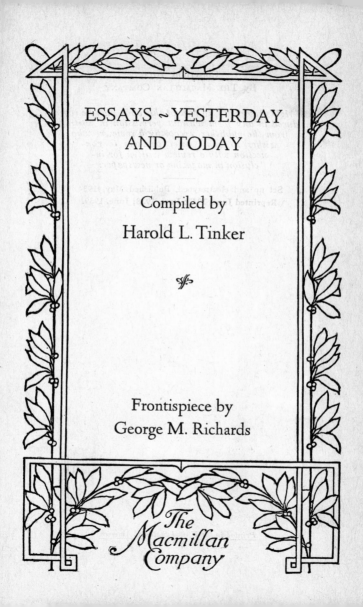

ESSAYS ~ YESTERDAY AND TODAY

Compiled by

Harold L. Tinker

❦

Frontispiece by
George M. Richards

*The
Macmillan
Company*

Printed in the United States of America

TO MY
FATHER AND MOTHER

ACKNOWLEDGMENT

GRATEFUL acknowledgment is hereby made to those who have so generously contributed to the formation of this volume by their friendly encouragement, criticism, and advice: my colleagues on the English faculty of The Choate School; Misses Lucy Roper and Ann Zetterholm of The Choate School secretarial staff; Professor Chauncey Brewster Tinker of Yale University; Dr. Ella P. Warner of Hillhouse High School, New Haven, Connecticut; Messrs. Frank W. Cushwa and Myron Williams of Phillips Exeter Academy, Exeter, N. H.; Mr. William Paxton of Moses Brown School, Providence, R. I.; Miss Marion Barnum of Commercial High School, New Haven; Dr. Bancroft Beatley of Simmons College; Dr. Charles Swain Thomas of Harvard University; and all those, authors and publishers alike, who have been so helpful in matters pertaining to copyrights.

TO THE STUDENT

Do you speak American?

Do you know that a single pair of house flies can have 5,598,720,000,000 descendants in five months?

Are you interested in athletics?

Have you ever tried to be like somebody else?

Do you know that the bee carries a pair of scissors on her knees?

Are you interested in the queer customs of foreign peoples?

Have you ever appeared in public in a hat much too large for you?

Do you enjoy bidding farewell to friends at railroad stations?

Are you in favor of war?

What would you think of a man who gave away a patent worth a fortune to retire to simple life in a shack in the woods?

If you are interested in these questions based on the essays which follow, you will not find the study of the essay so formidable as some students have thought it to be. The essay is not, as one boy put it, "a complicated, highbrow thing, over my head;" in its simplest terms it is but the statement of what one person thinks about something that interests him. Through the author's selection of subject and his manner of thinking about it, the reader soon gets to know what sort of person the author is. The essay is whatever the author is. Self-revelation is the basis of the essay form. Hence, the history of the essay is primarily the history of men who, by their differences, have molded the essay to express gayety, indignation, ridicule, scorn, as well as open admiration for the things in life which they have considered important.

In the biographical introductions to the essays included here, you will find clues to the influences which men of widely differing natures have exerted, and are still exerting, upon the essay form. To some of the essays, notes have been added, not as crutches upon which to lean but rather as a means of saving time in looking up references necessary to a full understanding of your reading.

You will doubtless disagree violently with some of the authors here presented. You will find that others have found expression for what you have often thought, and you will take satisfaction in agreeing with them. Out of your agreement and disagreement, it is hoped, will come that awareness of what you think about the world in which you live and the persons with whom you associate, which is the foundation of your education.

The Choate School   Harold L. Tinker
Wallingford, Connecticut
April, 1934.

TABLE OF CONTENTS

ix

ESSAYS—YESTERDAY AND TODAY

OF CUSTOM

Michel de Montaigne

The father of the essay form was MICHEL DE MON-
TAIGNE (1533–1592). The son of a prosperous herring-
merchant of Bordeaux, France, Montaigne was educated
privately by tutors, surrounded with all the cultural
advantages that money could buy. Waked in the morning by strains of soft music, surrounded by conversation in classical Latin throughout the day, trained to
decide for himself what he liked among his studies, Montaigne acquired, without knowing it, the instinct for the
familiar essay, a form not then known. At thirteen he began the study of law, and at nineteen became a member of
the Bordeaux Parliament. Then followed a successful career at court as an international lawyer. In 1571, his health
failed, and he retired to the family château outside Bordeaux to write. At that time the prevailing literary form
was the *leçon morale,* an impersonal prose form consisting
of anecdotes from the lives of the great men of ancient
Greece and Rome illustrating one moral or lesson, such as
bravery, honesty, wisdom. At first, Montaigne turned naturally to the *leçon morale* for expression, culling from his
fund of classical lore such material as would illustrate his
thought. After a few years, however, the sensitive nature
of Montaigne demanded fuller expression than the standard, impersonal form afforded; he then began to write
what *he* had seen, thought, believed. He began that revelation of himself which has come to be regarded as the true
test of the essayist. In 1580 his first volume appeared,

3

titled *Essais* and prefaced by his assertion, "It is myself that I portray," although less than half of the volume consisted of essays of the newer, revelative type. A second edition appeared in 1588 and showed still greater mastery of the more familiar style. To say that he was frank in his revelations is to understate. The *Essais* had great vogue in France, and were translated by John Florio for the English public. Their influence upon Bacon and other early English essayists was great; they were part of the literary background of the English Renaissance of the succeeding decades. After a return to public life as mayor of Bordeaux for a short time, Montaigne died in 1592. Three years later the complete revised edition of his works, containing the revisions and translations of quotations made by him just before his death, was published by his friend, Mlle. de Gournay. An excursion into these essays is like nothing else in the whole field of literature.

HE SEEMS to me to have had a right and true apprehension of the power of custom, who first invented the story of a country-woman who, having accustomed herself to play with and carry a young calf in her arms, and daily continuing to do so as it grew up, obtained this by custom, that, when grown to be a great ox, she was still able to bear it. For, in truth, custom is a violent and treacherous schoolmistress. She, by little and little, slily and unperceived, slips in the foot of her authority, but having by this gentle and humble beginning, with the benefit of time, fixed and established it, she then unmasks a furious and tyrannic countenance, against which we have no more the courage or the power so much as to lift

up our eyes. We see her, at every turn, forcing
and violating the rules of Nature:—

"Usus efficacissimus rerum omnium magister." [1]

I refer to her Plato's cave in his Republic, and
the physicians, who so often submit the reasons
of their art to her authority; as the story of that
king, who by custom brought his stomach to that
pass, as to live by poison, and the maid that Al-
bertus reports to have lived upon spiders. In that
new world of the Indies, there were found great
nations, and in very differing climates, who were
of the same diet, made provision of them, and
fed them for their tables; as also, they did grasshoppers, mice, lizards, and bats; and in a time of
scarcity of such delicacies, a toad was sold for
six crowns, all which they cook, and dish up with
several sauces. There were also others found, to
whom our diet, and the flesh we eat, were venomous and mortal.

These strange examples will not appear so
strange if we consider what we have ordinary
experience of, how much custom stupefies our
senses. We need not go to what is reported of
the people about the cataracts of the Nile; and
what philosophers believe of the music of the
spheres, that the bodies of those circles being
solid and smooth, and coming to touch and rub
upon one another, cannot fail of creating a mar-
vellous harmony, the changes and cadences of
which cause the revolutions and dances of the

stars; but that the hearing sense of all creatures here below, being universally, like that of the Egyptians, deafened, and stupefied with the continual noise, cannot, how great soever, perceive it. Smiths, millers, pewterers, forgemen, and armourers could never be able to live in the perpetual noise of their own trades, did it strike their ears with the same violence that it does ours.

My perfumed doublet gratifies my own scent at first; but after I have worn it three days together, 'tis only pleasing to the bystanders. This is yet more strange, that custom, notwithstanding long intermissions and intervals, should yet have the power to unite and establish the effect of its impressions upon our senses, as is manifest in such as live near unto steeples and the frequent noise of the bells. I myself lie at home in a tower, where every morning and evening a very great bell rings out the *Ave Maria*: the noise shakes my very tower, and at first seemed insupportable to me; but I am so used to it, that I hear it without any manner of offence, and often without awaking at it.

Plato reprehending a boy for playing at nuts, "Thou reprovest me," says the boy, "for a very little thing." "Custom" replied Plato, "is no little thing." I find that our greatest vices derive their first propensity from our most tender infancy, and that our principal education depends upon the nurse. Mothers are mightily pleased to see a child writhe off the neck of a chicken, or to please

itself with hurting a dog or a cat; and such wise
fathers there are in the world, who look upon it
as a notable mark of martial spirit, when they
hear a son miscall, or see him domineer over a
poor peasant, or a lackey, that dares not reply,
nor turn again; and a great sign of wit, when they
see him cheat and overreach his playfellow by
some malicious treachery and deceit. Yet these
are the true seeds and roots of cruelty, tyranny,
and treason; they bud and put out there, and
afterwards shoot up vigorously, and grow to prodigious bulk, cultivated by custom. And it is a
very dangerous mistake to excuse these vile inclinations upon the tenderness of their age, and
the triviality of the subject: first, it is nature that
speaks, whose declaration is then more sincere,
and inward thoughts more undisguised, as it is
more weak and young; secondly, the deformity
of cozenage does not consist nor depend upon the
difference betwixt crowns and pins; but I rather
hold it more just to conclude thus: why should he
not cozen in crowns since he does it in pins, than
as they do, who say they only play for pins, they
would not do it if it were for money? Children
should carefully be instructed to abhor vices for
their own contexture; and the natural deformity
of those vices ought so to be represented to them,
that they may not only avoid them in their actions, but especially so to abominate them in their
hearts, that the very thought should be hateful

to them, with what mask soever they may be disguised.

I know very well, for what concerns myself, that from having been brought up in my childhood to a plain and straightforward way of dealing, and from having had an aversion to all manner of juggling and foul play in my childish sports and recreations (and, indeed, it is to be noted, that the plays of children are not performed in play, but are to be judged in them as their most serious actions), there is no game so small wherein from my own bosom naturally, and without study or endeavour, I have not an extreme aversion from deceit. I shuffle and cut and make as much clatter with the cards, and keep as strict account for farthings, as it were for double pistoles; [2] when winning or losing against my wife and daughter, 'tis indifferent to me, as when I play in good earnest with others, for round sums. At all times, and in all places, my own eyes are sufficient to look to my fingers; I am not so narrowly watched by any other, neither is there any I have more respect to.

I saw the other day, at my own house, a little fellow, a native of Nantes, born without arms, who has so well taught his feet to perform the services his hands should have done him, that truly these have half forgotten their natural office; and, indeed, the fellow calls them his hands; with them he cuts anything, charges and discharges a pistol, threads a needle, sews, writes, puts off his hat, combs his head, plays at cards and dice, and all this with as much dexterity as any other could do who had more and more proper limbs to assist him. The money I gave him —for he gains his living by shewing these feats —he took in his foot, as we do in our hands. I have seen another who, being yet a boy, flourished a two-handed sword, and, if I may so say, handled a halberd with the mere motions of his neck and shoulders for want of hands; tossed them into the air, and caught them again, darted a dagger, and cracked a whip as well as any coachman in France.

But the effects of custom are much more manifest in the strange impressions she imprints in our minds, where she meets with less resistance. What has she not the power to impose upon our judgments and beliefs? Is there any so fantastic opinion (omitting the gross impostures of religions, with which we see so many great nations, and so many understanding men, so strangely besotted; for this being beyond the reach of human reason, any error is more excusable in such as are not endued, through the divine bounty, with an extraordinary illumination from above), but, of other opinions, are there any so extravagant, that she has not planted and established for laws in those parts of the world upon which she has been pleased to exercise her power? And therefore that ancient exclamation was exceeding just:—

"Non pudet physicum, id est speculatorem venatorem-
que naturae, ab animis consuetudine imbutis petere testi-
monium veritatis?" ³

NOTES

¹ Custom is the best master of all things. Pliny: *Natural
History*.

² Farthings are English coins worth a quarter of an English penny; pistoles, Spanish coins worth four dollars.

³ Is it not a shame for a natural philosopher, that is, for
an observer and hunter of nature, to seek testimony of the
truth from minds prepossessed by custom? Cicero: *Of the
Nature of Things*.

QUESTIONS

1. What customs have you retained from early youth?
2. What illustrations of the old *leçon morale* are found
in this essay?
3. What is your reaction to customs that differ from
yours?

OF STUDIES

FRANCIS BACON

When FRANCIS BACON entered Cambridge University in
1573 at the age of twelve, he embarked upon one of the
most brilliant careers in history. Already a member of the
English bar at the age of sixteen, he completed his education in France with the English ambassador, learning at
first hand the importance of political events at home and
abroad, which he emphasizes in his essay "Of Travel." In
the political arena of Queen Elizabeth his fortunes were
varied. His successes can be traced in part to his close
friendship with the Earl of Essex, the Queen's favorite,
and in part to the unusual sagacity of his brother, who was
perhaps the best informed man in European politics of the
period. His reverses were caused mainly by his undying en-
mity for Coke, the Attorney General under Elizabeth and
the bitter foe of Essex. At thirty-one Bacon wrote his famous letter to Lord Burleigh in which he announced, "I
have taken all knowledge to be my province," a boast
which he amply made good before his death in 1626. Pope,
the eighteenth-century satirist, called Bacon "the wisest,
brightest, and meanest of mankind"; and posterity as a
whole has accorded him a rank equalled by no man in the
world's history except Aristotle for eagerness and breadth
of mind. Bacon's first essays appeared in 1597 and were,
like Montaigne's earliest, chiefly moral reflections of his
reading, showing the old *leçon morale* influence. His later
essays, published in 1612 and 1625, show a gradual growth
away from the impersonal moral or aphorism toward the

greater revelation of his own thought and personality. This
present essay "Of Studies," without the italicized parts, is
as it appeared in 1597; the italics show the development
by Bacon for his 1625 edition. A striking picture of Bacon
as a man is presented in Lytton Strachey's *Elizabeth and
Essex*. There, better than anywhere else, may be seen the
human background of his essay "Of Travel."

STUDIES serve for delight, for ornament, and
for ability. Their chief use for delight is in pri-
vateness and retiring; for ornament, is in discourse; and for ability, is in the judgment *and
disposition of business*. For expert men can execute, *and perhaps judge of particulars, one by
one; but the general counsels, and the plots and
marshalling of affairs, come best from those that
are learned*. To spend too much time in studies is
sloth; to use them too much for ornament is
affectation; to make judgment wholly by their
rules is the humour of a scholar. They perfect
nature, and are perfected by experience: *for natural abilities are like natural plants, that need
pruning by study; and studies themselves do give
forth directions too much at large, except they
be bounded in by experience*. Crafty men condemn studies, simple men admire them, and wise
men use them; for they teach not their own use;
but that there is a wisdom without them, and
above them, won by observation. Read not to
contradict and confute; nor to believe *and take
for granted; nor to find talk and discourse;* but
to weigh and consider. Some books are to be

tasted, others to be swallowed, and some few to be chewed and digested; that is, some books are to be read only in parts; others to be read, but not curiously; and some few to be read wholly, and with diligence and attention. *Some books also may be read by deputy, and extracts made of them by others; but that would be only in the less important arguments, and the meaner sort of books; else distilled books are like common distilled waters, flashy things.* Reading maketh a full man; conference a ready man; and writing an exact man. And therefore, if a man write little, he had need have a great memory; if he confer little, he had need have a present wit: and if he read little, he had need have much cunning, to seem to know that he doth not. Histories make men wise; poets witty; the mathematics subtile; natural philosophy deep; moral grave; logic and rhetoric able to contend. *Abeunt studia in mores.*[1] *Nay, there is no stand or impediment in the wit but may be wrought out by fit studies; like as diseases of the body may have appropriate exercises. Bowling is good for the stone and reins; shooting for the lungs and breast; gentle walking for the stomach; riding for the head, and the like. So if a man's wit be wandering, let him study the mathematics; for in demonstrations, if his wit be called away never so little, he must begin again. If his wit be not apt to distinguish or find differences, let him study the Schoolmen; for they are cymini sectores.*[2] *If he be not apt to beat over matters, and to call up one thing to prove and illustrate another, let him study the lawyers' cases. So every defect of the mind may have a special receipt.*

NOTES

[1] Studies influence manners.
[2] Splitters of cummin seeds; hair splitters.

QUESTIONS

1. What sentences suggest the early date of this essay? See Introduction.
2. How would the title and content of this essay illustrate Bacon's statement that he took all knowledge as his field?

OF TRAVEL

Francis Bacon

Travel, in the younger sort, is a part of education; in the elder, a part of experience. He that travelleth into a country before he hath some entrance into the language, goeth to school, and not to travel. That young men travel under some tutor, or grave servant, I allow well; so that he be such a one that hath the language and hath been in the country before; whereby he may be able to tell them what things are worthy to be seen in the country where they go; what acquaintances they are to seek; what exercises or discipline the place yieldeth. For else young men shall go hooded, and look abroad little. It is a strange thing that in sea-voyages, where there is nothing to be seen but sky and sea, men should make diaries, but in land-travel, wherein so much is to be observed, for the most part they omit it; as if chance were fitter to be registered than observation. Let diaries therefore, be brought in use. The things to be seen and observed are: the courts of princes, specially when they give audience to ambassadors; the courts of justice, while they sit and hear causes, and so of consistories ecclesiastic; the churches and monasteries, with the monuments which are therein extant; the walls and fortifications of cities and towns, and so the havens and harbours; antiquities and ruins; libraries; colleges, disputations, and lectures, where any are; shipping and navies; houses and gardens of state and pleasure, near great cities; armories; arsenals; magazines; exchanges; bourses; warehouses; exercises of horsemanship, fencing, training of soldiers, and the like; comedies, such whereunto the better sort of persons do resort; treasuries of jewels and robes; cabinets and rarities; and, to conclude, whatsoever is memorable in the places where they go. After all which the tutors or servants ought to make diligent enquiry. As for triumphs, masques, feasts, weddings, funerals, capital executions, and such shews, men need not to be put in mind of them; yet are they not to be neglected. If you will have a young man to put his travel into a little room, and in short time to gather much, this you must do. First, as was said, he must have some entrance into the language, before he goeth. Then he must have such a servant, or tutor, as knoweth the country, as was likewise said. Let him carry with him also some card or book describing the country where he travelleth; which will be a good key to his enquiry. Let him keep also a diary. Let him not stay long in one city or town; more or less as the place deserveth, but not long: nay, when he stayeth in one city or town, let him

change his lodging from one end and part of the
town to another; which is a great adamant [1] of acquaintance. Let him sequester himself from the
company of his countrymen, and diet in such
places where there is good company of the nation
where he travelleth. Let him, upon his removes
from one place to another, procure recommendation to some person of quality residing in the
place whither he removeth; that he may use his
favour in those things he desireth to see or know.
Thus he may abridge his travel with much profit.
As for the acquaintance which is to be sought in
travel; that which is most of all profitable is acquaintance with the secretaries and employed
men of ambassadors; for so in travelling in one
country he shall suck the experience of many.
Let him also see and visit eminent persons in all
kinds, which are of great name abroad; that he
may be able to tell how the life agreeth with the
fame. For quarrels they are with care and discretion to be avoided: they are commonly for
mistresses, healths, place and words. And let a
man beware how he keepeth company with choleric and quarrelsome persons; for they will engage him into their own quarrels. When a traveller returneth home, let him not leave the countries
where he hath travelled altogether behind him,
but maintain a correspondence by letters with
those of his acquaintance which are of most
worth. And let his travel appear rather in his
discourse than in his apparel or gesture; and in

his discourse, let him be rather advised in his answers than forward to tell stories; and let it appear that he doth not change his country manners for those of foreign parts, but only prick in some flowers [2] of that he hath learned abroad into the customs of his own country.

NOTES

[1] Adamant here means a magnet, an obsolete use of the word.
[2] Embroider in some of the beauty.

SUGGESTIONS

1. Consider the highly organized tours of Cook or Whitcomb. Would Bacon approve of these? Give your reasons.
2. For a vivid, semi-historical view of Bacon, read Lytton Strachey's interesting novel *Elizabeth and Essex*. Therein Bacon practises what he preaches here. See also Maxwell Anderson's *Elizabeth the Queen*.

THE MASTER *

H. M. Tomlinson

HENRY MAJOR TOMLINSON was born in the East End of London in 1873 and early became familiar with London river traffic, working, as a young man, at "making out bills of lading for the *Cutty Sark* and all those 'now legendary clipper ships.'" Part-time writing during these early years found occasional publication in the London *Morning Leader,* for which paper he began full-time work in 1904. As war correspondent, as literary editor of *The Nation and Athenæum* (1917–1923), and as an independent essayist, he has earned a reputation as a finished craftsman interested more in ideas than in events. His boyhood enthusiasm for Emerson and Thoreau (whose *Walden* he used constantly to carry in his pocket) led to his pilgrimage to Concord in the spring of 1931, record of which was made in an essay in *The New York Herald Tribune.* This present essay, "The Master," is taken from Mr. Tomlinson's *London River,* which appeared in 1920.

THIS master of a ship I remember first as a slim lad, with a shy smile, and large hands that were lonely beyond his outgrown reefer jacket. His cap was always too small for him, and the soiled frontal badge of his line became a coloured

* Reprinted from *London River* by H. M. Tomlinson by permission of and special arrangement with Alfred A. Knopf, Inc., authorized publishers.

button beyond his forelock. He used to come home occasionally—and it was always when we were on the point of forgetting him altogether. He came with a huge bolster in a cab, as though out of the past and nowhere. There is a tradition, a book tradition, that the boy apprenticed to the sea acquires saucy eyes, and a self-reliance always ready to dare to that bleak extreme the very thought of which horrifies those who are lawful and cautious. They know better who live where the ships are. He used to bring his young shipmates to see us, and they were like himself. Their eyes were downcast. They showed no self-reliance. Their shyness and politeness, when the occasion was quite simple, were absurdly incommensurate even with modesty. Their sisters, not nearly so polite, used to mock them.

As our own shy lad was never with us for long, his departure being as abrupt and unannounced as his appearance, we could willingly endure him. But he was extraneous to the household. He had the impeding nature of a new and superfluous piece of furniture which is in the way, yet never knows it, and placidly stays where it is, in its wooden manner, till it is placed elsewhere. There was a morning when, as he was leaving the house, during one of his brief visits to his home, I noticed to my astonishment that he had grown taller than myself. How had that happened? And where? I had followed him to the door that morning because, looking down at his cap which he was nervously handling, he had told me he was going then to an examination. About a week later he announced, in a casual way, that he had got his master's ticket. After the first shock of surprise, caused by the fact that this information was an unexpected warning of our advance in years, we were amused, and we congratulated him. Naturally he had got his certificate as master mariner. Why not? Nearly all the mates we knew got it, sooner or later. That was bound to come. But very soon after that he gave us a genuine surprise, and made us anxious. He informed us, as casually, that he had been appointed master to a ship; a very different matter from merely possessing the licence to command.

We were even alarmed. This was serious. He could not do it. He was not the man to make a command for anything. A fellow who, not so long ago, used to walk a mile with a telegram because he had not the strength of character to face the lady clerk in the post office round the corner, was hardly the man to overawe a crowd of hard characters gathered by chance from Tower Hill, socialise them, and direct them successfully in subduing the conflicting elements of a difficult enterprise. Not he. But we said nothing to discourage him.

Of course, he was a delightful fellow. He often amused us, and he did not always know why. He was frank, he was gentle; but that large vacancy, the sea, where he had spent most of his young

life, had made him—well, slow. You know what
I mean. He was curiously innocent of those dangers of great cities which are nothing to us because we know they are there. Yet he was always
on the alert for thieves and parasites. I think he
enjoyed his belief in their crafty omnipresence
ashore. Proud of his alert and knowing intelligence, he would relate a long story of the way he
had not only frustrated an artful shark, but had
enjoyed the process in perfect safety. That we,
who rarely went out of London, never had such
adventures, did not strike him as worth a thought
or two. He never paused in his merriment to consider the strange fact that to him, alone of our
household, such wayside adventures fell. With a
shrewd air he would inform us that he was about
to put the savings of a voyage into an advertised
trap [1] which a country parson would have stepped
over without a second contemptuous glance.

He took his ship away. The affair was not discussed at home, though each of us gave it some
private despondency. We followed him silently,
apprehensively, through the reports in the *Shipping Gazette*. He made point after point safely—
St. Vincent, Gibraltar, Suez, Aden—after·him we
went across to Colombo, Singapore, and at length
we learned that he was safe at Batavia. He had
got that steamer out all right. He got her home
again, too. After his first adventure as master he
made voyage after voyage with no more excitement in them than you would find in Sunday

walks in a suburb. It was plain luck; or else navigation and seamanship were greatly overrated arts.

A day came when he invited me to go with him part of his voyage. I could leave the ship at Bordeaux. I went. You must remember that we had never seen his ship. And there he was, walking with me to the dock from a Welsh railway station, a man in a cheap mackintosh, with an umbrella I will not describe, and he was carrying a brown paper parcel. He was appropriately crowned with a bowler hat several sizes too small for him. Glancing up at his profile, I actually wondered whether the turmoil was now going on in his mind over that confession which now he was bound to make: that he was not the master of a ship, and never had been.

There she was, a bulky modern freighter, full of derricks and time-saving appliances, and her funnel lording it over the neighbourhood. The man with the parcel under his arm led me up the gangway. I was not yet convinced. I was, indeed, less sure than ever that he could be the master of his huge community of engines and men. He did not accord with it.

We were no sooner on deck than a man in uniform, grey-haired, with a seamed and resolute face, which anyone would have recognised at once as a sailor's, approached us. He was introduced as the chief officer. He had a tale of woe: trouble with the dock-master, with the stevedores, with

the cargo, with many things. He did not appear
to know what to do with them. He was asking
this boy of ours.

The skipper began to speak. At that moment
I was gazing at the funnel, trying to decipher a
monogram upon it; but I heard a new voice,
rapid and incisive, sure of its subject, resolving
doubts, and making the crooked straight. It was
the man with the brown paper parcel. That was still
under his arm—in fact, the parcel contained pink
pyjamas, and there was hardly enough paper. The
respect of the mate was not lessened by this.

The skipper went to gaze down a hatchway.
He walked to the other side of the ship, and in-
spected something there. Conned her length,
called up in a friendly but authoritative way to
an engineer standing by an amidship rail above.
He came back to the mate, and with an easy precision directed his will on others, through his
deputy, up to the time of sailing. He beckoned to
me, who also, apparently, was under his august
orders, and turned, as though perfectly aware
that in this place I should follow him meekly, in
full obedience.

Our steamer moved out at midnight, in a drive
of wind and rain. There were bewildering and un-
related lights about us. Peremptory challenges
were shouted to us from nowhere. Sirens blared
out of dark voids. And there was the skipper on
the bridge, the lad who caused us amusement at
home, with this confusion in the dark about him,

and an immense insentient mass moving with him at his will; and he had his hands in his pockets, and turned to tell me what a cold night it was. The pier-head searchlight showed his face, alert, serene, with his brows knitted in a little frown, and his underlip projecting as the sign of the pride of those who look direct into the eyes of an opponent, and care not at all. In my berth that night I searched for a moral for this narrative, but went to sleep before I found it.

NOTE

[1] A fraudulent scheme. Ministers and schoolmasters are popularly considered fair prey for frauds.

QUESTIONS

1. What moral would you attach to this essay? State it in one sentence.
2. How do you explain Tomlinson's last sentence?
3. How does this essay differ from the *leçon morale?* How does it resemble it?

THE KNOWLEDGE OF TREES *

A Fable

LINCOLN STEFFENS

LINCOLN STEFFENS (1866–   ) was born in San Francisco, California, was educated at the Universities of Berlin, Heidelberg, Leipzig, and Paris, and has been a journalist (on Metropolitan papers), magazine editor (*McClure's, American, Everybody's*), and a prominent free-lance writer. As correspondent for prominent papers, he has been intimately connected with national and international politics; as editor, he has been a clearing house for radical and conservative literature; as free-lance traveler and writer, he has studied, more deeply than most writers, foreign peoples and their philosophies. Confidant of statesmen, he is acutely aware of what forces combine to make and unmake nations. His writing is always provocative. (See *The Shame of the Cities, The Struggle for Self-Government, The Uplifters, The Last of These.*) His *Autobiography*, published in 1931, is an absorbing chronicle of one who, in a life unusually close to reality, found and drew forth good from individuals generally believed by society to be bad. His philosophy of intelligence and honesty will stir any reader who dares "to weigh and consider." "The Knowledge of Trees" well illustrates the elements of the fable, a fictitious story in which animals, or even inanimate objects, may talk and act like human beings.

* From *The Century Magazine*, December, 1924. Copyright by The Century Co.

SOME young fruit-trees were taken up out of the orchards of New England, shipped west, and replanted in California. There were hundreds of them, all chosen trees, selected with care and expert knowledge from the most famous orchards; chosen for their hardihood, quality, stock, and promise. An aristocracy they were, the best of their kind, and they came of breeds that had been picked over and transplanted before, many times before, and always for their fruitfulness. They were a real aristocracy.

Those trees might be expected to be all that trees can be, know in their fiber all that trees need know, behave as the wisest and most cultivated of trees would behave.

The test was hard. The change was great. They were to have every chance, all possible care. They were set out on the same side of just such hills as they had been born and bred on at home, and they were braced and watered, watched and nursed. Those precious baby trees were loved in California. But love and mere human thoughtfulness could not do everything for them. There were some things they had to do for themselves. And the greatest of these was to decide when to begin to bud and bear.

Now, it is not easy, even for a wise man—wise in the wisdom of plants and trees; it is indeed peculiarly difficult for a botanist, for example— to say when it is spring in California. The accepted signs are not always certain there. When the long drought of the summer is over, and the first fresh rains of the autumn fall upon and bathe and pour drink and hope into the famished soil, there spring to life plentiful plants, big and tiny, which in the cold East would wait for the snow to warm them and the perils of the winter to pass.

"So we don't know botanically," said the botanist, "when the spring is here, whether it is in the fall or in the spring."

And those young fruit trees did not know!

When they were of age, when the last terrible summer for strange trees was burned out, and the glad rains came down from the heavens, that new orchard had to act. They were ready, they were eager for the adventure; but, like all young things, they had to be wise. They had learned from their ancestors all that Mother Earth had been teaching them all through the ages. They knew what they knew. But in the circumstances they had to use their knowledge. They had to consider everything, and they did consider. The old orchardist saw them "think," he thought. He marked their natural impulse to bud; marked their halt of doubt; and, anxious himself, he declared that those beloved trees of his communed together, asked questions, answered them, argued. He said that they held a debate, and that everything that happened was turned into an argument. A cold shower was a cold shower upon the enthusiasts for spring; the warm drizzle of a hot day was a hot argument against the advocates of fall and the wait-for-winter party. Swayed by every wind that blew, moved by every bird that peeped, puzzled by the confusing variety of bugs that scratched conflicting signals on their hearkening barks, those cunning, knowing, sensitive trees held counsel day after day for weeks. And they did not, could not agree. They had to decide. It was a matter of life or death for them, and yet each little tree by itself had to answer for itself and act. And they did.

Some of them decided that it was spring, and they budded. Others held that it was fall, and they waited. And those that waited, lived and blossomed in the spring, and in the summer bore fruit; while those others that were sure it was spring and budded, were nipped by the frosts of winter and died.

MORAL

And so, you see, trees don't know any more than we do, not really.

QUESTIONS

1. How would you apply this fable to your educational life? to "the younger generation" problem?
2. What other applications of this fable can you make?

THE CLUB

RICHARD STEELE

The periodical essay originated in the eighteenth century, one of the "golden ages" of English literature, with SIR RICHARD STEELE (1672–1729). Born in Dublin in the same year in which Joseph Addison, later to become his famous co-worker, was born, Steele entered the Charterhouse School in London in 1684, at the age of twelve, and early formed that close friendship with and admiration for Addison which made possible some of the finest collaboration in all English literature. From Charterhouse, Steele went up to Christ's Church College, Oxford, but did not remain long enough to win his degree. Impulsive, ostentatious, impudent, generous, Steele could never be depended upon to follow any chosen course for long. The possibility of adventure in the army lured Steele away from his studies at Oxford without the knowledge and consent of his uncle-guardian, who promptly cut him off from the succession to his fine estate in Wexford, Ireland. After rising from the rank of cadet to that of captain, Steele ended his army career shortly after a duel with a Captain Kelly in Hyde Park in 1700, during which he seriously wounded his opponent and acquired a horror of dueling which was to be reflected later in his essays. The next year, in 1701, Steele produced his first play, *The Christian Hero,* which reflected the virtuous man whom Steele longed to be but, because of his many shortcomings, could not become. Therein we may find the beginnings of the famous *Tatler* and *Spectator* papers. Stung by the jibes of his associates at his conscious praising of virtue, Steele replied later the same year with a comedy, *The Funeral*, reconciling wit, good humor, and good breeding with virtuous conduct. After seven years of play producing, and serving his political apprenticeship by writing political pamphlets for *The Gazette*, he started *The Tatler* in 1709, a periodical newspaper appearing three times a week and signed with the name of Isaac Bickerstaff, which Steele appropriated from a satire by Jonathan Swift. The general purpose of *The Tatler*, according to its preface, was "to expose the false arts of life, to pull off the disguises of cunning, vanity, and affectation, and to recommend a general simplicity in our dress, our discourse, and our behaviour." His explanation of his pen-name appeared in the concluding number: "The general purpose of the whole," he says, "has been to recommend truth, innocence, honour, and virtue, as the chief ornaments of life; but I considered, that severity of manners was absolutely necessary to him who would censure others, and for *that reason, and that only*, chose to talk in a mask. I shall not carry my humility so far as to call myself a vicious man, but at the same time must confess, my life is at best but pardonable. And, with no greater character than this, a man would make but an indifferent progress in attacking prevailing and fashionable vices, which Mr. Bickerstaff has done with a freedom of spirit, that would have lost both its beauty and efficacy, had it been pretended to by Mr. Steele." The identity of Bickerstaff was guessed within two weeks by Addison, who was then in Ireland; and after the eighteenth number, Addison's contributions began and became increasingly numerous, though his total contributions, forty-two out of the total of two hundred and seventy-one, never approached Steele's own. In January, 1711, the publication of *The Tatler* suddenly stopped. The reason was soon evident. Two months later Steele started, with Addison, *The Spectator*, which appeared daily. Though greatly helped by the gifted Addison, Steele was the guiding, the creative, spirit in this venture, as he had been in *The Tatler*. For a long time Addison, by nature more suited to his age than Steele, enjoyed the reputation of being the greater of the two essayists. The more emotional Steele, however, has not been without his champions. John Gay wrote of him: "Bickerstaff ventured to tell the town, that they were a parcel of fops, fools, and vain coquettes; but in such a manner, as even pleased them, and made them more than half inclined to believe that he spoke the truth. Instead of complying with the false sentiments or vicious tastes of the age, either in morality, criticism, or good breeding, he has boldly assured them, that they were altogether in the wrong, and commanded them, with an authority which perfectly well became him, to surrender themselves to his arguments for virtue and good sense. It is incredible to conceive the effect his writings have had on the town; how many thousand follies they have either quite banished, or given a very great check to; how much countenance they have added to virtue and religion; how many people they have rendered happy, by showing them it was their own fault if they were not so; and, lastly, how entirely they have convinced our fops and young fellows of the value and advantages of learning." After experiencing political and financial success and failure, Richard Steele, the father of the English periodical essay, retired to his wife's estate in Wales where he died in 1729. Professor Hugh Walker has written of him: "There is such a thing as tone in writing, as well as style; and Steele at his best is as much superior to Addison in the former quality as he is inferior in the latter."

THE first of our Society is a Gentleman of Worcestershire, of antient Descent, a Baronet, his Name Sir ROGER DE COVERLEY. His great Grandfather was Inventor of that famous Country-Dance which is call'd after him.[1] All who know that Shire are very well acquainted with the Parts and Merits of Sir ROGER. He is a Gentleman that is very singular in his Behaviour, but his Singularities proceed from his good Sense, and are Contradictions to the Manners of the World, only as he thinks the World is in the wrong. However, this Humour creates him no Enemies, for he does nothing with Sourness or Obstinacy; and his being unconfined to Modes and Forms, makes him but the readier and more capable to please and oblige all who know him. When he is in town he lives in Soho Square.[2] It is said, he keeps himself a Batchelor by reason he was crossed in Love, by a perverse beautiful Widow of the next County to him. Before this Disappointment, Sir ROGER was what you call a fine Gentleman, had often supped with my Lord Rochester and Sir George Etherege,[3] fought a Duel upon his first coming to Town, and kick'd Bully Dawson[4] in a publick Coffee-house for calling him Youngster. But being ill used by the above-mentioned Widow, he was very serious for a Year and a half; and though, his Temper being naturally jovial, he at last got over it, he grew careless of himself, and never dressed afterwards; he continues to wear a Coat and Doublet of the same Cut that were in Fashion at the Time of his Repulse, which, in his merry Humours, he tells us, has been in and out[5] twelve Times since he first wore it. He is now in his Fifty-sixth Year, cheerful, gay, and hearty, keeps a good House

both in Town and Country; a great Lover of
Mankind; but there is such a mirthful Cast in his
Behaviour, that he is rather beloved than esteemed: His Tenants grow rich, his Servants look
satisfied, all the young Women profess Love to
him, and the young Men are glad of his Company. When he comes into a House he calls the
Servants by their Names, and talks all the way
up Stairs to a Visit. I must not omit that Sir
ROGER is a Justice of the *Quorum;* [6] that he fills
the chair at a Quarter-Session [7] with great Abilities, and three Months ago gain'd universal Applause by explaining a Passage in the Game-Act.

The Gentleman next in Esteem and Authority
among us, is another Batchelor, who is a Member
of the Inner Temple; [8] a man of great Probity,
Wit, and Understanding; but he has chosen his
Place of Residence rather to obey the Direction
of an old humoursome Father, than in pursuit of
his own Inclinations. He was placed there to study
the Laws of the Land, and is the most learned of
any of the House in those of the Stage. Aristotle
and Longinus are much better understood by him
than Littleton or Coke.[9] The Father sends up
every Post, Questions relating to Marriage-
Articles, Leases, and Tenures, in the Neighbourhood; all which Questions he agrees with an
Attorney to answer and take care of in the Lump:
He is studying the Passions themselves, when he
should be inquiring into the Debates among Men
which arise from them. He knows the Argument

of each of the Orations of Demosthenes and
Tully,[10] but not one Case in the Reports of our
own Courts. No one ever took him for a Fool,
but none, except his intimate Friends, knows he
has a great deal of Wit. This Turn makes him at
once both disinterested and agreeable: As few of
his Thoughts are drawn from Business, they are
most of them fit for Conversation. His Taste of
Books is a little too just for the Age he lives in;
he has read all, but approves of very few. His
Familiarity with the Customs, Manners, Actions,
and Writings of the Antients, makes him a very
delicate Observer of what occurs to him in the
present World. He is an excellent Critick, and
the Time of the Play is his Hour of Business;
exactly at five he passes thro' New-Inn, crosses
thro' Russell-Court, and takes a turn at Will's [11]
till the play begins; he has his Shoes rubbed and
his Perriwig powder'd at the Barber's as you go
into the Rose. It is for the Good of the Audience
when he is at a Play, for the Actors have an
Ambition to please him.

The Person of next Consideration is Sir AN-
DREW FREEPORT, a Merchant of great Eminence
in the City of London. A Person of indefatigable
Industry, strong Reason, and great Experience.
His Notions of Trade are noble and generous,
and (as every rich Man has usually some sly
Way of Jesting, which would make no great Fig-
ure were he not a rich Man) he calls the Sea the
British Common. He is acquainted with Com-

merce in all its Parts, and will tell you that it is a stupid and barbarous Way to extend Dominion by Arms; for true Power is to be got by Arts and Industry. He will often argue, that if this Part of our Trade were well cultivated, we should gain from one Nation; and if another, from another. I have heard him prove, that Diligence makes more lasting Acquisitions than Valour, and that Sloth has ruined more Nations than the Sword. He abounds in several frugal Maxims, among which the greatest Favourite is, "A Penny saved is a Penny got." A General Trader of good Sense is pleasanter company than a general Scholar; and Sir ANDREW having a natural unaffected Eloquence, the Perspicuity of his Discourse gives the same Pleasure that Wit would in another Man. He has made his Fortune himself; and says that England may be richer than other Kingdoms, by as plain Methods as he himself is richer than other Men; tho' at the same Time I can say this of him, that there is not a point in the Compass but blows home a Ship in which he is an Owner.

Next to Sir ANDREW in the Club-room sits Captain SENTRY, a Gentleman of great Courage, good Understanding, but invincible Modesty. He is one of those that deserve very well, but are very awkward at putting their Talents within the Observation of such as should take Notice of them. He was some Years a Captain, and behaved himself with great Gallantry in several

Engagements, and at several Sieges; but having a small Estate of his own, and being next Heir to Sir ROGER, he has quitted a Way of Life in which no Man can rise suitably to his Merit, who is not something of a Courtier as well as a Soldier. I have heard him often lament, that in a Profession where Merit is placed in so conspicuous a View, Impudence should get the better of Modesty. When he has talked to this Purpose I never heard him make a sour Expression, but frankly confess that he left the World, because he was not fit for it. A strict Honesty and an even Regular Behaviour, are in themselves obstacles to him that must press through Crowds, who endeavour at the same End with himself the Favour of a Commander. He will however in his Way of Talk excuse Generals, for not disposing according to Men's Desert, or inquiring into it: For, says he, that great Man who has a Mind to help me, has as many to break through to come at me, as I have to come at him. Therefore he will conclude, that the Man who would make a Figure, especially in a military Way, must get over all false Modesty, and assist his Patron against the Importunity of other Pretenders, by a proper Assurance in his own Vindication. He says it is a civil Cowardice to be backward in asserting what you ought to expect, as it is a military Fear to be slow in attacking when it is your Duty. With this Candour does the Gentleman speak of himself and others. The same Frankness runs through

all his Conversation. The military Part of his
Life has furnish'd him with many Adventures, in
the Relation of which he is very agreeable to the
Company; for he is never overbearing, though
accustomed to command Men in the utmost Degree below him; nor ever too obsequious, from
an Habit of obeying Men highly above him.

But that our Society may not appear a Set of
Humourists unacquainted with the Gallantries
and Pleasures of the Age, we have among us the
gallant WILL HONEYCOMB, a Gentleman who according to his Years should be in the Decline of
his Life, but having ever been very careful of his
Person, and always had a very easie Fortune,
Time has made but very little Impression, either
by Wrinkles on his Forehead, or Traces in his
Brain. His Person is well turn'd of a good Height.
He is very ready at that sort of Discourse with
which Men usually entertain Women. He has all
his Life dressed very well, and remembers Habits
as others do Men. He can smile when one speaks
to him, and laughs easily. He knows the History
of every Mode, and can inform you from which
of the French King's Wenches our Wives and
Daughters had this Manner of curling their Hair,
that Way of placing their Hoods; and whose
Vanity to show her Foot made Petticoats so short
in such a Year. In a Word, all his Conversation
and Knowledge has been in the female World:
As other Men of his Age will take Notice to you
what such a Minister said upon such and such an

Occasion, he will tell you when the Duke of Monmouth [12] danced at Court such a Woman was then smitten, another was taken with him at the Head of his Troop in the Park. In all these important Relations, he has ever about the same Time received a Glance or a Blow of a Fan from some celebrated Beauty, Mother of the Present Lord such-a-one. This way of talking of his very much enlivens the Conversation among us of a more sedate Turn; and I find there is not one of the Company but my self, who rarely speak at all, but speaks of him as that Sort of Man, who is usually called a well-bred fine Gentleman.

I cannot tell whether I am to account him whom I am next to speak of, as one of our Company; for he visits us but seldom, but when he does it adds to every Man else a new Enjoyment of himself. He is a Clergyman, a very philosophick Man, of general Learning, great Sanctity of Life, and the most exact good Breeding. He has the Misfortune to be of a very weak Constitution, and consequently cannot accept of such Cares and Business as Preferments in his Function would oblige him to: He is therefore among Divines what a Chamber-Counsellor is among Lawyers. The Probity of his Mind, and the Integrity of his Life, create him Followers, as being eloquent or loud advances others. He seldom introduces the Subject he speaks upon; but we are so far gone in Years, that he observes, when he is among us, an Earnestness to have him fall

on some divine Topick, which he always treats
with much Authority as one who has no Interests
in this World, as one who is hastening to the Object of all his Wishes, and conceives Hope from
his Decays and Infirmities. These are my ordinary
Companions.

NOTES

¹ The "Sir Roger de Coverley" was a square dance similar to the early American Virginia Reel.

² A fashionable quarter of London at the time.

³ Lord Rochester (1647–1680) who was a favorite of
dissolute King Charles I, died at 32, confessing that he
had been continually drunk for five years. Sir George
Etherege, a Restoration dramatist (1635–1691), fell down-
stairs while drunk and broke his neck.

⁴ Bully Dawson was a notorious, swaggering sharper of
the period.

⁵ That is, in and out of fashion.

⁶ A county Justice of the Peace.

⁷ County Courts, meeting every quarter.

⁸ One of the four legal societies which have the right to
admit English barristers to the practice of the law. The
other three, also named for their buildings, are the Middle
Temple, Lincoln's Inn, and Gray's Inn.

⁹ Longinus (213?–273) and Aristotle (384–322 B.C.)
were Greek critical writers. Sir Thomas Littleton (1402–
1481) and Sir Edward Coke (1552–1634) were English legal
authorities. The last named was the enemy of Francis
Bacon.

¹⁰ Demosthenes (384?–322 B.C.) and Marcus Tullius
Cicero (106–43 B.C.) were famous orators: the former,
Greek; the latter, Roman.

¹¹ Will's, in Russell Street near Drury Lane Theater, was
one of the more famous London coffee-houses of the period.

¹² Illegitimate son of King Charles II, much admired by
English society for his genteel manners.

QUESTIONS

1. What interests of Steele does this essay reflect?

2. What elements in this essay indicate the purpose which Steele avowed at the beginning of his venture in the essay field?

3. What qualities do you recognize here in eighteenth-century figures which present-day essayists are still criticizing?

THE SPECTATOR

JOSEPH ADDISON

After the severity of the Puritan Commonwealth, morality declined so sharply in the Restoration Period under Charles II that much of London felt "that something ought to be done about it." Blatant condemnation of sin would not do; the Puritans had done that, and it didn't last. So those of the Queen Anne periodical writers who wished that things might be different decided to use the more potent weapon of ridicule. The eighteenth-century periodical essay, then, represented a conscious effort of literary men to force men's customs or habits back into the patterns of morality. But to show the everyday man that he is no better than he ought to be, to make him realize the truth of the criticism instead of defeating it by sheer indignation and denial, demanded peculiar combinations of wisdom, patience, and genuine humor. Modern readers are all too conscious of the advertising which seeks to sell something by making it appear fashionable. Its appeal is, "Of course you have read, or bought Such and Such; Every One who IS ANYBODY has!" This modern method, in variant forms, was used by the eighteenth-century essayists, prominent among whom was JOSEPH ADDISON, who was born in 1672 when morality was out of style. "It is no small thing to make morality fashionable. Addison did it, and it remained in fashion," wrote one critic. Addison, the son of a clergyman who rose to the Deanship of the Cathedral at Lichfield, Doctor Samuel Johnson's birthplace, grew up in an atmosphere of refinement, scholarship, and piety, and early established a code of living from which he never deviated. After preparatory schooling in Lichfield, he entered Charterhouse School in London where he met Richard Steele, with whom he was destined to share fame as co-author of the *Tatler* and *Spectator* papers. At Oxford, his steadfast pursuit of learning led to high academic honors and a pension from the Crown to enable him to travel and study abroad as further preparation for a career in statecraft and political writing. Politics and authorship thus became intertwined, and upon his return to London, Addison, the Whig essayist, joined in that inimitable ridiculing of the stupidities and immoralities of the Tory lordlings and social figureheads, which exerted so profound an effect upon the manners of the English people. He contributed forty-two of the two hundred and seventy-one essays in Steele's *Tatler;* and two years later, now better schooled in the technique of the periodical essay, started with Steele *The Spectator* in which his most characteristic work appeared. Addison created the character of Sir Roger de Coverley, about whom many of the essays centered, Will Honeycomb, and part of the Spectator himself. In all, he wrote two hundred and seventy-four of the *Spectator* series to Steele's two hundred and thirty-six. More even in temperament than Steele, better disciplined in his thinking and smoother in expression, Addison immediately took his place as one of the most powerful forces in literary London. At Button's coffee-house, run by a former servant of Addison's, he met all the important literary and political figures of the day, and won their respect even though his cold aloofness prevented their giving him their affection. With his literary successes came political preferment, and he rose steadily in the councils of the Whigs until he became Secretary of State, in 1717. The year previously, he had married, after a prolonged courtship, the Countess Dowager of Warwick. Constantly failing health caused his retirement from public office to the splendor of Holland House, the Warwick mansion, where he died on June 17, 1719. It was characteristic of his entire life that he should call his dissolute stepson, the Earl of Warwick, to his death-bed and remark to him, "See how a Christian can die." He was buried with high honors in Westminster Abbey among England's great dead.

I HAVE observed that a reader seldom peruses a book with pleasure till he knows whether the writer of it be a black or a fair man, of a mild or choleric disposition, married or a bachelor, with other particulars of the like nature that conduce very much to the right understanding of an author. To gratify this curiosity, which is so natural to a reader, I design this paper and my next as prefatory discourses to my following writings, and shall give some account in them of the several persons that are engaged in this work. As the chief trouble of compiling, digesting, and correcting will fall to my share, I must do myself the justice to open the work with my own history. I was born to a small hereditary estate, which, according to the tradition of the village where it lies, was bounded by the same hedges and ditches in William the Conqueror's [1] time that it is at present, and has been delivered down from father to son whole and entire, without the loss or acquisition of a single field or meadow, during the space of six hundred years. There runs a story in the family, that my mother dreamt that she was brought to bed of a judge: whether this might proceed from a lawsuit which was then depending in the family, or my father's being a justice of the peace, I cannot determine; for I am not so vain as to think it presaged any dignity that I should arrive at in my future life, though that was the interpretation which the neighbourhood put upon it. The gravity of my behavior at my very first appearance in the world seemed to favor my mother's dream; for, as she has often told me, I threw away my rattle before I was two months old, and would not make use of my coral till they had taken away the bells from it.

As for the rest of my infancy, there being nothing in it remarkable, I shall pass over it in silence. I find that, during my nonage, I had the reputation of a very sullen youth, but was always a favorite of my school-master, who used to say "that my parts were solid and would wear well." I had not been long at the University before I distinguished myself by a most profound silence; for during the space of eight years, excepting in the public exercises of the college, I scarce uttered the quantity of an hundred words; and indeed do not remember that I ever spoke three sentences together in my whole life. Whilst I was in this learned body, I applied myself with so much diligence to my studies that there are few very celebrated books, either in the learned or the modern tongues, which I am not acquainted with.

Upon the death of my father, I was resolved to travel into foreign countries, and therefore left the University with the character of an odd, unaccountable fellow, that had a great deal of learning, if I would but show it. An insatiable thirst after knowledge carried me into all the countries of Europe in which there was anything new or strange to be seen; nay, to such a degree was my curiosity raised, that having read the controversies of some great men concerning the antiquities of Egypt, I made a voyage to Grand Cairo, on purpose to take the measure of a pyramid; and as soon as I had set myself right in that particular, returned to my native country with great satisfaction.

I have passed my latter years in this city, where I am frequently seen in most public places, though there are not above half a dozen of my select friends that know me; of whom my next paper shall give a more particular account. There is no place of general resort wherein I do not often make my appearance; sometimes I am seen thrusting my head into a round of politicians at Will's,[2] and listening with great attention to the narratives that are made in those little circular audiences. Sometimes I smoke a pipe at Child's,[3] and whilst I seem attentive to nothing but the *Postman*,[4] overhear the conversation of every table in the room. I appear on Sunday nights at St. James's [5] coffee-house, and sometimes join the little committee of politics in the inner room, as one who comes there to hear and improve. My face is likewise very well known at the Grecian, the Cocoa Tree,[6] and in the theatres both of Drury Lane and the Haymarket. I have been taken for a merchant upon the Exchange for above these ten years, and sometimes pass for a Jew in the assembly of stockjobbers at Jonathan's.[7] In short, wherever I see a cluster of people, I always mix with them, though I never open my lips but in my own club.

Thus I live in the world rather as a SPECTATOR of mankind than as one of the species; by which means I have made myself a speculative statesman, soldier, merchant, and artisan, without ever meddling with any practical part in life. I am very well versed in the theory of an husband or a father, and can discern the errors in the economy, business, and diversion of others better than those who are engaged in them: as standers-by discover blots which are apt to escape those who are in the game.[8] I never espoused any party with violence, and am resolved to observe a strict neutrality between the Whigs and Tories, unless I shall be forced to declare myself by the hostilities of either side. In short, I have acted in all the parts of my life as a looker-on, which is the character I intend to preserve in this paper.

I have given the reader just so much of my history and character as to let him see I am not altogether unqualified for the business I have undertaken. As for other particulars in my life and adventures, I shall insert them in following papers as I shall see occasion. In the mean time, when I consider how much I have seen, read, and heard, I begin to blame my own taciturnity: and since I have neither time nor inclination to communicate the fullness of my heart in speech, I am resolved to do it in writing, and to print myself out, if possible, before I die. I have been often told by my friends that it is pity so many useful discoveries which I have made, should be in the possession of a silent man. For this reason, therefore, I shall publish a sheetful of thoughts every morning for the benefit of my contemporaries; and if I can any way contribute to the diversion or improvement of the country in which I live, I shall leave it, when I am summoned out of it, with the secret satisfaction of thinking that I have not lived in vain.

There are three very material points which I have not spoken of in this paper, and which, for several important reasons I must keep to myself, at least for some time: I mean, an account of my name, my age, and my lodgings. I must confess, I would gratify my reader in anything that is reasonable; but, as for these three particulars, though I am sensible they might tend very much to the embellishment of my paper, I cannot yet come to a resolution of communicating them to the public. They would indeed draw me out of that obscurity which I have enjoyed for many years, and expose me in public places to several salutes and civilities which have been always very disagreeable to me; for the greatest pain I can suffer is the being talked to and being stared at. It is for this reason, likewise, that I keep my complexion and dress as very great secrets: though it is not impossible but I may make discoveries of both in the progress of the work I have undertaken.

After having been thus particular upon myself, I shall in to-morrow's paper give an account of those gentlemen who are concerned with me in this work; for, as I have before intimated, a plan of it is laid and concerted (as all other matters of importance are) in a club. However, as my friends have engaged me to stand in the front, those who have a mind to correspond with me may direct their letters to the SPECTATOR, at Mr. Buckley's in Little Britain.[9] For I must further acquaint the reader that, though our club meets only on Tuesdays and Thursdays, we have appointed a committee to sit every night, for the inspection of all such papers as may contribute to the advancement of the public weal.

NOTES

[1] William the Conqueror, Norman King, defeated King Harold of Britain at the Battle of Hastings in 1066.

[2] Will's famous coffee-house, near Drury Lane Theater in London.

[3] Child's coffee-house was located in St. Paul's Churchyard.

[4] *The Postman* was a news periodical of the time, appearing three times a week.

[5] A popular meeting place in St. James' Street, mainly for Whigs.

⁶ The Grecian, near the Strand, was for lawyers and scholars, while The Cocoa Tree, in St. James' Street, catered to Tories.

⁷ Jonathan's, near Cornhill, catered to brokers.

⁸ Backgammon, recently revived, was a popular game in the eighteenth century; blots were exposures of pieces so that they might be eliminated.

⁹ Samuel Buckley, publisher of the *Spectator* papers, had as his address The Dolphin Inn, in Little Britain, a section of London.

Questions

1. What difference does a knowledge of an author's life make in the reader's enjoyment of his work?

2. What difference does this make particularly in essay reading? What do you find in *The Spectator* that reflects Addison?

3. How can this character study be properly called an essay? What elements has it in common with the personal or familiar essay?

THE IMPORTANT TRIFLER

Oliver Goldsmith

One of the most picturesque figures in all English literary life is OLIVER GOLDSMITH. Born in County Longford, Ireland, in 1728 and tutored privately by teachers whom he either hated violently or worshiped, as he did Paddy Byrne who regaled him with stories and ballads of strange lands, he entered Trinity College, Dublin, in 1745 and early won a reputation for good-natured deviltry. Necessity forced him to work his way by doing menial tasks in the kitchen, and like Dr. Johnson, whom he was later to know intimately, quickly rebelled against the sneers of the more fortunate students. His escapades in college were characteristic of what was to follow. He studied for the ministry of the Church, but his lack of any real interest in the calling and his obvious shortcomings led those in authority to shake their heads dubiously when he appeared in scarlet breeches for ordination. He dabbled in medicine in Edinburgh. He traveled in Europe, tutoring, quarreling, playing the flute, and competing playfully in oratorical and debating contests. He would try anything. When, later, he proposed to publish a Natural History, Doctor Johnson remarked, "Goldsmith, sir, will give us a very fine book upon the subject; but if he can distinguish a cow from a horse, that, I believe, may be the extent of his knowledge of natural history." After writing some poetry and engaging in writing odd bits of biography and advertising matter for various publishers, Goldsmith met the great Doctor Johnson, who had published a Dictionary, had put the powerful Earl of Chesterfield in his place, and generally ruled the literary world. That was on May 31, 1761. Two years later, when Johnson started his famous Literary Club, Goldsmith was made a charter member, representing light literature, in spite of the opposition of certain members who deemed him unworthy of the honor of their intellectual company. There, as in the town proper, Goldsmith was the butt of many a joke; but fortified by the support of Johnson and by his own radiant good humor, he contrived to forge ahead in the circles where the opposition to him was strongest. Following Addison, Steele, and Johnson, he continued, in his *Citizen of the World*, to ridicule the weaknesses of society of his time, to reform through good-natured raillery. After the heaviness of some of the *Rambler* essays of Johnson, these lighter, more sprightly papers of Goldsmith did much to save the English essay from obesity and flat feet. He died in 1774 and was buried in the Court of the Middle Temple, most of literary London attending the simple rites. Washington Irving's *Life of Goldsmith* is a rich storehouse of anecdote about this picturesque and lovable man.

THOUGH naturally pensive, yet I am fond of gay company, and take every opportunity of thus dismissing the mind from duty. From this motive I am often found in the centre of a crowd; and wherever pleasure is to be sold, am always a purchaser. In those places, without being remarked by any, I join in whatever goes forward, work my passions into a similitude of frivolous earnestness, shout as they shout, and condemn as they happen to disapprove. A mind thus sunk for awhile below its natural standard, is qualified for stronger flights, as those first retire who would spring forward with greater vigour.

Attracted by the serenity of the evening, my friend and I lately went to gaze upon the company in one of the public walks near the city. Here we sauntered together for some time, either praising the beauty of such as were handsome, or the dresses of such as had nothing else to recommend them. We had gone thus deliberately forward for some time, when stopping on a sudden, my friend caught me by the elbow, and led me out of the public walk; I could perceive by the quickness of his pace, and by his frequently looking behind, that he was attempting to avoid somebody who followed; we now turned to the right, then to the left; as we went forward he still went faster, but in vain; the person whom he attempted to escape, hunted us through every doubling, and gained upon us each moment; so that at last we fairly stood still resolving to face what we could not avoid.

Our pursuer soon came up, and joined us with all the familiarity of an old acquaintance. "My dear Drybone," cries he, shaking my friend's hand, "where have you been hiding this half a century? Positively I had fancied you were gone down to cultivate matrimony and your estate in the country." During the reply, I had an opportunity of surveying the appearance of our new companion; his hat was pinched up with peculiar smartness; his looks were pale, thin, and sharp;

round his neck he wore a broad black ribbon, and in his bosom a buckle studded with glass; his coat was trimmed with tarnished twist;[1] he wore by his side a sword with a black hilt, and his stockings of silk, though newly washed, were grown yellow by long service. I was so much engaged with the peculiarity of his dress, that I attended only to the latter part of my friend's reply, in which he complimented Mr. Tibbs on the taste of his clothes, and the bloom in his countenance: "Psha, psha, Will," cried the figure, "no more of that if you love me; you know I hate flattery, on my soul I do; and yet to be sure an intimacy with the great will improve one's appearance, and a course of venison will fatten; and yet, faith, I despise the great as much as you do; but there are a great many damn'd honest fellows among them; and we must not quarrel with one half, because the other wants weeding. If they were all such as my Lord Muddler, one of the most good-natured creatures that ever squeezed a lemon, I should myself be among the number of their admirers. I was yesterday to dine at the Duchess of Piccadilly's; my lord was there. Ned, says he to me, Ned, says he, I'll hold gold to silver I can tell where you were poaching last night. Poaching, my lord, says I; faith you have missed already; for I staid at home, and let the girls poach for me. That's my way; I take a fine woman as some animals do their prey; stand still, and swoop, they fall into my mouth."

"Ah, Tibbs, thou art an happy fellow," cried my companion, with looks of infinite pity, "I hope your fortune is as much improved as your understanding in such company?"—"Improved," replied the other; "You shall know,—but let it go no further,—a great secret—five hundred a year to begin with.—My lord's word of honour for it —his lordship took me down in his own chariot yesterday, and we had a *tête-à-tête* dinner in the country; where we talked of nothing else."—"I fancy you forget, sir," cried I, "you told us but this moment of your dining yesterday in town!" —"Did I say so," replied he coolly, "to be sure if I said so it was so—dined in town; egad, now I do remember, I did dine in town; but I dined in the country too, for you must know, my boys, I eat two dinners. By the by, I am grown as nice as the devil in my eating. I'll tell you a pleasant affair about that: We were a select party of us to dine at Lady Grogram's, an affected piece, but let it go no further; a secret: well, there happened to be no asafœtida in the sauce to a turkey, upon which, says I, I'll hold a thousand guineas, and say done first, that—but, dear Drybone, you are an honest creature, lend me half-a-crown for a minute or two, or so, just till—but hearkee, ask me for it the next time we meet, or it may be twenty to one but I forget to pay you."

When he left us, our conversation naturally turned upon so extraordinary a character. His very dress, cries my friend, is not less extraordinary than his conduct. If you meet him this day you find him in rags, if the next in embroidery. With those persons of distinction, of whom he talks so familiarly, he has scarcely a coffee-house acquaintance.[2] However, both for the interest of society, and perhaps for his own, heaven has made him poor, and while all the world perceive his wants, he fancies them concealed from every eye. An agreeable companion because he understands flattery, and all must be pleased with the first part of his conversation, though all are sure of its ending with a demand on their purse. While his youth countenances the levity of his conduct, he may thus earn a precarious subsistence; but when age comes on, the gravity of which is incompatible with buffoonery, then will he find himself forsaken by all. Condemned in the decline of life to hang upon some rich family whom he once despised, there to undergo all the ingenuity of studied contempt, to be employed only as a spy upon the servants, or a bug-bear to frighten the children into obedience.

NOTES

[1] Twisted gold braid.
[2] Having seen, or possibly having been introduced casually to, them in a coffee-house.

QUESTIONS

1. What elements in this essay illustrate the eighteenth-century essayist's criticism of individuality?

2. What is the effect of using the name Tibbs? Look up *tibia* in the Dictionary.

3. Is the character of The Important Trifler still alive? What other petty bores could be satirized good-humoredly today?

IT SEEMS TO ME *

HEYWOOD BROUN

Since his leaving Harvard University in 1910 for having too great difficulty with Fraser and Squair's French Grammar, HEYWOOD BROUN has earned a wide reputation by his work on several of the metropolitan newspapers as sports writer, dramatic critic, and free-lance columnist. Today he is easily the Dean of the informal prose essay columnists, initiating with unerring skill such controversial topics as are sure to command the attention of the general public, inflaming portions of the public to ridicule and invective, only to start another topic when public interest begins to wane. Timely dissertations on popular philosophical subjects, politics, and manners—topics typical of the eighteenth-century periodical essay—Broun treats in such a way as to promote individualism rather than to suppress the individual or level him to the standard of society as a whole, as the eighteenth-century essayist sought to do. In 1923 when this present essay appeared, *The New York World* was easily the most brilliantly written newspaper in New York, with such leading writers as Walter Lippmann, editor; Franklin Pierce Adams, poet and columnist; Laurence Stallings, book reviewer; Heywood Broun, essayist-columnist; Alexander Woollcott, dramatic critic; Deems Taylor, music critic; Frank Sullivan, inventor of Martha Hepplethwaite and other creations of sheer nonsense; and Rollin Kirby, H. T. Webster, and Wortman, cartoonists.

* Reprinted by permission of the author. From *The New York World* of March 21, 1923.

This present essay is one of those starting a subject to foment popular interest. The digression on drinking, it will be noted, provokes the interest of those persons who might not be stirred by Mr. Broun's remarks on dancing. Mr. Broun now conducts his *It Seems To Me* column in *The New York World-Telegram* and is one of the leading spirits of the Algonquin Group, consisting of prominent metropolitan writers, actors, and wits who congregate for luncheons at the Algonquin Hotel. Mr. Broun was born in Brooklyn in 1888.

POSSIBLY we are growing more mature. This afternoon we threw into the wastebasket four letters which ended, "Of course, you won't dare print this."

In "Things Which Have Interested Me" (Doran), Arnold Bennett champions the younger generation. In his essay called "Dancing," he writes:

"As regards the spirit, the latest generation has rediscovered, or is rediscovering, the great secrets—lost since the Elizabethan Age—that the chief thing in life is to feel that you are fully alive, that continual repression is absurd, that dullness is a social crime, that the present is quite as important as the future, that life oughtn't to be a straight line but a series of ups and downs, and that moments of ecstasy are the finest moments and the summits of existence."

Mr. Bennett finds that "the most spectacular symptom of the new spirit is the revival and the full democratization of dancing."

"The curious and convenient thing," he writes, "is that dancing provides joy and ecstasy and the uplifting of the soul, and at the same time does positive moral, artistic and physical good to the dancer. It has practically none of the disadvantages which accompany other forms of diversion and exercise and discipline. You can get ecstasy out of a bottle of champagne or even a glass of beer (not to speak of six glasses), but the uplifting is no finer than what the dance affords; it is, in fact, less fine, and it has grave drawbacks, some of which may not be noticed for years, and some of which are very apt to be noticed the next morning. And dancing is a physical exercise quite as efficacious as, and far less tedious than, the ingenious contortions prescribed by training experts. Its effect upon the action of the skin is excellent; it develops the muscles; it renders the body lissom; and it fosters gracefulness of carriage. Further, it cannot fail to teach rhythm—an important matter which most citizens would remain quite ignorant of if they did not dance. The mere discipline of moving accurately to music is valuable; and so is the discipline of co-ordinating one's movements with the movements of another person."

This essay of Mr. Bennett's gives us just the inspiration which we have needed for some time to stiffen us in the resolve not to learn to dance. Or at any rate not learn all over again. As long as

dancing was regarded as depraved and vicious
we felt a moral obligation to participate. Once it
is revealed as nothing more than a new agency of
discipline we are satisfied to sit out and condemn
it. As something efficacious toward morality it is
just as easy to avoid tangoes as inspirational
talks.

Mr. Bennett has given his whole case away in
the points he has raised in his plea for fox-trotting
as something just as good and a little better than
alcohol. He admits the potential ecstasy which
lies in champagne and then seeks to compromise
it by pointing out that there is a price to pay. He
cites the very factor which has made drinking an
agreeable sport as one of the arguments against
it. Only the mean-spirited wish to be æsthetic
deadheads. Perhaps the most pleasurable sensation which comes to man, as he raises the cup, is
the thought, "Of course this is very bad for me;
I shall swear off next week." The glass is spiced
with danger.

The most tactless advertising campaign ever
conducted was that maintained by a great American distiller in the old days who hit upon the
slogan, "The whiskey without a headache." You
might as well expect big game hunters to flock to
a country in which all the lions were without
claws. The true Bacchian drinks, knowing full
well that he is going to feel fearfully the next day.
This prevision intensifies his interest in the pres-

ent. He clings to it more avidly than otherwise because the future threatens him.

But there is still another point to be raised against the advantages of dancing as presented by Arnold Bennett. It has many disadvantages which do not accompany other forms of diversion. For instance, golf is a much better game. It affords its ecstasies even to those who play badly. The complete joys of dancing (here we must have resort to a hypothesis which we cannot prove) are reserved for those who do it well. We fancy that most of the benefits, as enumerated by Mr. Bennett, will scarcely descend upon the man who dances badly. It may have an excellent "effect upon the action of his skin." Indeed it has been our observation that bad dancers profit more in this regard than others. But certainly the appearance of a duffer on the floor is not likely to promote grace in himself or anybody else.

"Moving accurately to music" may be valuable, but we fail to see just how the sum of human happiness is to be increased by the presence of those who do not move accurately. Save in certain rare instances it is possible that time, the great leveller, will tend to make even the most inept a little better. But this period of probation is too painful. The novice golfer does not have to go through this ordeal. By the process of handicapping he may meet the best of them upon even terms from the very beginning. As yet dancing has made no provision of this sort. Until there is some arrangement whereby we may receive two bisque per dance it is our intention to maintain an attitude of aloofness and contempt toward that great, earnest, swaying army of folk who are seeking to improve themselves through music.

Questions

1. What elements in this essay—in style or content—indicate its being directed toward the readers of the daily paper?

2. What portions of this essay reveal the differences between Mr. Broun and the eighteenth-century periodical essayists?

ON BEING A MARTIAL-FIGGER *

Arthur G. Staples

Arthur Gray Staples is known throughout Maine and northern New England as the owner-editor of the *Lewiston Journal*. For years his daily essay has turned what might otherwise be an impersonal news sheet into a living force among its readers. Sometimes he writes of some incident in his day, such as buying corn at a roadside stand from a lass with a twinkling eye; sometimes he reminisces about boyhood or college days; sometimes he wields a cudgel over some one who is trying to evade the laws of the land. Generally there is, in his essays, the trace of the editorial writer in his shaping the thought of his readers to support a decent, orderly standard of group living; but more apparent in all of his work is the true essayist's revelation of himself. Staples was born in Bowdoinham, Maine, in 1861, was graduated from Bowdoin College in 1882, and joined the staff of the *Lewiston Journal* the following year. Of his early journalistic work, he wrote in one of his more recent essays: "The *Journal*, the one live paper in Maine, had a city editor, a society editor, a city hall reporter, a baseball reporter, a prize-fight reporter, a specialist on weddings. I was it." He has continued to be it, and a great deal more besides. He is one of the best informed men politically in the state of Maine, and is, perhaps, closest to the minds of the people. Consequently, he is a power in journalistic and political fields, though he never runs

---

* Copyright by the *Lewiston Journal*. Reprinted by permission of the author.

ror office. He has cultivated Maine until he knows what idea will prosper in different localities; in return, his readers cherish him as one who is "Maine clear through." He is a diminutive man who likes to talk familiarly, though without affectation, about the Classics, political conditions, interesting personalities; and he is a past master at conducting a spelling-bee. He writes his essays rapidly and with little revision; he still considers his work as journalism rather than as literature. In this respect he is probably closer to the eighteenth-century periodical essayists in spirit than any other journalist writing in America today. The student will find, in the following essay, evidence of the editor's attempt to affect the thinking of his readers, by making them laugh at the militaristic spirit during the dark days of the World War. Mr. Staples has made selections from his essays from time to time and republished them in book form.

You rarely see an old chap like me or a sawed-off chap (one of the deferred-growth class), who has not a very strong martial spirit. They are certainly a warlike lot. And always were.

I used to march, in Masonic parades—or, at least, I did once. It was in Skowhegan. I have told the story once or twice to listening throngs, and most of the throng have been very patriotic, for quite a spell thereafter. If I could get it into a four-minute speech, I think it would sell bonds for liberty.

When we marched in Skowhegan, we had a short hike—only about thirty miles or so—on a medium warm day, say about 132 degrees in the shade. We were in light marching order—two luncheons, one dinner, three collations and the contents of four lemonade barrels in each man. Being a Sir Knight, I wore a *chapeau* several sizes too large, with a tendency to slip around sidewise and present a front view like Geo. Washington crossing the Delaware. Looked at from any angle, with the plume on the starboard side, and the knightly emblem of the cross on the port, I was a natty sight. I also wore a man-sized sword, which hung from a belt that was made for a large person, the outfit being borrowed. The sword hung down, therefore, in a sort of discouraged and depressed way; and the belt not having the proper friction against my abdomen (and I not having any· abdomen), it likewise slipped around in sympathy with my *chapeau* and got between my legs, so that really it was hard to tell sometimes which way I was marching; hard for me—harder for the Eminent Commander, who as much as said that I was no ornament to the parade. I wanted to be military and Knightly and I tried to be; but it was impossible, with only two hands, to keep my hat with the pointed end in front and my sword at my side. I kept both hands going and both legs going, and that was all any one Sir Knight could be expected to do.

I was in the rear rank. There were four of us in the rear rank: Two Sir Knights, a boy on a bicycle, and a man selling hot Frankfurts. It was very dusty. After we passed the fifteenth mile-post, the bicycle got a hot-box and fell out. On the twentieth mile, the Frankfurts began to ex-

plode with the heat, and one of them struck my
companion on the baldric and he fell out. After
that I brought up in the rear all alone. I never
saw it dustier. I hustled along working hands and
feet just as fast as lightning, now straightening
my hat and now pulling my sword out of my
shoes and leaping over it, anon—I will repeat
that word anon—doing my best. The head of the
parade was ahead of me; that much I knew.
Occasionally, I heard the far-off music of a
band. Now and then I saw the form of a comrade,
his plume nodding in the dust. And then, weary
of adjusting my hat, I let it slide where it would
over my nose and walked on, now in the darkness, now in the light, as the *chapeau* slid.

Along about six o'clock in the evening, as it
seemed to me, I met a man and asked him if he
had seen a Masonic parade. He said he understood it was yesterday. I told him that I thought
he was mistaken and would he inquire, because
I surely started today and if I had been walking
all night, I wanted to know it. He said he would;
and he did, and returning, said that I was right.
It was still today, not yesterday. He brought a
kind woman along; and she said she had seen the
parade, but that they all wore their hats differently. My sword then suddenly became tangled
in my legs as I endeavored to assume a military
appearance; and I stumbled visibly as I passed
on my way in the parade, leaving the man and
woman behind.

I caught up with my command at the twenty-ninth mile by getting a ride on a grocery cart, the boy driving frantically. I fell-in gracefully. Falling-in, or -over, was the best thing I did. I was received with enthusiasm. My appearance was surely *chic*. I was carrying my sword on my shoulder. That is all I remember until we were dressing up on the right, in front of the Skowhegan Town Hall and the band was playing "Onward, Christian Soldiers."

That night we had a dance in the Skowhegan Town Hall, and the next day we marched all day between Waterville and Fairfield, most of the time encircling graveyards. Since then I have not marched.

Today, I sit in my slippered years, thinking of my experiences in the battle-line. And I know that, if those old lines could be reformed and I could be attired as I was then, in that identical costume and placed on the Western Front, and the Germans could see me coming as I went through the streets of Skowhegan, the sight would so freeze the marrow of their bones as to give me free pathway to Berlin; and Berlin itself would evacuate and the Kaiser would plead louder than ever for peace.

QUESTIONS

1. What elements in this essay locate its date fairly definitely?

2. What elements make this essay independent of any given date?

LETTER TO LORD CHESTERFIELD

Samuel Johnson
(Feb. 7, 1755)

DOCTOR SAMUEL JOHNSON (1709–1784), the literary dictator of England in the latter part of the eighteenth century, derived most of his learning from browsing in his father's library and later informal study. When he went to London in 1737 to seek his literary fortune, he had to overcome the difficulties of a very trying period between two eras of prosperity—the one preceding offering considerable reimbursement to struggling authors for the dedication of a volume of poems, the one following offering financial rewards from public subscription to an author's product. In this dreary interval, however, Samuel Johnson, handicapped by poverty, by a mercurial temperament, and by a grotesque personal appearance, somehow managed to carve a career which has remained unique in the annals of English literature. So great had his reputation become in ten years that enterprising booksellers prevailed upon him to publish a Dictionary of the English Language, to appear in 1750. Responding to a friendly overture from Lord Chesterfield, one of the outstanding patrons of literature earlier in the century, Johnson formed an acquaintance with that fashionable and aristocratic Lord, and hoped, in spite of his independence of spirit, to secure from his new acquaintance some financial assistance in the work on the proposed Dictionary. The prospectus, or advance advertisement, of the Dictionary was published in 1747 and, as a gesture to win favor, was dedicated to Lord Chesterfield.

With the failure of the Dictionary to appear in 1750, however, the interest of Chesterfield gradually waned, impaired, no doubt, by the aristocrat's disapproval of the commoner's appearance and poor manners. When the Dictionary finally appeared in 1755 and won immediate acclamation on all sides, Chesterfield wrote a communication to one of the periodicals praising Johnson's work in glowing terms that practically sued for friendship. Johnson's reply, in the letter here presented, rebuffed the foremost literary patron of the day so completely as to inaugurate a period in which authors were freed from the domination of the patron. This letter might be called The Declaration of Independence of Authors.

To the Right Honourable the Earl of Chesterfield.

My Lord:

I have been lately informed by the proprietor of the World, that two papers, in which my Dictionary is recommended to the public, were written by your Lordship. To be so distinguished is an honour which, being very little accustomed to favours from the great, I know not well how to receive, or in what terms to acknowledge.

When, upon some slight encouragement, I first visited your Lordship, I was overpowered, like the rest of mankind, by the enchantment of your address, and could not forbear to wish that I might boast myself *Le vainqueur du vainqueur de la terre;* [1]—that I might obtain that regard for which I saw the world contending; but I found my attendance so little encouraged that neither pride nor modesty would suffer me to continue it. When I had once addressed your

Lordship in public, I had exhausted all the art of pleasing which a retired and uncourtly scholar can possess. I had done all that I could; and no man is well pleased to have his all neglected, be it ever so little.

Seven years, my Lord, have now passed since I waited in your outward rooms, or was repulsed from your door; [2] during which time I have been pushing on my work through difficulties, of which it is useless to complain, and have brought it, at last, to the verge of publication without one act of assistance, one word of encouragement, or one smile of favour. Such treatment I did not expect, for I never had a Patron before.

The shepherd in Virgil grew at last acquainted with Love, and found him a native of the rocks.

Is not a Patron, my Lord, one who looks with unconcern on a man struggling for life in the water, and when he has reached ground, encumbers him with help? The notice which you have been pleased to take of my labours, had it been early, had been kind; but it has been delayed till I am indifferent, and cannot enjoy it; till I am solitary, and cannot impart it; [3] till I am known, and do not want it. I hope it is no very cynical asperity not to confess obligations where no benefit has been received, or to be unwilling that the Public should consider me as owing that to a Patron, which Providence has enabled me to do for myself.

Having carried on my work thus far with so

little obligation to any favourer of learning, I shall not be disappointed though I should conclude it, if less be possible, with less; for I have been long wakened from that dream of hope, in which I once boasted myself with so much exultation,

My Lord,
Your Lordship's most humble,
Most obedient servant,
Sam. Johnson

NOTES

[1] The conqueror of the conqueror of the world.

[2] Macaulay's essay on the life of Samuel Johnson, in the *Encyclopædia Britannica,* gives the background of this statement. It is a classic in the field of the biographical essay.

[3] Tetty, Johnson's beloved wife, died three years earlier.

LETTER TO JEAN-JACQUES ROUSSEAU

JAMES BOSWELL

JAMES BOSWELL (1740–1795) is the outstanding biographer in English literature. Born in Edinburgh of a prominent Scotch family which traced its roots back to Tom
Boswell, a minstrel who died bravely in the battle of Flod-
den Field, James Boswell was never averse to telling of
his proud lineage, as this letter shows. At Edinburgh University he had the good fortune to become acquainted
with William Temple, who later became very prominent in
English political and literary circles. From that time on,
Boswell carefully cultivated the society of the prominent.
Macaulay's "Essay on the Life of Samuel Johnson" in the
Encyclopædia Britannica gives Boswell little credit for se-
lecting the truly great; calls him a coxcomb and a bore. It
is only recently that scholars have rescued Boswell from
the pit of ridicule and scorn into which Macaulay so sum-
marily pushed him. At the age of twenty Boswell went to
London and was introduced into London society, which he
amused and nettled by his capacity for doing untoward
things. In May, 1763, in Tom Davies' bookshop in London, he finally met Doctor Samuel Johnson, whom he had
stalked for weeks and whose name he was destined to make
immortal by his painstaking biography. With characteristic
promptness, he followed up the meeting with formal calls
and friendly visits, to the end that he soon won the heart
of "Dictionary" Johnson, the most powerful figure in the
English literary world. His slavish devotion to the great
man, his adroit questions which evoked the best that was

in Johnson, his persistence in the face of ridicule and scorn, are well known. Shortly after his meeting with Johnson, Boswell toured the Continent "in order to perfect himself." At that time Jean-Jacques Rousseau, eminent French philosopher and writer, was practising his theory of getting closer to nature (much as the American Thoreau did later), living in utter seclusion in the country. The world clamored to see Rousseau; he was not to be seen. Such a situation was Boswell's delight. How he won the coveted interview with the supposedly inaccessible Rousseau is shown in this present letter, written in French, which reflects the strength of personality which, in spite of the taunts of some of Johnson's more prominent friends, made him a figure to be reckoned with. The translation of Boswell's letter is by Professor Chauncey Brewster Tinker of Yale University, who has done much to restore to Boswell the credit that is his due.

Val de Traver, December 3, 1764.
Sir,

I am a gentleman of an ancient Scotch family. You know my rank. I am twenty-four years old. You know my age. It is sixteen months since I left Great Britain, a good islander, knowing hardly a word of French. I have been in Holland and in Germany, but not yet in France. You will therefore make allowance for my language. I am on my travels, with a true desire to bring myself to perfection. I have come here in the hope of seeing you.

I have heard, Sir, that you are exceedingly difficult of approach, that you have declined the visits of several persons of the highest distinction. For this, Sir, I respect you the more. Were you to admit everybody whose vanity makes him wish to say, 'I have seen him', your home would be no longer the retreat of exquisite Genius and of exalted Piety; and I should not press with such enthusiasm to be received there.

I present myself to you, Sir, as a man of unusual worth, as a man of sensibility, with a spirit both lively and melancholy. Ah! if all that I have suffered does not confer an unusual merit upon me in the eyes of Monsieur Rousseau, why have I been created as I am? why has he written as he has done?

Do you ask me for letters of introduction? With you is there need of any? In worldly associations, a recommendation is required in order to protect people without insight against impostors. But you, Sir, who have made such a study of human nature, is it possible that you should be deceived with respect to character? This is the notion that I have regarding you. Apart from the incomprehensible nature of the soul, you are perfectly acquainted with all the principles of both body and spirit, with their actions and their sentiments, in short with all that they can accomplish which exerts a genuine influence upon the man himself. It is for this reason, Sir, that I venture to introduce myself to you. I dare to submit to the test. In cities and in courts where there is a numerous society, a man may disguise himself, and on occasion may dazzle the eyes of the greatest philosophers. But I submit myself to the most difficult test. It is in the silence and solitude of your holy retreat that you shall judge of me; and think you that in such circumstances I shall be capable of dissimulation?

Your writings, Sir, have softened my heart, exalted my soul, kindled my imagination. Believe me, you will be delighted to see me. You are acquainted with the pride of the Scotch.—Sir, I come to you to render myself worthy of the nation which has produced a Fletcher of Saltoun [1] and a Lord Marischal. Pardon me, Sir, I am moved. I cannot restrain myself. O beloved St. Preux! inspired Mentor! eloquent and lovable Rousseau! I have a premonition that a truly noble friendship shall come into being this day.

I learn with great regret, Sir, that you are often indisposed. Possibly you may be so at this very time. But I beg you not to let this prevent you from receiving me. You will find in me a simplicity which will not disturb you, a cordiality which may contribute to make you forget your pains.

I have much to say to you. Although I am but a young man, I have had a varied life which will surprise you. I find myself in circumstances at once serious and delicate, regarding which I eagerly long for the advice of the author of the *Nouvelle Héloïse*.[2] If you are the charitable man that I believe you to be, you will not hesitate to give it me. Open, therefore, your door, Sir, to a man who dares to assure you that he has a right to enter. Have faith in a singular foreigner. You will not regret it. But I beg of you, be alone. Despite all my enthusiasm, after having written to you in this way, I am not sure that I would not rather give up seeing you for ever than see you for the first time in company. I await your answer with impatience.

Boswell.

TRANSLATOR'S NOTE

It would be futile to make a literal translation of Boswell's inaccurate and unidiomatic French. I have attempted, therefore, to render the meaning in such language as may suggest the English sentences which were floating in his mind as he painfully constructed his French letter.

NOTES

[1] Fletcher of Saltoun, Scottish gentleman soldier of fortune, who suffered banishment from Great Britain with the Duke of Monmouth, later returning to Scotland to worry the English rulers. He is famous particularly for his comment on the power of poetry: "Let me write the songs of a nation and I care not who makes its laws."

Earl Marischal, distinguished political figure, friend of Rousseau, from whom Boswell had recently learned that Rousseau was interested in the career of Fletcher of Saltoun.

[2] Boswell had, during the sixteen months thus far elapsed on the Continent, had a compromising love affair with the beautiful Isabella de Zuylen of Utrecht, the "Zelide" of his *Letters*. In July previous to this letter he had written her a masterly letter, full of brotherly advice and earnestly advising her to forget him.

QUESTIONS

1. Assuming the essay to contain a certain amount of self-revelation, can we rightly call this personal letter an essay? What qualities in Boswell does it reveal? How did Boswell differ from Johnson?

THE PRAISE OF CHIMNEY-SWEEPERS

CHARLES LAMB

The great master of the personal or familiar essay is "GENTLE CHARLES" LAMB (1775–1834). Born of a father who worked in the Inner Temple, one of the Inns of Court in London, he grew up in an atmosphere favorable to the love of books and literary people. At the age of seven he was sent to Christ's Hospital School, where the severity of the treatment only accentuated the gentleness of the boy and early made him known among his fellows as an exceedingly likable youth. There he made friends of boys who later became known in the literary world, particularly Coleridge and Leigh Hunt, and of Jem White, who appears in this essay. In November, 1789, when he was but fourteen, he was taken out of school and, soon after, went to work in a private office, the next year leaving to enter the South Sea House, importers, where his brother John worked. Finally in 1792 he entered the employ of the East India House as bookkeeper and remained in their employ for thirty-three years. In the winter of 1795, disappointment over love of Ann Simmons drove him temporarily insane and laid the basis of his unbounded sympathy for and devotion to his sister Mary, who later, in a fit of insanity, killed her mother. His sacrifice of himself and all that he might have wished for himself, in order to nurse Mary through her recurring insanity, has earned him the admiration of generations. His home and favorite coffee-houses were frequented by much of the best literary talent; his conversation and repartee became important in the literary life of the period. Slight of stature, dressed rather shabbily in outmoded clothes, given to punning in his humorous stammering, Lamb presented a figure closely associated with his literary work. Hazlitt called Lamb the best of indoor company. In 1820 the famous *Elia* essays appeared in the *London Magazine,* essays partly biographical, in which Lamb appeared as James Elia. It is upon these essays mainly that his fame rests. In 1834 he stumbled and fell and, lacking strength enough to recover from the blow, "sank into death placidly as into sleep". His grave is now cared for by a perpetual endowment from E. V. Lucas, a modern English essayist whose work reflects so much of the gentle Elia spirit. Lucas' *Life of Charles Lamb* is the best work on the subject. This present essay is typical of the whimsical tone of the *Elia* essays.

I LIKE to meet a sweep—understand me—not a grown sweeper—old chimney-sweepers are by no means attractive—but one of those tender novices, blooming through their first nigritude,[1] the maternal washings not quite effaced from the cheek—such as come forth with the dawn, or somewhat earlier, with their little professional notes sounding like the *peep-peep* of a young sparrow; or liker to the matin lark should I pronounce them, in their aerial ascents not seldom anticipating the sunrise?

I have a kindly yearning towards these dim specks—poor blots—innocent blacknesses—

I reverence these young Africans of our own growth—these almost clergy imps, who sport their cloth without assumption; and from their little pulpits (the tops of chimneys), in the nipping air of a December morning, preach a lesson of patience to mankind.

When a child, what a mysterious pleasure it was to witness their operation! to see a chit no bigger than one's self, enter, one knew not by what process, into what seemed the *fauces Averni* [2]—to pursue him in imagination, as he went sounding on through so many dark stifling caverns, horrid shades! to shudder with the idea that "now, surely he must be lost for ever!"— to revive at hearing his feeble shout of discovered day-light—and then (O fulness of delight!) running out of doors, to come just in time to see the sable phenomenon emerge in safety, the brandished weapon of his art victorious like some flag waved over a conquered citadel! I seem to remember having been told, that a bad sweep was once left in a stack with his brush, to indicate which way the wind blew. It was an awful spectacle, certainly; not much unlike the old stage direction in *Macbeth,* where the "Apparition of a child crowned, with a tree in his hand, rises."

Reader, if thou meetest one of these small gentry in thy early rambles, it is good to give him a penny,—it is better to give him two-pence. If it be starving weather, and to the proper troubles of his hard occupation, a pair of kibed heels [3] (no unusual accompaniment) be superadded, the demand on thy humanity will surely rise to a tester.

There is a composition, the ground-work of

which I have understood to be the sweet wood yclept [4] sassafras. This wood boiled down to a kind of tea, and tempered with an infusion of milk and sugar, hath to some tastes a delicacy beyond the China luxury. I know not how thy palate may relish it; for myself, with every deference to the judicious Mr. Read, who hath time out of mind kept open a shop (the only one he avers in London) for the vending of this "wholesome and pleasant beverage," on the south side of Fleet Street, as thou approachest Bridge Street —*the only Salopian house*—I have never yet adventured to dip my own particular lip in a basin of his commended ingredients—a cautious premonition to the olfactories [5] constantly whispering to me, that my stomach must infallibly, with all due courtesy, decline it. Yet I have seen palates, otherwise not uninstructed in dietetical elegancies, sup it up with avidity.

I know not by what particular conformation of the organ it happens, but I have always found that this composition is surprisingly gratifying to the palate of a young chimney-sweeper—whether the oily particles (sassafras is slightly oleaginous) do attenuate and soften the fuliginous concretions,[6] which are sometimes found (in dissections) to adhere to the roof of the mouth in these unfledged practitioners; or whether Nature, sensible that she had mingled too much of bitter wood in the lot of these raw victims, caused to grow out of the earth her sassafras for a sweet lenitive [7]

—but so it is, that no possible taste or odour to the senses of a young chimney-sweeper can convey a delicate excitement comparable to this mixture. Being penniless, they will yet hang their black heads over the ascending steam, to gratify one sense if possible, seemingly no less pleased than those domestic animals—cats—when they purr over a new-found sprig of valerian. There is something more in these sympathies than philosophy can inculcate.

Now albeit Mr. Read boasteth, not without reason, that his is the *only Salopian house;* yet be it known to thee, reader—if thou art one who keepest what are called good hours, thou art haply ignorant of the fact—he hath a race of industrious imitators, who from stalls, and under open sky, dispense the same savoury mess to humbler customers, at that dead time of the dawn, when (as extremes meet) the rake, reeling home from his midnight cups, and the hard-handed artizan leaving his bed to resume the premature labours of the day, jostle, not unfrequently to the manifest disconcerting of the former, for the honours of the pavement. It is the time when, in summer, between the expired and the not yet relumined kitchen-fires, the kennels of our fair metropolis give forth their least satisfactory odours. The rake, who wisheth to dissipate his o'ernight vapours in more grateful coffee, curses the ungenial fume, as he passeth;

but the artizan stops to taste, and blesses the fragrant breakfast.

This is Saloop—the precocious herb-woman's darling—the delight of the early gardener, who transports his smoking cabbages by break of day from Hammersmith to Covent Garden's famed piazzas [8]—the delight, and oh! I fear, too often the envy, of the unpennied sweep. Him shouldst thou haply encounter, with his dim visage pendent over the grateful steam, regale him with a sumptuous basin (it will cost thee but three-half-pennies) and a slice of delicate bread and butter (an added half-penny)—so may thy culinary fires, eased of the o'ercharged secretions from thy worse-placed hospitalities, curl up a lighter volume to the welkin—so may the descending soot never taint thy costly well-ingredienced soups—nor the odious cry, quick-reaching from street to street, of the *fired chimney*, invite the rattling engines from ten adjacent parishes, to disturb for a casual scintillation thy peace and pocket!

I am by nature extremely susceptible of street affronts; [9] the jeers and taunts of the populace; the low-bred triumph they display over the casual trip, or splashed stocking, of a gentleman. Yet can I endure the jocularity of a young sweep with something more than forgiveness.—In the last winter but one, pacing along Cheapside with my accustomed precipitation when I walk westward, a treacherous slide brought me upon my back in an instant. I scrambled up with pain and shame enough—yet outwardly trying to face it down, as if nothing had happened—when the roguish grin of one of these young wits encountered me. There he stood, pointing me out with his dusky finger to the mob, and to a poor woman (I suppose his mother) in particular, till the tears for the exquisiteness of the fun (so he thought it) worked themselves out at the corners of his poor red eyes, red from many a previous weeping, and soot-inflamed, yet twinkling through all with such a joy, snatched out of desolation, that Hogarth [10]—but Hogarth has got him already (how could he miss him?) in the March to Finchley, grinning at the pieman—there he stood, as he stands in the picture, irremovable, as if the jest was to last for ever—with such a maximum of glee, and minimum of mischief, in his mirth— for the grin of a genuine sweep hath absolutely no malice in it—that I could have been content, if the honour of a gentleman might endure it, to have remained his butt and his mockery till midnight.

I am by theory obdurate to the seductiveness of what are called a fine set of teeth. Every pair of rosy lips (the ladies must pardon me) is a casket presumably holding such jewels; but, methinks, they should take leave to "air" them as frugally as possible. The fine lady, or fine gentleman, who show me their teeth, show me bones. Yet must I confess, that from the mouth of a true sweep a display (even to ostentation) of

those white and shining ossifications, strikes me
as an agreeable anomaly in manners, and an
allowable piece of foppery. It is, as when

A sable cloud
Turns forth her silver lining on the night.[11]

It is like some remnant of gentry not quite extinct; a badge of better days; a hint of nobility:
—and, doubtless, under the obscuring darkness
and double night of their forlorn disguisement,
oftentimes lurketh good blood, and gentle conditions, derived from lost ancestry, and a lapsed
pedigree. The premature apprenticements of
these tender victims give but too much encouragement, I fear, to clandestine and almost infan-
tile abductions; the seeds of civility and true
courtesy, so often discernible in these young
grafts (not otherwise to be accounted for) plainly
hint at some forced adoptions; many noble
Rachels mourning for their children,[12] even in our
days, countenance the fact; the tales of fairy
spiriting may shadow a lamentable verity, and
the recovery of the young Montagu be but a
solitary instance of good fortune out of many
irreparable and hopeless *defiliations*.[13]

In one of the state-beds at Arundel Castle, a
few years since—under a ducal canopy—(that
seat of the Howards [14] is an object of curiosity
to visitors, chiefly for its beds, in which the late
duke was especially a connoisseur)—encircled
with curtains of delicatest crimson, with starry

coronets inwoven—folded between a pair of
sheets whiter and softer than the lap where Venus
lulled Ascanius [15]—was discovered by chance,
after all methods of search had failed, at noon-
day, fast asleep, a lost chimney-sweeper. The
little creature, having somehow confounded his
passage among the intricacies of those lordly
chimneys, by some unknown aperture had
alighted upon this magnificent chamber; and,
tired with his tedious explorations, was unable
to resist the delicious invitement to repose, which
he there saw exhibited; so creeping between the
sheets very quietly, laid his black head upon the
pillow, and slept like a young Howard.

Such is the account given to the visitors at the
Castle.—But I cannot help seeming to perceive
a confirmation of what I had just hinted at in this
story. A high instinct was at work in the case, or
I am mistaken. Is it probable that a poor child
of that description, with whatever weariness he
might be visited, would have ventured, under
such a penalty as he would be taught to expect,
to uncover the sheets of a Duke's bed, and deliberately to lay himself down between them,
when the rug, or the carpet, presented an obvious
couch, still far above his pretensions—is this
probable, I would ask, if the great power of nature, which I contend for, had not been mani-
fested within him, prompting to the adventure?
Doubtless this young nobleman (for such my
mind misgives me that he must be) was allured

by some memory, not amounting to full consciousness, of his condition in infancy, when he was used to be lapped by his mother, or his nurse, in just such sheets as he there found, into which he was but now creeping back as into his proper *incunabula*,[16] and resting-place.—By no other theory than by this sentiment of a pre-existent state (as I may call it), can I explain a deed so venturous, and, indeed, upon any other system, so indecorous, in this tender, but unseasonable, sleeper.

My pleasant friend Jem White [17] was so impressed with a belief of metamorphoses like this frequently taking place, that in some sort to reverse the wrongs of fortune in these poor changelings, he instituted an annual feast of chimney-sweepers, at which it was his pleasure to officiate as host and waiter. It was a solemn supper held in Smithfield, upon the yearly return of the fair of St. Bartholomew.[18] Cards were issued a week before to the master-sweeps in and about the metropolis, confining the invitation to their younger fry. Now and then an elderly stripling would get in among us, and be good-naturedly winked at; but our main body were infantry. One unfortunate wight, indeed, who, relying upon his dusky suit, had intruded himself into our party, but by tokens was providentially discovered in time to be no chimney-sweeper, (all is not soot which looks so,) was quoited out of the presence with universal indignation, as not having on

the wedding garment; but in general the greatest
harmony prevailed. The place chosen was a convenient spot among the pens, at the north side of
the fair, not so far distant as to be impervious to
the agreeable hubbub of that vanity, but remote
enough not to be obvious to the interruption of
every gaping spectator in it. The guests assembled
about seven. In those little temporary parlours
three tables were spread with napery, not so fine
as substantial, and at every board a comely
hostess presided with her pan of hissing sausages.
The nostrils of the young rogues dilated at the
savour. James White, as head waiter, had charge
of the first table; and myself, with our trusty
companion Bigod,[19] ordinarily ministered to the
other two. There was clambering and jostling,
you may be sure, who should get at the first table,
for Rochester [20] in his maddest days could not
have done the humours of the scene with more
spirit than my friend. After some general expression of thanks for the honour the company had
done him, his inaugural ceremony was to clasp
the greasy waist of old dame Ursula (the fattest
of the three), that stood frying and fretting, half-
blessing, half-cursing "the gentleman," and im-
print upon her chaste lips a tender salute, whereat
the universal host would set up a shout that tore
the concave, while hundreds of grinning teeth
startled the night with their brightness. O it was
a pleasure to see the sable younkers lick in the
unctuous meat, with his more unctuous sayings—

how he would fit the tit-bits to the puny mouths, reserving the lengthier links for the seniors—how he would intercept a morsel even in the jaws of some young desperado, declaring it "must to the pan again to be browned, for it was not fit for a gentleman's eating"—how he would recommend this slice of white bread, or that piece of kissing-crust, to a tender juvenile, advising them all to have a care of cracking their teeth, which were their best patrimony,—how genteelly he would deal about the small ale, as if it were wine, naming the brewer, and protesting, if it were not good, he should lose their custom; with a special recommendation to wipe the lip before drinking. Then we had our toasts—"the King,"—"the Cloth," [21]—which, whether they understood or not, was equally diverting and flattering; and for a crowning sentiment, which never failed, "May the Brush supersede the Laurel!" All these, and fifty other fancies, which were rather felt than comprehended by his guests, would he utter, standing upon tables, and prefacing every sentiment with a "Gentlemen, give me leave to propose so and so," which was a prodigious comfort to those young orphans; every now and then stuffing into his mouth (for it did not do to be squeamish on these occasions) indiscriminate pieces of those reeking sausages, which pleased them mightily, and was the savouriest part, you may believe, of the entertainment.

> Golden lads and lasses must,
> As chimney-sweepers, come to dust——[22]

James White is extinct, and with him these suppers have long ceased. He carried away with him half the fun of the world when he died—of my world at least. His old clients look for him among the pens; and, missing him, reproach the altered feast of St. Bartholomew, and the glory of Smithfield departed for ever.

NOTES

[1] blackness.

[2] the jaws of Hell.

[3] chapped, cracked.

[4] called. "In Heaven yclept Euphrosyne." Milton's *L'Allegro*.

[5] The olfactory nerves control the sense of smell.

[6] soot deposits.

[7] a mild laxative.

[8] open squares where the produce markets are held.

[9] With unpaved walks and streets, rainy London presented many opportunities for ruffians to elbow "quality" away from the inside of the walk—next the buildings, where there was shelter—and out into the splashings from passing carriages, or even into puddles.

[10] William Hogarth (1697–1764), excelled in comic and satiric painting and engraving.

[11] From Milton's *Comus*.

[12] See the story of Rachel in the Bible, 31st Chapter of Jeremiah.

[13] Lady Wortley Montagu's son Edward once ran away from school and became a chimney-sweep. Defiliations: losses of children.

[14] The Howards, dukes of Norfolk, rank next to royalty.

[15] Venus, the Goddess of Love and Beauty; Ascanius, the son of Æneas. *Æneid* Book I, lines 643 and following.

[16] incunabula: cradle or even swaddling clothes. It is now used to denote early printing, especially books before 1500.

[17] James White (1775–1820) attended Christ's Hospital with Lamb.

[18] This fair, started in the 12th century, was discontinued in 1855.

[19] An excellent appraisal of Lamb's friend Ralph Bigod, Esq. (John Fenwick) may be found in Lamb's essay *The Two Races of Men*.

[20] The second Earl of Rochester, companion and confidant of Charles II, was widely known for his wildness.

[21] The clergy.

[22] From Shakespeare's *Cymbeline*.

QUESTIONS

1. What parts of this essay illustrate the elements of "the familiar essay"?

2. What elements here account for Lamb's being called "gentle Charles"?

3. On what is Lamb's humor based—situation, character, or word-choice?

OLD CHINA

Charles Lamb

Adversity always seems more pleasant in retrospect. In this essay we find James Elia (Lamb) and his cousin Bridget (his sister Mary) looking back upon the years when they were less well off, and recapturing some of the romance of their earlier struggles. Old chinaware is only one of the delights they have sought earlier. There are other things in this essay which remind us that to recall past pleasures and disappointments is one of the best possible means of escaping sorrow. For further biographical detail about Lamb and what this situation with his sister meant to him, refer to the biography on pages 79-80.

I HAVE an almost feminine partiality for old china. When I go to see any great house, I inquire for the china-closet, and next for the picture-gallery. I cannot defend the order of preference, but by saying that we have all some taste or other, of too ancient a date to admit of our remembering distinctly that it was an acquired one. I can call to mind the first play, and the first exhibition, that I was taken to; but I am not conscious of a time when china jars and saucers were introduced into my imagination.

I had no repugnance then—why should I now

have?—to those little, lawless, azure-tinctured grotesques, that, under the notion of men and women, float about, uncircumscribed by any element, in that world before perspective—a china tea-cup.

I like to see my old friends—whom distance cannot diminish—figuring up in the air (so they appear to our optics), yet on *terra firma* still—for so we must in courtesy interpret that speck of deeper blue, which the decorous artist, to prevent absurdity, had made to spring up beneath their sandals.

I love the men with women's faces, and the women, if possible, with still more womanish expressions.

Here is a young and courtly Mandarin, handing tea to a lady from a salver—two miles off.[1] See how distance seems to set off respect! And here the same lady, or another—for likeness is identity on tea-cups—is stepping into a little fairy boat, moored on the hither side of this calm garden river, with a dainty mincing foot, which in a right angle of incidence (as angles go in our world) must infallibly land her in the midst of a flowery mead—a furlong off on the other side of the same strange stream!

Farther on—if far or near can be predicated of their world—see horses, trees, pagodas, dancing the hays.[2]

Here—a cow and rabbit couchant, and coextensive—so objects show, seen through the lucid atmosphere of fine Cathay.

I was pointing out to my cousin last evening, over our Hyson[3] (which we are old-fashioned enough to drink unmixed still of an afternoon), some of these *speciosa miracula*[4] upon a set of extraordinary old blue china (a recent purchase) which we were now for the first time using; and could not help remarking, how favourable circumstances had been to us of late years, that we could afford to please the eye sometimes with trifles of this sort—when a passing sentiment seemed to overshade the brows of my companion. I am quick at detecting these summer clouds in Bridget.[5]

"I wish the good old times would come again," she said, "when we were not quite so rich. I do not mean that I want to be poor; but there was a middle state"—so she was pleased to ramble on,—"in which I am sure we were a great deal happier. A purchase is but a purchase, now that you have money enough and to spare. Formerly it used to be a triumph. When we coveted a cheap luxury (and, O! how much ado I had to get you to consent in those times!), we were used to have a debate two or three days before, and to weigh the *for* and *against,* and think what we might spare it out of, and what saving we could hit upon, that should be an equivalent. A thing was worth buying then, when we felt the money that we paid for it.

"Do you remember the brown suit, which you made to hang upon you, till all your friends cried shame upon you, it grew so threadbare—and all because of that folio Beaumont and Fletcher,[6] which you dragged home late at night from Barker's in Covent Garden? Do you remember how we eyed it for weeks before we could make up our minds to the purchase, and had not come to a determination till it was near ten o'clock of the Saturday night, when you set off from Islington,[7] fearing you should be too late—and when the old bookseller with some grumbling opened his shop, and by the twinkling taper (for he was setting bedwards) lighted out the relic from his dusty treasures—and when you lugged it home, wishing it were twice as cumbersome—and when you presented it to me—and when we were exploring the perfectness of it (*collating* you called it)—and while I was repairing some of the loose leaves with paste, which your impatience would not suffer to be left till daybreak—was there no pleasure in being a poor man? or can those neat black clothes which you wear now, and are so careful to keep brushed, since we have become rich and finical, give you half the honest vanity with which you flaunted it about in that over-worn suit— your old corbeau [8]—for four or five weeks longer than you should have done, to pacify your conscience for the mighty sum of fifteen—or sixteen shillings was it?—a great affair we thought it then—which you had lavished on the old folio.

Now you can afford to buy any book that pleases you, but I do not see that you ever bring me home any nice old purchases now.

"When you came home with twenty apologies for laying out a less number of shillings upon that print after Leonardo, which we christened the *'Lady Blanch';* when you looked at the purchase, and thought of the money—and thought of the money, and looked again at the picture—was there no pleasure in being a poor man? Now, you have nothing to do but to walk into Colnaghi's, and buy a wilderness of Leonardos. Yet do you? [9]

"Then, do you remember our pleasant walks to Enfield, and Potter's Bar, and Waltham, when we had a holyday—holydays and all other fun are gone, now we are rich—and the little handbasket in which I used to deposit our day's fare of savoury cold lamb and salad—and how you would pry about at noon-tide for some decent house, where we might go in and produce our store—only paying for the ale that you must call for—and speculate upon the looks of the landlady, and whether she was likely to allow us a tablecloth—and wish for such another honest hostess as Izaak Walton has described many a one on the pleasant banks of the Lea, when he went a fishing—and sometimes they would prove obliging enough, and sometimes they would look grudgingly upon us—but we had cheerful looks still for one another, and would eat our plain food savourily, scarcely grudging Piscator his Trout Hall? [10] Now—when we go out for a day's pleasuring, which is seldom, moreover, we *ride* part of the way and go into a fine inn, and order the best of dinners, never debating the expense—which, after all, never has half the relish of those chance country snaps, when we were at the mercy of uncertain usage, and a precarious welcome.

"You are too proud to see a play anywhere now but in the pit. Do you remember where it was we used to sit, when we saw the *Battle of Hexham,* and the *Surrender of Calais,* and Bannister and Mrs. Bland in the *Children in the Wood* [11]—when we squeezed out our shillings apiece to sit three or four times in a season in the one-shilling gallery—where you felt all the time that you ought not to have brought me— and more strongly I felt obligation to you for having brought me—and the pleasure was the better for a little shame—and when the curtain drew up, what cared we for our place in the house, or what mattered it where we were sitting, when our thoughts were with Rosalind in Arden, or with Viola at the Court of Illyria? [12] You used to say that the gallery was the best place of all for enjoying a play socially—that the relish of such exhibitions must be in proportion to the infrequency of going—that the company we met there, not being in general readers of plays, were obliged to attend the more, and did attend, to what was going on, on the stage—because a word lost would have been a chasm, which it was impossible for them to fill up. With such reflections we consoled our pride then—and I appeal to you whether, as a woman, I met generally with less attention and accommodation than I have done since in more expensive situations in the house? The getting in, indeed, and the crowding up those inconvenient staircases, was bad enough,—but there was still a law of civility to woman recognized to quite as great an extent as we ever found in the other passages—and how a little difficulty overcome heightened the snug seat, and the play, afterwards! Now we can only pay our money, and walk in. You cannot see, you say, in the galleries now. I am sure we saw, and heard too, well enough then—but sight, and all, I think, is gone with our poverty.

"There was pleasure in eating strawberries, before they became quite common—in the first dish of peas, while they were yet dear—to have them for a nice supper, a treat. What treat can we have now? If we were to treat ourselves now— that is, to have dainties a little above our means, it would be selfish and wicked. It is the very little more that we allow ourselves beyond what the actual poor can get at, that makes what I call a treat—when two people living together, as we have done, now and then indulge themselves in a cheap luxury, which both like; while each apologizes, and is willing to take both halves of the blame to his single share. I see no harm in people making much of themselves in that sense of the word. It may give them a hint how to make much of others. But now—what I mean by the word—we never do make much of ourselves. None but the poor can do it. I do not mean the veriest poor of all, but persons as we were, just above poverty.

"I know what you were going to say, that it is mighty pleasant at the end of the year to make all meet,—and much ado we used to have every Thirty-first Night of December to account for our exceedings—many a long face did you make over your puzzled accounts, and in contriving to make it out how we had spent so much—or that we had not spent so much—or that it was impossible we should spend so much next year—and still we found our slender capital decreasing —but then, betwixt ways, and projects, and compromises of one sort or another, and talk of curtailing this charge, and doing without that for the future—and the hope that youth brings and laughing spirits (in which you were never poor till now), we pocketed up our loss, and in conclusion, with 'lusty brimmers' (as you used to quote it out of *hearty, cheerful Mr. Cotton*,[13] as you called him), we used to welcome in the 'coming guest.' Now we have no reckoning at all at the end of the old year—no flattering promises about the new year doing better for us."

Bridget is so sparing of her speech on most occasions, that when she gets into a rhetorical vein, I am careful how I interrupt it. I could not help, however, smiling at the phantom of wealth which her dear imagination had conjured up out of a clear income of a poor—hundred pounds a year. "It is true we were happier when we were poorer, but we were also younger, my cousin. I am afraid we must put up with the excess, for if we were to shake the superflux into the sea, we should not much mend ourselves. That we had much to struggle with, as we grew up together, we have reason to be most thankful. It strengthened and knit our compact closer. We could never have been what we have been to each other, if we had always had the sufficiency which you now complain of. The resisting power—those natural dilations of the youthful spirit, which circumstances cannot straiten—with us are long since passed away. Competence to age is supplementary youth, a sorry supplement indeed, but I fear the best that is to be had. We must ride, where we formerly walked: live better, and lie softer— and shall be wise to do so—than we had means to do in those good old days you speak of. Yet could those days return—could you and I once more walk our thirty miles a day—could Bannister and Mrs. Bland again be young, and you and I be young to see them—could the good old one-shilling gallery days return—they are dreams, my cousin, now—but could you and I at this moment, instead of this quiet argument, by our well-carpeted fireside, sitting on this luxurious sofa—be once more struggling up those inconvenient staircases, pushed about, and squeezed, and elbowed by the poorest rabble of poor gallery scramblers—could I once more hear those anxious shrieks of yours—and the delicious *Thank God, we are safe,* which always followed when the topmost stair, conquered, let in the first light of the whole cheerful theatre down beneath us—I know not the fathom line that ever touched a descent so deep as I would be willing to bury more wealth in than Crœsus had, or the great Jew R—— [14] is supposed to have, to purchase it. And now do just look at that merry little Chinese waiter holding an umbrella, big enough for a bed-tester over the head of that pretty insipid half-Madonna-ish chit of a lady in that very blue summer-house."

NOTES

[1] William Hogarth (1697–1764), a brilliant English engraver and painter, had done much to attract popular attention to perspective, through a series of prints which, for keenness of satire, have few equals.

[2] The hays is an old English folk dance.

[3] Hyson is a green tea.

[4] shining wonders.

[5] In the Elia essays, Lamb always refers to his sister Mary as his cousin Bridget.

[6] Francis Beaumont (1584–1616) and John Fletcher (1579–1625), Elizabethan dramatists, perhaps the most successful collaborators in English literary history. Those interested in linking dates will note that Beaumont and Shakespeare died in the same year, and that Fletcher died in the year of Bacon's last volume of essays.

[7] A suburb of London.

[8] corbeau—dark green, almost crow black.

[9] Leonardo da Vinci (1452–1519) one of the great masters of Renaissance painting. Colnaghi was a London art dealer.

[10] The favorite haunt of Piscator, main character of *The Compleat Angler* by Izaak Walton (1593–1683), was Trout Hall, "an honest ale-house."

[11] The first two plays mentioned here were by George Colman (1762–1836). *The Children in the Wood* was written by Thomas Morton (1764–1838). Bannister was a famous comedian of the day; Mrs. Bland, an actress.

[12] Rosalind and Viola are from Shakespeare's *As You Like It* and *Twelfth Night*.

[13] Charles Cotton (1630–1687), contributor to, and later the sustainer of, *The Compleat Angler* of Izaak Walton.

[14] The Great Jew R—— may be directed at Nathan Rothschild (1777–1836) founder of the English branch of that family, popularly supposed to be "as rich as Crœsus", the King of Lydia.

QUESTIONS

1. How would Lamb write an essay on "first nights" in New York theaters?

2. What objects have you collected? In what lies the value of things prized by a collector?

DREAM CHILDREN; A REVERIE

Charles Lamb

For the background of this essay, see the biographical introduction to "The Praise of Chimney-Sweepers" on pages 79-80.

This essay from *The Essays of Elia* was published in the *London Magazine* in January 1822, some two months after the death of Lamb's brother John, the "John L——— (James Elia)" of the essay. The "great-grandmother Field" is Lamb's grandmother, Mary Field, whom he visited during boyhood holidays in Hertfordshire. "Alice W———n" is Ann Simmons, boyhood love of Lamb. She married a Mr. Bartrum, a pawnbroker of London. "Bridget" is Lamb's sister Mary. Once familiar with the personal references involved here, the student should read "Dream Children" for the tenderness and restraint of its emotion.

CHILDREN love to listen to stories about their elders, when *they* were children; to stretch their imagination to the conception of a traditionary great-uncle, or grandame, whom they never saw. It was in this spirit that my little ones crept about me the other evening to hear about their great-grandmother Field, who lived in a great house in Norfolk (a hundred times bigger than that in which they and papa lived) which had been the scene—so at least it was generally believed in that part of the country—of the tragic incidents which they had lately become familiar with from the ballad of the Children in the Wood. Certain it is that the whole story of the children and their cruel uncle was to be seen fairly carved out in wood upon the chimney-piece of the great hall, the whole story down to the Robin Redbreasts, till a foolish rich person pulled it down to set up a marble one of modern invention in its stead, with no story upon it. Here Alice put out one of her dear mother's looks, too tender to be called upbraiding. Then I went on to say how religious and how good their great-grandmother Field was, how beloved and respected by everybody, though she was not indeed the mistress of this great house, but had only the charge of it (and yet in some respects she might be said to be the mistress of it too) committed to her by the owner, who preferred living in a newer and more fashionable mansion which he had purchased somewhere in the adjoining county; but still she lived in it in a manner as if it had been her own, and kept up the dignity of the great house in a sort while she lived, which afterwards, came to decay, and was nearly pulled down, and all its old ornaments stripped and carried away to the owner's other house, where they were set up, and looked as awkward as if some one were to carry away the old tombs they had seen lately at the Abbey, and stick them up in Lady C's tawdry

gilt drawing-room. Here John smiled, as much as
to say, "that would be foolish indeed." And then
I told how, when she came to die, her funeral was
attended by a concourse of all the poor, and some
of the gentry too, of the neighbourhood for many
miles round, to show their respect for her memory, because she had been such a good and religious woman; so good indeed that she knew all
the Psaltery by heart, ay, and a great part of the
Testament besides. Here little Alice spread her
hands. Then I told what a tall, upright, graceful
person their great-grandmother Field once was;
and how in her youth she was esteemed the best
dancer—here Alice's little right foot played an
involuntary movement, till, upon my looking
grave, it desisted—the best dancer, I was saying,
in the county, till a cruel disease, called a cancer,
came, and bowed her down with pain; but it
could never bend her good spirits, or make them
stoop, but they were still upright, because she
was so good and religious. Then I told how she
was used to sleep by herself in a lone chamber
of the great lone house; and how she believed
that an apparition of two infants was to be seen
at midnight gliding up and down the great stair-
case near where she slept, but she said "those
innocents would do her no harm"; and how
frightened I used to be, though in those days I
had my maid to sleep with me, because I was
never half so good or religious as she—and yet I
never saw the infants. Here John expanded all his

eyebrows and tried to look courageous. Then I told how good she was to all her grandchildren, having us to the great house in the holydays, where I in particular used to spend many hours by myself, in gazing upon the old busts of the twelve Cæsars, that had been Emperors of Rome, till the old marble heads would seem to live again, or I to be turned into marble with them; how I never could be tired with roaming about that huge mansion, with its vast empty rooms, with their worn-out hangings, fluttering tapestry, and carved oaken panels, with the gilding almost rubbed out—sometimes in the spacious old-fashioned gardens, which I had almost to myself, unless when now and then a solitary gardening man would cross me—and how the nectarines and peaches hung upon the walls, without my ever offering to pluck them, because they were forbidden fruit, unless now and then,—and because I had more pleasure in strolling about among the old melancholy-looking yew trees, or the firs, and picking up the red berries, and the fir-apples, which were good for nothing but to look at—or in lying about upon the fresh grass with all the fine garden smells around me—or basking in the orangery, till I could almost fancy myself ripening too along with the oranges and the limes in that grateful warmth—or in watching the dace that darted to and fro in the fish-pond, at the bottom of the garden, with here and there a great sulky pike hanging midway down the water in silent state, as if it mocked at their impertinent friskings,—I had more pleasure in these busy-idle diversions than in all the sweet flavours of peaches, nectarines, oranges, and such-like common baits of children. Here John slyly deposited back upon the plate a bunch of grapes, which, not unobserved by Alice, he had meditated dividing with her, and both seemed willing to relinquish them for the present as irrelevant. Then, in somewhat a more heightened tone, I told how, though their great-grandmother Field loved all her grandchildren, yet in an especial manner she might be said to love their uncle, John L——, because he was so handsome and spirited a youth, and a king to the rest of us; and, instead of moping about in solitary corners, like some of us, he would mount the most mettlesome horse he could get, when but an imp no bigger than themselves, and make it carry him half over the county in a morning, and join the hunters when there were any out—and yet he loved the old great house and gardens too, but had too much spirit to be always pent up within their boundaries—and how their uncle grew up to man's estate as brave as he was handsome, to the admiration of everybody, but of their great-grandmother Field most especially; and how he used to carry me upon his back when I was a lame-footed boy—for he was a good bit older than me—many a mile when I could not walk for pain;—and how in after life he became lame-footed too, and I did not always

(I fear) make allowances enough for him when he was impatient and in pain, nor remember sufficiently how considerate he had been to me when I was lame-footed; and how when he died, though he had not been dead an hour, it seemed as if he had died a great while ago, such a distance there is betwixt life and death; and how I bore his death as I thought pretty well at first, but afterwards it haunted and haunted me; and though I did not cry or take it to heart as some do, and as I think he would have done if I had died, yet I missed him all day long, and knew not till then how much I had loved him. I missed his kindness, and I missed his crossness, and wished him to be alive again, to be quarrelling with him (for we quarrelled sometimes), rather than not have him again, and was as uneasy without him, as he, their poor uncle, must have been when the doctor took off his limb.—Here the children fell a-crying, and asked if their little mourning which they had on was not for Uncle John, and they looked up, and prayed me not to go on about their uncle, but to tell them some stories about their pretty dead mother. Then I told how for seven long years, in hope sometimes, sometimes in despair, yet persisting ever, I courted the fair Alice W———n; and as much as children could understand, I explained to them what coyness, and difficulty, and denial, meant in maidens—when suddenly turning to Alice, the soul of the first Alice looked out at her eyes with such a reality of re-presentment, that I became in doubt which of them stood there before me, or whose that bright hair was; and while I stood gazing, both the children gradually grew fainter to my view, receding, and still receding, till nothing at last but two mournful features were seen in the uttermost distance, which, without speech, strangely impressed upon me the effects of speech: "We are not of Alice, nor of thee, nor are we children at all. The children of Alice call Bartrum father. We are nothing; less than nothing, and dreams. We are only what might have been, and must wait upon the tedious shores of Lethe millions of ages before we have existence, and a name"—and immediately awaking, I found myself quietly seated in my bachelor arm-chair, where I had fallen asleep, with the faithful Bridget unchanged by my side —but John L. (or James Elia) was gone for ever.

THE INHUMANITY OF ANGLERS

Leigh Hunt

Byron called Leigh Hunt "of the town, towny", meaning, perhaps, that he suggested the life of London streets
more than the more cultivated atmosphere of the university wits; and it was precisely this towny quality that
made Leigh Hunt an essayist set apart from the writers of
his day and enabled him to "carry over" into the next generation of essayists without sacrificing his own personality.
After his leaving Christ's Hospital School in London, Lamb
and Coleridge's school, at the age of 15, he continued
his education, not in the universities but rather on the
streets of London. His observations of life and character
made him a journalist rather than a periodical essayist,
and many political reforms close to the man in the street
were brought about through his partisan struggles for a
change. A leader of the liberals, he was frequenty sued for
libel, and was once imprisoned for two years in Horse-
monger Lane Prison in Sussex. There his friends—Hazlitt,
the Lambs, Byron, and Moore, and his relatives—visited
him and showered him with gifts of books and flowers. His
life, like those of most journalists of the period, fluctuated
between want and plenty, much of the latter being contributed by kind-hearted friends like Shelley, who, like
Keats, had been introduced to the public by Hunt. Lamb,
who should know what good indoor company was, called
Hunt "the most cordial-minded man I ever knew, and
matchless as a fireside companion." *The Town,* from which
this essay is an extract, appeared in 1848 and is perhaps

the fullest, richest handbook about London, its points of interest, gossip about the luminaries of the past, written as only a lover of the town could write it. Like most of his essays, it reflects the companionable presence of one who loved the best things and loved to share his enjoyment of them with his fellows. Hunt was born in Southgate, Middlesex, in 1784 and died in London in 1859.

A GREAT deal has been said lately of the merits and demerits of angling, and Izaak [1] has suffered in the discussion, beyond what is agreeable to the lovers of that gentle pleasure. Unfortunately the brothers of the angle do not argue ingenuously. They always omit the tortures suffered by the principal party, and affect to think you affected if you urge them; whereas their only reason for avoiding the point is, that it is not to be defended. If it is, we may defend, by an equal abuse of reason, any amusement which is to be obtained at another being's expense; and an evil genius might angle for ourselves, and twitch us up, bleeding and roaring, into an atmosphere that would stifle us. But fishes do not roar; they cannot express any sound of suffering; and therefore the angler chooses to think they do not suffer, more than it is convenient to him to fancy. Now it is a poor sport that depends for its existence on the want of a voice in the sufferer, and of imagination in the sportsman. Angling, in short, is not to be defended on any ground of reflection; and this is the worst thing to say of Izaak; for he was not unaware of the objections to his amusement, and he piqued himself upon being contemplative.

Anglers have been defended upon the ground of their having had among them so many pious men; but unfortunately men may be selfishly as well as nobly pious; and even charity itself may be practised, as well as cruelty deprecated, upon principles which have a much greater regard to a man's own safety and future comfort, than anything which concerns real Christian beneficence. Doubtless there have been many good and humane men anglers, as well as many pleasant men. There have also been some very unpleasant ones —Sir John Hawkins [2] among them. They make a well-founded pretension to a love of nature and her scenery; but it is a pity they cannot relish it without this pepper to the poor fish. Walton's book contains many passages in praise of rural enjoyment, which affect us almost like the fields and fresh air themselves, though his brethren have exalted it beyond its value; and his lives of his angling friends, the Divines, have been preposterously overrated. If angling is to be defended upon good and manly grounds, let it; it is no longer to be defended on any other. The best thing to be said for it (and the instance is worthy of reflection) is, that anglers have been brought up in the belief of its innocence, and that an inhuman custom is too powerful for the most humane. The inconsistency is to be accounted for on no other grounds; nor is it necessary or desirable that it should be. It is a remarkable illustration of what Plato said, when something was defended on the ground of its being a trifle, because it was a custom. 'But custom', said he, 'is no trifle'. Here, among persons of a more equivocal description, are some of the humanest men in the world, who will commit what other humane men reckon among the most inhuman actions, and make an absolute pastime of it. Let one of their grandchildren be brought up in the reverse opinion, and see what he will think of it. This, to be sure, might be said to be only another instance of the effect of education; but nobody, the most unprejudiced, thinks it a bigotry in Shakespeare and Steele [3] to have brought us to feel for the brute creation in general; and whatever we may incline to think for the accommodation of our propensities, there will still remain the unanswered and always avoided argument, of the dumb and torn fish themselves, who die agonized, in the midst of our tranquil looking on, and for no necessity.

John Whitney, author of the *Genteel Recreation, or the Pleasures of Angling*, a poem printed in the year 1700, recommends the lovers of the art to bait with the eyes of fish, in order to decoy others of the same species. A writer in the *Censura Literaria* exclaims, 'What a Nero of Anglers doth this proclaim John Whitney to have been! and how unworthy to be ranked as a lover of the same pastime, which had been so interestingly recommended by Izaak Walton, in his *Contemplative Man's Recreation.*'

But Izaak's contemplative man can content himself with impaling live worms, and jesting about the tenderness with which he treats them —using the worm, quoth Izaak, 'as if you loved him.' Doubtless John thought himself as good a man as Izaak. He poetizes, and is innocent with the best of them, and probably would not have hurt a dog. However, it must be allowed that he had less imagination than Walton, and was more cruel, inasmuch as he could commit a cruelty that was not the custom. Observe, nevertheless, that it was the customary cruelty which led to the new one. Why must these contemplative men commit any cruelty at all? The writer of the article in the *Censura* was, if we mistake not, one of the kindest of human beings, and yet he could see nothing erroneous in torturing a worm. 'A good man', says the Scripture, 'is merciful to his beast'. Therefore 'holy Mr. Herbert' [4] very properly helps a horse out of a ditch and is the better for it all the rest of the day. Are we not to be merciful to fish as well as beasts, merely because the Scripture does not expressly state it? Such are the inconsistencies of mankind, during their very acquirement of beneficence.

NOTES

[1] Izaak Walton (1593–1683), presiding genius of angling and author of *The Compleat Angler.*

[2] Sir John Hawkins (1532–1592) was a Rear-Admiral in the British Navy.

[3] Richard Steele (1672–1729), co-author with Joseph Addison of *The Tatler* and *The Spectator,* the leading periodical essays of the early eighteenth century. (See pages 30-32.)

[4] George Herbert (1593–1633) English poet and divine, whose poems, all published after his death, have been revived by an appreciative posterity.

QUESTIONS

1. What element in the nature of fishing renders it vulnerable as true sport? Is this true of hunting?

2. What other sports or activities may be challenged in this way? Could you satirize your favorite sport?

ON GOING A JOURNEY

William Hazlitt

William Hazlitt (1778–1830) studied first for the Unitarian ministry and later to be a painter. The real foundations for his literary career were not laid until the five years following his retirement from Hackney Theological College at the age of sixteen, years spent in doing just as he pleased about his father's house in Wem, a small town in Shropshire. "For many years of my life, I did nothing but think. I had nothing else to do but solve some knotty problem, or dip into some abstruse author, or look at the sky, or wander by the pebbled sea-side. I lived in a world of contemplation, and not of action." His entrance into the literary world as a journalist associated him with Leigh Hunt, for whom he wrote articles on politics and, later, his familiar essays. A friend of most of the literary figures of the day, Hazlitt appraised their work shrewdly and forcefully, and generally quite apart from their personalities. A liberal controversialist by nature, Hazlitt was fortunate in knowing Coleridge and Wordsworth at the time of their great revolt against the old conventions in poetry. Never a finished craftsman, he wrote naturally and conversationally, expressing his enthusiasms and his dislikes with a directness and vigor that drew from Keats the remark, "He is your only good damner, and if ever I am damned I should like to have him damn me." Discussing his own style, Hazlitt said, "No style is worth a farthing that is not calculated to be read out, or that is not allied to spirited conversation." The independence of his thought and the candor of his expression made Hazlitt one of the outstanding individualists among all the great English essayists. Like his friends Charles Lamb and Leigh Hunt, Hazlitt exemplifies the constant struggle of those who with native talents manage, through relentless self-education, to leave their impress on the world.

ONE of the pleasantest things in the world is going a journey; but I like to go by myself. I can enjoy society in a room; but out of doors, nature is company enough for me. I am then never less alone than when alone.

"The fields his study, nature was his book." [1]

I cannot see the wit of walking and talking at the same time. When I am in the country, I wish to vegetate like the country. I am not for criticizing hedge-rows and black cattle. I go out of town in order to forget the town and all that is in it. There are those who for this purpose go to watering-places and carry the metropolis with them. I like more elbow-room and fewer incumbrances. I like solitude, when I give myself up to it, for the sake of solitude; nor do I ask for

"—a friend in my retreat,
Whom I may whisper, solitude is sweet." [2]

The soul of a journey is liberty, perfect liberty, to think, feel, do, just as one pleases. We go a journey chiefly to be free of all impediments and of all inconveniences; to leave ourselves behind, much more to get rid of others. It is because I want a little breathing-space to muse on indifferent matters, where Contemplation

> "May plume her feathers and let grow her wings,
>   That in the various bustle of resort
>   Were all too ruffled, and sometimes impair'd," [3]

that I absent myself from the town for a while, without feeling at a loss the moment I am left by myself. Instead of a friend in a post-chaise or in a Tilbury,[4] to exchange good things with and vary the same stale topics over again, for once let me have a truce with impertinence. Give me the clear blue sky over my head, and the green turf beneath my feet, a winding road before me, and a three hours' march to dinner—and then to thinking! It is hard if I cannot start some game on these lone heaths. I laugh, I run, I leap, I sing for joy. From the point of yonder rolling cloud, I plunge into my past being and revel there, as the sun-burnt Indian plunges headlong into the wave that wafts him to his native shore. Then long-forgotten things, like "sunken wrack and sumless treasuries," [5] burst upon my eager sight, and I begin to feel, think, and be myself again. Instead of an awkward silence, broken by attempts at wit or dull commonplaces, mine is that undisturbed silence of the heart which alone is perfect eloquence. No one likes puns, alliterations, antitheses, argument, and analysis better than I do; but I sometimes had rather be without them. "Leave, oh leave me to my repose!" [6]

I have just now other business in hand, which would seem idle to you, but is with me "very stuff of the conscience." [7] Is not this wild rose sweet without a comment? Does not this daisy leap to my heart set in its coat of emerald? Yet if I were to explain to you the circumstance that has so endeared it to me, you would only smile. Had I not better then keep it to myself, and let it serve me to brood over, from here to yonder craggy point, and from thence onward to the far-distant horizon? I should be but bad company all that way, and therefore prefer being alone. I have heard it said that you may, when the moody fit comes on, walk or ride on by yourself and indulge your reveries. But this looks like a breach of manners, a neglect of others, and you are thinking all the time that you ought to rejoin your party. "Out upon such half-faced fellowship," [8] say I. I like to be either entirely to myself, or entirely at the disposal of others; to talk or be silent, to walk or sit still, to be sociable or solitary. I was pleased with an observation of Mr. Cobbett's,[9] that "he thought it a bad French custom to drink our wine with our meals, and that an Englishman ought to do only one thing at a time." So I cannot talk and think, or indulge in melancholy musing and lively conversation by fits and starts. "Let me have a companion of my way," says Sterne,[10] "were it but to remark how the shadows lengthen as the sun declines." It is beautifully said; but in my opinion, this continual comparing of notes interferes with the involuntary impression of things upon the mind and hurts the sentiment. If you only hint what you feel in a kind of dumb show, it is insipid; if you have to explain it, it is making a toil of a pleasure. You cannot read the book of nature without being perpetually put to the trouble of translating it for the benefit of others. I am for the synthetical method on a journey, in preference to the analytical. I am content to lay in a stock of ideas then, and to examine and anatomize them afterwards. I want to see my vague notions float like the down of the thistle before the breeze, and not to have them entangled in the briars and thorns of controversy. For once, I like to have it all my own way; and this is impossible unless you are alone, or in such company as I do not covet. I have no objection to argue a point with any one for twenty miles of measured road, but not for pleasure. If you remark the scent of a bean-field crossing the road, perhaps your fellow-traveller has no smell. If you point to a distant object, perhaps he is shortsighted, and has to take out his glass to look at it. There is a feeling in the air, a tone in the colour of a cloud which hits your fancy, but the effect of which you are unable to account for. There is then no sympathy, but an uneasy craving after it, and a dissatisfaction which pursues you on the way, and in the end probably produces ill humour. Now I never quarrel with myself, and take all my own conclusions for granted till I find it necessary to defend them against objections. It is not merely that you may not be of accord on the objects and circumstances that present themselves before you—these may recall a number of objects and lead to associations too delicate and refined to be possibly communicated to others. Yet these I love to cherish, and sometimes still fondly clutch them, when I can escape from the throng to do so. To give way to our feelings before company, seems extravagance or affectation; and, on the other hand, to have to unravel this mystery of our being at every turn, and to make others take an equal interest in it (otherwise the end is not answered) is a task to which few are competent. We must "give it an understanding, but no tongue." [11] My old friend Coleridge,[12] however, could do both. He could go on in the most delightful explanatory way over hill and dale, a summer's day, and convert a landscape into a didactic poem or a Pindaric ode. "He talked far above singing." [13] If I could so clothe my ideas in sounding and flowing words, I might perhaps wish to have someone with me to admire the swelling theme; or I could be more content, were it possible for me still to hear his echoing voice in the woods of All-Foxden.[14] They had "that fine madness in them which our first poets had"; and if they could have been caught by some rare instrument, would have breathed such strains as the following.

> —Here be woods as green
> As any, air likewise as fresh and sweet
> As when smooth Zephyrus plays on the fleet
> Face of the curled streams, with flow'rs as many
> As the young spring gives, and as choice as any;
> Here be all new delights, cool streams and wells,
> Arbours o'ergrown with woodbines, caves and dells;
> Choose where thou wilt, whilst I sit by and sing,
> Or gather rushes, to make many a ring
> For thy long fingers; tell thee tales of love;
> How the pale Phœbe, hunting in a grove,
> First saw the boy Endymion, from whose eyes
> She took eternal fire that never dies;
> How she convey'd him softly in a sleep,
> His temples bound with poppy, to the steep
> Head of old Latmos, where she stoops each night,
> Gilding the mountains with her brother's light,
> To kiss her sweetest.
>
> (*Faithful Shepherdess* by Fletcher)

Had I words and images at command like these, I would attempt to wake the thoughts that lie slumbering on golden ridges in the evening clouds; but at the sight of nature my fancy, poor as it is, droops and closes up its leaves, like flowers at sunset. I can make nothing out on the spot:—I must have time to collect myself.

In general, a good thing spoils out-of-door prospects; it should be reserved for table-talk. Lamb [15] is for this reason, I take it, the worst company in the world out of doors; because he is the best within. I grant, there is one subject on which it is pleasant to talk on a journey; and that is, what one shall have for supper when we

get to our inn at night. The open air improves
this sort of conversation or friendly altercation
by setting a keener edge on appetite. Every mile
of the road heightens the flavour of the viands we
expect at the end of it. How fine it is to enter
some old town, walled and turreted, just at the
approach of nightfall, or to come to some straggling village, with the lights streaming through
the surrounding gloom; and then after inquiring
for the best entertainment that the place affords,
to "take one's ease at one's inn!"[16] These event-
ful moments in our lives' history are too precious,
too full of solid, heartfelt happiness to be frittered
and dribbled away in imperfect sympathy. I
would have them all to myself, and drain them
to the last drop; they will do to talk of or to
write about afterwards. What a delicate speculation it is, after drinking whole goblets of tea,

> The cups that cheer, but not inebriate,[17]

and letting the fumes ascend into the brain, to
sit considering what we shall have for supper—
eggs and a rasher,[18] a rabbit smothered in onions,
or an excellent veal-cutlet! Sancho [19] in such a
situation once fixed on cow-heel; and his choice,
though he could not help it, is not to be dispar-
aged. Then, in the intervals of pictured scenery
and Shandean [20] contemplation, to catch the
preparation and the stir in the kitchen—*Procul,
O procul este profani!* [21] These hours are sacred
to silence and to musing, to be treasured up in

the memory, and to feed the source of smiling thoughts hereafter. I would not waste them in idle talk; or if I must have the integrity of fancy broken in upon, I would rather it were by a stranger than a friend. A stranger takes his hue and character from the time and place; he is a part of the furniture and costume of an inn. If he is a Quaker, or from the West Riding of Yorkshire, so much the better. I do not even try to sympathize with him, and he breaks no squares. I associate nothing with my travelling companion but present objects and passing events. In his ignorance of me and my affairs, I in a manner forget myself. But a friend reminds one of other things, rips up old grievances, and destroys the abstraction of the scene. He comes in ungraciously between us and our imaginary character. Something is dropped in the course of conversation that gives a hint of your profession and pursuits; or from having someone with you that knows the less sublime portions of your history, it seems that other people do. You are no longer a citizen of the world: but your "unhoused free condition is put into circumscription and confine." [22] The *incognito* of an inn is one of its striking privileges—"Lord of one's self, uncumber'd with a name." [23] Oh! it is great to shake off the trammels of the world and of public opinion, to lose our importunate, tormenting, everlasting personal identity in the elements of nature, and become the creature of the moment, clear of all ties—to hold to the universe only by a dish of sweetbreads, and to owe nothing but the score [24] of the evening—and no longer seeking for applause and meeting with contempt, to be known by no other title than *The Gentleman in the parlour!* One may take one's choice of all characters in this romantic state of uncertainty as to one's real pretensions, and become indefinitely respectable and negatively right-worshipful. We baffle prejudice and disappoint conjecture; and from being so to others, begin to be objects of curiosity and wonder even to ourselves. We are no more those hackneyed common-places that we appear in the world; an inn restores us to the level of nature and quits scores with society! I have certainly spent some enviable hours at inns—sometimes when I have been left entirely to myself and have tried to solve some metaphysical problem, as once at Witham-Common, where I found out the proof that likeness is not a case of the association of ideas; at other times, when there have been pictures in the room, as at St. Neot's (I think it was), where I first met with Gribelin's engravings of the Cartoons,[25] into which I entered at once, and at a little inn on the borders of Wales, where there happened to be hanging some of Westall's drawings, which I compared triumphantly (for a theory that I had, not for the admired artist) with the figure of a girl who had ferried me over the Severn, standing up in a boat between me and the twilight—at other times I might mention luxuriating in books, with a peculiar interest in this way, as I remember sitting up half the night to read *Paul and Virginia*,[26] which I picked up at an inn at Bridgewater, after being drenched in the rain all day; and at the same place I got through two volumes of Madame D'Arblay's *Camilla*. It was on the 10th of April, 1798, that I sat down to a volume of the *New Eloise*, at the inn at Llangollen, over a bottle of sherry and a cold chicken. The letter I chose was that in which St. Preux describes his feelings as he first caught a glimpse from the heights of the Jura of the Pays de Vaud, which I had brought with me as a *bon bouche*[27] to crown the evening with. It was my birthday, and I had for the first time come from a place in the neighborhood to visit this delightful spot. The road to Llangollen turns off between Chirk and Wrexham; and on passing a certain point, you come all at once upon the valley, which opens like an amphitheatre, broad, barren hills rising in majestic state on either side, with "green upland swells that echo to the bleat of flocks" below, and the river Dee babbling over its stony bed in the midst of them. The valley at this time "glittered green with sunny showers," and a budding ash-tree dipped its tender branches in the chiding stream. How proud, how glad I was to walk along the high road that overlooks the delicious prospect, repeating the lines which I have just quoted from Mr. Coleridge's poems!

But besides the prospect which opened beneath my feet, another also opened to my inward sight, a heavenly vision, on which were written, in letters large as Hope could make them, these four words, LIBERTY, GENIUS, LOVE, VIRTUE; which have since faded into the light of common day, or mock my idle gaze.

The beautiful is vanished, and returns not.[28]

Still I would return some time or other to this enchanted spot; but I would return to it alone.[29] What other self could I find to share that influx of thoughts, of regret and delight, the fragments of which I could hardly conjure up to myself, so much have they been broken and defaced! I could stand on some tall rock and overlook the precipice of years that separates me from what I then was. I was at that time going shortly to visit the poet whom I have above named. Where is he now? Not only I myself have changed; the world, which was then new to me, has become old and incorrigible. Yet will I turn to thee in thought, O sylvan Dee, in joy, in youth and gladness as thou then wert; and thou shalt always be to me the river of Paradise, where I will drink of the waters of life freely!

There is hardly anything that shows the short-sightedness or capriciousness of the imagination more than travelling does. With change of place we change our ideas; nay, our opinions and feelings. We can by an effort indeed transport our-

selves to old and long-forgotten scenes, and then
the picture of the mind revives again; but we
forget those that we have just left. It seems that
we can think but of one place at a time. The canvas of the fancy is but of a certain extent, and
if we paint one set of objects upon it, they immediately efface every other. We cannot enlarge our
conceptions, we only shift our point of view. The
landscape bares its bosom to the enraptured eye,
we take our fill of it and seem as if we could
form no other image of beauty or grandeur. We
pass on and think no more of it; the horizon that
shuts it from our sight, also blots it from our
memory like a dream. In travelling through a
wild, barren country, I can form no idea of a
woody and cultivated one. It appears to me that
all the world must be barren, like what I see of
it. In the country we forget the town, and in
town we despise the country. "Beyond Hyde
Park," says Sir Fopling Flutter,[30] "all is a desert." All that part of the map that we do not see
before us is a blank. The world in our conceit
of it is not much bigger than a nutshell. It is not
one prospect expanded into another, county
joined to county, kingdom to kingdom, lands to
seas, making an image voluminous and vast;—
the mind can form no larger idea of space than
the eye can take in at a single glance. The rest
is a name written in a map, a calculation of arithmetic. For instance, what is the true signification
of that immense mass of territory and population,

known by the name of China to us? An inch of pasteboard on a wooden globe, of no more account than a China orange! Things near us are seen of the size of life: things at a distance are diminished to the size of the understanding. We measure the universe by ourselves, and even comprehend the texture of our own being only piecemeal. In this way, however, we remember an infinity of things and places. The mind is like a mechanical instrument that plays a great variety of tunes, but it must play them in succession. One idea recalls another, but it at the same time excludes all others. In trying to renew old recollections, we cannot as it were unfold the whole web of our existence; we must pick out the single threads. So in coming to a place where we have formerly lived and with which we have intimate associations, everyone must have found that the feeling grows more vivid the nearer we approach the spot, from the mere anticipation of the actual impression: we remember circumstances, feelings, persons, faces, names that we had not thought of for years; but for the time all the rest of the world is forgotten!—To return to the question I have quitted above.

I have no objection to go to see ruins, aqueducts, pictures, in company with a friend or a party, but rather the contrary, for the former reason reversed. They are intelligible matters and will bear talking about. The sentiment here is not tacit, but communicable and overt. Salisbury

Plain is barren of criticism, but Stonehenge [31]
will bear a discussion antiquarian, picturesque,
and philosophical. In setting out on a party of
pleasure, the first consideration always is where
we shall go to; in taking a solitary ramble, the
question is what we shall meet with by the way.
"The mind is its own place"; [32] nor are we anxious to arrive at the end of our journey. I can
myself do the honours indifferently well to works
of art and curiosity. I once took a party to Oxford with no mean *éclat*—showed them that seat
of the Muses at a distance,

> The glistering spires and pinnacles adorn'd— [33]

descanted on the learned air that breathes from
the grassy quadrangles and stone walls of halls
and colleges—was at home in the Bodleian; and
at Blenheim quite superseded the powdered
ciceroni [34] that attended us, and that pointed in
vain with his wand to common-place beauties in
matchless pictures.—As another exception to the
above reasoning, I should not feel confident in
venturing on a journey in a foreign country without a companion. I should want at intervals to
hear the sound of my own language. There is an
involuntary antipathy in the mind of an Englishman to foreign manners and notions that requires
the assistance of social sympathy to carry it off.
As the distance from home increases, this relief,
which was at first a luxury, becomes a passion
and an appetite. A person would almost feel stifled

to find himself in the deserts of Arabia without friends and countrymen; there must be allowed to be something in the view of Athens or old Rome that claims the utterance of speech; and I own that the Pyramids are too mighty for any single contemplation. In such situations, so opposite to all one's ordinary train of ideas, one seems a species by one's-self, a limb torn off from society, unless one can meet with instant fellowship and support. Yet I did not feel this want or craving very pressing once, when I first set my foot on the laughing shores of France. Calais was peopled with novelty and delight. The confused, busy murmur of the place was like oil and wine poured into my ears; nor did the mariners' hymn, which was sung from the top of an old crazy vessel in the harbour, as the sun went down, send an alien sound into my soul. I only breathed the air of general humanity. I walked over "the vine-covered hills and gay regions of France," [35] erect and satisfied; for the image of man was not cast down and chained to the foot of arbitrary thrones; I was at no loss for language, for that of all the great schools of painting was open to me. The whole is vanished like a shade. Pictures, heroes, glory, freedom, all are fled: nothing remains but the Bourbons and the French people!—There is undoubtedly a sensation in travelling into foreign parts that is to be had nowhere else; but it is more pleasing at the time than lasting. It is too remote from our habitual associations to be a common topic of discourse or reference, and, like a dream or another state of existence, does not piece into our daily modes of life. It is an animated but a momentary hallucination. It demands an effort to exchange our actual for our ideal identity; and to feel the pulse of our old transports revive very keenly, we must "jump" all our present comforts and connexions. Our romantic and itinerant character is not to be domesticated. Doctor Johnson remarked how little foreign travel added to the facilities of conversation in those who had been abroad. In fact, the time we have spent there is both delightful and in one sense instructive; but it appears to be cut out of our substantial, downright existence, and never to join kindly on to it. We are not the same, but another, and perhaps more enviable individual, all the time we are out of our own country. We are lost to ourselves, as well as our friends. So the poet somewhat quaintly sings,

> Out of my country and myself I go.

Those who wish to forget painful thoughts do well to absent themselves for a while from the ties and objects that recall them; but we can be said only to fulfil our destiny in the place that gave us birth. I should on this account like well enough to spend the whole of my life in travelling abroad, if I could anywhere borrow another life to spend afterwards at home!

NOTES

1 From *The Farmer's Boy* by Robert Bloomfield (1766–1823).

2 From *Retirement* by William Cowper (1731–1800).

3 From *Comus* by John Milton (1608–1674).

4 A tilbury is a light two-wheeled carriage.

5 From Shakespeare's *Henry V*.

6 From *The Descent of Odin* by Thomas Gray (1716–1771).

7 From Shakespeare's *Othello*.

8 From Shakespeare's *Henry IV, Part I*.

9 William Cobbett (1762–1835), a political journalist and essayist.

10 Laurence Sterne (1713–1768), an English divine turned novelist, and reputed to have been one of the greatest plagiarists in English literature.

11 From Shakespeare's *Hamlet*.

12 Samuel Taylor Coleridge (1772–1834), friend of Wordsworth and one of the so-called Lake Poets who started the Romantic Movement in English poetry. See page 644.

13 From Beaumont and Fletcher's *Philaster*.

14 Where Hazlitt once visited Wordsworth and Coleridge.

15 "Gentle Charles" Lamb (1775–1834), one of the best of company in the evenings when he was freed from bookkeeping for the East India Company.

16 From Shakespeare's *Henry IV, Part I*.

17 This familiar quotation is from William Cowper's *The Task*.

18 A rasher is a thin slice of bacon.

19 Sancho Panza was the squire to that famous dreamer, Don Quixote, in Cervantes' novel.

20 Tristram Shandy, in the novel of the same name by Laurence Sterne, could never bring himself to the point, but digressed for pages at a time on material which was exasperatingly but amusingly irrelevant.

21 "Away! Away! You Unhallowed"; from Virgil's *Æneid*.

22 From Shakespeare's *Othello*.

[23] Incognito; unrecognized or unknown, hence disguise. The quotation here is a paraphrase of Dryden.

[24] score or reckoning; a bill for dinner and wine.

[25] The cartoons or sketches made by Raphael (1483–1520), Renaissance master painter, as designs for tapestries.

[26] seq. *Paul and Virginia*, a romance by Bernadine St. Pierre, 1788. *Camilla*, by Madame D'Arblay (Frances Burney), (1752–1840), friend of Doctor Samuel Johnson. *The New Heloise*, by Jean-Jacques Rousseau (1712–1778), French philosopher, deals with love letters between St. Preux and his love Julie. Rousseau will prove important enough for the student to look up his life in any standard encyclopedia. See also Boswell's first letter to Rousseau on page 74.

[27] A dainty morsel.

[28] Coleridge's translation from Schiller's *Wallenstein's Tod*.

[29] Contrast this with Wordsworth's poem "Tintern Abbey," in which he expresses his preference for sharing the joys of nature with a friend. Also Keats' sonnet on "Solitude."

[30] This character from Sir George Etherege's comedy *The Man of Mode* illustrates the seventeenth- and eighteenth-century tendency to characterize persons by their names. Watch for further illustrations in the essays of that period.

[31] Prehistoric Druid monument on Salisbury Plain, Dorsetshire, England.

[32], [33] From Milton's *Paradise Lost*.

[34] A ciceroni is a guide. The Bodleian Library is at Oxford University Blenheim is the town house of the Duke of Marlborough, and named after the battle.

[35] From a *Song* by William Roscoe (1753–1831).

QUESTIONS

1. What sections of this essay reflect that independence and candor that made Hazlitt one of the greatest nineteenth-century essayists?

2. What are the differences between this essay and those

by Montaigne and Bacon; in expression, in personal qualities, in manner of thinking?

3. Has Hazlitt restricted his writing to the subject of his title?

4. Does Hazlitt's own style satisfy his definition of style quoted in the biographical introduction to this essay?

5. What sentences in this essay would you consider significant enough to learn and quote?

6. What evidence is shown here of Hazlitt's art education?

SEEING PEOPLE OFF *

Max Beerbohm

Max Beerbohm, "the incomparable Max", is almost as well known for his cartoons and lithographs as for the delicacy of satire which makes his essays so prominent in modern English literature. One of the leaders of the *Yellow Book* group, whose publication was one of the leading English periodicals in the 1890's, Beerbohm developed the fine art of satire until no one of prominence in the English literary and political fields was safe from his pen or drawing pencil. In fact, to be caricatured by "the incomparable Max" was one of the surest gauges of a man's importance. As an accomplished writer and artist in his own right and as one of the most penetrating dramatic critics, as which he succeeded Bernard Shaw on *The Saturday Review*, Beerbohm has romped through the related fields of the arts with Puckish delight and mischief. This present essay is characteristic of but one, and that a slight, side of this many-sided writer. A more penetrating essay will be found in "The Fire" in *Yet Again;* his more sustained satire is, perhaps, best shown in his novel *Zuleika Dobson* with its shrewd appraisal of English university life and the American Rhodes Scholar. Beerbohm was born in London in 1872 and was educated at Merton College, Oxford. He now lives in Rapallo, Italy, and seldom contributes to the literary circles in which he formerly played so prominent a part.

---

* Reprinted by permission of Curtis Brown, Ltd.

I AM not good at it. To do it well seems to me one of the most difficult things in the world, and probably seems so to you, too.

To see a friend off from Waterloo to Vauxhall were easy enough. But we are never called on to perform that small feat. It is only when a friend is going on a longish journey, and will be absent for a longish time, that we turn up at the railway station. The dearer the friend, and the longer the journey, and the longer the likely absence, the earlier do we turn up, and the more lamentably do we fail. Our failure is in exact ratio to the seriousness of the occasion, and to the depth of our feeling.

In a room, or even on a doorstep, we can make the farewell quite worthily. We can express in our faces the genuine sorrow we feel. Nor do words fail us. There is no awkwardness, no restraint, on either side. The thread of our intimacy has not been snapped. The leave-taking is an ideal one. Why not, then, leave the leave-taking at that? Always, departing friends implore us not to bother to come to the railway station next morning. Always, we are deaf to these entreaties, knowing them to be not quite sincere. The departing friends would think it very odd of us if we took them at their word. Besides, they really do want to see us again. And that wish is heartily reciprocated. We duly turn up. And then, oh then, what a gulf yawns! We stretch our arms vainly across it. We have utterly lost touch. We have nothing at all to say. We gaze at each other as dumb animals gaze at human beings. We 'make conversation'—and such conversation! We know that these are the friends from whom we parted overnight. They know that we have not altered. Yet, on the surface, everything is different; and the tension is such that we only long for the guard to blow his whistle and put an end to the farce.

On a bleak morning of last week I duly turned up at Euston, to see off an old friend who was starting for America.

Overnight, we had given him a farewell dinner, in which sadness was well mingled with festivity. Years probably would elapse before his return. Some of us might never see him again. Not ignoring the shadow of the future, we gaily celebrated the past. We were as thankful to have known our guest as we were grieved to lose him; and both these emotions were made evident. It was a perfect farewell.

And now, here we were, stiff and self-conscious on the platform; and framed in the window of the railway carriage was the face of our friend; but it was as the face of a stranger—a stranger anxious to please, an appealing stranger, an awkward stranger. 'Have you got everything?' asked one of us, breaking the silence. 'Yes, everything,' said our friend, with a pleasant nod. 'Everything,' he repeated, with the emphasis of an empty brain. 'You'll be able to lunch on the train,' said I, though this prophecy had already been made more than once. 'Oh yes,' he said with conviction. He added that the train went straight through to Liverpool. This fact seemed to strike us as rather odd. We exchanged glances. 'Doesn't it stop at Crewe?' asked one of us. 'No,' said our friend, briefly. He seemed almost disagreeable. There was a long pause. One of us, with a nod and a forced smile at the traveller, said 'Well!' The nod, the smile, and the unmeaning monosyllable were returned conscientiously. Another pause was broken by one of us with a fit of coughing. It was an obviously assumed fit, but it served to pass the time. The bustle of the platform was unabated. There was no sign of the train's departure. Release— ours, and our friend's—was not yet.

My wandering eye alighted on a rather portly middle-aged man who was talking earnestly from the platform to a young lady at the next window but one to ours. His fine profile was vaguely familiar to me. The young lady was evidently American, and he was evidently English; otherwise I should have guessed from his impressive air that he was her father. I wished I could hear what he was saying. I was sure he was giving the very best advice; and the strong tenderness of his gaze was really beautiful. He seemed magnetic, as he poured out his final injunctions. I could feel something of his magnetism even where I stood. And the magnetism, like the profile, was vaguely familiar to me. Where had I experienced it?

In a flash I remembered. The man was Hubert

le Ros. But how changed since last I saw him! That was seven or eight years ago, in the Strand. He was then (as usual) out of an engagement, and borrowed half-a-crown. It seemed a privilege to lend anything to him. He was always magnetic. And why his magnetism had never made him successful on the London stage was always a mystery to me. He was an excellent actor, and a man of sober habit. But, like many others of his kind, Hubert le Ros (I do not, of course, give the actual name by which he was known) drifted seedily away into the provinces; and I, like every one else, ceased to remember him.

It was strange to see him, after all these years, here on the platform of Euston, looking so prosperous and solid. It was not only the flesh he had put on, but also the clothes, that made him hard to recognise. In the old days, an imitation fur coat had seemed to be as integral a part of him as were his ill-shorn lantern jaws. But now his costume was a model of rich and sombre moderation, drawing, not calling, attention to itself. He looked like a banker. Any one would have been proud to be seen off by him.

'Stand back, please.' The train was about to start, and I waved farewell to my friend. Le Ros did not stand back. He stood clasping in both hands the hands of the young American. 'Stand back, sir, please!' He obeyed, but quickly darted forward again to whisper some final word. I think there were tears in her eyes. There certainly were

tears in his when, at length, having watched the
train out of sight, he turned round. He seemed,
nevertheless, delighted to see me. He asked me
where I had been hiding all these years; and si-
multaneously repaid me the half-crown as though
it had been borrowed yesterday. He linked his
arm in mine, and walked me slowly along the platform, saying with what pleasure he read my dramatic criticisms every Saturday.

I told him, in return, how much he was missed
on the stage. 'Ah yes,' he said, 'I never act on the
stage nowadays.' He laid some emphasis on the
word 'stage,' and I asked him where, then, he did
act. 'On the platform,' he answered. 'You mean,'
said I, 'that you recite at concerts?' He smiled.
'This,' he whispered, striking his stick on the
ground, 'is the platform I mean.' Had his mysterious prosperity unhinged him? He looked quite
sane. I begged him to be more explicit.

'I suppose,' he said presently, giving me a light
for the cigar which he had offered me, 'you have
been seeing a friend off?' I assented. He asked me
what I supposed *he* had been doing. I said that I
had watched him doing the same thing. 'No,' he
said gravely. 'That lady was not a friend of mine.
I met her for the first time this morning, less than
half an hour ago, *here,*' and again struck the platform with his stick.

I confessed that I was bewildered. He smiled.
'You may,' he said, 'have heard of the Anglo-
American Social Bureau?' I had not. He ex-

plained to me that of the thousands of Americans who annually pass through England there are many hundreds who have no English friends. In the old days they used to bring letters of introduction. But the English are so inhospitable that these letters are hardly worth the paper they are written on. 'Thus,' said Le Ros, 'the A.A.S.B. supplies a long-felt want. Americans are a sociable people, and most of them have plenty of money to spend. The A.A.S.B. supplies them with English friends. Fifty per cent of the fees is paid over to the friends. The other fifty is retained by the A.A.S.B. I am not, alas, a director. If I were, I should be a very rich man indeed. I am only an employee. But even so I do very well. I am one of the seers-off.'

Again I asked for enlightenment. 'Many Americans,' he said, 'cannot afford to keep friends in England. But they can all afford to be seen off. The fee is only five pounds (twenty-five dollars) for a single traveller; and eight pounds (forty dollars) for a party of two or more. They send that in to the Bureau, giving the date of their departure, and a description by which the seer-off can identify them on the platform. And then— well, then they are seen off.'

'But is it worth it?' I exclaimed. 'Of course it is worth it,' said Le Ros. 'It prevents them from feeling "out of it." It earns them the respect of the guard. It saves them from being despised by their fellow-passengers—the people who are going

to be on the boat. It gives them a *footing* for the
whole voyage. Besides, it is a great pleasure in
itself. You saw me seeing that young lady off.
Didn't you think I did it beautifully?' 'Beautifully,' I admitted. 'I envied you. There was I—'
'Yes, I can imagine. There were you, shuffling
from foot to foot, staring blankly at your friend,
trying to make conversation. I know. That's how
I used to be myself, before I studied, and went
into the thing professionally. I don't say I'm perfect yet. I'm still a martyr to platform fright. A
railway station is the most difficult of all places
to act in, as you have discovered for yourself.'
'But,' I said with resentment, 'I wasn't trying to
act. I really *felt*.' 'So did I, my boy,' said Le Ros.
'You can't act without feeling. What's-his-name,
the Frenchman—Diderot, yes—said you could;
but what did *he* know about it? Didn't you see
those tears in my eyes when the train started? I
hadn't forced them. I tell you I was *moved*. So
were you, I dare say. But you couldn't have
pumped up a tear to prove it. You can't express
your feelings. In other words, you can't act. At
any rate,' he added kindly, 'not in a railway station.' 'Teach me!' I cried. He looked thoughtfully
at me. 'Well,' he said at length, 'the seeing-off season is practically over. Yes, I'll give you a course.
I have a good many pupils on hand already; but
yes,' he said, consulting an ornate notebook, 'I
could give you an hour on Tuesdays and Fridays.'

His terms, I confess, are rather high. But I do not grudge the investment.

QUESTIONS

1. From what does Beerbohm mostly derive his humor—character, situation, or choice of word?
2. What other situations common to everyday life could be similarly treated in an essay?
3. Would you compare, or contrast, Beerbohm's humor with that of Arthur G. Staples? (See page 65.) Give your reasons with specific references to their essays.

A PHILOSOPHER THAT FAILED *

E. V. Lucas

EDWARD VERRAL LUCAS is well known as traveler, critic
of the arts and letters, novelist, poet, essayist, biographer,
publisher, and authority on cricket. His *Wanderer in
Paris, Wanderer in London,* and others in the *Wanderer*
series are among the best of travel and art books; his biography of Charles Lamb is far and away the best work
on that essayist, whom he resembles so much in spirit; but
he is best known as a master of the light, familiar essay.
As such he reveals himself as a lover of books, of the out-
of-doors, of galleries and cathedrals, of foreign lands and
customs, of prize-fighters, of the companionship of all
sorts of people. As the head of Methuen and Company,
English publishers, and as an active club man in London,
he has the reputation of knowing practically everybody of
note in English literary life. A native of Brighton (born
1868), Lucas was educated at University College, London,
and immediately entered journalism. He is assistant editor
of the celebrated London *Punch* and a contributor to various leading periodicals. This essay, "A Philosopher That
Failed", from *Character and Comedy*, is but one of many
that reflect his devotion to Boswell's *Life of Samuel Johnson*, the gold mine of many another essayist. Lovers of
Charles Lamb see more than a gesture in Lucas' endowing
the grave of Lamb with perpetual care.

* From *Character and Comedy* by E. V. Lucas. Reprinted by
permission of The Macmillan Company.

OF OLIVER EDWARDS, nothing, I believe, is known beyond the fact that he had been at Pembroke College with Dr. Johnson; that he was a solicitor in Barnard's Inn; that he married twice; that he lived on a little farm of sixty acres near Stevenage and came to London twice a week; and that he wore grey clothes and a wig with many curls, and went to church on Good Fridays. We know of Edwards' life only this, and of his speech we have only some dozen sentences; and yet he will live for ever, by virtue of having crossed the stage of literature on one fine morning one hundred and twenty-nine years ago. He might be likened to the bird with which the Venerable Bede [1] compared the life of man in a famous and beautiful passage: the bird that flies out of the dark void into the lighted banqueting hall and out again into the void once more. So with Edwards: for sixty years he was not; then he met Dr. Johnson and his Boswell in Butcher Row, stayed with them for an hour; and was not again. But the hour was sufficient: it gave him time to make his one deathless remark. By virtue of that remark he lives, and will live.

Edwards' day was Good Friday, April 17, 1778—"a delightful day," says Boswell. How little the good Edwards can have thought, as he climbed out of his bed in Barnard's Inn that morning and donned his grey clothes and his curly wig, that he was about to become immortal. He spent, I take it, the early hours in his office, reading conveyances or deeds and writing letters; then he went to church, whither Dr. Johnson and Boswell had also gone, to St. Clement's, which through some strange stroke of luck is standing, with the Doctor's pew intact within it, to this dark, irreverent, rebuilding day.

On the way Boswell (who could grow the flower quite easily now, having obtained much seed) remarked that Fleet Street was the most cheerful scene in the world, adding, skilfully as he thought, "Fleet Street is, in my mind, more delightful than Tempe!" [2] The Doctor, however, having the same dislike of the imitator that most teachers and all cynics possess, had his dash of cold water ready. "Ay, ay, but let it be compared with Mull." [3] So they passed on to church, where the Doctor was pleased to see so numerous a congregation.

It was after church that they met Edwards, whom Johnson had not seen for forty years. The recognition came from the lawyer, a talkative, friendly, and not easily daunted man, who thereafter quickly got to work and enlarged to Boswell on the pleasure of living in the country. Boswell, again in the true Johnsonian manner, replied, "I have no notion of this, sir. What you have to entertain you is, I think, exhausted in half an hour." But Edwards was deeper and more sincere. "What," he said, "don't you love to have hope realized? I see my grass, and my corn, and my trees growing. Now, for instance, I am curious to see if this frost has not nipped my fruit trees."

Johnson, who had been in a reverie, possibly missing the familiar scent of incense,—for, in spite of Boswell's innuendoes to the contrary, Edwards does not appear to have been at all impressed by the magnitude and lustre of his old friend,—here remarked, "You find, sir, you have fears as well as hopes;" and I am glad he did so, for it gave Boswell the opportunity to add the reflection, "So well did he see the whole when another saw but the half of a subject." And yet it is more than likely that Edwards saw the whole too.

Being comfortably seated in the Bolt Court library on this sunny Good Friday, Edwards, who had already commented with delightful bluntness, but perfect innocence, on the Doctor's age, remarked, "Sir, I remember you would not let us say 'prodigious' at college. For even then," he added, turning to Boswell, "he was delicate in language, and we all feared him." Johnson said nothing of this at the time, but to his Boswell said afterwards, in private, "Sir, they respected me for my literature"—meaning by "they" the undergraduates—"and yet it was not great but by comparison. Sir, it is amazing how little literature there is in the world." That was one hundred and twenty-nine years ago, and it is amazing still.

The conversation with Edwards then turned to money, and it came out that the lawyer had given much away. He also admitted to a longing to be a parson and live in comfort and comparative idleness. Johnson had an opening here, and took it.

"I would rather have Chancery suits upon my hands," he said, "than the care of souls. No, sir, I do not envy a clergyman's life as an easy life, nor do I envy the clergyman who makes it an easy life." Edwards, however, did. There is no evidence that the Doctor convinced him. My impression is that he was never convinced by anyone's arguments. I picture him as the kind of man who goes through life contentedly, secure in his own opinion.

Nothing could daunt Edwards, and so innocent and happy was he that he had no notion he was not observing the strict rules of the game. The rules of the Johnson conversational game made it imperative that you should utter only questions or provocative opinions, and then wait for the answer and receive it humbly. But Edwards smilingly broke them all. He asked questions, it is true, but long before the Doctor could reply he had volunteered, with appalling hardihood, scraps of autobiography. If there is one thing an autobiographer like Johnson cannot stand it is the autobiography of others. And yet the Doctor, with his great human imagination, knew that Edwards was a pearl of sincerity and candour, and in his heart, I am sure, valued him accordingly. "I have been twice married, Doctor," said Edwards, apropos of nothing, cheerily adding the terrifying sentiment, "You, I suppose, have never known what it was to have a wife?" This—to Johnson! We can see Boswell shivering on his chair's edge. "Sir," said Dr. Johnson, "I have known what it was to have a wife, and (in a solemn, tender, faltering tone) I have known what it was to lose a wife. It had almost broke my heart." Edwards was unabashed. He said instantly, "How do you live, sir?" adding, "For my part, I must have my regular meals and a glass of good wine." Dr. Johnson replied suitably—the kind of reply that would usually settle the matter among his guests—"I now drink no wine, sir. Early in life I drank wine; for many years I drank none. I then for some years drank a great deal." Edwards rose to a fine height of irreverence here, to the immense dismay, I have no doubt, of Boswell, who, with all his advantages, had not been at Pembroke with his hero. He cut in with, "Some hogsheads, I warrant you." The Doctor succeeded in taking no notice (quite possibly he was secretly flattered; we all like to be credited with great deeds), and continued his dull alimentary history; but the victory was Edwards', for the Doctor, when asked if he ate supper, merely and very uncharacteristically said "No," leaving it for his visitor to remark, with something of the great man's own manner made human, "For my part, now, I consider supper as a turnpike through which one must pass in order to get to bed."

That is good enough; but it is not the single remark by which Edwards is known—on which his deathless fame rests. That had come earlier. "You are a philosopher, Dr. Johnson," said Edwards. "I have tried, too, in my time to be a philosopher; but I don't know how; cheerfulness was always breaking in." That was Edwards' great speech. By virtue of that candid confession he takes his place with the shining company of simple souls, the hierarchy of the ingenuous. It was too much for Boswell, who had no eye for children, young or old. But on repeating it to Mr. Burke,[4] Sir Joshua Reynolds, Mr. Courtenay, Mr. Malone, and, indeed, all the eminent men he knew, they said with one accord that "it was an exquisite trait of character." He therefore refrained from belittling it in the book.

To Boswell's intense relief, Edwards at last went. He had begun by calling Dr. Johnson (who was sixty-nine) old; he left with another reference to his age. Looking him full in the face, he said, "You'll find in Dr. Young the line,

'O my coevals! remnants of yourselves.' "

When he was gone, Boswell came to himself again, and quickly remarked that he thought him a weak man; and the Doctor smarting under the imputation of senility, was, I regret to say, weak enough to agree. But they were both wrong. Edwards was a strong man—strong in his cheerfulness and his transparency.

NOTES

[1] The Venerable Bede (673–735), author of *Ecclesiastical History of England*, source book of earliest English history.

[2] The Vale of Tempe, sacred to Apollo, was one of the famed beauty spots in ancient Greece.

[3] One of the desolate islands in the Hebrides group off the northwest coast of Scotland.

[4] In Dr. Johnson's Literary Club, Burke represented politics; Reynolds, art. Courtenay and Malone were literary acquaintances of Johnson.

Questions

1. What makes Edwards' remark about philosophy and cheerfulness "deathless"?

2. What qualities in Edwards denote strength of character?

3. What does this essay reveal about the character of Lucas?

THE MOWING OF A FIELD *

HILAIRE BELLOC

Few contemporary essayists can approach HILAIRE BEL-
LOC in spinning some fragile trifle into an enduring fabric.
Through him moments become timeless; the merest gesture of a man becomes character, and with so light a
touch that one is scarcely conscious of the development of
any theme. In this respect, his essays differ from his other
works; in his histories (five of them) and in his controversial papers against George Bernard Shaw (over Social-
ism and Bolshevism) and against H. G. Wells (over
Catholicism and inaccuracies in Wells' *Outline of History*)
he writes with a heavier hand, leaving the reader in no
doubt about his theme and his steps in developing it.
Once a member of Parliament, he retired from political
life to be better able to criticize it from without. His association with Gilbert Chesterton in defending the Catholic
Church from the onslaughts made upon it by George Bernard Shaw has so linked his name with Chesterton's in the
public mind that the two seem almost inseparable. Shaw
refers to them as "the Chesterbelloc, an animal with four
legs, capable of doing infinite harm." Belloc was born near
Paris in 1870, the son of a prominent French barrister and
an English mother. He was educated at Egbaston Oratory
School and at Balliol College, Oxford. He served his French
military term in Artillery, but later became an English citizen. He lives in the country, about twenty miles from

* From *Hills and the Sea*. Reprinted by permission of Charles
Scribner's Sons, publishers.

London, at Horsham, and bases his convictions about social and economic changes upon his own knowledge of country life and folk-ways. The essay here presented, "The Mowing of a Field," reflects a love of the soil not unlike that of America's Robert Frost.

THERE is a valley in South England remote from ambition and from fear, where the passage of strangers is rare and unperceived, and where the scent of the grass in summer is breathed only by those who are native to that unvisited land. The roads to the Channel do not traverse it; they choose upon either side easier passes over the range. One track alone leads up through it to the hills, and this is changeable: now green where men have little occasion to go, now a good road where it nears the homesteads and the barns. The woods grow steep above the slopes; they reach sometimes the very summit of the heights, or, when they cannot attain them, fill in and clothe the coombes.[1] And, in between, along the floor of the valley, deep pastures and their silence are bordered by lawns of chalky grass and the small yew trees of the Downs.

The clouds that visit its sky reveal themselves beyond the one great rise, and sail, white and enormous, to the other, and sink beyond that other. But the plains above which they have traveled and the Weald [2] to which they go, the people of the valley cannot see and hardly recall. The wind, when it reaches such fields, is no longer a gale from the salt, but fruitful and soft, an inland breeze; and those whose blood was nourished here feel in that wind the fruitfulness of our orchards and all the life that all things draw from the air.

In this place, when I was a boy, I pushed through a fringe of beeches that made a complete screen between me and the world, and I came to a glade called No Man's Land. I climbed beyond it; and I was surprised and glad, because from the ridge of that glade, I saw the sea. To this place very lately I returned.

The many things that I recovered as I came up the countryside were not less charming than when a distant memory had enshrined them, but much more. Whatever veil is thrown by a longing recollection had not intensified nor even made more mysterious the beauty of that happy ground; not in my very dreams of morning had I, in exile, seen it more beloved or more rare. Much also that I had forgotten now returned to me as I approached—a group of elms, a little turn of the parson's wall, a small paddock beyond the graveyard close, cherished by one man, with a low wall of very old stone guarding it all round. And all these things fulfilled and amplified my delight, till even the good vision of the place, which I had kept so many years, left me and was replaced by its better reality. "Here," I said to myself, "is a symbol of what some say is reserved for the soul: pleasure of a kind which cannot be imagined save in a moment when at last it is attained."

When I came to my own gate and my own field, and had before me the house I knew, I looked around a little (though it was already evening), and I saw that the grass was standing as it should stand when it is ready for the scythe. For in this, as in everything that a man can do—of those things at least which are very old—there is an exact moment when they are done best. And it has been remarked of whatever rules us that it works blunderingly, seeing that the good things given to a man are not given at the precise moment when they would have filled him with delight. But, whether this be true or false, we can choose the just turn of the seasons in everything we do of our own will, and especially in the making of hay. Many think that hay is best made when the grass is thickest; and so they delay until it is rank and in flower, and has already heavily pulled the ground. And there is another false reason for delay, which is wet weather. For very few will understand (though it comes year after year) that we have rain always in South England between the sickle and the scythe, or say just after the weeks of east wind are over. First we have a week of sudden warmth, as though the south had come to see us all; then we have the weeks of east and southeast wind; and then we have more or less of that rain of which I spoke, and which always astonishes the world. Now it is just before, or during, or at the very end of, that rain—but not later—that grass should be cut for

hay. True, upland grass, which is always thin,
should be cut earlier than the grass in the bottoms
and along the water meadows; but not even the
latest, even in the wettest seasons, should be left
(as it is) to flower and even to seed. For what we
get when we store our grass is not a harvest of
something ripe, but a thing just caught in its
prime before maturity; as witness that our corn
and straw are best yellow, but our hay is best
green. So also Death should be represented with a
scythe and Time with a sickle; for Time can take
only what is ripe, but Death comes always too
soon. In a word, then, it is always much easier to
cut grass too late than too early; and I, under
that evening and come back to these pleasant
fields, looked at the grass and knew that it was
time. June was in full advance; it was the beginning of that season when the night has already
lost her foothold of the earth and hovers over it,
never quite descending, but mixing sunset with
the dawn.

Next morning, before it was yet broad day, I
awoke, and thought of the mowing. The birds
were already chattering in the trees beside my
window, all except the nightingale, which had left
and flown away to the Weald, where he sings all
summer by day as well as by night in the oaks
and the hazel spinneys,[3] and especially along the
little river Adur, one of the rivers of the Weald.
The birds and the thought of the mowing had
awakened me, and I went down the stairs and

along the stone floors to where I could find a
scythe; and when I took it from its nail, I remembered how, fourteen years ago, I had last gone out
with my scythe, just so, into the fields at morning.
In between that day and this were many things,
cities and armies, and a confusion of books,
mountains and the desert, and horrible great
breadths of sea.

When I got out into the long grass, the sun was
not yet risen, but there were already many colors
in the eastern sky, and I made haste to sharpen
my scythe, so that I might get to the cutting before the dew should dry. Some say that it is best
to wait till all the dew has risen, so as to get the
grass quite dry from the very first. But, though it
is an advantage to get the grass quite dry, yet it
is not worth while to wait till the dew has risen.
For, in the first place, you lose many hours of
work (and those the coolest), and next—which is
more important—you lose that great ease and
thickness in cutting which comes of the dew. So I
at once began to sharpen my scythe.

There is an art also in the sharpening of the
scythe, and it is worth describing carefully. Your
blade must be dry, and that is why you will see
men rubbing the scythe-blade with grass before
they whet it. Then also your rubber must be quite
dry, and on this account it is a good thing to lay it
on your coat and keep it there during all your
day's mowing. The scythe you stand upright, with
the blade pointing away from you, and put your

left hand firmly on the back of the blade, grasping it: then you pass the rubber first down one side of the blade-edge and then down the other, beginning near the handle and going on to the point and working quickly and hard. When you first do this you will, perhaps, cut your hand; but it is only at first that such an accident will happen to you.

To tell when the scythe is sharp enough, this is the rule. First the stone clangs and grinds against the iron harshly; then it rings musically to one note; then, at last, it purrs as though the iron and stone were exactly suited. When you hear this, your scythe is sharp enough; and I, when I heard it that June dawn, with everything quite silent except the birds, let down the scythe and bent myself to mow.

When one does anything anew, after so many years, one fears very much for one's trick or habit. But all things once learnt are easily recoverable, and I very soon recovered the swing and power of the mower. Mowing well and mowing badly—or rather not mowing at all—are separated by very little; as is also true of writing verse, of playing the fiddle, and of dozens of other things, but of nothing more than of believing. For the bad or young or untaught mower without tradition, the mower Promethean, the mower original and contemptuous of the past, does all these things: He leaves great crescents of grass uncut. He digs the point of the scythe hard into the

ground with a jerk. He loosens the handles and
even the fastening of the blade. He twists the
blade with his blunders, he blunts the blade, he
chips it, dulls it, or breaks it clean off at the tip.
If any one is standing by, he cuts him in the
ankle. He sweeps up into the air wildly, with
nothing to resist his stroke. He drags up earth
with the grass, which is like making the meadow
bleed. But the good mower who does things just
as they should be done and have been for a hundred thousand years, falls into none of these fool-
eries. He goes forward very steadily, his scythe-
blade just barely missing the ground, every grass
falling; the swish and rhythm of his mowing are
always the same.

So great an art can only be learnt by continual
practice; but this much is worth writing down,
that, as in all good work, to know the thing with
which you work is the core of the affair. Good
verse is best written on good paper with an easy
pen, not with a lump of coal on a whitewashed
wall. The pen thinks for you; and so does the
scythe mow for you if you treat it honorably and
in a manner that makes it recognize its service.
The manner is this. You must regard the scythe
as a pendulum that swings, not as a knife that
cuts. A good mower puts no more strength into
his stroke than into his lifting. Again, stand up to
your work. The bad mower, eager and full of
pain, leans forward and tries to force the scythe
through the grass. The good mower, serene and

able, stands as nearly straight as the shape of the
scythe will let him, and follows up every stroke
closely, moving his left foot forward. Then also
let every stroke get well away. Mowing is a thing
of ample gestures, like drawing a cartoon. Then,
again, get yourself into a mechanical and repeti-
tive mood: be thinking of anything at all but
your mowing, and be anxious only when there
seems some interruption to the monotony of the
sound. In this, mowing should be like one's
prayers—all of a sort and always the same, and
so made that you can establish a monotony and
work them, as it were, with half your mind: that
happier half, the half that does not bother.

In this way, when I had recovered the art after
so many years, I went forward over the field, cutting lane after lane through the grass, and bringing out its most secret essences with the sweep of
the scythe until the air was full of odors. At the
end of every lane I sharpened my scythe and
looked back at the work done, and then carried
my scythe down again upon my shoulder to begin
another. So, long before the bell rang in the
chapel above me—that is, long before six o'clock,
which is the time for the Angelus—I had many
swathes already lying in order parallel like sol-
diery; and the high grass yet standing, making a
great contrast with the shaven part, looked dense
and high. As it says in the Ballad of Val-ès-
Dunes, where—

The tall son of the Seven Winds
Came riding out of Hither-hythe,

and his horse-hoofs (you will remember) tram-
pled into the press and made a gap in it, and his
sword (as you know)

was like a scythe
In Arcus when the grass is high
And all the swathes in order lie,
And there's the bailiff standing by
A-gathering of the tithe.

So I mowed all that morning, till the houses
awoke in the valley, and from some of them rose
a little fragrant smoke, and men began to be seen.

I stood still and rested on my scythe to watch
the awakening of the village, when I saw coming
up to my field a man whom I had known in older
times, before I had left the Valley.

He was of that dark silent race upon which all
the learned quarrel, but which, by whatever
meaningless name it may be called—Iberian, or
Celtic, or what you will—is the permanent root of
all England, and makes England wealthy and preserves it everywhere, except perhaps in the Fens
and in a part of Yorkshire. Everywhere else you
will find it active and strong. These people are intensive; their thoughts and their labors turn inward. It is on account of their presence in these
islands that our gardens are the richest in the
world. They also love low rooms and ample fires
and great warm slopes of thatch. They have, as I

believe, an older acquaintance with the English air than any other of all the strains that make up England. They hunted in the Weald with stones, and camped in the pines of the green-sand. They lurked under the oaks of the upper rivers, and saw the legionaries go up, up the straight paved road from the sea. They helped the few pirates to destroy the towns, and mixed with those pirates and shared the spoils of the Roman villas, and were glad to see the captains and the priests destroyed. They remain; and no admixture of the Frisian pirates, or the Breton, or the Angevin and Norman conquerors, has very much affected their cunning eyes.

To this race, I say, belonged the man who now approached me. And he said to me, "Mowing?" And I answered, "Ar." Then he also said, "Ar," as in duty bound; for so we speak to each other in the Stenes [4] of the Downs.

Next he told me that, as he had nothing to do, he would lend me a hand; and I thanked him warmly, or, as we say, "kindly." For it is a good custom of ours always to treat bargaining as though it were a courteous pastime; and though what he was after was money, and what I wanted was his labor at the least pay, yet we both played the comedy that we were free men, the one granting a grace and the other accepting it. For the dry bones of commerce, avarice and method and need, are odious to the Valley; and we cover them up with a pretty body of fiction and observances.

Thus, when it comes to buying pigs, the buyer does not begin to decry the pig and the vendor to praise it, as is the custom with lesser men; but tradition makes them do business in this fashion:—

First the buyer will go up to the seller when he sees him in his own steading, and, looking at the pig with admiration, the buyer will say that rain may or may not fall, or that we shall have snow or thunder, according to the time of the year. Then the seller, looking critically at the pig, will agree that the weather is as his friend maintains. There is no haste at all; great leisure marks the dignity of their exchange. And the next step is, that the buyer says: "That's a fine pig you have there, Mr.——" (giving the seller's name). "Ar, powerful fine pig." Then the seller, saying also "Mr." (for twin brothers rocked in one cradle give each other ceremonious observance here), the seller, I say, admits, as though with reluctance, the strength and beauty of the pig, and falls into deep thought. Then the buyer says, as though moved by a great desire, that he is ready to give so much for the pig, naming half the proper price, or a little less. Then the seller remains in silence for some moments; and at last begins to shake his head slowly, till he says: "I don't be thinking of selling the pig, anyways." He will also add that a party only Wednesday offered him so much for the pig—and he names about double the proper price. Thus all ritual is duly accomplished; and the solemn act is entered upon with reverence and in a spirit of truth. For when the buyer uses this phrase: "I'll tell you what I *will* do," and offers within half a crown of the pig's value, the seller replies that he can refuse him nothing, and names half a crown above its value; the difference is split, the pig is sold, and in the quiet soul of each runs the peace of something accomplished.

Thus do we buy a pig or land or labor or malt or lime, always with elaboration and set forms; and many a London man has paid double and more for his violence and his greedy haste and very unchivalrous higgling. As happened with the land at Underwaltham, which the mortgagees had begged and implored the estate to take at twelve hundred and had privately offered to all the world at a thousand, but which a sharp direct man, of the kind that makes great fortunes, a man in a motor-car, a man in a fur coat, a man of few words, bought for two thousand three hundred before my very eyes, protesting that they might take his offer or leave it; and all because he did not begin by praising the land.

Well, then, this man I spoke of offered to help me, and he went to get his scythe. But I went into the house and brought out a gallon jar of small ale for him and for me; for the sun was now very warm, and small ale goes well with mowing. When we had drunk some of this ale in mugs called "I see you," we took each a swathe, he a little be-

hind me because he was the better mower; and
so for many hours we swung, one before the other,
mowing and mowing at the tall grass of the field.
And the sun rose to noon and we were still at our
mowing; and we ate food, but only for a little
while, and we took again to our mowing. And at
last there was nothing left but a small square of
grass, standing like a square of linesmen who
keep their formation, tall and unbroken, with all
the dead lying around them when the battle is
over and done.

Then for some little time I rested after all those
hours; and the man and I talked together, and a
long way off we heard in another field the musical
sharpening of a scythe.

The sunlight slanted powdered and mellow over
the breadth of the valley; for day was nearing its
end. I went to fetch rakes from the steading; and
when I had come back the last of the grass had
fallen, and all the field lay flat and smooth, with
the very green short grass in lanes between the
dead and yellow swathes.

These swathes we raked into cocks to keep
them from the dew against our return at daybreak; and we made the cocks as tall and steep as
we could, for in that shape they best keep off the
dew, and it is easier also to spread them after the
sun has risen. Then we raked up every straggling
blade, till the whole field was a clean floor for the
tedding and the carrying of the hay next morning.
The grass we had mown was but a little over two

acres; for that is all the pasture on my little tiny farm.

When we had done all this, there fell upon us the beneficent and deliberate evening; so that as we sat a little while together near the rakes, we saw the valley more solemn and dim around us, and all the trees and hedgerows quite still, and held by a complete silence. Then I paid my companion his wage, and bade him a good night, till we should meet in the same place before sunrise.

He went off with a slow and steady progress, as all our peasants do, making their walking a part of the easy but continual labor of their lives. But I sat on, watching the light creep around towards the north and change, and the waning moon coming up as though by stealth behind the woods of No Man's Land.

NOTES

[1] narrow, ravine-like valleys.
[2] wold, or open country. Here, a wooded district extending over the southern countries of Kent, Surrey, and Sussex.
[3] copses or thickets of hazel.
[4] twisted or contorted vowel sounds.

SUGGESTIONS

1. Note especially the selection of detail in this essay. Nothing is included that would detract from the simple operation with which Belloc is here concerned.

2. Compare the subtle use of exposition here; the blending of exposition and narrative, without the stiffness of ordinary exposition.

3. Look up David Grayson's essay "The Mowing" in *Adventures in Contentment*.

SELECTIONS FROM
THE PRIVATE PAPERS OF
HENRY RYECROFT

GEORGE GISSING

GEORGE GISSING (1857–1903), English novelist, is best
known for his stories of the poorer classes of London. His
emphasis upon the hopeless struggle of poverty-ridden people against the relentlessness of fate and the conflict between education and the force of circumstance, is the
result of his own struggles with poverty during young man-
hood. He was born in Wakefield, and was sent to a
Quaker Boarding School at Alderly Edge and later attended Owens College, Manchester, where he excelled in
classical studies. After college, Gissing removed to London
where he soon learned to know the hearts of the poor
through his struggles, with them, against privation and
hunger. His *Private Papers of Henry Ryecroft,* which appeared in 1903, the year of his death, is a partly autobiographical record of an educated person's conflict with circumstances beyond his control. In his critical study of
Gissing, Frank Swinnerton says that Gissing lost, in his
deep wish for the comforts of life, the deeper significance
of want. But to a generation such as ours, which has seen
painters and sculptors bartering their creations for food and
dental work, this excerpt from Gissing's *Private Papers* will
not seem exaggerated. A comparison of the essays of Swinnerton, Gissing, Stevenson, Martin, and Thoreau will shed
light on this conflict of attitudes.

I

"SIR," said Johnson,[1] "all the arguments which are brought to represent poverty as no evil, show it to be evidently a great evil. You never find people labouring to convince you that you may live very happily upon a plentiful fortune."

He knew what he was talking of, that rugged old master of common sense. Poverty is of course a relative thing. The term has reference, above all, to one's standing as an intellectual being. If I am to believe the newspapers, there are title-bearing men and women in England, who, had they an assured income of five-and-twenty shillings per week, would have no right to call themselves poor, for their intellectual needs are those of a stable-boy or scullery wench. Give me the same income and I can live, but I am poor indeed.

You tell me that money cannot buy the things most precious. Your commonplace proves that you have never known the lack of it. When I think of all the sorrow and the barrenness that has been wrought in my life by want of a few more pounds per annum than I was able to earn, I stand aghast at money's significance. What kindly joys have I lost—those simple forms of happiness to which every heart has claim—because of poverty! Meetings with those I loved made impossible year after year; sadness, misunderstanding, nay, cruel alienation, arising from inability to do the things I wished, and which I might have done had a little money helped me; endless instances of homely pleasure and contentment curtailed or forbidden by narrow means. I have lost friends merely through the constraints of my position; friends I might have made have remained strangers to me; solitude of the bitter kind, the solitude which is enforced at times when mind or heart longs for companionship, often cursed my life solely because I was poor. I think it would scarce be an exaggeration to say that there is no moral good which has not to be paid for in coin of the realm.

"Poverty," said Johnson again, "is so great an evil, and pregnant with so much temptation, so much misery, that I cannot but earnestly enjoin you to avoid it."

For my own part, I needed no injunction to that effort of avoidance. Many a London garret knows how I struggled with the unwelcome chamber-fellow. I marvel she did not abide with me to the end. It is a sort of inconsequence in Nature, and sometimes makes me vaguely uneasy through nights of broken sleep.

II

To-day I have read *The Tempest*. It is perhaps the play that I love best, and, because I seem to myself to know it so well, I commonly pass it over in opening the book. Yet, as always in regard to Shakespeare, having read it once more, I find that my knowledge was less complete than I supposed. So it would be, live as long as one might; so it would ever be, whilst one had strength to turn the pages and a mind left to read them.

I like to believe that this was the poet's last work, that he wrote it in his home at Stratford, walking day by day in the fields which had taught his boyhood to love rural England. It is ripe fruit of the supreme imagination, perfect craft of the master hand. For a man whose life's business it has been to study the English tongue, what joy can equal that of marking the happy ease wherewith Shakespeare surpasses, in mere command of words, every achievement of those even who, apart from him, are great? I could fancy that, in *The Tempest,* he wrought with a peculiar consciousness of this power, smiling as the word of inimitable felicity, the phrase of incomparable cadence, was whispered to him by the Ariel [2] that was his genius. He seems to sport with language, to amuse himself with new discovery of its resources. From king to beggar, men of every rank and every order of mind have spoken with his lips; he has uttered the lore of fairyland; now it pleases him to create a being neither man nor fairy, a something between brute and human nature, and to endow its purposes with words. These words, how they smack of the moist and spawning earth, of the life of creatures that cannot rise above the soil! We do not think of it enough; we stint our wonder because we fall short in appreciation. A miracle is worked before us, and we scarce give heed; it has become familiar to our minds as any other of nature's marvels, which we rarely pause to reflect upon. *The Tempest* contains the noblest meditative passage in all the plays; that which embodies Shakespeare's final view of life, and is the inevitable quotation of all who would sum the teachings of philosophy. It contains his most exquisite lyrics, his tenderest love passages, and one glimpse of fairyland which —I cannot but think—outshines the utmost beauty of *A Midsummer Night's Dream:* Prospero's farewell to the "elves of hills, brooks, standing lakes, and groves." Again a miracle; these are things which cannot be staled by repetition. Come to them often as you will, they are ever fresh as though new minted from the brain of the poet. Being perfect, they can never droop under that satiety which arises from the perception of fault; their virtue can never be so entirely savoured as to leave no pungency of gusto for the next approach.

Among the many reasons which make me glad to have been born in England, one of the first is that I read Shakespeare in my mother tongue. If I try to imagine myself as one who cannot know him face to face, who hears him only speaking from afar, and that in accents which only through the labouring intelligence can touch the living soul, there comes upon me a sense of chill discouragement, of dreary deprivation. I am wont to think that I can read Homer, and, assuredly, if any man enjoys him, it is I; but can I for a moment dream that Homer yields me all his music, that his word is to me as to him who walked by the Hellenic shore when Hellas lived? I know that there reaches me across the vast stretches of time no more than a faint and broken echo; I know that it would be fainter still, but for its blending with those memories of youth which are as a glimmer of the world's primeval glory. Let every land have joy of its poet; for the poet is the land itself, all its greatness and its sweetness, all that incommunicable heritage for which men live and die. As I close the book, love and reverence possess me. Whether does my full heart turn to the great Enchanter, or to the Island upon which he has laid his spell? I know not. I cannot think of them apart. In the love and reverence awakened by that voice of voices, Shakespeare and England are but one.

III

In the last ten years I have seen a good deal of English inns in many parts of the country, and it astonishes me to find how bad they are. Only once or twice have I chanced upon an inn (or, if you like, hotel) where I enjoyed any sort of comfort. More often than not, even the beds are unsatisfactory—either pretentiously huge and choked with drapery, or hard and thinly accoutred. Furnishing is uniformly hideous, and there is either no attempt at ornament (the safest thing) or a villainous taste thrusts itself upon one at every turn. The meals, in general, are coarse and poor in quality, and served with gross slovenliness.

I have often heard it said that the touring cyclist has caused the revival of wayside inns. It may be so, but the touring cyclist seems to be very easily satisfied. Unless we are greatly deceived by the old writers, an English inn used to be a delightful resort, abounding in comfort, and supplied with the best of food; a place, too, where one was sure of welcome at once hearty and courteous. The inns of to-day, in country towns and villages, are not in that good old sense inns at all; they are merely public-houses. The landlord's chief interest is the sale of liquor. Under his roof you may, if you choose, eat and sleep, but what you are expected to do is to drink. Yet, even for drinking, there is no decent accommodation. You will find what is called a bar-parlour, a stuffy and dirty room, with crazy chairs, where only the sodden dram-gulper could imagine himself at ease. Should you wish to write a letter, only the worst pen and the vilest ink is forthcoming; this, even in the "commercial room" of many an inn which seems to depend upon the custom of travelling tradesmen. Indeed, this whole business of inn-keeping is incredibly mismanaged. Most of all does the common ineptitude or brutality enrage one when it has possession of an old and picturesque house such as reminds you of the best tradition, a house which might be made as comfortable as house can be, a place of rest and mirth.

At a public-house you expect public-house manners, and nothing better will meet you at most of the so-called inns or hotels. It surprises me to think in how few instances I have found even the pretence of civility. As a rule, the landlord and landlady are either contemptuously superior or boorishly familiar; the waiters and chambermaids do their work with an indifference which only softens to a condescending interest at the moment of your departure, when, if the tip be thought insufficient, a sneer or a muttered insult speeds you on your way. One inn I remember, where, having to go in and out two or three times in a morning, I always found the front door blocked by the portly forms of two women, the landlady and the barmaid, who stood there chatting and surveying the street. Coming from within the house, I had to call out a request for passage; it was granted with all deliberation, and with not a syllable of apology. This was the best "hotel" in a Sussex market town.

And the food. Here, beyond doubt, there is grave degeneracy. It is impossible to suppose that the old travellers by coach were contented with entertainment such as one gets nowadays at the table of a country hotel. The cooking is wont to be wretched; the quality of the meat and vegetables worse than mediocre. What! Shall one ask in vain at an English inn for an honest chop or steak? Again and again has my appetite been frustrated with an offer of mere sinew and scrag. At a hotel where the charge for lunch was five shillings, I have been sickened with pulpy potatoes and stringy cabbage. The very joint—ribs or sirloin, leg or shoulder—is commonly a poor, underfed, sapless thing, scorched in an oven; and as for the round of beef, it has as good as disappeared—probably because it asks too much skill in the salting. Then again one's breakfast bacon; what intolerable stuff, smelling of saltpetre, has been set before me when I paid the price of the best smoked Wiltshire! It would be mere indulgence of the spirit of grumbling to talk about poisonous tea and washy coffee; every one knows that these drinks cannot be had at public tables; but what if there be real reason for discontent with one's pint of ale? Often, still, that draught from the local brewery is sound and invigorating; but there are grievous exceptions, and no doubt the tendency is here, as in other things—a falling off, a carelessness, if not a calculating dishonesty. I foresee the day when Englishmen will have forgotten how to brew beer; when one's only safety will lie in the draught imported from Munich.

IV

Every one, I suppose, is subject to a trick of mind which often puzzles me. I am reading or thinking, and at a moment, without any association or suggestion that I can discover, there rises before me the vision of a place I know. Impossible to explain why that particular spot should show itself to my mind's eye; the cerebral impulse is so subtle that no search may trace its origin. If I am reading, doubtless a thought, a phrase, possibly a mere word, on the page before me serves to awaken memory. If I am otherwise occupied, it must be an object seen, an odour, a touch; perhaps even a posture of the body suffices to recall something in the past. Sometimes the vision passes, and there an end; sometimes, however, it has successors, the memory working quite independently of my will, and no link appearing between one scene and the next.

Ten minutes ago I was talking with my gardener. Our topic was the nature of the soil, whether or not it would suit a certain kind of vegetable. Of a sudden I found myself gazing at —the Bay of Avlona. Quite certainly my thoughts had not strayed in that direction. The picture that came before me caused me a shock of surprise, and I am still vainly trying to discover how I came to behold it.

A happy chance that I ever saw Avlona. I was on my way from Corfu to Brindisi. The steamer sailed late in the afternoon; there was a little wind, and as the December night became chilly, I soon turned in. With the first daylight I was on deck, expecting to find that we were near the Italian port; to my surprise, I saw a mountainous shore, towards which the ship was making at full speed. On inquiry, I learnt that this was the coast of Albania. Our vessel not being very sea-worthy, and the wind still blowing a little (though not enough to make any passenger uncomfortable), the captain had turned back when nearly half across the Adriatic, and was seeking a haven in the shelter of the snow-topped hills. Presently we steamed into a great bay, in the narrow mouth of which lay an island. My map showed me where we were, and with no small interest I discovered that the long line of heights guarding the bay on the southern side formed the Acroceraunian Promontory. A little town visible high up on the inner shore was the ancient Aulon.

Here we anchored, and lay all day long. Provisions running short, a boat had to be sent to land, and the sailors purchased, among other things, some peculiarly detestable bread—according to them, *cotto al sole*.[3] There was not a cloud in the sky; till evening the wind whistled above our heads, but the sea about us was blue and smooth. I sat in hot sunshine, feasting my eyes on the beautiful cliffs and valleys of the thickly-wooded shore. Then came a noble sunset; then night crept gently into the hollows of the hills, which now were coloured the deepest, richest green. A little lighthouse began to shine. In the perfect calm that had fallen, I heard breakers murmuring softly upon the beach.

At sunrise we entered the port of Brindisi.

NOTES

[1] Doctor Samuel Johnson, eighteenth-century literary dictator of England, most quoted of English authors, thanks to his devoted biographer James Boswell. (See pp. 69-70, 73-74.)

[2] Ariel was the spirit attendant of Prospero in Shakespeare's *The Tempest*. A modern use of this character may be found in André Maurois' *Ariel,* a novelized biography of Shelley.

[3] sun-baked.

QUESTIONS

1. How polite can one reasonably expect public servants to be? What is service?

2. Which of these criticisms of English inns hold true in America today?

3. Which would you prefer, reasonable ease or riches? Give your real reasons, avoiding those which are obviously derived from reading, memory, or what you think people expect.

4. What sort of personality does this essay reveal?

QUALITIES THAT MAKE OR MAR
SUCCESS *

Knute K. Rockne

South Bend, Indiana, and Notre Dame University more readily suggest Knute K. Rockne to American readers than Voss, Norway, where he was born in 1888. Brought to the United States at the age of five and educated in the public schools and at Notre Dame University, he was, after his graduation from college in 1914, the coach of that university's crack football teams. Through his articles in *Collier's Magazine* and the moving picture "The Four Horsemen of Notre Dame," most Americans have become aware of his unusual success at developing teams that won victories. This paper is part of a speech delivered at a convention of Studebaker automobile salesmen in Detroit early in 1931. Mr. Rockne was killed in an airplane crash in April, 1931.

I don't know anything about selling automobiles; I never sold one in my life; but perhaps a few remarks here on the psychology that is necessary for success in a football organization might not be out of place, because it seems to me that the same psychology that makes for success in a football organization will make for success in any

* Reprinted by permission of The Studebaker Corporation.
181

organization, particularly in a selling organization.

Now, in the fall when we make our first call for the team, for the lads to come out, about three hundred and fifty of them assemble in a large room in the library somewhat like this one; and it is my idea to talk to them on the correct psychology before I take them out on the field. I talk to them on ambition and I tell them that most of that which I read about ambition is bunk. There is not plenty of room at the top. There is very little room at the top. There is room at the top only for the few who have the ability, the imagination, the daring, the personality, and the energy that make them stand out from their fellow-men. But there is success for any man in his own job if he does as well as it can be done. As far as I am able to observe, the greatest satisfaction I can get on this earth is to do the particular job I am doing as well as it can be done; and I think that holds good for any one. There may be other things that are easier, but they generally leave a headache or a heartache the day after.

I tell the lads there are six types that I do not want. The first type I have in mind is the swelled head, the man who was a success a year ago, who is content to rest on his laurels, who wants to play on his reputation. Dry rot sets in, and he ceases to make an effort. To that kind of boy there will come quite a shock, because the chances are there will be some one playing in his place.

The second type of lad is the chronic complainer. He crabs everyone but himself. And I say no organization can afford to have that type of man, because he is infectious. He is in for a shock, too, because as soon as I find out who he is, some day when he comes out for practice—there will be no suit in his locker.

And third is the quitter. The quitter is the fellow who wishes he could play, but is not willing to pay the price. And I tell the boys if any of that type is there, he might just as well quit then and not wear out the equipment.

Fourth, I don't want boys to dissipate, physically or emotionally. I tell them that I hold no brief against playing pool long hours in the afternoon, dancing half the night, or learning to drive an automobile with one hand; but I tell them that they have no time for it. If they are going to compete with organizations which do not do that sort of thing and which are saving all their energy for the contest, I say, they should not dissipate any energy emotionally. And by that I mean that they should not give way to emotions such as jealousy, hatred, or anything of that sort. That sort of thing destroys any organization.

And then I tell them that they should look upon one another in a friendly way, look for the good in one another, and be inspired by the fine qualities in those around them and forget about their faults. I tell them that the chances are that I will notice the faults—and won't stutter when I mention them to the particular individual who has them. The man who lacks friendliness is the fifth.

There is a sixth type of undesirable; he suffers from an inferiority complex. He generally comes from a small community and he says to himself, "What chances have I got to get on the first string of thirty-three men here, when there are three hundred and fifty boys trying out for it? I don't believe I've got a chance; I don't believe I can make it." "If there are any among you who feel that way," I say, "forget about it, and get a superiority complex. You are just as good as any man out here. And by getting a superiority complex you can show the coach you belong at the top of the thirty-three men where you would like to be."

I remember about four years ago I divided the men on the field into groups—the ends, tackles, guards, centers, quarter-backs, and so forth. I walked to the group of guards. Now, guard is a position demanding a certain amount of physical ruggedness. There were fifteen good-sized boys in the group and one little chap whose name was Metzger. I said to him. "Aren't you a little slight and small to be playing guard?" "Yes," he answered, "but I'm a little rough." That confidence enabled him last fall, in spite of the fact that he weighed only one hundred and forty-nine pounds, to hold his own against any opponent whether he weighed two hundred pounds or more.

In two weeks I call them together again and I tell them that there are certain among them that have great potentialities, but that they have not shown any improvement. There are certain ones among them that I do not want unless they change.

The first is the chap who alibis, who justifies his own failure. And I tell them that a boy who does this had better watch out or he will get into another class, that of feeling sorry for himself, in which case the bony part of his spine turns into a soft colloidal substance known as "soap", and he is absolutely worthless.

The second class of lad—I generally have very few of them—is the slicker, the mucker, who tries to get by by playing unfair football. And I tell that type of boy that we cannot afford to have him on the team, for he will bring discredit on the school and on our organization. I also impress on him that slugging and unfairness do not pay, either in a game or in life after leaving school.

Then, third, there is the boy who lacks courage, who is afraid. What is courage? Courage means to be afraid to do something but still to go ahead and do it. If a man has character, the right kind of energy and mental ability, he will learn that fear is something to overcome and not to run away from.

Before the first game of the year I talk to them again on ambition. I say ambition, the right kind of ambition, means the ability to coöperate with the men around them, men who are working with them. It is my observation that ability to coöperate is more essential than individual technique. In this day no individual stands alone any more; he must coöperate in every sense of the word: and that is not a very easy thing to do in football, because in our colleges we often get boys who have been spoiled by the local press in their high school days. They kick the ball well, pass pretty well, and once in a while they run with it. They are all pretty good. If you don't believe it, they have clippings along with them to prove it. Teaching coöperation is not always the easiest thing in the world, especially to a group of boys. I remember one lad who looked good in practice, and we decided to start him the first game of the year.

I remember the contest well. Three times they called this chap's number and three times he made long runs for touchdowns—sixty, seventy, and eighty yards in length. Of course, on each of these runs he had excellent coöperation from his teammates. The next morning I picked up the local paper to see if the local sports writer had given credit where credit was due. Did he say that the outstanding feature of the game was the wonderful blocking and tackling, unusual for so early in the season? No! this sports writer knew his public, and he wrote what he thought they would like. In big headlines across the paper were the following—"New Horseman Looms on the Horizon of Fame—The Kokomo Flash." That was his home town. They had full length pictures of him —front view, side view, and rear view—and they had five columns telling all about it.

Well, this young man never had anything like that happen to him before in his life, so the first thing we knew, he was suffering from that disease which we call in athletics "elephantiasis of the occipital lobe"; not a very dangerous malady, but it renders the victim useless for the time being. We gave him the usual serum treatment, which is ridicule from his team-mates, the student body, and his best girl. That usually reduces the fever and the swelling.

A few weeks later we went East to play the Army, up there on the plains above the Hudson River. By that time we had forgotten that young man at half-back. We thought he had recovered from the malady, so we decided to play him. We had a beautiful setting; clouds of variegated colors were floating overhead; and the boy's father and mother were there to see the boy play, and I think a couple of aunts. Anyhow, after about ten minutes, during which time this young man posed around, evidently wondering how he looked from the grandstand, I put in the game a third string half-back who was anxious to go out and do his bit for the team; and we were lucky enough to nose out the Army.

After that contest we left for home, getting into South Bend late Sunday afternoon. Well, Monday after the classes were over, we had our first practice after the game. "The Kokomo Flash" was sulking over in a corner of the field. I did not pay any attention to him. Tuesday he was still sulking. I still ignored him.

Wednesday he came over to me and he said, "Coach, I think I will turn in my suit."

"Well," I said, "I was just thinking of asking you for it."

"This is the most unfair treatment I ever received in my life. You disgraced and humiliated me in front of my folks."

I said, "Don't you know why I took you out?" He did not seem to know. "I will refresh your memory," I said. "On two occasions when the Army kicked to us and after we failed three times to make any gain, George Gipp dropped back in punt formation and sent one of those long spirals soaring down the field. Every one of your teammates ran down the field just as fast as he could in order that the Army quarter-back might not bring the ball back an inch. All but you, the fancy prima donna. You were gamboling leisurely down the field. You were saving yourself for later on when they were to call your number. With the aid of your ten team-mates you were going to make good and get headlines in the New York papers. We overlooked that phase.

"However, the Army fumbled on their own twenty-yard line and we recovered the ball. We lined up just twenty yards from the Army's goal line and little Joe Brandy, quarter-back, turned to the team and said, 'This is our chance; now is the time to drive it right over.' And he barked out the signals clear, crisp, and staccato, calling for a play where the ball comes to you and you take it around right end. The ball came to you and you started around right end; but running just in front of you was your pal and team-mate, the other half-back, George Gipp, and his particular responsibility on that play was to take the right end out and keep him out. He did; and you wriggled and squirmed for eleven yards before you were finally tackled on the Army's nine yard line. I remember the cheering of the crowd, mentioning just your name as the team lined up for the next play. Again Joe Brandy called signals, calling for the same play, except this time around the other end. The same play, except this time George Gipp was to carry the ball. You were expected to do for him and for the team what he did for you—take the Army right end out of the play and keep him out. And what did you do? You did not even annoy him, and George Gipp was tackled for a four yard loss. The team lined up and the same play was called again. You were given a second chance to see if you could fulfill your obligation to your team. And what did you do? The second time you went out there and leaned against the end, who tackled Gipp a second time for a loss. So I took you out, not because we failed to score at that particular moment, but because you did not have the sense of responsibility to coöperate, the sense of obligation, not so much to me as to your pals on the team."

Well, the lad had character. He was well-bred, and he learned his lesson and came out and did his bit for the team. The next year he developed into an All-American half-back, if that means anything.

In any organization no one man can enjoy the spotlight all the time while the rest of the boys are doing the chores. Each one has to take his turn doing the chores.

After that I began the practice of putting up signs in the locker rooms where the boys had to read them. I put up a half dozen signs, figuring that would impress certain things on their minds. One sign which applied in this particular case read "Success is based on what the team does, not on how you look." The result is I have had little trouble along that line since, although now and then I may have to hang up that sign in an individual locker. And when I do, the boy brings the sign back to me and says, "You got me all wrong, Coach." And I say, "Was that hanging in your locker? Oh, I beg your pardon." But it has its effect just the same.

Later on after a game or two, and particularly after a game where I have seen the lads give up, I talk to them further on ambition. I tell them that there can be no ambition without perseverance. By perseverance I mean the ability to stick in there and keep giving the best of one's self.

There can be no success, no reward, unless every man has the ability to stay in there until the last whistle blows.

I was down in New York a few years ago; and in the company of Lawrence Perry, the author, I visited the Players' Club. He was showing me through the Club and was telling me about its being founded by Booth, the famous Shakespearean actor, and how Booth was the first president, and how under his guidance the club had always maintained a very fine high standard of membership. As we were going through, we came to a room where there was a table and chair, and Perry told me that Booth was wont to go there, when he was tired, to read and study. One afternoon while sitting and reading, he died. The table and chair were left in the same place in memory of Booth, and the book has been left open at the very place where he was reading at the time he passed away. Out of curiosity, I stepped up to find out what he had been reading at that particular moment. It was Pope's *Essay on Man*. You all remember it. The first line reads —"Hope springs eternal in the human breast." Glancing quickly down the page I read the last line. It said, "But if hope eludes you, all is lost."

Going back to Notre Dame, I carried that message to the boys. I talked to them about it, until I felt that every one of them was thoroughly imbued with that psychology. That year our last game was with Southern California in Los Angeles. With but seven or eight minutes to play we were ahead seven to six. I, of course, thought the game was pretty well over, and felt that the one point lead we had was sufficient to win; but just then the Southern California boys began to collect themselves and started an irresistible drive down the field. I changed my guards, tackles; but still on they came, three and four yards at a time, over our goal line for a touchdown. And although they missed the goal, that made the score 12 to 7 in favor of Southern California with about three minutes to play. "Well," I said, "I guess it is all over but the shouting."

We elected to receive the kick-off, and brought the ball back to the twenty yard line. Here we tried three plays without making an inch; so, finally, on the fourth down, kicked down the field to Southern California, who punted the ball right back, as if to say, "There it is; what are you going to do with it?" We had seventy yards to go. In those three plays on the twenty yard line I had seen something I had hoped I wouldn't see. I saw ten men still doggedly trying for all they were worth; but the eleventh lad, a little third-string quarter-back was through. As far as he was concerned, the game was over. Hope had eluded him. I don't blame him, for he was just a normal young lad nineteen years old. I turned around to a little chap sitting behind me on the bench, who had been injured earlier in the season and had not played much, little Art Parisien; and I said,

"Art, how do you feel? Do you think if I put you in there you can pull old 83 and 84, those left-handed passes of yours, and maybe still pull the game out of the fire?" Before I had finished talking, he had his head-gear on and was already on the field. As he was leaving, he turned around and hollered back to me, "Coach, it's a cinch."

That may sound like egotism, but it wasn't. A man once defined egotism to me as "the anæsthetic that deadens the pain of one's stupidity." You can be assured that that was not the case with this lad. He felt that he could do it, for he had done it just a short time previously against Northwestern in Chicago. He felt that he could do it, because he was filled with hope. On the first play he pulled a play of nine yards straight through the line, after which he called time out. Then he called those ten lads around him (for he could not talk to them until after the first play), and you could see him imbuing them with his optimism. He lifted those ten team-mates of his; and to my surprise, they lined up and did pull old 83, that left-handed pass, which was good for a gain of twenty-three yards. I thought that was fine, but I still didn't see how we had a chance. There were now left only two minutes and a quarter to play. Next he pulled a side-end run to the right side of the field for position, and there was less than a minute to play. Then he pulled old 84, that left-handed pass to a lad named Niemic, who went over for the winning touchdown. Winning

the game is not important, although interesting.
The important thing to me was the fact that this
team wouldn't be beaten, and proved to me that
the team, or the individual, that *will not* be beaten
can not be beaten.

QUESTIONS

1. What qualities in himself did Rockne reveal in this
speech?

2. How can we rightly call this speech an essay?

3. Do you agree that sports can, and do, develop the
qualities mentioned by Mr. Rockne?

ATHLETICS *

PERCY MARKS

Anyone who has read PERCY MARKS' *Which Way Parnassus?* or has heard him speak to a group of students about college problems, knows his broad interests and sympathetic understanding of the student mind. A sports enthusiast as well as a scholar, Mr. Marks treats the problem of collegiate athletics from two points of view. He was graduated from the University of California in 1912, and after graduate work at Harvard University served as Supervisor of Education at the Massachusetts State Infirmary in Tewksbury, Massachusetts, and as Instructor in English at the Massachusetts Institute of Technology, Dartmouth College, and Brown University. Since 1923 Mr. Marks has devoted his time exclusively to writing. In addition to his novels, he has contributed stories and essays to such magazines as *College Humor, Harpers, Scribner's,* and *The Saturday Evening Post*. His *The Plastic Age,* a vivid treatment of student problems published in 1924, attracted wide attention and was for years the center of animated discussion.

PRACTICALLY every freshman, unless restrained by a ban from the throne, will write a theme on the benefits of athletics. He will begin his theme by writing: "The benefits of athletics are three-

---

fold: physical, mental, and moral." The second paragraph will, of course, be devoted to the physical benefits, the third to the mental benefits, the fourth to the moral benefits, and the fifth to the conclusion, which invariably reads: "Thus we see that the benefits of athletics are threefold: physical, mental, and moral." I have endured such themes by the score, and that trinity of athletic virtues has been so impressed upon me that no one could possibly persuade me that they did not exist. Also, it is impossible for me to think of athletics except in the form of a freshman theme. The form has become a part of my thinking, so completely a part that I cannot discuss athletics independently until I have expressed the point of view of the undergraduates in their own way and manner. If the reader wishes, let him skip the theme that follows. It isn't really a part of this essay; it is merely a mental purgative written to make the essay itself possible.

The Benefits of Athletics

The benefits of athletics are threefold: physical, mental, and moral. They benefit a man physically because they develop his body, mentally because they teach him to think fast, and morally because an athlete develops a fine character.

If a man is going to be a good athlete, he has to have a fine body. No weakling can be an athlete. Only fellows with fine physiques make good athletes, and a fellow can't be a good athlete unless he takes care of his body. You can't smoke and drink and play around with loose women and be a good athlete. You've got to take care of yourself. Training develops your body. It makes you stronger. Therefore, since a fellow has to have a fine body to be a good athlete and he has to take care of it and go straight, athletics develop a man physically.

Athletics develop a man mentally because they teach him to think fast. All good athletes think fast. You can't think slow and get football signals. You've got to work fast or you will confuse the whole team. Tennis players and basketball players think fast too. Therefore, since athletics teach a man to think fast, they develop you mentally.

Athletics develop you morally because you've got to go straight if you're going to be a good athlete. You can't dissipate and be a good athlete. An athlete has to learn team play, which makes him know what good sportsmanship is. Therefore, since athletics teach a man to go straight and teach him the value of team play, athletics develop a man morally.

Thus we see that the benefits of athletics are threefold: physical, mental, and moral. They benefit him physically by developing his body, mentally by making him think fast, and morally because he's got to work with the other fellow and go straight if he's going to be a good athlete.

Little as one may think of the freshman method, the validity of most of his ideas must be admitted. His logic is not entirely perfect, and his thesis is hardly established; basically, however, he is talking sense. The physical benefits of athletics are too obvious to need justification. I am inclined to be a bit dubious about the mental benefits, since the kind of thinking that athletics demand is rarely of the highest order. An instantaneous and sure physical reaction to a stimulus is necessary to satisfactory athletic results, but such a reaction can be called thinking only by stretching definitions grotesquely. It is safe, however, to say that a healthy body makes for a clear mind, and so we can grant the freshman the right to say that athletics at least help a man mentally. Athletics do arouse in their participants a realization of the value of team play, they do impel some men toward clean living; and some forms of them, tennis for example, hold up a standard of good sportsmanship that is altogether admirable: some of them, on the other hand—football, for example—do nothing of the sort.

Before I say some unpleasant things about athletics, let me assure the reader that I am enthusiastic about all kinds of sports and that I do not believe that intercollegiate athletics should be abolished. I can, and do, make a fool of myself at all athletic contests, baseball excepted, and my excitement at a good football game is completely idiotic and altogether delightful. Only bad baseball games interest me; not enough happens in a good one. Six home runs, three pitchers knocked out of the box, and about a dozen errors make a baseball game that has enough action to be interesting; a pitcher's battle may be exciting to the umpire, but to the spectator—to me, at least—a sand lot game of one ol' cat provides ten times the drama. I hope, however, that my confessed lack of enthusiasm for baseball will not disqualify me to discuss athletics in general without undue bias.

If professionalism could be done away with, no argument worth a moment's notice could be brought against athletics. Their virtues are many, but professionalism is a sin so heavy that it almost balances the virtues; it is an octopus with such long arms that it grips not only the men paid but in some ways the entire student body. For the moment, however, let us ignore the faults of athletics and pay tribute to the color and enjoyment that they bring both to the college and to the general public as well. I confess to no great interest in the general public's pleasure in college athletics, but that pleasure is so obvious that it must at least receive recognition.

For most of us the pageantry of college life is something rich and beautiful, from the parade of the faculty in cap and gown at the beginning of the year to the final parade at commencement. Nearly all academic rituals are lovely, partly because most of them are simple and unaffected, and partly because they have dignity. The undergraduate parades usually are lacking in dignity, but they have color and to spare. No one, I am sure, would willingly part with them—no one, that is, except those so arid emotionally that they shrink from the boisterous high jinks so naturally a part of youth. To me undergraduates are ridiculous only when they adopt a code of serene maturity. Harvard is great, perhaps our greatest university, and no one bows more humbly before its faculty and its equipment than I do. I wish, though, that the undergraduates could forget that they are Harvard *men* and remember that they are American boys. Harvard Yard would be a pleasanter place if one occasionally saw some boisterous youngsters playing catch on its shaded lawns or if one were ever startled by hundreds of them whirling madly under the elms in a spontaneous rally. It is quite possible to be an earnest student and a kid at the same time, and most Harvard undergraduates are not so lost in study that they cannot afford an occasional hour for natural play. Plenty of Harvard boys play tennis, and the socially élite, of course, play golf at various country clubs; but otherwise athletics seem to be confined to the teams and the extremely thin college life to the Yale game—and the Yale game as a spectacle is nothing to get panegyric about.

At its best a football game is the most impressive pageant that American life affords, and I, for one, would not willingly forego that pageantry. True, it is almost always done badly in the East, so badly, in fact, that one wonders how the participants can ignore their opportunities so blindly. Harvard again furnishes a convenient example. In the last few years, it has blundered to the extent of countenancing an excellent band, but the band forgot itself so far as to appear in white flannels and red sweaters. Worse yet, it paraded on the field. It paraded very nicely, true, and went through rather intricate and interesting evolutions with fine rhythm and precision. This simple attempt at pageantry invariably delighted the Stadium crowds, but the *Crimson* (the Harvard undergraduate daily paper) broke out in a cold sweat of indignation in editorial protest. Such small college antics were beneath the dignity of Harvard, and so on and so on, with self-conscious smugness and childish pomposity. The band, I believe, still marches, but it alone lends any color to a Harvard game. The pageantry comes from the enormous crowds only. Good singing and good cheering would smack too much, I suppose, of vulgar efficiency. At any rate, at all the eastern colleges both the cheering and the singing are offensively bad. The leaders run up and down like drunken clowns—O dignity!—and the undergraduates yowl cheers and songs with aristocratic indifference to pitch and rhythm.

The middle western colleges manage such athletic occasions far better, but it is only on the Pacific Coast that the true pageantry of a football game is understood. No public occasion in this country is so overwhelmingly gorgeous as a California-Stanford game. It blazes with color. The California cheering section is an enormous rectangle of blue and gold, the Stanford section a corresponding rectangle of flaming red. Everywhere there are flowers, chrysanthemums in thousands. The stage management is frankly obvious from the buglers on the highest part of the stadium to the marchings and countermarchings of the two excellent bands. Nor do the colleges scorn to do well what they have set out to do: the cheer leaders do not race idiotically up and down like gymnastic buffoons; they stand still and direct their tremendous choirs. And how those choirs sing! The California cheering section is probably the largest male chorus in the world, and until one has heard those thousands of young men sing "Hail to California," he has yet to learn how stirringly splendid mass singing can be. I suppose the "stunts" would horrify an eastern college man— that is, if they didn't make his blasé eyes bulge naïvely with wonder and admiration. He might learn, too, that a cheering section properly trained and properly conducted can produce meaningless sounds with such thumping vigor and crackling rhythm that they can lift the most flaccid listener out of his seat. Outside of the football game itself, the spectacle is tremendously impressive—and it is beautiful.

Am I too ingenuously enthusiastic? I doubt it. As a nation we are too self-conscious to know how to play; we act like old men before we have had our fill of instinctive gamboling. A people that cannot "make believe," that cannot dramatize its life into something more romantic than it is in itself, is a people lacking in vitality, in imagination. Communal play is healthy and invigorating; without it a nation soon grows old and stale. Perhaps it is a remaining trace of the Spanish influence that makes Californians lose themselves so completely and joyously in any kind of fiesta, but whatever the reason, the carnival spirit lives there abundantly and brings with it a spontaneous ardor in living that is lacking in the drabber East.

It is not less of this kind of "rah-rah spirit" that I am asking for, but more of it. Let us have all the pageantry we can get, and the more gorgeous it is, the more completely it justifies itself. And if the football games turn mature, sedate men into howling, happy fools for a couple of hours, the greater their virtue. Any one incapable of realizing the drama of an athletic contest or incapable of reacting to it is a person to be pitied— or scorned; I don't know which. Such people wander importantly around art galleries admiring this statue or that and never see the finer, more living beauty of a half-back poised to throw a forward pass; they applaud a dancer moving with mechanical accuracy to an orchestra's sharp beat and miss the subtler and more wonderful art of a tennis player flashing across a court with spontaneous grace; they listen raptly to a symphonic poem and never hear the breath-taking rhythm of a sprinter's spikes; they go to the theater and learnedly discuss suspense and dénouement and see no drama in a tie score, the bases full, two men out, three balls and two strikes. I don't believe such people really care for art or music or drama; they have neither eyes that see, nor ears that hear nor hearts that beat; they are poseurs fooling themselves, "finished and finite clods untroubled by a spark." When a man gets too old to play, too sophisticated to lose himself in the delight and drama of others' play, it is time for him to die; if he was never capable of losing himself in his own play or that of others, he never had enough imagination or vitality to live. Life without play would be intolerable; life without pageantry would be ugly; and life without many a place where we can give ourselves completely to vivid excitement, whether it be theater, concert hall, or football stadium, would be hell. The more such places, the better. They afford release that is necessary, delightful, and often beautiful—and the beauty of an athletic contest is often rare and fine, as the Greeks so well knew.

Nor do I object to the great stadia and the vast sums spent on maintaining them. Primarily, the stadia exist for football alone, and in most colleges football supports not only itself and its particular stadium but most of the other athletic teams as well. What difference does it make whether a large crowd or a small one watches a football game just so long as the college itself does not have to expend its precious dollars to make the game possible? I do object to the large salaries paid to coaches, especially football coaches, partly because they tend to glorify the coaches into a splendor they have not earned and partly because athletics can confer all their benefits without any such absurd expenditure of money. The amount of money that coaches can, and do, demand comes, I think, from a false valuation of athletics and from mistaken loyalty to the college. In the first place, "crack" teams are in no way responsible for the various athletic virtues that I have just granted; those virtues come not from expertness but from the contest itself. Any two small colleges that cannot afford expensive coaches get just as much good and just as much thrill from their annual game as California and Stanford do, or Harvard and Yale. If Harvard and Yale dropped their professional coaches tomorrow, the attendance at their game next year would be just as large as ever and the enthusiasm just as great. Alumni coaches would serve in the end quite as satisfactorily as professional coaches—and the professional coach, who is nothing more or less than a hired man, would lose the godlike prestige that he enjoys at present. A college coach of a successful team is idolized so idiotically that many of the undergraduates seem to get him confused with God. The mental process seems to be this: athletic success brings the college glorious prestige; the coach makes the prestige possible; ergo, the coach is a man with well-nigh divine powers.

The reasoning is false on every count. First, athletic success does not bring a college prestige of any moment; at best, it is passing, and a college can hold its prestige with very bad athletic teams, a fact of which Harvard furnishes ample proof. Secondly, no coach has the power within himself to make a fine football team out of commonplace material. Great athletes are born just as truly as poets are. Expert coaches *can* devise strategic plays, they can weld a group of competent players into a formidable unit, and they can develop the gifts of individual players; but more they cannot do. That, the reader may say, is quite enough; and from a professional point of view, it is. No one asks a horse trainer to *make* a good horse out of a bad one, but college folk do expect their high-priced coaches to make good football players and good football teams out of boys who have little aptitude for football. Percy Haughton, marvelous coach though he was, could give Columbia nothing but a mediocre team. He didn't have time to develop his system, the newspapers explained. My guess is that he didn't have football players.

In a way the expensive coach is symbolical of the whole professional attitude which is destroying the value of college athletics. There is altogether too much interest in winning and not enough in the game. Let us keep our attention on football for the present, since it is the worst offender. The coach is paid a high salary to produce winning teams, and produce them he must or lose his salary. The result is that he trains his squad as if it were composed of race horses. I am not complaining of the training rules but of the time taken and the point of view adopted. Football isn't played for sport; it is played as a desperately serious business, and the players have to give hours of attention to it daily as if the next game were their sole interest in life. A star player once said to me: "I wish I knew how to get off the team. It isn't that I want to quit playing football. I like it, but I'm sick of playing it as if my life depended on it. It's too damned serious. There's no fun." Certainly the rigorous training can't be much fun for most of the players, and if they don't get practically continuous enjoyment from the game its basic value is gone, since the pleasure that it gives to the spectators must be considered as secondary.

In other words, the spirit of football is wrong. "Win at any cost" is the slogan of most teams, and the methods used to win are often abominable. I have heard of one college team that made a practice—at least, so several of its members asserted—of rubbing the lime from the lines into their opponents' eyes at every opportunity. In nearly every scrimmage the roughest kind of unsportsmanlike play is indulged in, and the broken arms and ankles are often intentional rather than accidental. Worst of all, the players are trained to take such rotten ethics as a natural part of the game. A few months ago I had a long talk with a famous eastern football star whom I shall call Peters. He told me quite casually in the course of our conversation about football that Jones of X College had kicked him in the face in a game the preceding season. Now, Peters and

Jones had gone to preparatory school together and had been friends for years. It happened that I knew Jones very well, and I protested that I did not believe that he would deliberately kick any one in the face, especially a friend who happened to be on an opposing team.

"Oh, it was all right," Peters explained. "You remember Smith (a team-mate of Jones) got kicked in the face in our game last year, and the whole bunch was out to get back at us."

He bore no resentment against Jones; in fact, he frankly considered that he had whitewashed his friend completely.

Perhaps he had, but I am just chicken-hearted enough to doubt it. Jones, notwithstanding his size and strength, is one of the gentlest souls I have ever met. If he kicked Peters in the face, and I am perfectly willing to believe that he did, he did it for one of two reasons: either years of football playing had persuaded him that brutality was necessary and inevitable, or the telegram that every member of his football team received just before the game excited him to merciless revenge. The telegrams came from an alumni club, and each one read, "Remember Smith."

Football might well learn a lesson in sportsmanship from tennis, in which the code is high and reverently observed. College tennis players strive to win, of course, but they strive with dignity and courtesy. Good feeling is absolutely necessary to a tennis match—and it is significant,

I think, that an umpire isn't. No one is going to cheat under any circumstances, and most players are more than willing to sacrifice a dubious point. Even too much earnestness is rather bad form; the game is the thing. I remember watching a college match in which one of the participants was too serious. He played fairly, he was perfectly courteous, but he looked downcast when he made a poor shot, and he never expressed by look or word admiration for a good play by his opponent. A youth sitting beside me, a member of the team, finally ejaculated in disgust: "Just watch that guy, will you? You'd think he was playing for money."

Well, football players act as if they were playing for money, and many of them are. What is the sense in the constant hypocrisy about paid athletes? There is nothing amateur about most college athletics, football especially, either in spirit or in fact. Nearly every college athlete that I have ever known (and I have known dozens of them) who wasn't financially independent received money for his services to some team. The payment is often disguised so that it is hard to detect, but the money is given as payment nevertheless. For instance, a loyal alumnus employs an impecunious athlete to work in his office. The work is remarkably light; in fact, it usually takes practically no time at all—and the salary is splendid. Some athletes receive free room and board from their fraternities. Occasionally the fraternities bear the burden; often alumni pay the athletes' bills. Unless I have been lied to repeatedly, there is one college where the entire football squad is established in a hotel during the season, fed and roomed gratis, and paid thirty-five dollars a week. I asked a trainer last summer why so few good football players seemed to be coming to his college. He smiled sardonically and replied: "They all go to Z or X."

"Why," I demanded, "are they going to those two colleges all at once?"

"They pay them so well. It cost X over $20,000 to put its freshman team on the field last year."

As a rule, the players' salaries are disguised as jobs, but sometimes money is offered outright. I shall always remember the amusement of an athletic friend of mine who was thinking of leaving college for reasons that had nothing to do with football. He called on me to discuss his troubles, finally decided to stay in college, and returned to his room at midnight. He found three members of the local alumni club waiting for him—with one hundred dollars.

It is needless to labor the argument. Many college athletes are directly or indirectly paid—and everybody intimately in touch with colleges knows it. Furthermore, some of the athletes come to college for the money they receive and for no other reason. It is these outright professionals who give rise to the tradition that all athletes are numskulls. Let me pause long enough to ridicule that idea. Brains and brawn are in no wise incompatible, and some of the best students I have ever had were athletes. Most of the members of any team in a high-grade college are quite as intelligent as the average undergraduate, and some are far more intelligent; on the other hand, there are always a few brilliant performers who were devised by the all-wise Creator to be longshoremen. They flock into the "snap" courses; they receive money from alumni for tutoring and more direct aid from friendly undergraduates. Sometimes they even graduate, but usually they are "flunked out" and go to another college to earn an easy living for another year. What could be more anachronistic and repellent than a college team winning in an *amateur* sport by virtue of the prowess of hired morons?

The professionalizing of athletes and the playing of the game for winning's sake rather than for the game's sake give rise to an hysterical over-valuation of the importance of athletics in every way. A game of any kind is important for the pleasure it gives the performers and observers, and for no other reason. College athletes ought to take part in various sports mainly for the pleasure and benefits they derive from sportsmanlike competition and vigorous exercise. And if college athletics were not professionalized into a state of businesslike expertness, perhaps it would be possible for the majority of undergraduates to indulge in them instead of a scanty few. "Making the team" ought not to be so important in the end as making health and pleasure, but in nearly every college the equipment for sport is largely limited to the use of the teams. Let us take as an example the University of California, the largest university in the world. When I entered there in 1908, the registration was about 2500; and the gymnasium was inadequate. Now each year there are about 3000 freshmen, and the same old gymnasium has to serve—but California has a stadium as large as the Yale Bowl and a practice football field. There are at most twelve tennis courts. Harvard has had its famous stadium for many years, but consider the Hemenway Gymnasium! Yale is making plans, I understand, for a large gymnasium, but the Bowl, useless most of the year, seats its 70,000. And so it is in most colleges; enormous amounts of money are spent on the teams and very little on the rest of the students. As I said earlier, I have no objections to the stadia in themselves, but I do object to the neglect of the majority in order that an insignificant minority may be trained like race horses and exhibited like prize Pomeranian pups.

Most colleges do make an attempt to encourage intramural sports. There are interfraternity baseball games and class competitions, but except in country colleges, most of the undergraduates do not get enough outside play. The teams are parasites that hog most of the equipment and money.

(My metaphor is sadly mixed, but I decline to surrender either "parasites" or "hog." Both words are too exact.) Every one has to make way for the sacred team practice. While the season is on, the football field must not be used because the turf will be cut; besides, the team is on it most of the hours free for play. Nor must the baseball diamond be used, for exactly the same reasons. The little space in the gymnasium must be given over to the basketball team when setting-up exercises are not being held. At Dartmouth and Williams, the situation is almost exactly the reverse of what I have been describing, but the boys at those colleges have all out-of-doors for their playground—and at most colleges the play area is strictly limited.

In the end, all the faults come back to professionalism. Without the professional athlete and the professional coach most of the evils now clinging to athletics could be easily brushed aside. It is time our college people, alumni and undergraduates, were impressed with the fact that "amateur" is derived from the much-conjugated *amare* and that it means "to love." An amateur is one who does a thing purely for the love of it, who plays a game as well as he can because he loves it and gets a lover's delight in playing it well. A true amateur, furthermore, plays like a gentleman; he cares too much for the game to smudge it with dirty practices. And he plays hard to win; but if he loses he loses happily because, after all, it was good sport.

If American alumni and undergraduates ever learn the meaning and spirit of the word "amateur," the benefits of athletics may become truly threefold: physical, mental, and moral.

QUESTIONS

1. What is an amateur? What does the amateur spirit foster that is rarely achieved without it?

2. Just how important should we consider organized sport? Would you give it more, or less, importance than it now enjoys?

3. How far is being average a virtue? When does it become a vice?

4. What subjects other than *The Benefits of Athletics* have become victims of the stock theme treatment?

THE BEE'S KNEES *

CHARLES D. STEWART

Few better illustrations of George Moore's dictum that "All Education Is Self-Education" could be found than CHARLES D. STEWART. Born in Zanesville, Ohio, he soon moved to Wisconsin, with which state his name is widely associated through his reputation as "The Wisconsin Philosopher." With very little formal schooling, Mr. Stewart has educated himself to enter several fields not usually penetrated by the self-taught. From his first publication, *The Fugitive Blacksmith* in 1905 to his essays in the *Atlantic Monthly* in 1933, he has utilized most of the literary forms, including a scholarly thesis on *Some Textual Difficulties in Shakespeare*, done under the auspices of the Elizabethan Club of Yale University. "The Bee's Knees" clearly illustrates how deeply a student may enter any intellectual field and still keep the amateur spirit, in the fullest sense of the term. Mr. Stewart now lives in Hartford, Wisconsin, and contributes to the leading magazines.

A BEE in the field is engaged in gathering three sorts of raw material—flour, varnish, and syrup; all of them commodities which present problems in handling and transportation.

That the yellow pollen of the flowers is simply flour to a bee may be gathered from the fact

* Reprinted by permission of the author and the *Atlantic Monthly*.

that beekeepers, in seasons when pollen is scarce, set out little troughs of rye flour which serves the bees instead and induces them to raise young earlier in the season than they otherwise would. Young bees, like young children, cannot thrive and develop on sweets alone; and so the pollen, a highly nitrogenous product, is the food of the young bee during the days when it is truly a baby in the cradle, occupying the open cell in larval form. Honey, a form of sugar, supplies the bee, as it does the human worker, with a vast amount of heat and energy; but it lacks the elements needed in repair and growth. The older bees eat the pollen in small quantity also, a certain proportion of it being necessary to health.

As for varnish, the bee gets hers from the same source that man does—the resinous exudation of trees. But the bee finds the readiest supply on sticky buds such as those of the balm of Gilead tree, and, in lesser quantity, on the buds of poplar, horse-chestnut, willow, and hollyhock. While we are accustomed to think of the bee as a hoarder of honey, entirely possessed with her passion for sweets, the fact is that every worker bee has varnish on her mind. She will gather it as eagerly and hurry home with it in as high a state of happiness as if she were working in nectar or in pollen. A swarm of bees that has found suitable quarters in the decayed hollow of a tree will clean it out scrupulously, removing every particle of loose dirt and rubbish, and may then repair its surface until they have given it a complete coat of varnish. Those that are kept in the usual "patent" hives stop up every crack and crevice with their resin; and they cement the lid on so tight that the beekeeper has to carry a special tool to pry it off. Mixed with wax it makes the wax stickier and hardens it, and this preparation they use as a basis and buttress with which to fasten their combs securely. If a mouse, or other large unwieldy animal, invades the hive and dies there, a problem in sanitary engineering has to be met and dealt with. Varnish-gatherers set to work at once, and in a short time they have the mouse coated over and made odorless—virtually embalmed in their sweet-smelling resins. Usually bees deal with any objectionable object by dragging it out of the door and casting it overboard; but there are cases when such measures are not practicable.

Some years ago, on a bright warm day in spring, I set to work to varnish a sponson canoe and get it in shape for another season's use on the lake on which I live. I had not plied the brush long when I became aware that a number of bees were keeping me company. Then more and more bees. After a while they became so numerous, and were flying about in such a highly excited state of mind, that I put down the brush and began to worry. At that time I knew a great deal about bees, or thought I did; and so I was perfectly aware that bees gather the resinous *propolis* at

great expenditure of time and labor. But up to
the time when I met the bees in a common concern over the same sort of work, I did not really
know what I had learned. This *propolis* was a
word which kept itself in a different department
of my mind from that in which I deal with my
everyday work; and so I did not know, as these
particular bees did, that it was the same sort of
stuff that I was putting on my canoe. But then—
who would ever suspect that a bee could know so
much about Greek! This little episode taught me
a lesson in writing; I decided that if I ever wrote
anything about bees I would use the plain word
"varnish."

A bee carries her varnish in her pollen basket,
so called because she also packs her flour in it.
She gathers it when it is in such a warm, sticky
condition that it will draw out in a thread; and
when she has loaded up with all the sticky stuff
she can handle, she hurries home and applies it to
the hive while it is yet in a workable state. Commercial beekeepers, when they have worked a
while with their hives, taking off lids and handling
frames, find their hands covered with a gummy
tenacious substance which soap and water has
little effect upon. Following the advice of their
Langstroth, or other work on practical beekeeping, they use "turpentine or alcohol" to get it off.
A bee's varnish resembles man's in the embarrass-
ing qualities of stickiness and insolubility; and
so, if a bee can get it off her bristly body without

using any special recipe out of a bee book, I think it is evident that she knows how to handle varnish. I am quite willing to believe that she could make use of canoe varnish, even though it is guaranteed to set dust free in a few hours and to be glass hard in a day or two.

The nectar from the blossoms is the bee's true food. While much of it finds its way into her stomach to supply her present needs, much more is retained in her honey bag, or crop, to be carried home in the form of sap and evaporated to honey in the cells. A bee that is engaged in field work never eats honey so long as the nectar is to be had. She simply stores it up for future use, and for the support of the bees that work in the hive. As a certain part of the swarm, the younger bees, stay at home and devote themselves to household specialties,—wax-making, comb-building, nursing, and ventilating,—they have to be supported on honey by the workers in the field. This current consumption alone is enough to keep them busy, especially when there is comb being built; besides which there must be a good supply of honey sealed up for time of need.

In hot weather a number of bees in every hive are acting in the capacity of electric fans, their wings working away at a great rate while they drive the air in just the directions needed in a well-calculated ventilating system. In front of any hive, holding their proper stations at the narrow entrance, a detachment of these ventilating bees may be seen. Their heads are always turned toward the entrance so that the air is kept moving past them toward the rear, the reason for this position being that these bees are drawing out the foul air from the hive. On the inside of the hive, their heads turned also toward the entrance, is another file of bees propelling the air past them toward the interior. These bees are sucking in fresh air to take the place of the foul air. It is a double ventilating system based upon good mechanical principles.

To get the full effect of ventilation, it is not enough to admit a steady supply of fresh air at such an opening; it is also desirable to keep the whole mass of air in motion. Building engineers who specialize on such problems as are presented by theatres, moving-picture houses, and other human hives, have recently announced as an interesting discovery that there is a vivifying influence imparted to air simply by keeping it in motion; and this in addition to, or independent of, any new supply of oxygen. Whether there is any truth in these conclusions or not, bees fulfill all the requirements necessary to take advantage of them; for inside the hive are other detachments of bees steadily agitating the air. A bee has two pairs of wings, the rear pair and the forward pair being placed so close together that their edges almost touch. The wings are hooked together in flying, and to this end there is a row of little hooks on the forward edge of the rear wing and a stiff pleat on the edge of the front wing in which the little hooks may readily engage. A single pair of broad wings would be quite as serviceable in flying, but such a pair would not go into a cell. For this purpose they unhook and fold together like a fan. It has been observed that, in ventilating, bees do not have the wings hooked together.

The effect of this well-directed activity is not only to give a supply of life-sustaining oxygen to the multitude of workers in the hive, but also to keep down the temperature when there is danger of the comb melting; and, in addition, to evaporate the surplus water from the honey stored in the cells, which are never sealed shut till the product is properly "ripened." The nectar in some seasons is more watery than at other periods; but whatever its condition in this regard the bees bring it in and store it in the open cells and then fan it to the right consistency. The watery product is held in the uncapped cells largely by capillary attraction; but the bees have a tendency to build the cells with a dip toward the rear. When they are building cells especially for the storage of honey this dip is more pronounced, as if they considered it an advantage; but they also use brood cells which have hatched their young and been cleaned out, and here the tendency is not so pronounced. The practice of building the caps from the bottom up, after the manner of a dam, also helps them in filling the cells full without leakage. Their care in evaporating the honey till it is a highly concentrated food-product is an economic one, due to the high cost of wax. It takes from seven to fifteen pounds of honey to make one pound of wax; and this means that, in addition to all the time and energy spent in gathering the honey, there is the time spent in digesting it into wax. They cannot afford to use such an expensive product for the storage of water.

As this work of driving air in and out of the door is very exhausting, other bees take the places of any that have grown tired, and so the ventilating crew gradually changes. The hotter the day or the more liquid the nectar, the more fanning there is in the hive. If the entrance is stopped up, by way of experiment, the whole populace will set their wings a-going. It is apparent that the ventilating bees are not specialists, except as they specialize for a while on this part of the work. They are volunteers, taking their places among the files at the entrance or manning the forces of the interior as circumstances require. And what influence is it, or what supreme authority, that picks this bee and that one for the task, sets some to fanning the interior, sends others to complete the files of the fresh-air crew or the foul-air gang, and keeps up the balanced quota at the door? I am afraid we shall have to call this a mystery.

Indeed, we have now been led to the point where all study of bees, in any of their various activities, must inevitably lead us. At first we are shrewd observers, duly careful and skeptical in our conclusions, but led on by fact after fact until, just as we are about to reach the point of knowledge, we must admit that we are baffled. Unless we throw our scientific caution to the winds and turn poet or romancer, there is little to do but wonder. And I do not know but this latter outcome marks a man's deepest knowledge of nature. Especially as the wonder must beget a certain reverence, and a due humility of mind in the presence of the unknowable.

II

A bee needs so many tools in the day's work—such a variety of combs, brushes, pincers, shears, and what not—that her body is fairly covered with handy appliances. Any skilled workman, however little he might know about nature, would quickly conclude from an examination of the working parts of a bee that here was a fellow factory-hand who knew the tricks of some highly technical trade. Every hair and joint from head to foot has some special development which makes it an ingenious combination-tool without interfering with the proper working of the bee's own person.

The leg of the bee—and I am not here forgetting that there are six of them—has a greater number of joints than has the leg of a human being. Midway between the knee and the joints of the foot there is another articulation, or knee, that is particularly interesting. In each of the three pairs of legs this knee is differently developed so as to furnish the bee with three sorts of very useful tools—pincers, crowbar, and comb.

On the first, or front, pair of legs, there is just below this joint a self-threading needle arrangement so equipped as to make a combination comb and scraper for keeping the antenna clean and in condition. It consists of a deep notch, constituting somewhat more than half a circle, in the horny shell of the leg; and the open part of this notch is closed, or bridged over, by means of a strong little piece of horny substance opening and closing by means of a hinge. The principle of this contrivance is, as I have said, that of a self-threading needle—though it is more finely and mechanically made than most of man's contrivances. Its object is to allow the bee's antenna to be slipped into the notch when the little bridge-like piece is raised; and then to be held in place, like a thread in the eye of a needle, as the little piece is dropped down and pressed into position. The interior of this notch is furnished with a comb, the fine, long, rounded teeth of which are set close together in a single row all round the half circle. The little horny piece which closes the opening does not carry any teeth, but has a sharpened edge. When the bee's feeler, or antenna, is slipped into the opening and drawn through, the little horny piece presses it down against the teeth.

As a bee's feelers carry its "smell hollows" and the fine, peculiarly designed hairs which serve somehow as a means of communication between bees, it is important that they be kept free from sticky substances and the accumulation of a summer's dust. With these comb-and-scraper devices placed so conveniently on the front legs—one for each antenna to right and left—the bee can slip her feelers into these self-threading inventions alternately and so keep her means of communication in working order with a minimum of time and trouble.

Looking now at the middle pair of legs, and turning our attention to this same joint upon either one of them, we find a very different sort of arrangement. Sprouting out from beneath the hard shell of the leg, at the edge just above the joint, is a process or prong which I can best describe as being a diminutive elephant's tusk. It has the same curve, proportions, and general appearance of utility. This is the bee's combination pick and crowbar; and she uses it particularly for loosening the close-packed pollen in her pollen basket—which she carries upon her hind pair of legs—and pushing it out into the cell in which it is to be stored.

Anyone who has had even a little experience in gardening knows how a packed soil may be loosened with a single tine of a potato fork; or how the worker in the most stubborn soils easily conquers with the point of a pick. For a better illustration, watch the grocer as he separates a pound of dates from the close-packed mass, and observe that it may be pried loose only with a single-pointed instrument which acts as pick and crowbar. Nature had like knowledge of adapting the means to the end, of fitting the tool to the trade, when she equipped the bee with this prong for loosening her load of pollen. Burroughs [1] says that when a bee has brought a load of pollen to the hive "he advances to the cell in which it is to be deposited and kicks it off as one might his overalls or rubber boots, making one foot help the other." It is not done in quite so loose and easy a manner as this description would imply. The tusklike tool is working to pry the pollen loose, the one on the left leg serving to unload the right, and the right doing a like service for the left. "He," as Mr. Burroughs here uses it, must be a grammatical he. No male bee ever gathered any pollen or honey or did any work around a hive. The drone is strictly a gentleman of leisure.

This brings us to the hind legs of the bee, the longest, strongest, and most elaborate of the three pairs; and here we confine our attention to the pair of knees which correspond to the ones we have been studying on the other two pairs of legs. The hind legs of the bee differ from the others in the fact that they become much wider and spatulate toward their lower extremities, somewhat like a sailor's trousers when well pressed. Rather they are like oars with broad generous blades. Of the three principal divisions of the leg, the upper one is round like the haft of an oar, and the next two sections are flattened so that each is like a blade or paddle. The joint or knee we are now considering unites these two broad, paddlelike sections of the leg. These are hinged together only at one edge, the result being that when this particular knee is bent, it opens a wide, gaping mouth with sharp, serrated edges. This is the bee's combination shears and pincers. With these she seizes and disattaches the flattened wax which extrudes from between the joints of the body, on the abdomen, and furnishes her with building material.

In considering the supplies which the bee in the field is engaged in gathering, no mention was made of wax, because it is a product of the hive. It is manufactured like fat in the bee's body, out of honey which is eaten in large quantities for the purpose. On each side of the abdomen are four little wax-pockets situated in the joints of the hard-surfaced body; and here the supply of wax may be seen issuing, the flat, light-colored wax appearing somewhat like a letter which a man has tucked up under his waistcoat.

When there is comb to be built, certain bees will hang themselves up in festoons from the roof of the hive and remain there quiescently while wax forms and pushes its way out from the pockets. It takes about twenty-four hours for a stomachful of honey to be converted into wax, the bee having gorged herself with honey for the purpose. And it is the younger bees, which seem to have the most vigorous digestion and wax-forming ability, that take this specialty upon themselves. The festoons consist of loops like a watch chain, each bee hanging by the claws or hooks on her forelegs to the extended hind legs of the bee above her; and the whole loop is supported by the bees that have hold of the ceiling. At first they form chains hanging straight down; and then two chains uniting at the bottom form a loop.

When the appointed time has been fulfilled and the bee feels that her wax is ready for delivery, she separates herself from the others and proceeds to a part of the roof where building is to begin; and now she detaches the wax from her abdomen, macerates it,—for which purpose she seems to moisten it with some form of fluid or saliva,—and sticks it against the ceiling. Bee after bee comes here and does likewise until a little wall of wax has been built up—a crude blank wall on which the architects have not gone to work. From this it will be seen that the shears and pincers on the hind legs serve a bee to disattach the wax from her own body—not from the body of another bee. Sometimes the floor of the hive will be littered with these wax scales, in which case the worker bees pick them up and carry them to the work, regarding them as so much useful lumber. As the hive is warmed by the bodies of so many busy workers, the wax is rendered pliable and soft, so that it is easily united to the edge of a growing cell and worked into shape by the strong, blunt mandibles of the bee.

The wax shears, as we have seen, are a development of the joint itself; and now, for further interesting developments, we must turn our attention to the broad, paddlelike sections of the leg above and below this particular joint. They are made thus broad in order that there may be room on them for all the devices needed in the reaping and loading of pollen. On the upper one is the pollen basket. It is situated, like a pocket, on the side of the leg away from the bee's body. On the lower one is the pollen-reaping or gathering device; and this is on the side *toward* the bee's body. The pollen basket is most frequently referred to as being on the bee's "thigh," or on her "hip," but this is far from correct. It is on the tibia, which is the section below the thigh; and the pollen-gathering device is on the section next below that. It is important that these devices be low down on the leg, at a considerable distance from the bee's body, in which position they have free scope and reaching power. A bee loads her left pollen basket with her right leg, and her right one with her left leg; and I dare say anyone will see the difficulty in reaching a hip pocket by means of the opposite shin. Bees that carry their pollen in that position are poetical bees, not the work of a practical mechanic.

The pollen basket, so far as its bottom is concerned, consists of the broad, smooth side of this section called the tibia, its surface being slightly concave. It is fenced round by a row of spines or bristles that serve like the stakes around a wagon bed; and there are longer hairs curving inward and over the top and serving to keep the pollen from falling out.

The pollen packs firmly into this place like flour or snow; and being held by the row of stiff spines which fence it in, and the long incurving hairs which clasp it down, there is evident need for the little tusk or crowbar on each of the middle pair of legs. Without this it would be difficult to unload.

On the broad section of the leg next below the one which holds the pollen basket, and, as we have already noted, on the inner side instead of the outer, we find the pollen-gathering and loading device. Arranged across this part of the leg is a series of combs, yellowish brown in color, and looking for all the world like the side combs which women use to hold the hair in place.[2] Each comb has its teeth slightly raised from the surface of the leg, and partially overlapping the next comb below. These combs, by being constantly plied over the bee's breast, serve to gather the grains of pollen which adhere to the feathered hairs on this part of the bee's body; and then, when the combs are full, to transfer it to the pollen basket on the opposite leg. The bee bends the knee and wipes or draws the row of combs across the back of the opposite leg just as a man might draw his shinbone lengthwise across the back of his thigh; the little stakes or spines which surround the pollen basket pass between the teeth of the combs and clean them out; and thus the pollen basket, after many such combfuls, is well packed with pollen, and the bee is ready to go home and unload. The whole device works together with the ingenuity and perfect fitness of a piece of agricultural machinery.

The feathered hairs on parts of the body are an indispensable part of the machine. These are hairs which have other little hairs growing all over them, giving them a feathered or mosslike appearance. They serve to entangle and hold the grains of pollen better than ordinary smooth hairs would do. On other parts of the bee's body the hairs are smooth; but these are of different sizes and proportions according to the functions they serve, and are grouped, as we have seen, with various objects in view. On the front pair of legs is an arrangement of hairs which serves the bee as an eye-brush. As bees have no eyelids on their compound eyes, and are always thrusting their heads into the flour bins of the summer's blossoms, they would seem to have need of some such convenience.

A bee's sting consists of two separate spears or shafts, each with nine barbs. It will be more readily comprehended by viewing it as a single spear which has been accurately split down the middle so that the two halves move smoothly up and down on one another, and the shafts are enclosed in a neat-fitting sheath which holds them together and guides them when thus working. There is a muscle belonging to the sting which gives the spears a pumping motion in the sheath, first one and then the other; and this muscle is able to keep up the pumping motion to a certain extent even after the sting has become disattached from the bee. The consequence is that when the sting is thrust slightly into the flesh the barbs take hold, and the barbs on one spear hold the sting firmly in place while the other spear is thrust deeper, and so on, alternately. The sting works its way in by its own power, and thus goes deeper than the bee could thrust it with her light weight and the limited hold of the little claws and gumlike pads on her feet. Attached to the sting also is the poison sac, which feeds the spears with poison by a groove in their working surfaces.

III

Readers who have read anything whatever about bees are probably familiar with the queen bee and the sexual peculiarities of the swarm. These things belong to the better-known facts in bee life such as are to be found in any treatise on beekeeping; but I shall repeat a few of them here, partly because of their intrinsic interest and partly because they lead on to some further considerations regarding the bee's tools.

In a swarm of bees, numbering anywhere from ten thousand to a hundred thousand individuals, there is but one female, the 'queen bee.' During her whole life she does nothing but lay eggs. She does not even feed herself, but is accompanied by a guard of fifteen or twenty bees who watch over her and attend to her wants; and when she thrusts her tongue out, they put honey upon it. A few days after she is hatched, she leaves the hive and goes forth on her wedding flight; and when she comes back, she can lay fertile eggs during all the rest of her life—as many as a million eggs—with but the one impregnation. Except for this wedding flight and the flight she takes when she goes out with the swarm to a new home, a queen bee has no experience in the outer world. While the other bees go forth for work, for exercise, and for cleansing flights, she sees nothing of the world of daylight. She lays eggs; and she goes out of that little door for no purpose whatsoever. And as she builds no comb, lays up no honey, takes no part in the rearing of the young, and does nothing but go from cell to cell laying eggs, she has no opportunity for experience or development in the work of the hive.

The workers, usually called neuter bees, are really females that are sexually undeveloped. They do all the work, of whatever sort, including the "nursing" which consists in feeding the larvae in their cells and tending to all the needs of the young. Dean Inge,[3] dealing with social questions in a recent number of the *Atlantic,* referred to the bee community as a "socialistic gynæcocracy of maiden aunts." It is a phrase which deserves to be perpetuated.

The males, or drones, of which there are only a few hundred in the hive, are non-workers. They do not bother to support themselves, but depend upon the others to keep plenty of stores in the hive. But they do go outdoors and enjoy themselves generally. They loaf about on the porch like true gentlemen—each a potential husband of the queen. And when the days of plenty are over and winter is in sight, the worker bees have a day of slaughter and kill every last drone. They also go over the comb and murder all the baby drones in their cells.

The queen has an appearance quite different from that of a worker. She is longer and slimmer and has wings that are shorter in proportion to her size, though she is a powerful flier. And yet the queen bee is hatched from the same sort of egg as is a worker bee. Usually a queen is hatched in a cell especially designed for the purpose; but

if the bees find themselves queenless at a time
when there is no royal cell with an egg in it, they
proceed to raise a queen from one of the eggs in
an ordinary worker cell, for which purpose they
give the egg more room by tearing away some of
the adjoining cells. The larva is then fed exclusively on a predigested food, called 'royal jelly,'
up to the time when it is sealed in to undergo its
metamorphosis into a bee. Ordinarily that larva
would have received predigested food, a sort of
mother's milk, for only a short time, after which
its food would become bee bread, or pollen mixed
with a little honey. But by this different feeding,
the egg that was intended to become a worker has
its destiny changed and becomes a bee with different tools, different instincts, and a different
form. They can make this change even after the
larva has been started out in its small cell as a
young worker bee, providing the process has not
been too long delayed.

This brings us around again to the interesting
subject of the bee's tools. A queen has no pollen
basket; she is not intended for that sort of work.
And, lacking the pollen basket, she is also wanting in that set of combs for gathering and loading
the grains; in short, she lacks the whole mechanism for reaping the crop. The drone, not being
intended for work, also lacks it.

A queen lacks the eight wax-pockets on the
abdomen which a worker has; and the drone, as
he does no building, lacks them also. The antenna

of a female bee or worker has thirteen joints, while that of a drone has one more. The sting of a queen bee is curved, and with it she kills rival queens. The sting of the worker is straight and serves to defend the hive. The drone, as he is not a sentinel or soldier, has no sting at all; and as he is killed at the end of the honey season, so that he may not consume any of the winter stores, it is a good thing for the others that he has no weapon and cannot fight back. In the wonderful compound eyes of the worker bees there are six thousand facets; but a drone has more than twice as many. And his antennae have more "smell hollows" than do the antennae of the other bees.

From what we have observed of the sexual arrangements of the hive, it will be seen that a queen is the daughter of a father and a mother neither of whom has had any experience in the work of the bee, either in the hive or out; and these fathers and mothers were descended from others who never had any experience in those things which make up the marvelous mechanism of the swarm. Consequently they can have no acquired traits or habits, or responses to environment, or effects of the use or disuse of organs to transmit to their offspring. And the neuter bees, who have all the struggles with life, and most of the special fitness which makes the swarm survive, cannot transmit to their offspring any new results of experience, or developments of habit, or gradual conformation to environment—simply because they have no offspring to transmit them to.

Right here is where Darwin's [4] theory of evolution went on the rocks. To any theory of evolution, heredity—the ability to transmit evolved traits to offspring—is absolutely necessary. A "law" that does not account for all cases that it is supposed to cover is no law at all; consequently the law of evolution has to succeed here or fail to be a law. Knowing this, Darwin was much perturbed when, about the two hundred and fiftieth page of his *Origin of Species,* he came to this problem of the neuter insect. As he says, it is a difficulty "which at first appeared to me insuperable and actually fatal to the whole theory." In fact, he must here submit a theory which seems plausible, or acceptable as a working hypothesis, or it is the end of his theory of evolution—or, for that matter, any other theory of evolution. And so, while his theory went on the rocks at this point, he set to work manfully to pull it off and get it into some sort of working condition.

He lays aside the idea of animals which vary from generation to generation and which transmit these advantageous changes to their offspring, and supposes instead the ability of a queen, somehow acquired, to *lay eggs* which vary in this advantageous way. Queens which laid such eggs survived because their swarms had advantages which caused them to survive. As to how such queens came to lay eggs with these peculiar potentialities, and different from the eggs of other queens, he puts the whole stress here on "spontaneous" variation—by which he means variation which we do not understand and cannot account for. Thus the theory went ahead again, but without having been really cleared up even by this supposition. While he had to account for all neuter insects, he was dealing especially with ants; and among ants the neuter insects in a community are not all alike, but have definite classes or castes, quite different from one another in structure and instinct. Here the theory would have to be stretched pretty far—almost too far. For how did a queen ant, simply employed in laying eggs, get this ability to lay eggs in which the whole intricate plan of the community, with its various instincts and different physical structure, was all latent and ready to spring forth from this egg and that? How does "evolution" account for such a thing? Darwin never got quite over the difficulty here, as can be seen in his recapitulation, where he refers to it with an evidently dissatisfied mind.

IV

However, all this is a difficult and recondite subject for the layman to employ himself upon, and he would never know his own opinion of evolution if he had to consider and weigh such obscure and questionable facts. If he wishes to bring his mind to the testing-point, he must get at it more directly.

Here on this front leg of the bee is that self-threading, combined comb and scraper for the bee's antenna. It is not in the patent-applied-for stage of invention, but is a complete and perfect working device. The whole affair would be quite likely to receive papers from the United States Patent Office; but a lawyer would have to draw up his basic claims pretty carefully to keep some useful point from being stolen. It might be the invention of some assiduous Yankee—though it is doubtful whether he would get it so perfect that it would not need further improvement and repairing.

Considering this now as a mere "fortuitous" falling-together of raw material, a mere happening or series of coincidences, a result of pure blind chance, the human mind simply refuses to take that position. In anything like this we see preconception. And preconception is mind, intelligent force. It is something quite different from material.

"Darwin considered natural selection, operating by means of small fortuitous individual variations, as the most important factor in organic evolution."

So says the *New International Dictionary*, very correctly including the *fortuitous*. Indeed, blind chance is of the very essence of the theory; for the survival of the fittest, as the result of advantageous variation, implies that other animals had variations which did not happen to be advantageous. The advantageous variation is one which happens to coincide with some feature of the environment; and so natural selection is a theory which gives an animal a "spontaneous" tendency to vary in all sorts of aimless and undirected ways, and then builds the animal up from some primitive or one-celled form by a long series of coincidences. Essentially it is "fortuitous."

The human mind, accepting this theory and starting out to give it definite application, is immediately brought to a halt. A man simply *will* ask questions—it is part of his nature; and so he wants to know whether the bee's antenna existed first and needed a cleaner for long periods of time, or whether the cleaner happened first and was in need of something to clean. As to the gradual evolution of tools, here is a bothersome thought! Some tools are of such a nature that they are not of use till they are complete. A wheelbarrow without a wheel, a pipe wrench without a jaw, would be an entirely unevolved piece of evolution. The *idea* might be there, but—! The antenna-cleaner seems to belong to this class of tools. One cannot imagine its progressive stages and see how any one of the imaginary states of incompletion would give its possessor any advantage over other insects in the struggle for existence.

One sees now why evolutionists have more recently taken up the theory of "mutations," which is that individuals may acquire new characteristics suddenly, all at a birth. This would be a much better way for such tools to happen—all at once, and overnight as it were, answering the need of an antenna that ought to be cleaned. And so it would appear that the antenna and the cleaner must have been made together—in fact, maybe they were made at the same time the bee was made! But this will not do, for this is not evolution at all. Evolution is opposed to *special creation;* that is its very definition as set down by the evolutionists. We must not imagine any such thing because it is against the law of evolution. So there we are again—the human mind refusing to meet the conditions. For my part, I must admit that I am completely frustrated; and so I shall proceed to drop the subject.

Practically, it is like an argument about infinity. Eternity is difficult to admit; a thing without end is beyond the reach of thought. On the other hand, it is just as difficult to admit that there could be an end to time or space—beyond which point there would be neither time nor space. Both are impossible.

Evolution, practically, is something in the same line. At first it is a supreme act of faith, under the guise of a "working hypothesis"; and very soon it has become a sort of theology, disbelieving which you are a heretic. Right here is the ground of complaint as set forth by Funda-

mentalists and others. They say that evolution
has become a dogma, a creed of science, set forth
as if it were truth instead of a mere theory. The
"working hypothesis," which belongs in the
laboratory of the trained investigator, has got
itself mixed up in our educational programme. It
is a school of thought. Young men and women,
instead of being brought face to face with the
unknowable, and trained in any sort of contemplation or reflection, are wholly neglected in that
important department of their natures.

For my part, I cannot contemplate a wasp, a
spider, or a bee without being confronted with
absolute Mystery. At the end of every telescope,
beneath every microscope, at the bottom of every
marl pit, is Mystery pure and simple. Science reveals more for me to wonder at, but solves nothing. This may not be religion exactly, but it is
a continual reminder of my own position in the
universe. And so I think that a system of education which takes the attitude of accounting for
all things, or being just upon the point of accounting for them when the scientists have discovered just a few more facts, is not education
at all. It stops just short of the truth; and therefore it is not exactly honest.

NOTES

[1] John Burroughs (1837–1921), American naturalist.
[2] This essay was published in 1926.
[3] "The gloomy Dean" of St. Paul's Cathedral, London.

[4] Charles Darwin (1809–1882), author of *Origin of Species*, crystallized the theory of evolution.

SUGGESTIONS

1. Notice how the last paragraph demands a reconsideration of the essay as a whole. Does this challenge strengthen or weaken, in your estimation, the connection between science and religion?

2. Select some natural phenomenon with which you are familiar and determine what is back of it, mystery or proof.

WASTEFUL NATURE *

ALEXANDER PETRUNKEVITCH

ALEXANDER PETRUNKEVITCH has been Professor of Zoology at Yale University since 1917. He was born at Pliski, Russia, in 1875, was educated at Gymnasiums (preparatory schools) at Kiev, Tuver, Moscow, and at the University of Moscow. He has received the degree of Doctor of Philosophy from the Universities of Freiburg and Porto Rico, and belongs to most of the learned societies in America. Prior to his teaching at Yale, he taught Zoölogy at Harvard University and the University of Indiana. Readers of Professor Petrunkevitch's occasional essays in *The Yale Review* have come to expect from him more than mere scientific reporting; there is always the suggestion of the philosopher standing at the scientist's elbow as he writes.

THAT man is wasteful is a truism. Not only does he waste his own time and energy; he wastes the energy and the resources of the world. When he seeks to increase productivity he constructs machines and makes them to do his work wherever he can. Now, it is an easy thing to show that, in doing this, man wastes resources and energy in favor of time. For, after all, his own organism

---

* Reprinted from *The Yale Review*, copyright, Yale University Press, by permission of the editors.

as a machine is vastly superior to and more efficient than the best machine constructed by his
hands; and the work produced by his brain and
his muscles represents a considerably greater return of energy received than ever will be produced
by a man-made engine. So man is in an eternal
quandary whether to save his resources by wasting his time, or to save his time by wasting his
resources.

But is Nature herself economical? We hear the
statement repeated very often that Nature does
not waste anything. This was taught long ago by
Lucretius in his *De rerum natura,* a remarkable
philosophical poem, too soon forgotten by the
world and too little known to the scholar of to-
day. The so-called principle of preservation of
matter, neglected for many centuries, was demonstrated by the experiments of the distinguished
Russian man of science and letters, Lomonosov,
and later independently arrived at by the French
chemist Lavoisier in the last quarter of the eighteenth century. The work of more modern physicists established the principle of preservation of
energy, perhaps the most important principle that
was ever revealed to human mind. Both principles
are now universally accepted and form the basis
of our conceptions of Nature.

The biologist, too, is often heard making the
statement that Nature wastes nothing. But his
point of view differs from that of the chemist or
the physicist. He deals, not with the transforma-

tion of matter and energy as such, but with the manifestations of life. The ultimate equation of matter and energy received and spent will show a perfect balance, but the balance may be in favor of something else than the individual. The biologist should beware lest he give a wrong interpretation to natural phenomena. When he contemplates Nature, he is apt to admire the end result and to forget the process by which Nature has arrived at that result. Yet it is the process, the method, which determines the efficiency; and the methods pursued by Nature are often appallingly inefficient. Nature is wasteful. She is lavish; she is ruthless in her waste!

Look at the wastefulness of Nature in her devious ways of preserving the existence of some species of animals. All that is required to prevent the extinction of the species is that the number of the progeny should always be the same as that of the progenitors. As long as the ratio is maintained, the species is safe from extinction. If the ratio were changed ever so little in favor of the progenitors, the progeny would begin to decrease and the species would embark upon the course of a gradual, but sure, destruction. What does Nature do to solve this mathematically simple problem? She displays a bewildering ingenuity in increasing the ratio in favor of the progeny to an almost unbelievable proportion and then cuts it down to the normal by all means at her disposal. Let us consider a few examples.

The common house-fly—the nursling of garbage, filth, and manure—lays on the average 120 eggs, half of which are females. From the time that the eggs are deposited to the time when the newly developed generation of flies will deposit eggs in their turn, some twenty days will elapse. At the end of five months, if the ratio were maintained and if all individuals were to survive, there would be 5,598,720,000,000 descendants of a single pair of flies. This is about the total possible yearly increase, since flies do not reproduce in cold weather. And only two of this number are destined to survive. What an appalling waste! Those who see wisdom in Nature should pause for a moment to consider whether it would not have been both wise and more economical, more efficient, not to employ such methods of wanton destruction where partial restriction of productive powers and a slight perfection in organs and instincts of defense would have achieved just the same end.

But the case of the house-fly is neither exceptional, nor in any way extraordinary. There are hundreds of insects and of other animals that present the same picture. In many cases even this ratio seems to have been insufficient, and Nature with her inexhaustible means and rampant imagination conceived the idea of increasing the ratio by making it possible for some insects to multiply without males. Whereas in other instances a pair of individuals is needed for the

act of reproduction, in so-called "parthenogen-
esis" every individual is a female and produces
either eggs or young, as the case may be, auto-
matically at a certain stage in her life. The plant-
lice furnish the most common example of such
reproduction during the summer months when
from eight to eleven generations, always females,
never a male, follow in swift succession one after
the other. As each female produces on the average
about 90 young, the number of individuals descended from a single female after eight generations would reach the incredible figure of 4,353,-
039,202,247,190; or—if only the individuals of
the last generation survived—4,304,672,100,-
000,000.

One shudders to think what would happen if
even one per cent of all animals born and of all
eggs laid in the world were to survive. The famine
in Russia would be as nothing in comparison with
the devastation and ruin that would result in a
few weeks. Americans are aware of the damage
done yearly, as it is, to their crops and their gardens, to their cotton fields and forests. They know
only too well the ravages of the boll-weevil, of the
San José scale, of the gypsy moth, of the potato
beetle, of the clothes moth, of the bark beetles,
and of hundreds of other insects causing losses
running into millions of dollars. All of these have
to be combated by man year after year. But there
are numerous instances of a sudden increase in
the numbers of some species of insects which are

usually kept in check by other agencies than man. Thus we have the account of the invasion of Belgium in 1834 by hostile armies, not of Germans but of plant-lice. They appeared on September 28 of that year between Bruges and Ghent as an immense cloud obstructing the light of the sun. The creatures descended upon the buildings in Ghent in such quantities that it was impossible to discern the color of the walls. The road between Antwerp and Ghent became, for a time, practically impassable. People were forced to put on spectacles and to protect their heads with kerchiefs to avoid the maddening sensation of tickling produced by the feet of the alighting insects.

The European May-beetle or cockchafer, as it is often called, a species closely related to and slightly larger than our common June-bug, suddenly developed in such quantities in some parts of Germany in 1860, that at least one thrifty farmer offered to pay a good price for large quantities of these beetles to be used as fertilizer on his fields. A computation showed that between the ninth and the thirtieth of May he bought nearly 22,000,000 beetles, and the number of beetles which remained was still so great that it would have been profitable to collect them had it not been too late in the season to make use of them as fertilizer. In 1804 millions of May-beetles were carried by the wind and drowned in the Lake of Zurich in Switzerland, and the stench as they decomposed was almost unendurable. In 1841

May-beetles flew over the river Saône in France
and descended upon the vineyards of Mâcon.
The bridges across the river became impassable
with them and remained so until the people had
cleared the way with shovels. It is said that in
1688 in the County of Galway in Ireland the
May-beetles appeared in such quantities that all
vegetation was destroyed and the unfortunate
population was forced to use the beetles for food.
There is a delightful account of court proceedings
against May-beetles which caused a famine in
Lausanne, Switzerland, in the year 1479. The
prosecuting attorney named Friburg was so eloquent in his denunciation of the wicked little
criminals that the court pronounced a sentence of
banishment against them.

Dragon-flies, like butterflies, may at times appear in unusual numbers. In the summer of 1895
I observed for several hours an uninterrupted
stream of them over the city of Moscow, and in
1909 I saw on three successive days a similiar
stream of butterflies over the green expanse of the
jungles of the Isthmus of Tehuantepec in Mexico.
But the most spectacular and most terrifying
spectacle is afforded by the migrating locust of
Southern Europe and Northern Africa. Pliny the
Elder reports in his *Natural History,* published
about 77 A.D., that in Cyrenaica and on the Island
of Lemnos special laws had to be passed for the
destruction of locusts. The Bible speaks of them
as one of the ten scourges of Egypt. The monk

Alvarez, who encountered locusts in Ethiopia in the sixteenth century, describes in a charmingly naïve way how he ordered some of the insects to be brought alive to him and how he then chanted a charm over them, which he composed during the preceding night. "I threatened," he writes, "I expostulated, I excommunicated them, I adjured them to leave the fields within three hours and to go either to the sea or to the country of the Moors, avoiding Christian countries. In case they should disobey, I conjured all the birds under the heavens, all the creatures on land and all the storms of the air to come, disperse, destroy, and annihilate them. Then I ordered a few more insects brought to me. I told them to listen attentively to my words and then released them that they might carry my words to their kin."

In 1613 three thousand quintals of locusts' eggs were destroyed in Southern France by the peasants in their crusade against the creatures—about 5,250,000,000 eggs! In 1709 the retreating army of Charles the Twelfth of Sweden was stopped by locusts in Southern Russia. Fifteen hundred and eighteen sacks of locusts, weighing 68,861 kilograms, were once destroyed in the district of Saintes-Maries on the Mediterranean coast of France. And in 1878 a detachment of Russian troops on a military expedition met with locusts near Elizavetpol and fled in disorder.

Nature accomplishes the same result in an astonishing variety of ways. Either the number of eggs produced by a single female is so tremendous that it almost surpasses imagination; or the tempo of egg production, the number of generations per year, is increased; or both sexes are united in the same individual, as is the rule in so many parasitic and other worms; or the necessity of producing males is obviated; or a-sexual reproduction may regularly alternate with sexual reproduction. All this occurs continually everywhere on land, in fresh water, in the sea, even among parasites inhabiting our own bodies. Always Nature produces as great a progeny as possible; always she is lavish to the point of endangering her own creations.

And then, having given all living creatures such potentialities of reproduction, Nature proceeds to destroy them incessantly by day and night, in winter and in summer, year after year, century after century, and millennium after millennium. The number of individuals for each species in each locality remains stationary, and a perceptible increase is noticeable only in isolated cases. Usually when the sun-rays grow warm enough to call dormant beings back to activity and the early spring flowers gladden our hearts, animal life, in our latitude at least, starts from the same level as at the corresponding time the year before. Should the production of new individuals one year by chance be excessive, the food supply needed for their existence becomes insufficient. The animals may then migrate to better fields, leaving devastation and ruin behind them. Such migrations are known for locusts, brown-tail moths in the caterpillar stage, blister-beetles, and many other creatures. Yet famine among animals must be much more common than with man, and its consequences are even more serious. For man takes precautions against drought and devastation. Or if people in one part of the world fail to do so, others are ready to come to their assistance. But animals eat as long as they find food, and when the food is gone their only salvation lies in migrating and searching for food elsewhere. Rarely will animals eat other food than that to which they are accustomed. Keepers in zoölogical gardens must often have recourse to tricks to induce an animal to swallow perfectly wholesome and palatable food, but food to which that animal is not accustomed when living in its free state. Thus thousands of animals sometimes perish amidst a plenty of food.

We are often told that cannibalism in man, at least where it is commonly practised, is a sign of a very low stage of development. This may be doubted, considering that the nearest relatives of man among the apes are not cannibals. And yet among other animals cannibalism is widespread. Indeed, in some cases, it is the normal way of handling not only the weaker enemy but one's own kin as well. Higher animals will not normally resort to it; but still wolves will devour wounded companions, and mice and rats often destroy their own helpless young. Some male birds will break and suck the eggs laid by their own mates, and older fish swallow young fish of the same species. Among invertebrates cannibalism is of daily occurrence. In a way it is all right if the children make a meal of their mother, as is the case regularly with some round worms and the insect known as the earwig. The work of the mother is accomplished when she has perpetuated her kind, and it looks almost like economy when she gives her body into the bargain as food for her young. But more often brothers and sisters succumb to the stronger one in the battle in which each adversary regards the other only as an enemy or a prospective supply of food. Indeed, love itself is not always powerful enough to restrain the hunger of the strong female, who may make a meal of her wooer if he comes at an inopportune moment. It has even been observed that in the case of one common European spider the wooing male offers his prospective bride a neatly swathed fly before he ventures to whisper to her his protestations of love.

But here is a strange case. Consider some of the parasites whose food is derived from their host. The relation between the two is very remarkable. The host furnishes the living abode and the necessary supply of food. He protects the parasite within him from sure death, by fighting the enemies in whose stomach the parasite would perish. Yet his own life is often imperilled by the parasite. In fact, in many instances the host himself must be killed and devoured to permit the parasite to continue normal development. Tapeworms of the *genus Ligula* have at times caused the death of great number of fresh-water fish by spontaneously leaving their body cavity in which they had grown for two years, nourished and protected by the host. The *Ligulae* will finish their own strange lives in a few days in the alimentary tract of some aquatic bird which swallows them mistaking them for proper food, such as earthworms, but does not derive any benefit whatsoever from them. Whether the bird suffers any harm in this case is also doubtful. Twenty-four hours after having thus involuntarily established its domicile in the alimentary tract of the bird, the *Ligula* begins to lay eggs. On reaching the water, these eggs develop into little free swimming *larvae* within a few days if the temperature of the water is sufficiently warm—there may be a delay of several weeks if the water is cold. When developed, the *larvae* may continue their existence in the free state for ten days, swimming about in the water. None can live longer unless swallowed by some unlucky fish; swallowed entirely by chance, for the *larvae* are much too small to be seen. Thus at the time when failure to be swallowed by a fish will mean death to the parasite, the opportunity of being swallowed has been considerably impaired by the wholesale destruction of fish caused by the migration of the nearly adult parasite from the fish into the water.

In all parasites which require two hosts for the completion of their life cycle and in which part of this life cycle is entirely dependent upon the feeding habits of the final hosts, the chance of survival of the parasite is infinitesimal. This is self-evident, for there is no provision here for putting the opportunity of getting into the host, so to say, at the disposal of the parasite. Moreover, such a provision would be self-restricting. If man, for example, eats too much pork or ham infected with *larvae* of *trichina,* he is sure to die of the effects produced on his system by the worms, and consequently the entire progeny of the swallowed parasites themselves are doomed to perish with him because they migrate from the alimentary system to the muscles and cannot develop otherwise than by being swallowed together with the muscles by some new host. *Trichina* may develop in almost any animal, but only such omnivorous animals as rats and pigs will normally perpetuate her race. All the innumerable individuals that may be swallowed by other animals will represent nothing but frightful waste.

This is true of the majority of similar parasites. There is, for example, a small tapeworm living in domestic cats. The *larvae* of this tapeworm are found in the liver of mice and rats. They reach this organ after they have developed from eggs swallowed by the mouse or rat. The tapeworm produces hundreds of thousands of eggs; and the unfortunate animal that swallows too many of them will die in less than two weeks after the meal, as may be demonstrated without any difficulty in laboratory experiments. Who could see any economy or foresight in Nature in the case of that terrible tapeworm which in its adult stage lives as a comparatively harmless creature in the alimentary tract of dogs, but whose *larvae* can develop only in the brain of sheep, causing the disease known as gid or staggers, so cruel and fatal in its effects? The *larvae* develop from eggs swallowed by the sheep with grass. They are carried all over the body by the blood and lodge in all kinds of organs only to perish there sooner or later. Not so with those that reach the brain. There they will grow and increase in number. Yet they, too, will perish unless swallowed with the brain by a dog.

Some zoölogists try to avoid the difficulty in the way of explaining such inconsistencies of Nature by reversing the problem. They say that Nature has increased the productivity of parasites precisely because the tremendous loss due to the slight chance of being swallowed would in the end imperil the existence of the species. In other words, that the more difficult the transmission of a parasite is, the greater must be the production of eggs if the parasite is to survive. Such a view is, however, merely a statement of fact; and itself begs the question. Reproduction is one of the fundamental attributes of all living beings, plants as well as animals. It is a strange inconsistency to decrease the chance of transmission by limiting the number of animal species and of organs which may be successfully infected by a given parasite, to meet the resulting danger of extinction by enormously increasing productivity, and then to make such productivity itself a further cause imperilling the existence of the parasite. Would it not be much more efficient, for example, if it were possible, to give the gid-bladder worm the ability to develop in other organs than the brain and in other animals than sheep alone? Yet that is not the case.

But death is not the only effect working against the advantage to the parasite without at the same time giving any advantage to the host. Many animals are made permanently incapable of reproduction by the parasite, which, nevertheless, cannot develop in any other species. Especially, insects and crabs show this quite commonly when infected by parasites living in their body cavity. This fact has an even greater effect than death. For whereas in the case of death in consequence of infection, the infected animal may have performed its function of reproduction previous to infection, in the case of parasites of the type now being considered, invasion of the host is accomplished before reproductive maturity of the host; and while the life of the infected individual is not necessarily imperilled, its reproductive function is obliterated forever. This of course decreases the number of individuals that may be infected.

But Nature is also wasteful in the process of

reproduction itself. At the expense of food, eggs are produced in numbers without being capable of further development. In the case of domestic fowl, man has utilized this extravagance of Nature by making unfertilized eggs a staple article of food for himself. But we know a great many instances where eggs are laid only because the female as an egg-producing machine cannot help doing so.

Similarly the production of male generative cells is in every respect wasteful. It requires a single male reproductive cell to fertilize an egg; and not only is this true, but if by chance more than one such cell enters the egg, all such excessive cells either perish or imperil development, causing either death or the production of monstrosities. Yet what do we see in reality? Millions of male reproductive cells are wasted to ensure the fertilization sometimes of a single egg! Is this efficiency? And to avoid the danger of overfertilization Nature is forced to endow the egg with special means to prevent it. This is especially true in the case of all vertebrates, but applies also to many invertebrates. There is nothing easier than to overfertilize eggs of sea urchins, starfish, oysters, or scallops in laboratory experiments by adding too much sperm to the water.

In some insects, as for instance bees, the so-called queen is once only in her life fertilized by a male or drone. The sperm is stored in a special receptacle in the body of the queen and must suffice during the four or five years of the queen's normal life. Here indeed it seems as if Nature had found a provision against squandering the sperm, for only those eggs have to be fertilized which will develop into workers and queens. A wonderful apparatus admits a small quantity of the fluid to each egg as it passes by the duct of the receptacle while the rest of the precious treasure is again locked up. Nevertheless, far more than one sperm-cell are allowed to act upon each egg. Usually several of them enter each egg, and all but one are used by the egg itself as so much food. As these cells are exceedingly small, their nutritive value is quite negligible, while their reproductive function has been nullified and the cells themselves wasted. There is sufficient sperm in the receptacle of the queen to last for about four years of her egg-laying activity, after which she can lay only unfertilized eggs developing into drones—a danger to the existence of the entire beehive—and yet Nature was unable to perfect the apparatus of the queen, or at any rate did not do so; and thus day after day and year after year goes on wasting several hundred per cent of her own capital stock.

The reproductive function is, however, not the only one which is wasteful. There is no really perfectly functioning organ in the body of an animal. Take, for instance, the alimentary canal. Is it not of primary value to every animal that food should be used in such a manner as to leave no waste whatsoever? And yet no animal seems to be able to extract all the nutritive elements from its normal food. This is evidenced best of all by the existence of insects that make their meal exclusively of excrements of higher animals. Out of this apparently useless material some of the most permanent and most beautiful colors in the wings of dungbeetles are produced. Nor is oxygen entirely extracted from the air in the process of respiration. A great deal of it is wasted by all mammals, although in birds we find a more perfect arrangement because of the existence of the so-called airsacs. Again, a great deal of energy and material is spent on the daily growth of hair without which life would be quite possible, while at the same time the ability to produce new teeth has been lost in all mammals, although teeth are indeed very much needed.

In the life of an individual, wastefulness is increased by the imperfection of its instincts. We admire the squirrels as they lay by a store of nuts and acorns for the coming winter. But a great deal of their time is also spent in burying nuts in places where they will be forgotten and never again recovered. Similarly the nuthatches are busy all day long in hiding seeds and nuts in little crevices in the bark of trees, only to have these discovered and eaten by the more lazy and greedy squirrels. Even the construction of those wonderful geometric webs made by spiders is accompanied by considerable waste. For the spider constructs first a complete web of common silk before it attempts to weave into it the special silk with adhesive drops which alone can capture insects. To do this properly, the spider has to remove the first structure, thread by thread, rolling it up in a little ball which is then dropped to the ground.

Misdirected instincts, instincts productive of altogether wasteful and often fatal results, are only too common. In addition to cannibalism, infanticide has been observed in various animals and birds, as, for instance, in the common herring gull. The rigidity, the machine-like precision of instincts, which is always praised so highly by students of Nature, is in itself a source of danger. After a rain the earthworms crawl out on to the sidewalks in the city only to perish miserably from lack of moisture. The cat cleans itself daily by licking its fur and infects itself with a tapeworm the *larvae* of which live in fleas and lice. The honeybee attacks any intruder, no matter how harmless, and gives her life for the protection of the hive, when it is in no danger and needs no protection. She falls a victim, not to the resentment of the enemy attacked, but to the normal function of the perfectly absurd structure of her sting, supplied with barbs which bring about automatic self-mutilation when the bee tries to withdraw the sting and fly away from the animal stung and tears herself free, bleeding to death of her wound.

The queen bee produces thousands of drones,

far in excess of the females, although a single
drone only is accepted by a queen, and all others
perish without having performed the function of
reproduction. But the successful drone also pays
with his life for the fulfilment of his desire, being
unable to tear himself from the female without
mortal injury to himself. Worker bees are incapable of reproduction under normal conditions,
but may be artificially induced to lay eggs in an
orphaned hive. These eggs will develop into drones
only, because they are unfertilized; and the hive
will ultimately perish because of the absence of a
queen; and yet if some other queen is placed in
the orphaned hive, the workers, instead of wel-
coming her as a savior, will instantly attack her
and kill her with their stings. Only special precautions taken by the bee-keeper in the interest
of the hive can prevent such fatal results.

Thus Nature works incessantly against her own
best interests and wastes her own energy. Not
guided by any principle of efficiency, an animal or
a plant performs its various functions to capacity,
regardless of any benefit or harm to itself or to
others, until all inherent possibilities and all the
stored up energy are completely exhausted. The
limitation in every direction is not that of efficiency but of counter-action exerted by other
forces. And why should there be any economy,
any efficiency in any particular case, when to the
universe as a whole no force, no energy, however
inefficiently spent, is ever lost? The principles

of efficiency are applicable only to the limited, to the machine, to the individual. As a self-perpetuating principle, Life is perhaps worthy of admiration; but it is certainly highly inefficient.

SUGGESTIONS

1. Note the qualities revealed in Petrunkevitch through the quality of his thinking.

2. Correlate this with "The Bee's Knees" by Charles D. Stewart.

3. Note other evidence of this same theme in your daily reading of the newspaper.

4. What does the location of the scientific news in the newspapers indicate about popular interest in science?

ON MULTIPLE PERSONALITIES

(A Selection from *The Autocrat of The Breakfast Table*)

OLIVER WENDELL HOLMES

"I was just going to say when I was interrupted" is one of the famous lines in American literature. It appeared as the opening of OLIVER WENDELL HOLMES' *Autocrat of the Breakfast Table* in the first issue of the *Atlantic Monthly*. When James Russell Lowell was asked in 1856 to edit a new magazine for a group of Boston publishers, he accepted on the condition that he have the assistance of Oliver Wendell Holmes. The famous *Autocrat* and *Professor at the Breakfast Table* are the fortunate result of that respect for Holmes' ability. Holmes was born in Cambridge, Massachusetts, in 1809, the son of a clergyman. Educated at Phillips Andover Academy and at Harvard, class of 1829, he first came to public notice shortly after his graduation through his stirring poem objecting to the War Department's order to scrap the historic frigate, The Constitution. Public indignation aroused by the poem caused the War Department to recant and save the ship, which has ever since served as a symbol of American liberty. After studying medicine in France for two years, Holmes returned to Boston and took up practice. But the social graces and fun-loving wit of the young physician soon created the impression that he was not serious enough for such a learned profession. He then began lecturing on anatomy at Dartmouth College, and some years later accepted the chair of Professor of Anatomy and Physiology at Harvard University. His attendant duties in departments associated with this led him to refer to his new position as "not a chair but a settee in the school." His wife, Amelia Lee Jackson, was a daughter of the Honorable Charles Jackson (1775–1855) who served the state of Massachusetts with ability as Associate Justice of the Massachusetts Supreme Court. Their son Oliver Wendell, Junior, is well known to the present generation for his distinguished legal career ending with his retirement in 1932, an outstanding Liberal and Justice of the United States Supreme Court, the highest court in the land. With the exception of summers, which he spent at Pittsfield or at Beverly Farms, Massachusetts, Holmes spent his life in Boston, publishing biological treatises filled with the same sly humor that characterizes his work as the essayist of the *Atlantic Monthly*. His lectures at Harvard were frequently scheduled, it is said, for late afternoon, Holmes being the most capable of keeping weary students awake by his fresh, lively wit. His circle of friends in Boston included the best of the literary group. He belonged to the Saturday Club, which included such lights as Ralph Waldo Emerson, Henry Wadsworth Longfellow (then teaching at Harvard), James Russell Lowell, John Greenleaf Whittier, Charles Sumner (the Senator from Massachusetts and ardent proponent of the Abolition of Slavery), and Louis Agassiz (the eminent biologist, then teaching at Harvard). Of this group, Lowell said that Holmes was easily the most interesting conversationalist. Holmes died in 1894 and was buried in Mount Auburn cemetery, Boston.

SOME persons seem to think that absolute truth, in the form of rigidly stated propositions, is all that conversation admits. This is precisely as if a musician should insist on having nothing but perfect chords and simple melodies,—no diminished fifths, no flat sevenths, no flourishes, on any account. Now it is fair to say, that, just as music must have all these, so conversation must have its partial truths, its embellished truths, its exaggerated truths. It is in its higher forms an artistic product, and admits the ideal element as much as pictures or statues. One man who is a little too literal can spoil the talk of a whole tableful of men of *esprit.*—"Yes," you say, "but who wants to hear fanciful people's nonsense? Put the facts to it, and then see where it is!"—Certainly, if a man is too fond of paradox, —if he is flighty and empty,—if, instead of striking those fifths and sevenths, those harmonious discords, often so much better than the twinned octaves, in the music of thought,—if, instead of striking these, he jangles the chords, stick a fact into him like a stiletto. But remember that talking is one of the fine arts,—the noblest, the most important, and the most difficult,—and that its fluent harmonies may be spoiled by the intrusion of a single harsh note. Therefore conversation which is suggestive rather than argumentative, which lets out the most of each talker's results of thought, is commonly the pleasantest and the most profitable. It is not easy, at the best, for two persons talking together to make the most of each other's thoughts, there are so many of them.

The company looked as if they wanted an explanation.[1]

When John and Thomas, for instance, are talking together, it is natural enough that among the six there should be more or less confusion and misapprehension.

Our landlady turned pale;—no doubt she thought there was a screw loose in my intellects, —and that involved the probable loss of a boarder. A severe-looking person, who wears a Spanish cloak and a sad cheek, fluted by the passions of the melodrama, whom I understand to be the professional ruffian of the neighboring theatre, alluded, with a certain lifting of the brow, drawing down of the corners of the mouth, and somewhat rasping *voce di petto*,[2] to Falstaff's nine men in buckram. Everybody looked up; I believe the old gentleman opposite was afraid I should seize the carving-knife; at any rate, he slid it to one side, as it were carelessly.

I think, I said, I can make it plain to Benjamin Franklin here, that there are at least six personalities distinctly to be recognized as taking part in that dialogue between John and Thomas.

Three Johns.	1. The real John; known only to his Maker.
	2. John's ideal John; never the real one, and often very unlike him.
	3. Thomas' ideal John; never the real John, nor John's John, but often very unlike either.
Three Thomases.	1. The real Thomas.
	2. Thomas' ideal Thomas.
	3. John's ideal Thomas.

Only one of the three Johns is taxed; only one can be weighed on a platform-balance; but the other two are just as important in the conversation. Let us suppose the real John to be old, dull, and ill-looking. But as the Higher Powers have not conferred on men the gift of seeing themselves in the true light, John very possibly conceives himself to be youthful, witty, and fascinating, and talks from the point of view of this ideal. Thomas, again, believes him to be an artful rogue, we will say; therefore he *is*, so far as Thomas' attitude in the conversation is concerned, an artful rogue though really simple and stupid. The same conditions apply to the three Thomases. It follows, that, until a man can be found who knows himself as his Maker knows him, or who sees himself as others see him, there must be at least six persons engaged in every dialogue between two. Of these, the least important, philosophically speaking, is the one that we have called the real person. No wonder two disputants often get angry, when there are six of them talking and listening all at the same time.

A very unphilosophical application of the above remarks was made by a young fellow answering to the name of John, who sits near me at table. A certain basket of peaches, a rare vegetable, little known to boarding-houses, was on its way to me *via* this unlettered Johannes. He appropriated the three that remained in the basket, remarking that there was just one apiece for him. I convinced him that his practical inference was hasty and illogical, but in the mean time he had eaten the peaches.

NOTES

[1] The company around the table in the boarding-house of *The Autocrat of the Breakfast Table*.

[2] A harsh voice.

SUGGESTION

Link this essay with "The Difficult Art of Self-Expression" by L. P. Jacks and "Every Man's Natural Desire to Be Somebody Else" by Samuel McChord Crothers, which follow.

THE DIFFICULT ART OF
SELF-EXPRESSION *

L. P. JACKS

What Wordsworth and Coleridge did for poetry; what
H. G. Wells and James Truslow Adams have done for history; what Charles D. Stewart and Petrunkevitch have
done for science; so much has DR. L. P. JACKS done,
through his essays, for philosophy. He has freed the materials of his subject from the shackles of technical and
complicated terms and re-stated them in terms which "the
man in the street" can grasp. No mere popularizer of
philosophy, Dr. Jacks interprets the passing show of modern life with a simplicity that renders age-old problems
familiar to the lay reader. Dr. Jacks was born in Notting-
ham, England, in 1860. After a particularly successful ministry in the Unitarian Church, he resigned, in 1902, to
found and edit *The Hibbert Journal.* The following year
he became instructor in philosophy at Manchester College,
Oxford, and served as such until 1915, when he was
elected principal of that college. Dr. Jacks is best known
to Americans, perhaps, through his frequent contributions
to the magazine section of *The New York Times* and
through his appearances on the lecture platform.

THEORETICALLY and in the abstract I have no
objection to raise against the modern doctrine of

---

* Published by permission of the author and *The New York
Times.*

self-expression, whether as defining the end of life for all men or as a principle for the education of the young. On the contrary, I consider it as sound as any other of the doctrines which have been laid down either for life or for education, and a good deal sounder than some of them. At the same time, it needs to be pointed out—and this is seldom done—that in application and practice no doctrine is more difficult to carry out. To suppose that by choosing the path of self-expression we are taking an easy road to some sort of paradise is the silliest of delusions, though by no means an uncommon one. Any one who adopts the doctrine under that delusion will only succeed in getting his life into an appalling mess, as, I am sorry to say, some of my young friends, who say they have adopted it, seem to be doing.

A successful self-expressionist must put himself under the severest discipline. For long periods of his life he must scorn delights and live laborious days. The best examples of self-expression I know of are to be found in the work of the great artists, Kreisler playing the violin or Pavlowa in one of her exquisite dances—easy and beautiful arts of self-expression, but founded on a self-control attained by long years of self-discipline. To attain self-expression otherwise, no matter in what walk of life you attempt it, is impossible. One might as well try to play the violin without learning one's notes or to execute a Pavlowa dance on a pair of wooden legs.

There is no more difficult life in the universe than the life of self-expression. Stern adhesion to the law of duty, or social service for the happiness of others, is certainly not more difficult and probably less so. Let those who want an "easy" life (which is not "easily" attainable nowadays) avoid self-expression as the most difficult of all the paths that lead to it. The other day a man who had been reading Bertrand Russell's [1] "Conquest of Happiness" said to me: "Rather than endure all the botheration involved in conquering happiness, I would do without happiness altogether."

The difficulty largely arises from the fact that it needs an exceptionally wise man to know for certain whether he is really expressing himself or not. For my own part, I have to confess that I am not wise enough—at least, in my own case. If any reader of this article were to ask me: "Are you really expressing yourself in what you are writing at this moment?" I should have to answer: "I think so, I hope so; but I can't prove it either to you, to myself or to anybody else." Or if, putting the question more generally, he were to ask: "How far, after your rather long life, have you succeeded in realizing that self of yours?" my answer would be: "God only knows. I must wait till the Day of Judgment to find out."

But while I am uncertain about myself, I feel pretty sure that some of my emancipated young friends, alluded to above, who have adopted the doctrine of self-expression, are not acting up to their creed. They think they are expressing themselves by their wild goings-on (especially in sex matters), while in reality they are only imitating the fashions of a wild set into whose company they happen to have fallen. Nothing is easier than to imagine we are expressing ourselves when we are only following a fashionable craze for something new.

After all, there is nothing more vital in the "self" of any one, man or woman, than the sense of decency, which Professor Gilbert Murray [2] has lately been telling us is quite as strong in the youth of our day as ever it was, as strong if not stronger. So vital is this sense of decency in the make-up of normal human nature, especially in youth, that any mode of life which fails to express it is not real self-expression, but only a miserable counterfeit of it. Professor Murray calls it the "inner censor," [3] and I think he is right in saying that we can trust it (in the long run) to correct the silly aberrations into which the counterfeit article is now leading so many of our delightful young people to indulge themselves.

In the meantime, however, they run a risk of making a horrible mess of their lives and fools of themselves in the bargain. After a few years of that sort of self-expression—the "go-as-you-please" variety—they will get themselves into impossible tangles with other folk, who, incidentally, will not stand their goings-on. They will discover that what they have been "expressing" is not their "selves" at all, and they will curse themselves for fools.

"The good life," said Aristotle, "is a very difficult affair." So, too, he might have added, is the bad life, though for different reasons; and it seems a pity he didn't say so—as the Bible so frequently does. "The way of the transgressors is hard," says the Book of Proverbs, in which respect the way of transgressors bears a remarkable resemblance to the way of the saints. On the score of hardness it may be doubted whether there is a pin to choose between the good life and the bad, or between the best life and the worst. Who could say that the life of a Chicago gangster is easier, taking it all around, than the life of the sternest moralist in that city? Or that the life of "free love" is easier than that of the strictest monogamous fidelity? Both, taken in the broad and large, are very difficult.

Two criminals were recently executed in England. One had killed his nagging wife, to whom he had always been faithful, because he had found the monogamous relationship intolerable; the other, who had six mistresses, killed one of them because she was making herself a nuisance in his relations with the other five. Neither the monogamist nor the free lover found his way of life an easy one, nor his principles easy to carry out.

What principles are? Even the principle of

having no principle, which is what some self-expressionists seem to affect, is extremely difficult to carry out, and especially so when sex relations are concerned.

No easy solution of the "sex problem" has ever been discovered and none ever will be. From the foundations of the world it was ordained that this problem should be difficult for the sons and daughters of men. Nobody has yet been able to circumvent nature at that point. Socrates seems to have recognized this when he replied to the young man who consulted him about getting married, "Whether you marry or refrain from marrying, you will regret it afterward." Should we not all be in a better position for dealing with the sex problem if we frankly recognized from the outset that we were up against "a very difficult affair" and that a short and easy cut to the solution is impossible for everybody? Here, if nowhere else, nature seems to have resolved that mankind shall be put upon its mettle to the end of the chapter. There is no escape for anybody, not even for the self-expressionist.

I have dwelt upon this matter of sex relations because it seems to be the chief theatre in which self-expressionism is now operating—witness the enormous amount of popular novels and plays which turn exclusively on this theme. It seems a pity that self-expressionism should have fallen into that net, for there is a profound truth in self-expression, which might have been put to better and, I will even add, to more enjoyable uses. The self of a human being is a complicated and many-sided affair, in which the sex element, though always present and unquestionably important, is only one of a thousand demands which have to be satisfied before anything worthy to be called self-expression can be attained. In complete self-expression, sex would not destroy or poison the other elements, as it does in sex novels and pornographic cinemas, but would vitalize them all, as it does in the highest art, for example, in Sophocles, Dante, and Goethe, all of whose work is sex-vitalized, sex-illuminated, and sex-glorified.

Man, by nature, is a skill-hungry animal. His nature is defined by his function; and his function, as revealed alike by the structure of his body and his mind, is the exercise of skill. Taking the "self" all round, it seems to me that its hunger for skill is the most salient and universal feature of it. This is why the finest examples of self-expression are to be found in the great arts. Here it is that the self most completely attains the joyous satisfaction of its deepest needs, while satisfying at the same time the needs of the social environment, with which it is integrally one. Without some form of skillful activity on lines that are socially valuable, self-expression is impossible. Education is the discipline of the self which leads to that result. But no "easier" than other disciplines, which still hold their ground on the educational field, without leading to results at all comparable to social value. As an educational principle, self-expression means education for skill—that or nothing.

In all this I must not be understood as arguing against the modern doctrine of self-expression. On the contrary, I regard it as thoroughly sound in principle. At the same time it seems to me a doctrine that needs exceptional skill, courage, and wisdom in the application of it, and singularly exposed to the danger of being misapplied, more exposed, indeed, than almost any other philosophy of life I know of, which is saying a good deal. This danger is what I have been pointing out. By way of summing up what has been said, I will offer the following hints to any self-expressionist who may happen to read these lines.

1. Make sure that the self you are expressing is your whole self and not a fragment of it, nor a phase of it, nor a mood of it, nor a merely spectacular element of it. Be on your guard against fragments of your self—like the sex element, for example, or the money-making element—which masquerade as the whole of it. Take particular care to include your sense of decency in the whole self you are expressing. If you leave out the sense of decency, if you fail to express that, later on this left-out element will repudiate the whole of your self-expression up to date as a miserable fraud perpetrated on yourself.

2. In trying to get your whole self into expression, be careful to include the time factor along

with the sense of decency. Your whole self includes what you have been in the past, what you are in the present, and what you are going to be in the future. By neglecting this, and treating your present or momentary self as though it were the whole, you will get into that horrible mess referred to above, which characterizes so much of the "self-expression" going on at the present day. There is the self of youth, the self of maturity and the self of old age.[4] The whole self is the synthesis of all three. But see the muddle that many self-expressionists are making of it—expressing the self of youth in ways which leave them, by the time they come to middle age, with hardly any self at all to express, and which old age repudiates as perfectly idiotic; or, worse still, expressing the self of middle age in ways which their youthful sense of decency, buried but not dead, looks upon with loathing.

3. Lastly, make sure that you have not been betrayed into adopting the creed of self-expression by the belief that you will find it easier than the doctrines presented by stern, old-fashioned moralists. More likely than not, you will find that, so far as difficulty is concerned, you got out of the frying pan into the fire when you made the change from old-fashioned morality to self-expression. All philosophies of life are difficult to carry out, those that preach emancipation from all morality, like "eat and drink for tomorrow you die," being, probably, the most difficult of all—especially when

the time factor is taken into account. All the same the difficulty of self-expression should not be taken as a point against it. Man was born for a difficult life of skillful activity, and it is only through skillful activity that self-expression can be attained by any one.

NOTES

[1] Bertrand Russell (1872–   ) has been Professor of Philosophy at Trinity College, Cambridge, and is a prominent figure in scientific and educational circles throughout the English-speaking world.

[2] Gilbert Murray (1866–   ) is the Regius Professor of Greek at Oxford and a leading exponent of world peace. See his essay, "Satanism and the World Order," later in this volume.

[3] Those interested in the problems of writing should read Francis Hackett's essay "The Invisible Censor" in his volume of that title.

[4] Wilfrid Scawen Blunt divided his life into these three periods, devoting them in turn to feeling, to action, and to reflection. See Robert Browning's poem "Rabbi Ben Ezra".

QUESTIONS

1. What does Doctor Jacks mean by a "skill-hungry animal"?

2. What, in your own words, are Doctor Jacks' three hints to self-expressionists?

3. How may this essay be linked to the eighteenth-century periodical essays?

EVERY MAN'S NATURAL DESIRE TO BE
SOMEBODY ELSE *

SAMUEL MCCHORD CROTHERS

One of the most consistently readable essayists America
has produced is SAMUEL MCCHORD CROTHERS (1857–
1927). Readers of any one of his volumes will find a deep
undercurrent of interest in human conduct, of liberty for
individuals without impairing the rights of others, of
whimsical appreciation of the incongruous, that makes the
writer's presence a pleasant and comforting reality. What
he once wrote about Agnes Repplier is equally applicable
to himself: "I am inclined to think that leisure is not a
condition but an art. Some people who have very little to
do and no great desire to do it, are yet always in a hurry.
Coming duties cast their shadows before, and there is always a sense of being driven. Other people have learned to
protect themselves. There is always a little film of free
time around them, which prevents undue friction. Some
essayists have learned this art, much to their own and their
readers' advantage. Though they have only a little space at
their disposal, they do not allow it to be crowded. There
is no rude jostling of ideas. There is time to follow out
any suggestion. Among American writers Agnes Repplier
has this un-American accomplishment." Dr. Crothers' firm
tolerance for the convictions of others and his own independence of thinking, which, with his gentle humor, per-

* Reprinted by permission of and special arrangement with
Houghton Mifflin Company, publishers.

vade his essays, have their roots deep in the life of the
man. He was born in Oswego, Illinois, and studied for the
Presbyterian ministry at the College of New Jersey, now
Princeton. After a few years in the West, ministering to
people whose religious convictions differed widely from his
own, he severed his connection with his Church and devoted a year to close scrutiny of what he really believed.
At the end of that time he entered the Unitarian ministry
and served churches in Brattleboro, Vermont, and St. Paul,
Minnesota, before he was called to the First Church in
Cambridge, Massachusetts, in 1894, where he remained until his death. His philosophy of common sense and humor,
in his life and his writing, reflects the sort of man who
"walks softly among events yet influences them."

SEVERAL years ago a young man came to my
study with a manuscript which he wished me to
criticize.

"It is only a little bit of my work," he said
modestly, "and it will not take you long to look
it over. In fact it is only the first chapter, in which
I explain the Universe."

I suppose that we have all had moments of
sudden illumination when it occurred to us that
we had explained the Universe, and it was so
easy for us that we wondered why we had not
done it before. Some thought drifted into our
mind and filled us with vague forebodings of om-
niscience. It was not an ordinary thought that
explained only a fragment of existence. It explained everything. It proved one thing and it
proved the opposite just as well. It explained why
things are as they are; and if it should turn out

that they are not that way at all, it would prove that fact also. In the light of our great thought chaos seemed rational.

Such thoughts usually occur about four o'clock in the morning. Having explained the Universe, we relapse into satisfied slumber. When, a few hours later, we rise, we wonder what the explanation was.

Now and then, however, one of these highly explanatory ideas remains to comfort us in our waking hours. Such a thought is that which I here throw out, and which has doubtless at some early hour occurred to most of my readers. It is that every man has a natural desire to be somebody else.

This does not explain the Universe, but it explains that perplexing part of it which we call Human Nature. It explains why so many intelligent people, who deal skillfully with matters of fact, make such a mess of it when they deal with their fellow creatures. It explains why we get on as well as we do with strangers, and why we do not get on better with our friends. It explains why people are so often offended when we say nice things about them, and why it is that, when we say harsh things about them, they take it as a compliment. It explains why people marry their opposites and why they live happily ever afterwards. It also explains why some people don't. It explains the meaning of tact and its opposite.

The tactless person treats a person according

to a scientific method as if he were a thing. Now, in dealing with a thing, you must first find out what it is, and then act accordingly. But with a person, you must first find out what he is and then carefully conceal from him the fact that you have made the discovery.

The tactless person can never be made to understand this. He prides himself on taking people as they are without being aware that that is not the way they want to be taken.

He has a keen eye for the obvious, and calls attention to it. Age, sex, color, nationality, previous condition of servitude, and all the facts that are interesting to the census-taker, are apparent to him and are made the basis of his conversation. When he meets one who is older than he, he is conscious of the fact, and emphasizes by every polite attention the disparity in years. He has an idea that at a certain period in life the highest tribute of respect is to be urged to rise out of one chair and take another that is presumably more comfortable. It does not occur to him that there may remain any tastes that are not sedentary. On the other hand, he sees a callow youth and addresses himself to the obvious callowness, and thereby makes himself thoroughly disliked. For, strange to say, the youth prefers to be addressed as a person of precocious maturity.

The literalist, observing that most people talk shop, takes it for granted that they like to talk shop. This is a mistake. They do it because it is the easiest thing to do, but they resent having attention called to their limitations. A man's profession does not necessarily coincide with his natural aptitude or with his predominant desire. When you meet a member of the Supreme Court you may assume that he is gifted with a judicial mind. But it does not follow that that is the only quality of mind he has; nor that when, out of court, he gives you a piece of his mind, it will be a piece of his judicial mind that he gives.

My acquaintance with royalty is limited to photographs of royal groups, which exhibit a high degree of domesticity. It would seem that the business of royalty when pursued as a steady job becomes tiresome, and that when they have their pictures taken they endeavor to look as much like ordinary folks as possible—and they usually succeed.

The member of one profession is always flattered by being taken for a skilled practitioner of another. Try it on your minister. Instead of saying, "That was an excellent sermon of yours this morning," say, "As I listened to your cogent argument, I thought what a successful lawyer you would have made." Then he will say, "I did think of taking to the law."

If you had belonged to the court of Frederick the Great, you would have proved a poor courtier indeed if you had praised His Majesty's campaigns. Frederick knew that he was a Prussian general, but he wanted to be a French literary man. If you wished to gain his favor, you should have told him that in your opinion he excelled Voltaire.

We do not like to have too much attention drawn to our present circumstances. They may be well enough in their way, but we can think of something which would be more fitting for us. We have either seen better days or we expect them.

Suppose you had visited Napoleon in Elba [1] and had sought to ingratiate yourself with him.

"Sire," you would have said, "this is a beautiful little empire of yours, so snug and cosy and quiet. It is just such a domain as is suited to a man in your condition. The climate is excellent. Everything is peaceful. It must be delightful to rule where everything is arranged for you and the details are taken care of by others. As I came to your dominion, I saw a line of British frigates guarding your shores. The evidences of such thoughtfulness are everywhere."

Your praise of his present condition would not have endeared you to Napoleon. You were addressing him as the Emperor of Elba. In his own eyes he was Emperor, though in Elba.

It is such a misapprehension which irritates any mature human being when his environment is taken as a measure of his personality.

The man with a literal mind moves in a perpetual comedy of errors. It is not a question of two Dromios.[2] There are half a dozen Dromios under one hat.

How casually introductions are made, as if it were the easiest thing in the world to make two human beings acquainted! Your friend says, "I want you to know Mr. Stifflekin," and you say that you are happy to know him. But does either of you know the enigma that goes under the name of Stifflekin? You may know what he looks like and where he resides and what he does for a living. But that is all in the present tense. To really know him, you must not only know what he is but what he used to be; what he used to think he was; what he used to think he ought to be and might be if he worked hard enough. You must know what he might have been if certain things had happened otherwise, and you must know what might have happened otherwise if he had been otherwise. All these complexities are a part of his own dim apprehension of himself. They are what make him so much more interesting to himself than he is to any one else.

It is this consciousness of the inadequacy of our knowledge which makes us so embarrassed when we offer any service to another. Will he take it in the spirit in which it is given?

That was an awkward moment when Stanley,[3] after all his hardships in his search for Dr. Livingstone, at last found the Doctor by a lake in Central Africa. Stanley held out his hand and said stiffly, "Dr. Livingstone, I presume?" Stanley had heroically plunged through the equatorial forests to find Livingstone and to bring him back to civilization. But Livingstone was not particularly anxious to be found, and had a decided objection to being brought back to civilization. What he wanted was a new adventure. Stanley did not find the real Livingstone till he discovered that the old man was as young at heart as himself. The two men became acquainted only when they began to plan a new expedition to find the source of the Nile.

II

The natural desire of every man to be somebody else explains many of the minor irritations of life. It prevents that perfect organization of society in which every one should know his place and keep it. The desire to be somebody else leads us to practice on work that does not strictly belong to us. We all have aptitudes and talents that overflow the narrow bounds of our trade or profession. Every man feels that he is bigger than his job, and he is all the time doing what theologians call "works of supererogation."

The serious-minded housemaid is not content to do what she is told to do. She has an unexpended balance of energy. She wants to be a general household reformer. So she goes to the desk of the titular master of the house and gives it a thorough reformation. She arranges the papers according to her idea of neatness. When the poor gentleman returns and finds his familiar chaos transformed into a hateful order, he becomes a reactionary.

The serious manager of a street railway company is not content with the simple duty of transporting passengers cheaply and comfortably. He wants to exercise the functions of a lecturer in an ethical culture society. While the transported victim is swaying precariously from the end of a strap, he reads a notice urging him to practice Christian courtesy and not to push. While the poor wretch pores over this counsel of perfection, he feels like answering as did Junius to the Duke of Grafton, "My Lord, injuries may be atoned for and forgiven, but insults admit of no compensation."

A man enters a barber's shop with the simple desire of being shaved. But he meets with the more ambitious desire of the barber. The serious barber is not content with any slight contribution to human welfare. He insists that his client shall be shampooed, manicured, massaged, steamed beneath boiling towels, cooled off by electric fans, and, while all this is going on, that he shall have his boots blacked.

Have you never marveled at the patience of people in having so many things done to them that they don't want, just to avoid hurting the feelings of professional people who want to do more than is expected of them? You watch the

stoical countenance of the passenger in a Pullman
car as he stands up to be brushed. The chances
are that he doesn't want to be brushed. He would
prefer to leave the dust on his coat rather than
to be compelled to swallow it. But he knows what
is expected of him. It is a part of the solemn
ritual of traveling. It precedes the offering.

The fact that every man desires to be somebody else explains many of the aberrations of
artists and literary men. The painters, dramatists,
musicians, poets, and novelists are just as human
as housemaids and railway managers and porters.
They want to do "all the good they can to all the
people they can in all the ways they can." They
get tired of the ways they are used to and like to
try new combinations. So they are continually
mixing things. The practitioner of one art tries to
produce effects that are proper to another art.

A musician wants to be a painter and use his
violin as if it were a brush. He would have us see
the sunset glories that he is painting for us. A
painter wants to be a musician and paint sym-
phonies, and he is grieved because the uninstructed cannot hear his pictures, although the
colors do swear at each other. Another painter
wants to be an architect and build up his picture
as if it were made of cubes of brick. It looks like
brick-work, but to the natural eye it doesn't look
like a picture. A prose-writer gets tired of writing
prose, and wants to be a poet. So he begins every

line with a capital letter, and keeps on writing prose.

You go to the theatre with the simple-minded Shakespearean idea that the play's the thing. But the playwright wants to be a pathologist. So you discover that you have dropped into a gruesome clinic. You sought innocent relaxation, but you are one of the non-elect and have gone to the place prepared for you. You must see the thing through. The fact that you have troubles of your own is not a sufficient claim for exemption.

Or you take up a novel expecting it to be a work of fiction. But the novelist has other views. He wants to be your spiritual adviser. He must do something to your mind, he must rearrange your fundamental ideas, he must massage your soul, and generally brush you off. All this in spite of the fact that you don't want to be brushed off and set to rights. You don't want him to do anything to your mind. It's the only mind you have and you need it in your own business.

III

But if the desire of every man to be somebody else accounts for many whimsicalities of human conduct and for many aberrations in the arts, it cannot be lightly dismissed as belonging only to the realm of comedy. It has its origin in the nature of things. The reason why every man wants to be somebody else is that he can remember the time when he was somebody else. What we call personal identity is a very changeable thing, as all of us realize when we look over old photographs and read old letters.

The oldest man now living is but a few years removed from the undifferentiated germ-plasm, which might have developed into almost anything. In the beginning he was a bundle of possibilities. Every actuality that is developed means a decrease in the rich variety of possibilities. In becoming one thing, it becomes impossible to be something else.

The delight in being a boy lies in the fact that the possibilities are still manifold. The boy feels that he can be anything that he desires. He is conscious that he has capacities that would make him a successful banker. On the other hand, there are attractions in a life of adventure in the South Seas. It would be pleasant to lie under a bread-fruit tree and let the fruit drop into his mouth, to the admiration of the gentle savages who would gather about him. Or he might be a saint—not a commonplace modern saint who does chores and attends tiresome committee meetings, but a saint such as one reads about, who gives away his rich robes and his purse of gold to the first beggar he meets, and then goes on his carefree way through the forest to convert interesting robbers. He feels that he might practice that kind of unscientific charity, if his father would furnish him with the money to give away.

But by and by he learns that making a success in the banking business is not consistent with excursions to the South Seas or with the more picturesque and unusual forms of saintliness. If he is to be in a bank he must do as the bankers do.

Parents and teachers conspire together to make a man of him, which means making a particular kind of man of him. All mental processes which are not useful must be suppressed. The sum of their admonitions is that he must pay attention. That is precisely what he is doing. He is paying attention to a variety of things that escape the adult mind. As he wriggles on the bench in the school-room, he pays attention to all that is going on. He attends to what is going on out-of-doors; he sees the weak points of his fellow pupils, against whom he is planning punitive expeditions; and he is delightfully conscious of the idiosyncrasies of the teacher. Moreover, he is a youthful artist, and his sketches from life give acute joy to his contemporaries when they are furtively passed around.

But the schoolmaster says sternly, "My boy, you must learn to pay attention; that is to say, you must not pay attention to so many things, but you must pay attention to one thing, namely, the second declension."

Now, the second declension is the least interesting thing in the room, but unless he confines his attention to it he will never learn it. Education demands narrowing of attention in the interest of efficiency.

A man may, by dint of application to a particular subject, become a successful merchant or real estate man or chemist or overseer of the poor. But he cannot be all these things at the same time. He must make his choice. Having in the presence of witnesses taken himself for better or worse, he must, forsaking all others, cleave to that alone. The consequence is that, by the time he is forty, he has become one kind of man, and is able to do one kind of work. He has acquired a stock of ideas true enough for his purposes, but not so transcendentally true as to interfere with his business. His neighbors know where to find him, and they do not need to take a spiritual elevator. He does business on the ground floor. He has gained in practicality, but has lost in the quality of interestingness.

The old prophet declared that the young men dream dreams and the old men see visions, but he did not say anything about the middle-aged men. *They* have to look after the business end.

But has the man whose working hours are so full of responsibilities changed so much as he seems to have done? When he is talking shop is he "all there"? I think not. There are elusive personalities that are in hiding. As the rambling mansions of the old Catholic families had secret panels opening into the "priest's hole," to which the family resorted for spiritual comfort, so in the mind of the most successful man there are secret chambers where are hidden his unsuccessful ventures, his romantic ambitions, his unfulfilled promises. All that he dreamed of as possible is somewhere concealed in the man's heart. He would not for the world have the public know how much he cares for the selves that have not had a fair chance to come into the light of day. You do not know a man until you know his lost Atlantis, and his Utopia [4] for which he still hopes to set sail.

When Dogberry [5] asserted that he was "as pretty a piece of flesh as any is in Messina," and "one that hath two gowns and everything handsome about him," he was pointing out what he deemed to be quite obvious. It was in a more intimate tone that he boasted, "and a fellow that hath had losses."

When Julius Caesar rode through the streets of Rome in his chariot, his laurel crown seemed to the populace a symbol of his present greatness. But gossip has it that Caesar at that time desired to be younger than he was, and that before appearing in public he carefully arranged his laurel wreath so as to conceal the fact that he had had losses.

Much that passes for pride in the behavior of the great comes from the fear of the betrayal of emotions that belong to a simpler manner of life. When the sons of Jacob saw the great Egyptian officer to whom they appealed turn away from

them they little knew what was going on. "And
Joseph made haste, for his bowels did yearn upon
his brother: and he sought where to weep, and
he entered into his chamber, and wept there. And
he washed his face, and went out, and refrained
himself." Joseph didn't want to be a great man.
He wanted to be human. It was hard to refrain
himself.

IV

What of the lost arts of childhood, the lost
audacities and ambitions and romantic admira-
tions of adolescence? What becomes of the sympathies which make us feel our kinship to all
sorts of people? What becomes of the early curiosity in regard to things which were none of our
business? We ask as Saint Paul asked of the
Galatians, "Ye began well; who did hinder you?"

The answer is not wholly to our discredit. We
do not develop all parts of our nature because we
are not allowed to do so. Walt Whitman [6] might
exult over the Spontaneous Me. But nobody is
paid for being spontaneous. A spontaneous switch-
man on the railway would be a menace to the
traveling public. We prefer some one less tem-
peramental.

As civilization advances and work becomes
more specialized, it becomes impossible for any
one to find free and full development for all his
natural powers in any recognized occupation.

What then becomes of the other selves? The answer must be that playgrounds must be provided for them outside the confines of daily business. As work becomes more engrossing and narrowing, the need is more urgent for recognized and carefully guarded periods of leisure.

The old Hebrew sage declared, "Wisdom cometh from the opportunity of leisure." It does not mean that a wise man must belong to what we call the leisure classes. It means that, if one has only a little free time at his disposal, he must use that time for the refreshment of his hidden selves. If he cannot have a sabbath rest of twenty-four hours, he must learn to sanctify little sabbaths, it may be of ten minutes' length. In them he shall do no manner of work. It is not enough that the self that works and receives wages shall be recognized and protected; the world must be made safe for our other selves. Does not the Declaration of Independence say that every man has an inalienable right to the pursuit of happiness?

The old-time minister, after he had exhorted the believers at considerable length, used to turn to a personage who for homiletical purposes was known as the Objector. To him he addressed his most labored arguments. At this point I am conscious of the presence of the Objector.

"All you say," he remarks, "in praise of your favorite platitude is true to a fault. But what has all this to do with the War? There is only one thing in these days worth thinking about—at least, it is the only thing we *can* think about."

"I agree with you, courteous Objector. No matter where we start, we all come back to this point: Who was to blame for the War, and how is it coming out? Our explanatory idea has a direct bearing on the question before us. The Prussian militarists had a painstaking knowledge of facts, but they had a contempt for human nature. Their tactlessness was almost beyond belief. They treated persons as if they were things. They treated facts with deadly seriousness, but had no regard for feelings. They had spies all over the world to report all that could be seen, but they took no account of what could not be seen. So, while they were dealing scientifically with the obvious facts and forces, all the hidden powers of the human soul were being turned against them. Prussianism insists on highly specialized men who have no sympathies to interfere with their efficiency. Having adopted a standard, all variation must be suppressed. It is against this effort to suppress the human variations that we are fighting. We don't want all men to be reduced to one pattern."

"But what about the Kaiser? Does your formula explain him? Does he want to be somebody else?"

"I confess, dear Objector, that it is probably a new idea to him; but he may come to it."

Notes

¹ Island in the Mediterranean to which the defeated Napoleon was exiled in 1814 for a period of two years.

² Dromio of Ephesus and Dromio of Syracuse were twin brothers in Shakespeare's *Comedy of Errors.*

³ Sir Henry Morton Stanley (1841–1904), the British explorer, found David Livingstone (1813–1873), the famous missionary-explorer who was "lost" in the African jungle. Stanley's *Darkest Africa* still makes interesting reading.

⁴ Atlantis, a lost island in the eastern Atlantic where, it is presumed, civilization formerly flourished; Utopia, the imaginary kingdom wherein everything is as one would wish it to be. See Sir Thomas More's *Utopia* and decide how you would change it.

⁵ Dogberry was the constable in Shakespeare's comedy *Much Ado about Nothing.*

⁶ Walt Whitman (1819–1892), self-educated poet, one of the greatest influences in American literature.

Question

1. What portions of this essay were obviously derived from reading? From observation? From reflection?

THE MUCKER POSE *

JAMES TRUSLOW ADAMS

JAMES TRUSLOW ADAMS, whose *The Adams Family, The Epic of America,* and *The March of Democracy* have amply proved that histories may become best-sellers, is a former Wall Street stockbroker. Born in Brooklyn in 1878 and educated at the Brooklyn Polytechnic Institute and at Yale University, he devoted twelve years to a Stock Exchange house before history claimed his major interest. Early in the World War he served with the Colonel House Commission, gathering and preparing data for the Peace Conference, later entered the Intelligence Division of the General Staff of the United States Army and was assigned to special duty at the Peace Conference in Paris in 1919. His best-known works have been written since the War. This essay, from *Our Business Civilization,* is characteristic of one who is passionately devoted to arousing a thinking electorate to form standards for public life commensurate with the fundamental genius of our people. The recent efforts in the United States toward a planned civilization are, in part, an illustration of what can be done when leaders seek to bring government into line with the fundamental needs of the people. It is difficult to say how influential Mr. Adams' histories have been during the major depression in the United States; certainly it is not too much to assume that many readers were, through them,

---

* Reprinted from *Our Business Civilization* by permission of the publishers, Albert & Charles Boni, Inc.

brought to an assurance of the underlying greatness of their country at a time when such assurance had become a crying need.

THIS borrowed title expresses better than any I have been able to devise for myself a problem which has recently been put to me by several of my American friends, men who on account of both their profession and positions are familiar with the more cultured portion of the American scene. The question which they put is one that I have been hesitatingly asking myself as I contrast the scene on successive returns from abroad with the one very obviously to be observed in this respect in France or England. "Why," they ask, "is it that a gentleman in America nowadays seems afraid to appear as such; that even university men try to appear uncultured; and that the pose of a gentleman and a scholar is that of the man in the street?" A few nights ago another friend of mine, a literary editor of some importance in New York, complained in the course of the evening's talk that the verbal criticism of many of the writers whom he knew had descended to the moronic classifications of "hot stuff," "bully," "rot," and so on. These writers, often meticulous in the artistry of their own work and thoroughly competent to criticise acutely and intelligently that of others, appeared afraid to do so lest they be considered as literary poseurs. The real pose in their cases was in talking like newsagents on a railroad train; but that appeared to them to be safe, whereas vague danger lurked in conversing as would any intelligent French or English critic.

The mucker-poseurs do not content themselves with talking like uneducated half-wits. They also emulate the language and manners of the bargee and the longshoreman, although where the profanity of the latter is apt to have at least the virtue of picturesqueness, the swearing of the mucker-poseur is apt to be merely coarse. A member of a most distinguished family and a young graduate of one of our best known Eastern universities was overheard the other day in his university club in New York describing his new position in the banking world. The nearest to analysis or description of his work this young scion of American aristocracy with every social and educational advantage could reach was to tell his friends that it was "the God-damnedest most interesting job in the world." Both among men and women of the supposedly cultivated classes such profanity is much on the increase. I know of a man who has recently declined to take foreign visitors to his club for luncheon or dinner any longer on account of the unfortunate impres-
·sion which would be made upon them by the hard swearing of the American gentlemen, mucker-poseurs, at the surrounding tables. One of the finest scholars in the country, a man who once had distinguished manners, has not only become extremely profane, but exceedingly addicted to

smutty stories, both apparently, in the effort to make himself considered a good mixer and as a bid for popularity. If one wishes to acquire an extensive and varied vocabulary of the most modern sort, one has merely to watch the young ladies of the mucker-poseur type playing tennis at Southampton or Newport.

Again, the mucker-poseur aims to act like the lowest of muckers when he—and frequently she —gets drunk. Drinking in this country has ceased to add any charm or grace to social life. On a recent sailing from New York on the *Aquitania* at midnight I counted twelve women first-cabin passengers brought on board, all so drunk that they could not get up the gangway without help. Many years ago, when I was a small boy of twelve, I attended "Field Day" at one of the most exclusive private boarding schools in the East. In the course of the day an address was made by an old graduate on the subject of alcohol. To the surprise and horror of the clerical head of the school, the good-natured but somewhat inebriated speaker said nothing to condemn drinking but he threw out the comment, which is all I can now recall of his speech, that "when you boys do drink, remember always to get drunk like gentlemen." That is something which our present generation of drinkers have completely forgotten. They act in country clubs in a way which would have been considered a disgrace to the patrons and patronized in a disorderly house of a generation ago. It is not a question of mere decline in manners but of consciously striven-for pose.

In the case of the young this is more understandable, just as it is more international. I am not here concerned, however, with (or at) the vagaries of the younger and, in so many respects, admirable generation. I am concerned with their elders, men who have lived long enough to have developed personalities of their own, men who appreciate the value of cultivating both mind and manners. Why should they be afraid to appear as cultured gentlemen and assume as a protective coloration the manners and level of thought of those who are beneath them?

The question would be a futile one unless we believed that manners and culture possess genuine significance, a significance for society as a whole as well as for the individual. It is all too evident that a large proportion of dwellers in our United States do not believe so, but there is a large minority which does. Not to do so argues a failure to think things through and ignorance of history and human nature. This article deals with the contemporary attitude of many believers, and we can but glance briefly, before passing to them, at the non-believers.

II

One of the most suggestive methods of modern study has been the comparative. By the use of

none other, however, are the unwary and the untrained so likely to come to logical grief over a
non sequitur.[1] The comparative study of habits
and customs has revealed that both moral and
social conventions have varied from age to age,
from place to place, and from race to race.[2] Immediately the unwary and untrained jump to the
conclusion that because there appear to be no
eternal or universal standards of morals and manners there is, therefore, no value in a local, temporary, and but slowly changing one—a conclusion by no logical possibility to be drawn from
the premises. The result of this particular and, at
the moment, very popular *non sequitur* has been
to cause in many persons a headlong jettisoning
of their whole cargo of morals, manners, and conventions, and the bringing about of a muckerly
chaos which arouses mirth or terror according to
the temperament of the social observer.

It would seem as though no sane person with
a knowledge of the past of his own species and
any adequate insight into human nature could
fail to believe in the absolute need of *some* standards, *some* established values to save us from a
derelict wallowing about in the welter of sensa-
tions, impulses, attractions, and repulsions which
form so much of this strange dream we call life.
The standards, the values, will undoubtedly alter
from time to time and from place to place; but
that does not invalidate the need of having some
of them at any one given time and place. Even

the now much scorned minor conventions have their effective influence upon conduct, remote or proximate. A story [3] is told of an English gentleman who was sent out as governor of an island where the entire population save for his sole self was black and savage. He dressed for his solitary dinner every night as carefully as though he were about to take a taxi to the smartest residence in Park Lane. He did so not from habit but from a knowledge of human nature. "If," he said, "I should drop this convention of civilized society, I should find myself some day having dropped one and another of the more important conventions, social and moral, and lower myself to the level of the blacks whom I govern. Evening clothes are far more important here than they ever were in London."

As for the second point, lack of culture, it is most evident in the extreme slovenliness in America in the use of the English language. There is, of course, some slang which is not slovenly but which has been born in some flash of genuine insight; and the language is always being enriched by absorbing many such words from below, much as the English aristocracy is by marrying or admitting commoners. But this is not true of the vast mass of slang words and cheap and easy expressions which are intellectually slovenly and nothing else; and anyone habitually using them impairs the keenness of his mind as much as he would the strength of his body by lolling in a

hammock all his life. There is no question but
that the use of slang, hackneyed phrases, and
clichés worn smooth makes for intellectual laziness, and if constantly used blurs the sense of
discrimination. The very first step toward a cultivated mind is the development of the ability
rationally to discriminate, to distinguish between
varying values and qualities. It is not easy, and
most of us Americans rarely achieve it in the cultural field. I have often been struck by the different replies one receives from an American and a
Frenchman if you ask them what sort of person
so-and-so is. The American will usually find himself helpless and toss off a mere "good scout," "a
great guy," "a good egg," whereas the Frenchman, with a moment's reflection, will give you in
half a dozen sentences a sharply etched sketch of
the man's distinctive characteristics, or what he
believes to be such, and classify him accurately
as to type. To describe anything accurately—
book, picture, man, or woman—so as to bring out
their unique individual qualities, calls for mental
exercise of no mean order. One has to train one's
self to do it and keep in training; yet the ability
to distinguish, if one of the first steps toward
culture, is also, in its higher forms, one of its
most perfect fruits. If one dodges every call for
discrimination, if one gets no farther in describing
a book than "hot stuff," one loses the power after
a while even if one ever possessed it. Slovenly
language corrodes the mind.

These few observations as to manners and culture are well enough understood by any cultivated person who has had social and intellectual training and who has thought things through. He knows that there are both values and dangers in life, that some things are more valuable than others, and that if he has achieved any such social and intellectual training he cannot lower himself to the general level again without risk. If manners and culture have no value, there is no question involved; but if they have—and we shall now assume that they have—the man who possesses them is above, in those respects at least, the vast mass of men who do not possess them. Why then should he pretend not to, and assume the manners and mental lazzaronism [4] of the crowd? It may be that there is no answer to the question, but as I find those better qualified than myself asking it, it is worth pondering over; and I have come to think that there may be three fundamental influences at work in America which will help us to solve it. One is democracy as we have it, another is business, and the third is the extreme mobility of American life.

III

In civilization no man can live wholly to or for himself; and whoever would achieve power, influence, or success must cater to the tastes and whims of those who have the granting of these things in their hands. In a democracy, speaking broadly, those who have the power to grant are the whole people; and the minds and manners of the people as a whole are of necessity below those of the chosen few who have risen above the average level by gifts of nature or happy opportunity. Every social class everywhere has always had its own standards of morals, manners, and culture. When such classes are separated by wide social or economic chasms, the only influences they exert upon one another are apt to be negative. Each lives in a world of its own, supported by the only public opinion for which it cares, that of its own class. Each also tends to react against the manners or morals of the other. The aristocrats of an earlier day looked down upon the common people and were more than ever satisfied with their own codes. The common people, in turn, feeling themselves despised, bolstered up their *egos* by despising the manners and morals of the class which looked down upon them. Much of the Puritan movement in England and elsewhere has here its roots. By no possibility could an ordinary laborer attain to the manners, social ease, or knowledge of the world of a duke. Ergo,[5] the laborer by unconscious mental processes well understood by modern psychology, asserted his own worth by denying worth to the qualities of the classes above him. He could not have the manners of a duke; therefore, those manners were undesirable anyway. He could not travel and he could not gain the most valuable sort of education, that of association with great or cultivated men; therefore, such things were of no importance. So long as the classes remain separated, as I said above, their influence upon one another is largely negative; but when class distinctions disappear in a democracy, the mutual influences of members of those former classes or their vestiges in later generations become as complex in their action as the currents where tide and river meet.

The effects of democracy in America have been emphasized by three factors not present in any of the great democracies of Europe. In the first place, the Americans started wholly fresh. Here were no thousand-year-old institutions and forms of government and society to be reckoned with as impediments. America was a clean slate. The settlers did indeed bring with them habits, information, and memories gained in the Old World, but they brought them to a wilderness.

In the second place, America has been built up exclusively by the middle and lower classes, from which practically all of us have descended. Scarcely a man has ever come and settled here who did not belong to one or the other; and the most distinguished American families form no exceptions. Every class in history has had its good and bad attributes which have varied with class, country, and period. The English middle class, upper and lower, from which the character of America, with some modifications, has essentially

been built up, had admirable qualities, but it
lacked some of those enjoyed by the aristocracy.
For our purpose here we need mention only one.
The genuine aristocrat insists upon being himself
and is disdainful of public opinion. The middle
class, on the other hand, has always been notoriously timid socially. It rests in terror not only
of public but even of village opinion. If the religious refugees of New England be held an exception, it may be noted that the genuine ones
were far fewer than used to be supposed, and that
as a whole the New England immigration may be
considered as part of the great economic exodus
from England which took thirty thousand Englishmen to Barbados and little St. Kitts while
only twelve thousand were settling Massachusetts. Religious refugees have formed an infinitesimal part of American immigration as compared with the economic ones.

The third great influence upon American democracy has been the frontier, whose line was
lapped by the waves of the Atlantic in 1640 and
after retreating three thousand miles to the Pacific
was declared officially closed only in 1890. In the
hard rough life of the frontier, manners and culture find no home. As Pastorius,[6] the most learned
man who came to America before 1700, said,
"Never have metaphysics or Aristotelian logic
earned a loaf of bread." When one is busy killing
Indians, clearing the forest, and trekking farther
westward every decade, a strong arm, an axe, and

a rifle are worth more than all the culture of all
the ages. Not only has the frontiersman no leisure
or opportunity to acquire manners and culture,
but also, because of their apparent uselessness,
and in true class spirit, he comes to despise them.
They are effete, effeminate, whereas he and his
fellows are the "real men". The well-dressed, cultivated gentleman becomes the "dude," object of
derision, who, so far from exerting any ameliorat-
ing social or intelligent influence, is heartily
looked down upon; and culture itself is relegated
to idle women as something with which no real
man would concern himself.

These are some of the special attributes of
American democracy, and of any democracy in a
new land, which it shows in addition to those it
would show in any case merely as democracy. In
America it was slow in gathering into its hands
the reins of power. For many generations the
English aristocratic tradition in part survived,
and it may be recalled that we were a part of the
British Empire for a longer period than we have
been independent. In general, the "appeal to the
people" throughout the colonial period and the
years of the early republic was an appeal to "the
best people" only. The first two presidents, Washington and Adams, were as little democratic in
doctrine as they were by nature. Jefferson's doc-
trinal democracy was largely offset in practice by
his being an aristocrat to his finger tips by nature,
and it was not until Andrew Jackson that "the

people" in the democratic sense came into their own. At his inaugural reception in the White House his followers climbed upon the silken chairs in their muddy boots to get a look at him, rushed the waiters to grab champagne, broke the glasses, and in the joy of victory gave a number of ladies bloody noses, and even the President himself had to be rescued from his admirers and hurried out through a back door. This historic episode may be taken to mark the turning-point in American manners. These people had made a president. Thereafter their tastes would form one of the national influences.

IV

It is this new democracy, a hundred times richer and a shade less raw, which is in the saddle today. What has it done in the way of influencing manners and thought? Leaving all else aside, even at the risk of drawing a false picture, we shall consider only those points which may help to answer our first question. For one thing, then, it has knocked the dignity of its elected officials into a cocked hat. Leaving out of the scene many of its chosen, such as the mayor of Chicago or its favorite, Bryan, it forces men to play the mountebank and whatever the character of the man himself, to appear as one of "the people". Washington was a very human man, but he never forgot that he was a gentleman. He was adored by his soldiers, but he won their deep affection without ever for a moment losing the dignity of his character and manner. One has only to imagine what would have happened had a group of his men shouted "Atta Boy, Georgie!" to realize the gulf between his day and ours. When John Quincy Adams was president, he declined to attend a county fair in Maryland, remarking privately that he did not intend that the president of the United States should be made a side-show at a cattle fair. To-day, the people insist that the president be a side-show; and Roosevelt, with amused understanding, in his cowboy suit and his Rough-rider uniform, used his "properties" as does an actor. Even the supremely conventional Coolidge had to dress up in a ten-gallon hat and chaps, although utterly out of character, and looking so. Just as I write these lines, my attention is called to an announcement in large type in this morning's *New York Times* that it will publish next Sunday "photographs of Herbert Hoover in workaday clothes and a panorama of his ranch." So he, too, is cast for the comedy. Democracy cracks the whip, and even the most conservative of candidates and officials must dance. In the campaign of 1916 it is said that Hughes was politely asked to shave his beard to suit the people. He balked and consented only so far as to trim it. But then, he lost the election.

The people want officials in their own image. Such men as Elihu Root, Joseph Choate, or John

Hay [7] are rarely elected, only appointed. To get anywhere in elective politics one must be a "good mixer", and to be a good mixer one must shed a good part of one's culture and a good part of one's manners. Dignity to a considerable degree must be discarded. One must conceal one's knowledge of English and learn the vernacular, except for "orations." Henry Adams,[8] when he became a newspaper correspondent in Washington, said that he had to "learn to talk to Western congressmen, and to hide his own antecedents." It is what every gentleman who desires to take part in elective public life on a large or small stage in the country to-day has to do to some extent except for happy accidents.

Our democracy has fostered education, at least to the extent of almost fabulously increasing the numbers of the reading public. What has been, for the purpose of the present argument, the effect of that? There has been one effect, at least, germane to this discussion. It has greatly lowered the tone of our public press. Such newspaper men as I know agree with me that there has been a most marked decline even in the last twenty years, and they agree with me as to the cause. In the old days a newspaper was largely a personal organ, and what appeared in it reflected for good or ill upon the editor who was known by name to all its readers. In New York the *Sun* was Charles A. Dana. The *Tribune* was Horace Greeley. To-day we know no editors, only owners.

The newspaper of to-day aims only at circulation, and with every increase in circulation the quality has to be lowered. The case is well known of the purchaser a few years ago of what had been one of the country's most distinguished journals, who told his staff that thereafter they would have to "cut the high-brow" and write down to the level of the increased public he intended to go after. First the "yellow press," then the tabloids, taught the older newspapers what fortunes awaited those who would stoop to pick them up by catering to the masses. One of the worst tabloids has a circulation of a million copies a day. A newspaper depends on its advertising for its profits. Advertising quantity and rates depend on circulation. Increased circulation spells decreased quality. There is the vicious circle which has been drawn for us by the huge mob which has become literate but not educated.

The discovery of the possibilities of mass circulation has caused the advertisers to raise their demands. Some will not advertise at all in journals with a circulation of less than half a million. Advertising is withdrawn from those journals which heroically venture to maintain their quality at the expense of not increasing their circulation. Financial ruin usually results. The people are evidently getting the kind of papers they want, but in doing so they are depriving the cultured class of the sort *they* want, and used to get before America became so "educated." We get for-

eign cables about the Prince of Wales dancing
with Judy Grady, or the doings of sex perverts
in Berlin, and the treatment of our domestic news
is beneath contempt. The other night I examined
what used to be one of the leading papers not only
in New York but in the whole country, and I
found no headline on three consecutive pages
which did not refer to scandal or to crime. It has
been said that the new reading public has not in-
terfered with the old, that there are simply vast
numbers of new readers of a different type who
are being supplied with what they want. That is
not wholly true, and the competition of the new
market has had a heavily detrimental influence
on the older journals. To-day if a man wishes to
succeed in a journalistic career on the daily press
he has to scrap even more of his qualities as a
gentleman and a scholar than he has to in a career
of politics.

The democratic spread of education has also
had detrimental effects in other ways. The necessity of finding instruction for the enormous numbers who now go to school, high school, and college has caused a demand for teachers which has
far outrun the supply of those qualified to teach.
Great numbers of these teachers have even less
social and cultural background than have their
students. Under them the students may learn the
facts of some given subject, but they gain nothing
in breadth of culture or even in manners. It is
an old story that Charles Eliot Norton [9] once

began a lecture at Harvard by saying, "I suppose that none of you young men has ever seen a gentleman." The remark was hyperbolic, as was intended; but it is only too likely to-day that many young men can go through some of our newer "institutions of learning" without seeing at least what used to be called a gentleman. In the professions, more particularly medicine and law, complaint is rampant that they are being swamped by young men who know only the facts of the profession (when they know those) and have no cultural, ethical, or professional standards. A few such could be ignored. When they come, as they are coming now, in shoals, they lower the tone of the whole profession and, without standards themselves, force an unfair competition upon those who try to maintain them.

V

Perhaps the greatest pressure on the individual to force him to be wary of how he appears to others is in business, for the overwhelming mass of Americans are in the varied ranks of business of some sort or another. One who has reached the top and "made his pile" may, perhaps, do more or less as he pleases, subject only to milder forms of social pressure; but for those on the way the road is beset with pitfalls. Nearly every man wants to make himself popular with his employers, his fellow-workers, his office superiors, or his customers. These are made up of all sorts of men, but the sprinkling of gentlemen and scholars among them is so slight as to be almost negligible for the purpose of helping one's advancement. In America, to an extent known nowhere else, organization is used for every purpose. It is hardly too much to say that there can hardly be an American who is not a member of from one to a dozen organizations, ranging from Rotary, Lions, Kiwanis, Red Men, Masons, Mechanics, the Grange, and dozens more, to Bar Associations, Bankers' Clubs, and social and country clubs innumerable. Some of the larger corporations, notably the banks and trust companies in New York, now have clubs made up entirely of members of their own staffs, with obvious intent. In many lines of business the effect produced by one's personality at the annual "convention" is of prime importance. For business reasons it is essential that men should be at least moderately popular at all such organizations or meetings. On an unprecedented scale, tacitly understood but not openly acknowledged, there is competition for personal popularity. In many lines, such as stock brokerage where the service is almost wholly personal, it is needful to "play with your customers," the necessity varying not with their social congeniality but with the size of their account. In salesmanship of all sorts the results of the "personal approach" are, of course, of the first importance.

In order to gain popularity with a very large proportion of business men, many of whom have to-day risen from nothing to riches since the War, one thing is fundamentally necessary. You must never appear to be superior even if you are. Not long ago one of the New York banks added a new vice president. He was chosen not for his ability but for his hearty vulgarity, so that he could "make contacts" with the bank's new sort of customers! Too perfect an accent in English may be almost as dangerous in business as a false one in Latin used to be in the House of Lords. To display a knowledge or taste in art or literature not possessed by your "prospect" may be fatal. On the whole, it is safest to plump yourself down to his level at once, whatever that may be, to talk his talk, and only about what he talks. This pressure of the majority on one's personal tastes was amusingly exemplified to me the other day when I was looking for a house to rent in a pleasant Jersey suburb. In the house shown me—as is the case in all the suburbs of New York I know—there was nothing to mark where my lawn might end and my neighbor's begin. All was as open to the public gaze as the street itself. I thought of delightful English or French gardens, surrounded by hedge or wall, screened from the public, where one could putter absurdly over one's plants, read one's book, or have one's supper as much to one's self as in the house. In fact they are out-door rooms, infinitely more attractive than the American "sun parlor." I knew well that no such attempt could be made here, but, nevertheless, I remarked to the "realtor" that it would be pleasant to have a hedge and privacy, but I supposed it could not be done on account of the neighbors. "I say No," he answered with pained surprise; "if you are going to be 'high hat' you won't last long here." Just so, and so many things in this country are "high hat" which in other lands simply make for sane and cultivated living that it is no wonder that the business man whose car and cellarette, if not bread and butter, depend so often on his popularity, has to walk warily.

Just why having a garden-wall, speaking one's native tongue correctly, or being able to discriminate in matters of art or literature should be the Gallic equivalent of "high hat" would puzzle a Frenchman; but so it often is in the land of the free. And no one knows his way about the land of the free better than the business man. The pressure may vary with his position and the kind of business he is in; but in general he will soon discover that in any business where personal contact is a factor, the people with whom he deals and upon whose good will he has to lean will insist upon his not being too different from themselves. In Greenwich Village [10] a man may wear a flowing tie and a Spanish hat, but it would be suicidal for a bond broker. One has to conform or one is lost. Our two most successful business men are perhaps John D. Rockefeller and Henry

Ford. Rockefeller says it is a "religious duty" to make as much money as you can, and Ford has informed us that "history is bunk." The one standard of success in business—and perhaps its stark and easily grasped simplicity is what attracts many Americans—is the amount of money you make from it. There are no foolish nuances. Most Americans are business men. Whatever ideals they may have had in college, and to a considerable extent whatever manners they may have inherited or acquired, they begin to shed, unless their niche is an unusually sheltered one, when the real nature of the excoriating modern business competition dawns upon them. Little by little as they "learn the game" they conform to their customers or associates.

VI

Another characteristic of American life is its extreme mobility. People move up and down in the social scale and round about the country like bubbles in a boiling kettle. Social life everywhere here is in constant flux. I left Wall Street, where I was in business, and a certain suburb where I then lived, fifteen years ago. To-day the personnel of "the Street" as I remember it is almost as completely changed as are the symbols on the ticker. In the suburb where I once knew everyone, at least by name, I know scarcely half a dozen households. People are forever making or losing money, arriving in new social sets, living in Pittsburgh or a mining camp one year and in Los Angeles or St. Paul the next. This has a marked effect on social independence. When a family has lived for many generations in the same place, or, as have many county families in England for centuries, they acquire a social position almost wholly independent of their individual members at a given time. Indeed, a member is almost an accident and may be as erratic and independent as he pleases. He still remains a so-and-so of so-and-so, known to all the country-side. An old hereditary title accomplishes the same result. Here and there in New England villages or in the South there are families who approximate this happy condition, but in the constant movement of the life of most Americans it is necessary for them to depend wholly upon the effect of their personalities and bank accounts. A man whose family has lived in the "big house" in a small Massachusetts town for a century or two is sufficiently "somebody" there almost to be independent; but should business require him to move to Kalamazoo he is nobody until he "shows them." The social reputation, immunity, and freedom which long residence in one place gives without effort or thought has to be built again from the ground up, and warily, when one moves to another town where they know not Joseph.[11] One joins the organizations in the new town, and, again, one conforms. To begin in a new place by being "different" is dangerous; to begin by being too superior, even if actually, unconsciously, and with no wish to appear so, may be fatal. Like myself, had I gone to that Jersey suburb and made a little privacy round my garden, the new-comer might be voted "high hat" and not "last long."

In assuming the "mucker pose" the gentleman and scholar does not, of course, descend as low as the "mucker"; but he does, in self-defense, for the sake of peace and quiet, for business success, and for the sake of not offending the motley crowd of all sorts whom his neighbors are apt to be in the seething, changing society everywhere to-day, shed enough of his own personality not to offend the average. He avoids whatever others may think "high hat" in manners or culture as he would the plague. Like Henry Adams he will find himself hiding his antecedents if they happen to be better than the neighbor's.

This possible answer to my friends' question does not necessarily indict democracy and Ameri-can life. Both have brought new values into the world of other sorts. I am merely pointing to one of the possible losses. For it *is* a loss when a man deliberately uses worse manners than he knows how to use, when he tries to cover up his intel-lectual abilities or when he tries to be average when he is above it. A business-democracy has accomplished a great task in levelling up the ma-terial condition of its people. It may be asked, however, whether there is no danger of a levelling down of manners and culture. Perhaps the new values gained offset the old ones in some danger of being lost, but it may, even in America, be left to one to question, to ponder, and to doubt. Is the mucker pose really forced on one? People adopt it, evidently, because they think it is the thing to do and essential to make them quickly popular. It does not always work, even in business. A dignified man of science was recently explaining to an applicant for a position some new research work he had been doing. The young Ph.D.[12] was intensely interested. When the scientist concluded he asked the flower of our highest university training what he thought of it. "Hot Dog!" was the immediate and enthusiastic answer, which, in this case, promptly blasted the young man's career in *that* laboratory. It would not have done so generally, however, and we come back to business as conducted to-day, and the character and background of our business leaders as, perhaps, the main contributing cause of forcing the mucker pose.

We can prate as we like about the idealism of America, but it is only money success which really counts. What are ideals or culture or charming manners as compared with business? What in the last Presidential campaign did two leaders of opinion tell us, one from the Pacific and the other from the Atlantic coast? Mr. Hoover, in his address replying to the welcome given him by the people of San Francisco, told them that the most precious possession of their great city was—what? —*their foreign trade!* In New York, the *Sun* in its editorial explaining its intention to support the Republican party, admitted that the prohibition question was "a live campaign topic," and that present conditions might be "intolerable" and "a morass of lawbreaking," but asked whether it was well to risk loss of prosperity for the possible reform of those conditions. In America to-day business life is not the basis for a rational social life, but social life is manipulated as the basis for an irrational business one. One makes acquaintances and tries for popularity in order to get ahead downtown. To an unprecedented extent the people who have money in all lines of business are newcomers from far down in the social scale, men with no culture and no background, and often no manners. We may note our new class of multimillionaire landlords who have built fortunes out of shoestrings since the War. Two of our now greatest industries have been wholly evolved in the last two decades, and one certainly does not look for culture among the kings in the motor and moving-picture trades. The "people" who came into political power under Jackson made a huge grab at economic power under Grant, but it has been reserved for the present to "make the world safe for democracy." The old class which has inherited manners and culture as essential to an ordered life has abdicated mainly for mere lack of funds. In business for the last decade it has been for the most part the conservatives, who had much to lose, who have lost, and the reckless who have won.

Business may explain the mucker pose, but it may be asked whether those who adopt it are not traitors to all that is best in the world and which has been so hardly built up. An impoverished aristocrat may sell his title in marriage for one generation to rehabilitate his house, but Americans who sell their culture and their breeding to truckle to the unbred in business, who shed these things of the spirit for motor cars and all the rest of the things of the body, are taking refuge in a yet more ignominious surrender. They may thus pick up some of the golden drippings from the muckers' tables, but they do not gain the respect of the muckers whom they imitate and may yet awake to the fact that they have properly forfeited even their own.

NOTES

[1] An argument that does not follow logically.

[2] An interesting account of differing customs will be found in Montaigne's essay.

[3] "The Outstation" from *The Casuarina Tree* by W. Somerset Maugham. The lover of an unusual story will do well to look this one up.

[4] Beggary.

[5] Therefore.

[6] Francis Daniel Pastorius (1651–1719), great Quaker teacher who settled in Philadelphia in 1683 and became one of the founders of Germantown, Pennsylvania.

[7] Elihu Root (1845–   ), outstanding international law-

yer and former Secretary of War and Secretary of State.
Joseph Choate (1832–1917), distinguished lawyer and dip-
lomat, Ambassador to the Court of St. James. John Hay
(1838–1905), private secretary to President Lincoln and
later Secretary of State under Presidents McKinley and
Roosevelt, founder of The Open Door Policy with China.

[8] Henry Adams (1838–1918), Harvard professor, magazine editor, and author of *The Education of Henry Adams*.

[9] Charles Eliot Norton (1827–1908), professor of Art
History at Harvard University.

[10] Downtown section in New York popularly known as
the resort of artists and writers.

[11] A reflection of the story of Joseph (*Exodus* XVIII)
whose prominence kept his people free as long as his reputation lasted.

[12] Ph.D. abbreviation of the degree of Doctor of Philosophy, given by leading universities for advanced research
in any chosen field.

QUESTIONS

1. State briefly in your own words what constitutes
"the mucker pose".

2. What are the causes of "the mucker pose"?

3. What are the three factors which have contributed to
democracy in the United States?

4. What are the advantages of a democratic point of
view? What are its disadvantages?

5. What evidence of "the mucker pose" have you
found in your own observation of persons around you? in
yourself?

6. What is a gentleman? What are the bounds or limits
that define what he should do, what he should be?

7. Do you believe in the free expression of individual
personality or in the adherence to some standard?

8. Would L. P. Jacks agree with Mr. Adams about this
"mucker pose"?

SELF-RELIANCE *

RALPH WALDO EMERSON

RALPH WALDO EMERSON (1803–1882) was born in Boston. His father, from whom he derived his love of letters and his sense of humor, died when Ralph was eight, and left his widow with six children under the age of ten to educate. At ten Emerson entered Boston Latin School, and at fourteen entered Harvard University as the president's freshman, a sort of messenger boy to the president, and received free lodging in the president's house for services rendered. He earned his way by waiting on table and tutoring other students, and read widely and diffusely rather than tending strictly to his prescribed courses. During vacations he worked as teacher's assistant in the school of his uncle, Samuel Ripley, in Waltham. After his graduation in 1821, he taught in his brother William's school for four years and then studied for the ministry and served parishes in Waltham, Massachusetts, Concord, New Hampshire, and other New England towns. In 1833, after some misgivings about his beliefs, he left the ministry and traveled for a year abroad, forming friendships with Coleridge, Wordsworth, and particularly Carlyle, who influenced him greatly and crystallized his belief in the dignity of the soul and the need for simplifying one's desires. During this period, also, he read the works of Swedenborg, from which he derived the conception of man as the center of Nature, a belief he was later to re-affirm so strongly as leader of

---

* Abridged.

the Transcendentalist Group of philosophers. Upon his return to America, he settled in Concord, Massachusetts, where he became the leader of the Concord Group, comprising Bronson Alcott, Thoreau, Hawthorne, and Margaret Fuller. There he followed a strict routine of writing in the mornings, walking alone in the afternoons, and talking with friends or lecturing in the evenings. His Phi Beta Kappa Oration at Harvard University in 1837 on *The American Scholar* and an address to the Divinity College at Harvard the following year aroused so much criticism of his plea for the cultivation of self-reliance as a new revelation of God, that he was considered *tabu* in Cambridge for thirty years. In 1840 he began his contributions to *The Dial,* edited by Margaret Fuller, and engaged more actively in lecturing upon the subjects of his essays. As a lecturer, even more than as an essayist, he exerted a powerful influence upon men of his time. A tall, dignified man with a kindly smile, he read his lectures without gesture, and with a calm assurance and gentle humor won disbelievers to him by sheer force of personality. In 1872, when his home in Concord was destroyed by fire, devoted friends and followers contributed a fund to restore it. Probably no other man contributed more, by his personality and thought, to his generation than did Emerson. He died in 1882 and was buried in Concord near his eminent pupil, Thoreau.

Man is his own star, and the soul that can
Render an honest and a perfect man,
Command all light, all influence, all fate,
Nothing to him falls early or too late.
Our acts our angels are, or good or ill,
Our fatal shadows that walk by us still.
            —Epilogue to Beaumont and Fletcher's
                Honest Man's Fortune.

I READ the other day some verses written by an eminent painter which were original and not conventional. The soul always hears an admonition in such lines, let the subject be what it may. The sentiment they instil is of more value than any thought they may contain. To believe your own thought, to believe that what is true for you in your private heart is true for all men—that is genius. Speak your latent conviction, and it shall be the universal sense; for the inmost in due time becomes the outmost, and our first thought is rendered back to us by the trumpets of the Last Judgment. Familiar as the voice of the mind is to each, the highest merit we ascribe to Moses, Plato, and Milton is that they set at naught books and traditions and spoke not what men, but what they, thought. A man should learn to detect and watch that gleam of light which flashes across his mind from within more than the luster of the firmament of bards and sages. Yet he dismisses without notice his thought, because it is his. In every work of genius we recognize our rejected thoughts; they come back to us with a certain alienated majesty. Great works of art have no more affecting lesson for us than this. They teach us to abide by our spontaneous impression with good-humored inflexibility the most when the whole cry of voices is on the other side. Else, tomorrow a stranger will say with masterly good sense precisely what we have thought and felt all the time, and we shall be forced to take with shame our own opinion from another.

Trust thyself; every heart vibrates to that iron string. Accept the place the Divine Providence has found for you, the society of your contemporaries, the connection of events. Great men have always done so, and confided themselves child-like to the genius of their age, betraying their perception that the absolutely trustworthy was seated at their heart, working through their hands, predominating in all their being. And we are now men and must accept in the highest mind the same transcendent destiny; and not minors and invalids in a protected corner, not cowards fleeing before a revolution, but guides, redeemers, and benefactors, obeying the Almighty effort, and advancing on Chaos and the Dark.

The nonchalance of boys who are sure of a dinner and would disdain as much as a lord to do or say aught to conciliate one is the healthy attitude of human nature. A boy is in the parlor what the pit [1] is in the playhouse; independent, irresponsible, looking out from his corner on such people and facts as pass by, he tries and sentences them on their merits, in the swift, summary way of boys, as good, bad, interesting, silly, eloquent, troublesome. He cumbers himself never about consequences, about interests; he gives an independent, genuine verdict. You must court him; he does not court you. But the man is, as it were, clapped into jail by his consciousness. As soon as he has once acted or spoken with *éclat*, he is a committed person, watched by the sympathy or the hatred of hundreds, whose affections must now enter into his account. There is no Lethe[2] for this. Ah, that he could pass again into his neutrality! Who can thus lose all pledges and, having observed, observe again from the same unaffected, unbiased, unbribable, unaffrighted innocence must always be formidable. He would utter opinions on all passing affairs, which being seen to be not private, but necessary, would sink like darts into the ear of men, and put them in fear.

Whoso would be a man must be a nonconformist. He who would gather immortal palms must not be hindered by the name of goodness, but must explore if it be goodness. Nothing is at last sacred but the integrity of your own mind. Absolve you to yourself, and you shall have the suffrage of the world. I remember an answer which when quite young I was prompted to make to a valued adviser who was wont to importune me with the dear old doctrines of the church. On my saying, "What have I to do with the sacredness of traditions, if I live wholly from within?" my friend suggested, "But these impulses may be from below, not from above." I replied, "They do not seem to me to be such; but if I am the Devil's child, I will live then from the Devil." No law can be sacred to me but that of my nature. Good and bad are but names very readily transferable to that or this; the only right is what is after my constitution; the only wrong, what is against it. A man is to carry himself in the presence of all opposition as if everything were titular and ephemeral but him! I am ashamed to think how easily we capitulate to badges and names, to large societies and dead institutions. Every decent and well-spoken individual affects and sways me more than is right. I ought to go upright and vital, and speak the rude truth in all ways.

What I must do is all that concerns me, not what the people think. This rule, equally arduous in actual and in intellectual life, may serve for the whole distinction between greatness and meanness. It is the harder, because you will always find those who think they know what is your duty better than you know it. It is easy in the world to live after the world's opinion; it is easy in solitude to live after our own; but the great man is he who in the midst of the crowd keeps with perfect sweetness the independence of solitude.

For nonconformity the world whips you with its displeasure. And therefore a man must know how to estimate a sour face. The bystanders look askance on him in the public street or in the friend's parlor. If this aversion had its origin in contempt and resistance like his own, he might well go home with a sad countenance; but the sour faces of the multitude, like their sweet faces, have no deep cause, but are put on and off as the wind blows and a newspaper directs. Yet is the discontent of the multitude more formidable than that of the senate and the college. It is easy enough for a firm man who knows the world to brook the rage of the cultivated classes. Their rage is decorous and prudent, for they are timid, as being very vulnerable themselves. But when to their feminine rage the indignation of the people is added, when the ignorant and the poor are aroused, when the unintelligent brute force that lies at the bottom of society is made to growl and mow, it needs the habit of magnanimity and religion to treat it godlike as a trifle of no concernment.

The other terror that scares us from self-trust is our consistency, a reverence for our past act or word because the eyes of others have no other data for computing our orbit than our past acts, and we are loath to disappoint them. A foolish consistency is the hobgoblin of little minds, adored by little statesmen and philosophers and divines. With consistency a great soul has simply nothing to do. He may as well concern himself with his shadow on the wall. Speak what you think now in hard words, and tomorrow speak what tomorrow thinks in hard words again, though it contradict everything you said today. "Ah, so you shall be sure to be misunderstood." Is it so bad, then, to be misunderstood? Pythagoras was misunderstood, and Socrates, and Jesus, and Luther, and Copernicus, and Galileo, and Newton, and every pure and wise spirit that ever took flesh. To be great is to be misunderstood.

I hope in these days we have heard the last of conformity and consistency. Let the words be gazetted and ridiculous henceforward. Instead of the gong for dinner, let us hear a whistle from the Spartan fife. Let us never bow and apologize more. A great man is coming to eat at my house. I do not wish to please him; I wish that he should wish to please me. I will stand here for humanity, and though I would make it kind, I would make it true. Let us affront and reprimand the smooth mediocrity and squalid contentment of the times and hurl in the face of custom, and trade, and office, the fact which is the upshot of all history, that there is a great responsible Thinker and Actor working wherever a man works, that a true man belongs to no other time or place, but is the center of things. Where he is, there is nature.

Let a man, then, know his worth, and keep things under his feet. Let him not peep or steal, or skulk up and down with the air of a charity-boy, or an interloper, in the world which exists for him. But the man in the street, finding no worth in himself which corresponds to the force which built a tower or sculptured a marble god, feels poor when he looks on these. To him a palace, a statue, or a costly book have an alien and forbidding air, much like a gay equipage, and seem to say like that, "Who are you, sir?" Yet they all are his, suitors for his notice, petitioners to his faculties that they will come out and take possession. The picture waits for my verdict; it is not to command me, but I am to settle its claim to praise. That popular fable of the sot who was picked up dead drunk in the street, carried to the duke's house, washed and dressed and laid in the duke's bed, and, on his waking, treated with all obsequious ceremony like the duke, and assured that he had been insane, owes its popularity to the fact that it symbolizes so well the state of man who is in the world a sort of sot, but now and then wakes up, exercises his reason, and finds himself a true prince.

Every man discerns between the voluntary acts of his mind and his involuntary perceptions, and knows that to his involuntary perceptions a perfect faith is due. He may err in the expression of them, but he knows that these things are so, like day and night, not to be disputed. My wilful actions and acquisitions are but roving; the idlest reverie, the faintest native emotion command my curiosity and respect. Thoughtless people contradict as readily the statement of perceptions as of opinions, or rather much more readily; for they do not distinguish between perception and notion. They fancy that I choose to see this or that thing. But perception is not whimsical, but fatal. If I see a trait, my children will see it after me, and in course of time, all mankind, although it may chance that no one has seen it before me. For my perception of it is as much a fact as the sun.

And now at last the highest truth on this subject remains unsaid; probably cannot be said; for all that we say is the far off remembering of the intuition. That thought, by what I can now nearest approach to say it, is this. When good is near you, when you have life in yourself, it is not by any known or accustomed way; you shall not discern the footprints of any other; you shall not see the face of man; you shall not hear any name; the way, the thought, the good, shall be wholly strange and new. It shall exclude example and experience. You take the way from man, not to man. All persons that ever existed are its forgotten ministers. Fear and hope are alike beneath it. There is somewhat low even in hope. In the hour of vision there is nothing that can be called gratitude, nor properly joy. The soul raised over passion beholds identity and eternal causation, perceives the self-existence of Truth and Right, and calms itself with knowing that all things go well. Vast spaces of nature, the Atlantic Ocean, the South Sea, long intervals of time, years, centuries are of no account. This which I think and feel underlay every former state of life and circumstances, as it does underlie my present, and what is called life, and what is called death.

Life only avails, not the having lived. Power ceases in the instant of repose; it resides in the moment of transition from a past to a new state, in the shooting of the gulf, in the darting to an aim. This one fact the world hates, that the soul *becomes;* for that forever degrades the past, turns all riches to poverty, all reputation to a shame, confounds the saint with the rogue, shoves Jesus and Judas equally aside. Why, then, do we prate of self-reliance? Inasmuch as the soul is present, there will be power not confident but agent.[3] To talk of reliance is a poor external way of speaking. Speak rather of that which relies because it works and is. Who has more obedience than I masters me, though he should not raise his finger. Round him I must revolve by the gravitation of spirits. We fancy it rhetoric when we speak of eminent virtue. We do not yet see that virtue is Height, and that a man or a company of men, plastic and permeable to principles, by the law of nature must overpower and ride all cities, nations, kings, rich men, poets who are not.

This is the ultimate fact which we so quickly reach on this, as on every topic, the resolution of all into the ever-blessed ONE. Self-existence is the attribute of the Supreme Cause, and it constitutes the measure of good by the degree in which it enters into all lower forms. All things real are so by so much virtue as they contain. Commerce, husbandry, hunting, whaling, war, eloquence, personal weight, are somewhat, and engage my respect as examples of its presence and impure action. I see the same law working in nature for conservation and growth. Power is in nature the essential measure of right. Nature suffers nothing to remain in her kingdoms which cannot help itself. The genesis and maturation of a planet, its poise and orbit, the bended tree recovering itself from the strong wind, the vital resources of every animal and vegetable are demonstrations of the self-sufficing, and therefore self-relying, soul.

If any man consider the present aspects of what is called by distinction *society*, he will see the need of these ethics. The sinew and heart of man seem to be drawn out, and we are become timorous, desponding whimperers. We are afraid of truth, afraid of fortune, afraid of death, and afraid of each other. Our age yields no great and perfect persons. We want men and women who shall renovate life and our social state; but we see that most natures are insolvent, cannot satisfy their own wants, have an ambition out of all proportion to their practical force, and do lean and beg day and night continually. Our housekeeping is mendicant; our arts, our occupations, our marriages, our religion we have not chosen, but society has chosen for us. We are parlor soldiers. We shun the rugged battle of fate where strength is born.

If our young men miscarry in their first enterprise, they lose all heart. If the young merchant fails, men say he is ruined. If the finest genius studies at one of our colleges and is not installed in an office within one year afterwards in the cities or suburbs of Boston or New York, it seems to his friends and to himself that he is right in being disheartened, and in complaining the rest of his life. A sturdy lad from New Hampshire or Vermont, who in turn tries all the professions, who teams it, farms it, peddles, keeps a school, preaches, edits a newspaper, goes to Congress, buys a township, and so forth, in successive years, and always, like a cat, falls on his feet, is worth a hundred of these city dolls. He walks abreast with his days and feels no shame in not "studying a profession," for he does not postpone his life, but lives already. He has not one chance, but a hundred chances. Let a stoic open the resources of man and tell men they are not leaning willows, but can and must detach themselves; that with the exercise of self-trust, new powers shall appear; that a man is the word made flesh, born to shed healing to the nations; that he should be ashamed of our compassion, and that the moment he acts from himself, tossing the laws, the books, idolatries, and customs out of the window, we pity him no more but thank and revere him; and that teacher shall restore the life of man to splendor, and make his name dear to all history.

It is for want of self-culture that the superstition of traveling, whose idols are Italy, England, Egypt, retains its fascination for all educated Americans. They who made England, Italy, or Greece venerable in the imagination did so by sticking fast where they were, like an axis of the earth. In manly hours we feel that duty is our place. The soul is no traveler; the wise man stays at home, and when his necessities, his duties, on any occasion call him from his house, or into foreign lands, he is at home still, and shall make men sensible by the expression of his countenance that he goes, the missionary of wisdom and virtue, and visits cities and men like a sovereign, and not like an interloper or a valet.

I have no churlish objection to the circumnavigation of the globe for the purposes of art, of study, and benevolence, if the man is first domesticated, or does not go abroad with the hope of finding somewhat greater than he knows. He who travels to be amused, or to get somewhat which he does not carry, travels away from himself, and grows old even in youth among old things. In Thebes, in Palmyra, his will and mind have become old and dilapidated as they. He carries ruins to ruins.

Traveling is a fool's paradise. Our first journeys discover to us the indifference of places. At home I dream that at Naples, at Rome, I can be intoxicated with beauty and lose my sadness. I pack my trunk, embrace my friends, embark on the sea, and at last wake up in Naples, and there beside me is the stern fact, the sad self, unrelenting, identical, that I fled from. I seek the Vatican and the palaces; I affect to be intoxicated with sights and suggestions, but I am not intoxicated. My giant goes with me wherever I go.

But the rage of traveling is a symptom of a

deeper unsoundness affecting the whole intellectual action. The intellect is vagabond, and our system of education fosters restlessness. Our minds travel when our bodies are forced to stay at home. We imitate; and what is imitation but the traveling of the mind? Our houses are built with foreign taste; our shelves are garnished with foreign ornaments; our opinions, our tastes, our faculties lean and follow the past and the distant. The soul created the arts wherever they have flourished. It was in his own mind that the artist sought his model. It was an application of his own thought to the thing to be done and the conditions to be observed. And why need we copy the Doric or the Gothic model? Beauty, convenience, grandeur of thought, and quaint expression are as near to us as to any, and if the American artist will study with hope and love the precise thing to be done by him, considering the climate, the soil, the length of the day, the wants of the people, the habit and form of the government, he will create a house in which all these will find themselves fitted, and taste and sentiment will be satisfied also.

Insist on yourself; never imitate. Your own gift you can present every moment with the cumulative force of a whole life's cultivation; but of the adopted talent of another, you have only an extemporaneous half possession. That which each can do best, none but his Maker can teach him. No man yet knows what it is, nor can, till that person has exhibited it. Where is the master who could have taught Shakespeare? Where is the master who could have instructed Franklin, or Washington, or Bacon, or Newton? Every great man is unique. Do that which is assigned you and you cannot hope too much or dare too much. There is at this moment for you an utterance brave and grand as that of the colossal chisel of Phidias, or trowel of the Egyptians, or the pen of Moses, or Dante, but different from all these. Not possibly will the soul, all rich, all eloquent, with thousand-cloven tongue, deign to repeat itself; but if you can hear what these patriarchs say, surely you can reply to them in the same pitch of voice, for the ear and the tongue are two organs of one nature. Abide in the simple and noble regions of thy life, obey thy heart, and thou shalt reproduce the foreworld again.

As our religion, our education, our art look abroad, so does our spirit of society. All men plume themselves on the improvement of society, and no man improves.

Society never advances. It recedes as fast on one side as it gains on the other. It undergoes continual changes; it is barbarous, it is civilized, it is Christianized, it is rich, it is scientific; but this change is not amelioration. For everything that is given, something is taken. Society acquires new arts, and loses old instincts. What a contrast between the well-clad, reading, writing, thinking American, with a watch, a pencil, and a bill of exchange in his pocket, and the naked New Zealander, whose property is a club, a spear, a mat, and an undivided twentieth of a shed to sleep under! But compare the health of the two men, and you shall see that the white man has lost his aboriginal strength. If the traveler tell us truly, strike the savage with a broad ax, and in a day or two the flesh shall unite and heal as if you struck the blow into soft pitch, and the same blow shall send the white to his grave.

The civilized man has built a coach, but has lost the use of his feet. He is supported on crutches, but lacks so much support of muscle. He has a fine Geneva watch, but he fails of the skill to tell the hour by the sun. A Greenwich nautical almanac he has, and so being sure of the information when he wants it, the man in the street does not know a star in the sky. The solstice he does not observe; the equinox he knows as little; and the whole bright calendar of the year is without a dial in his mind. His note-books impair his memory; his libraries overload his wit; the insurance-office increases the number of accidents; and it may be a question whether machinery does not encumber; whether we have not lost by refinement some energy by a Christianity intrenched in establishments and forms, some vigor of wild virtue. For every stoic was a stoic; but in Christendom where is the Christian?

Society is a wave. The wave moves onward, but the water of which it is composed does not.

The same particle does not rise from the valley to the ridge. Its unity is only phenomenal. The persons who make up a nation today next year die, and their experience with them.

And so the reliance on property, including the reliance on governments which protect it, is the want of self-reliance. Men have looked away from themselves and at things so long, that they have come to esteem the religious, learned, and civil institutions as guards of property, and they deprecate assaults on these, because they feel them to be assaults on property. They measure their esteem of each other by what each has, and not by what each is. But a cultivated man becomes ashamed of his property out of new respect for his nature. Especially he hates what he has, if he see that it is accidental, or come to him by inheritance, or gift, or crime; then he feels that it is not having; it does not belong to him, has no root in him, and merely lies there, because no revolution or no robber takes it away. But that which a man is does always by necessity acquire a living property, which does not wait the beck of rulers, or mobs, or revolutions, or fire, or storm, or bankruptcies, but perpetually renews itself wherever the man breathes. "Thy lot or portion of life," said the Caliph Ali, "is seeking after thee; therefore be at rest from seeking after it."

So use all that is called Fortune. Most men gamble with her, and gain all, and lose all, as her wheel rolls. But do thou leave as unlawful these winnings, and deal with Cause and Effect, the chancellors of God. In the Will work and acquire, and thou hast chained the wheel of Chance, and shalt sit hereafter out of fear from her rotations. A political victory, a rise of rents, the recovery of your sick, or the return of your absent friend, or some other favorable event raises your spirits, and you think good days are preparing for you. Do not believe it. Nothing can bring you peace but yourself. Nothing can bring you peace but the triumph of principles.

NOTES

[1] The pit in the earlier theaters was filled by those who now fill the galleries of the theater and the bleachers of a ball park.

[2] The River of Forgetfulness.

[3] active.

QUESTIONS

1. Do you agree with Emerson about consistency's being "the hobgoblin of little minds"?

2. What evidence of self-reliance have you noticed in others? What lack of it?

3. What are the evils of conformity? What are the advantages?

4. How would you relate this essay to those by L. P. Jacks and Samuel McChord Crothers?

ON A CERTAIN CONDESCENSION IN FOREIGNERS *

James Russell Lowell

James Russell Lowell's life (1819–1891) gave, in its early stages, little promise of the prominence he was later to achieve. Indeed, had it not been for the influence of two women and a group of unusual men, it is doubtful whether this versatile man would ever have accomplished so much. A desultory student at Harvard, from which he was graduated in 1838 as class poet, he followed his academic course with two years of law study, and for several years drifted aimlessly, apparently undecided upon any one field of endeavor. Then he met Maria White, of Watertown, Massachusetts, the sister of a college classmate. Her passionate interest in poetry and the anti-slavery movement fired his devotion to the cause that was soon to link him with Ralph Waldo Emerson, Henry David Thoreau, and John Greenleaf Whittier. His contributions to various periodicals, in both prose and verse, widened his circle of friends to include Henry Wadsworth Longfellow and Oliver Wendell Holmes. Maria White, now Mrs. Lowell, did much to cement the friendship of Lowell with this group of men who were then dominating the American literary world. When Longfellow left Harvard University's faculty in 1854, Lowell was offered the position as his successor as Smith Professor of French and Spanish Literature, which he accepted after a year of preparatory study

---

* Abridged.

on the Continent. The first Mrs. Lowell having died in
1853, Lowell married, in 1857, Frances Dunlap, govern-
ess to his daughter Mabel and a woman whose intellectual
and social gifts did much to sustain his position in what
was, perhaps, the foremost intellectual and literary circle
in America at the time. The *Atlantic Monthly* began publication the same year, with Lowell as its editor-in-chief,
aided by Oliver Wendell Holmes, who was retained before
publication as a regular contributor, and by the rest of
Lowell's august circle of friends. The *Atlantic Monthly*
and, later, the *North American Review* played important
rôles in forming the political and social thought of the day
and brought to Lowell, as editor, a prestige which made
his selection as Minister to the Court of Spain in 1877 a
logical one. There he served for three years until he was
transferred to the Court of St. James. That he soon made
lasting friendships with the leading political and literary
men in England, in spite of his earlier criticisms of the
British attitude toward Americans (such as the essay presented here), is a tribute to the affectionate and whimsical
manner which covered the more serious part of his nature.
This Ambassadorship to Great Britain he held until shortly
after the death of the second Mrs. Lowell in 1885. The remaining six years of his life Lowell spent in travel and at
his home in Cambridge, Massachusetts. He died in 1891 in
the same house in Cambridge in which, seventy-two years
earlier, he had been born. "On a Certain Condescension in
Foreigners" is characteristic of the more serious side of
Lowell, relieved by his gift of satire.

WALKING one day toward the Village, as we
used to call it in the good old days when almost
every dweller in the town had been born in it, I
was enjoying that delicious sense of disenthral-
ment from the actual which the deepening twilight brings with it, giving as it does a sort of ob-

scure novelty to things familiar. For the moment,
I was enjoying the blessed privilege of thinking
without being called on to stand and deliver what
I thought to the small public who are good
enough to take any interest therein. I love old
ways, and the path I was walking felt kindly to
the feet it had known for almost fifty years. And
as I felt more and more the soothing magic of
evening's cool palm upon my temples, as my
fancy came home from its revery, and my senses,
with reawakened curiosity, ran to the front windows again from the viewless closet of abstraction, and felt a strange charm in finding the old
tree and shabby fence still there under the trav-
esty of falling night, nay, were conscious of an
unsuspected newness in familiar stars and the
fading outlines of hills, my earliest horizon, I was
conscious of an immortal soul, and could not but
rejoice in the unwaning goodliness of the world
into which I had been born without any merit of
my own. I remembered people who had to go over
to the Alps to learn what the divine silence of
snow was, who must run to Italy before they were
conscious of the miracle wrought every day under
their very noses by the sunset, who must call
upon the Berkshire hills to teach them what a
painter autumn was, while close at hand the Fresh
Pond meadows made all oriels cheap with hues
that showed as if a sunset-cloud had been wrecked
among their maples. One might be worse off than
even in America, I thought. There are some things

so elastic that even the heavy roller of democracy cannot flatten them altogether down. The mind can weave itself warmly in the cocoon of its own thoughts and dwell a hermit anywhere. A country without traditions, without ennobling associations, a scramble of *parvenus*,[1] with a horrible consciousness of shoddy running through politics, manners, art, literature, nay, religion itself? I confess, it did not seem so to me there in that illimitable quiet, that serene self-possession of nature. Traditions? Granting that we had none, all that is worth having in them is the common property of the soul,—an estate in gavelkind [2] for all the sons of Adam,—and, moreover, if a man cannot stand on his two feet (the prime quality of whoever has left any tradition behind him), were it not better for him to be honest about it at once, and go down on all fours? And for associations, if one have not the wit to make them for himself out of native earth, no ready-made ones of other men will avail much. Lexington is none the worse to me for not being in Greece, nor Gettysburg that its name is not Marathon. "Blessed old fields," I was just exclaiming to myself, "dear acres, innocently secure from history, which these eyes first beheld, may you be also those to which they shall at last slowly darken!" when I was interrupted by a voice which asked me in German whether I was the Herr Professor, Doctor, So-and-so? The "Doctor" was to make the grade easier to my pocket.

One feels so intimately assured that he is made up, in part, of shreds and leavings of the past, in part of the interpolations of other people, that an honest man would be slow in saying *yes* to such a question. But "my name is So-and-so" is a safe answer, and I gave it. While I had been romancing with myself, the street-lamps had been lighted, and it was under one of these detectives that have robbed the Old Road of its privilege of sanctuary after nightfall that I was ambushed by my foe.

I knew perfectly well what was coming. It is seldom that debtors or good Samaritans waylay people under gas-lamps in order to force money upon them, so far as I have seen or heard. I was also aware, from considerable experience, that every foreigner is persuaded that, by doing this country the favor of coming to it, he has laid every native thereof under an obligation, pecuniary or other, as the case may be, whose discharge he is entitled to on demand duly made in person or by letter. Too much learning (of this kind) had made me mad in the provincial sense of the word. I had begun life with the theory of giving something to every beggar that came along. But moralists, sociologists, political economists, and taxes have slowly convinced me that my beggarly sympathies were a sin against society.

But I am leaving my new acquaintance too long under the lamp-post. That which had betrayed me to him revealed to me a well-set young man of about half my own age, as well dressed, so far as I could see, as I was, and with every natural qualification for getting his own livelihood as good, if not better, than my own. He had been reduced to the painful necessity of calling upon me by a series of crosses beginning with the Baden Revolution (for which, I own, he seemed rather young,—but perhaps he referred to a kind of revolution practiced every season at Baden-Baden),[3] continued by repeated failures in business, for amounts which must convince me of his entire respectability, and ending with our Civil War. During the latter, he had served with distinction as a soldier, taking a main part in every important battle, with a rapid list of which he favored me, and no doubt would have admitted that, impartial as Jonathan Wild's [4] great ancestor, he had been on both sides, had I baited him with a few hints of conservative opinions on a subject so distressing to a gentleman wishing to profit by one's sympathy and unhappily doubtful as to which way it might lean. For all these reasons and, as he seemed to imply, for his merit in consenting to be born in Germany, he considered himself my natural creditor to the extent of five dollars, which he would handsomely consent to accept in greenbacks, though he preferred specie. The offer was certainly a generous one, and the claim presented with an assurance that carried conviction. But, unhappily, I had been led to remark a curious natural phenomenon. If I was ever weak enough to give anything to a petitioner of whatever nationality, it always rained decayed compatriots of his for a month after. I accordingly made up my mind to deny the debt, and modestly did so, pleading a native bias towards impecuniosity to the full as strong as his own. He took a high tone with me at once, such as an honest man would naturally take with a confessed repudiator. He even brought down his proud stomach so far as to join himself to me for the rest of my townward walk, that he might give me his views of the American people, and thus inclusively of myself.

I know not whether it is because I am pigeon-livered and lack gall, or whether it is from an overmastering sense of drollery, but I am apt to submit to such bastings with a patience which afterwards surprises me, being not without my share of warmth in the blood. Perhaps it is because I so often meet with young persons who know vastly more than I do, and especially with so many foreigners whose knowledge of this country is superior to my own. However it may be, I listened for some time with tolerable composure as my self-appointed lecturer gave me in detail his opinions of my country and its people. America, he informed me, was without arts, science, literature, culture, or any native hope of supplying them. We were a people wholly given to money-getting, and who, having got it, knew no other use for it than to hold it fast. I am fain to confess that I felt a sensible itching of the biceps, and that my fingers closed with such a grip as he had just informed me was one of the effects of our unhappy climate. But happening just then to be where I could avoid temptation by dodging down a by-street, I hastily left him to finish his diatribe to the lamp-post, which could stand it better than I. That young man will never know how near he came to being assaulted by a respectable gentleman of middle age, at the corner of Church Street. I have never felt quite satisfied that I did all my duty by him in not knocking him down. But perhaps he might have knocked *me* down, and then?

The capacity of indignation makes an essential part of the outfit of every honest man, but I am inclined to doubt whether he is a wise one who allows himself to act upon its first hints. It should be rather, I suspect, a *latent* heat in the blood, which makes itself felt in character a steady reserve for the brain, warming the *ovum* of thought to life, rather than cooking it by a too hasty enthusiasm in reaching the boiling-point. As my pulse gradually fell back to its normal beat, I reflected that I had been uncomfortably near making a fool of myself,—a handy salve of euphuism for our vanity, though it does not always make a just allowance to Nature for her share in the business. What possible claim had my Teutonic friend to rob me of my composure? I am not, I think, specially thin-skinned as to other people's opin-

ions of myself, having, as I conceive, later and
fuller intelligence on that point than anybody else
can give me. Life is continually weighing us in
very sensitive scales, and telling every one of us
precisely what his real weight is to the last grain
of dust. Whoever at fifty does not rate himself
quite as low as most of his acquaintance would be
likely to put him, must be either a fool or a great
man, and I humbly disclaim being either. But if I
was not smarting in person from any scattering
shot of my late companion's commination, why
should I grow hot at any implication of my country therein? Surely *her* shoulders are broad
enough, if yours or mine are not, to bear up under
a considerable avalanche of this kind. It is the bit
of truth in every slander, the hint of likeness in
every caricature, that makes us smart. How did
your blade know its way so well to that one loose
rivet in our armor? I wondered whether Americans were over-sensitive in this respect, whether
they were more touchy than other folks. On the
whole, I thought we were not. Plutarch, who at
least had studied philosophy, if he had not mastered it, could not stomach something Herodotus
had said of Bœotia, and devoted an essay to
showing up the delightful old traveler's malice
and ill-breeding. French editors leave out of Montaigne's "Travels" some remarks of his about
France, for reasons best known to themselves.
Pachydermatous Deutschland, covered with tro-
phies from every field of letters, still winces under

that question which Père Bouhours put two centuries ago, *Si un Allemand peut être bel-esprit?* [5]
John Bull grew apoplectic with angry amazement at the audacious persiflage of Pückler-Muskau. To be sure, he was a prince,—but that was not all of it, for a chance phrase of gentle Hawthorne sent a spasm through all the journals of England. Then this tenderness is not peculiar to *us?* Console yourself, dear man and brother; whatever else you may be sure of, be sure at least of this, that you are dreadfully like other people. Human nature has a much greater genius for sameness than for originality, or the world would be at a sad pass shortly. The surprising thing is that men have such a taste for this somewhat musty flavor, that an Englishman, for example, should feel himself defrauded, nay, even outraged, when he comes over here and finds a people speaking what he admits to be something like English, and yet so very different from (or, as he would say, to) those he left at home. Nothing, I am sure, equals *my* thankfulness when I meet an Englishman who is *not* like every other, or, I may add, an American of the same odd turn.

It seems to be the common opinion of foreigners that Americans are *too* tender upon this point. Perhaps we are; and if so, there must be a reason for it. Have we had fair play? Could the eyes of what is called Good Society (though it is so seldom true either to the adjective or noun) look upon a nation of democrats with any chance of receiving an undistorted image? Were not those, moreover, who found in the old order of things an earthly paradise, paying them quarterly dividends for the wisdom of their ancestors, with the punctuality of the seasons, unconsciously bribed to misunderstand if not to misrepresent us? For more than a century the Dutch were the laughing-stock of polite Europe. They were butter-firkins, swillers of beer and schnapps, and their *vrouws* from whom Holbein painted the all-but loveliest of Madonnas, Rembrandt the graceful girl who sits immortal on his knee in Dresden, and Rubens his abounding goddesses, were the synonyms of clumsy vulgarity. Meanwhile, during that very century of scorn, they were the best artists, sailors, merchants, bankers, printers, scholars, jurisconsults, and statesmen in Europe, and the genius of Motley [6] has revealed them to us, earning a right to themselves by the most heroic struggle in human annals. But, alas! they were not merely simple burghers who had fairly made themselves High Mightinesses, and could treat on equal terms with anointed kings; their commonwealth carried in its bosom the germs of democracy. They even unmuzzled, at least after dark, that dreadful mastiff, the Press, whose scent is, or ought to be, so keen for wolves in sheep's clothing and for certain other animals in lions' skins. They made fun of Sacred Majesty, and what was worse, managed uncommonly well without it. In an age when periwigs made so large a part of the natural dignity of man, people with such a turn of mind were dangerous. How could they seem other than vulgar and hateful?

In the natural course of things we succeeded to this unenviable position of general butt. The Dutch had thriven under it pretty well, and there was hope that we could at least contrive to worry along. And we certainly did in a very redoubtable fashion. Perhaps we deserved some of the sarcasm more than our Dutch predecessors in office. We had nothing to boast of in arts or letters, and were given to bragging over-much of our merely material prosperity, due quite as much to the virtue of our continent as to our own. Till we had succeeded in some higher way than this, we had only the success of physical growth. Our greatness, like that of enormous Russia, was greatness on the map,—barbarian mass only; but had we gone down, like that other Atlantis, in some vast cataclysm, we should have covered but a pin's point on the chart of memory, compared with those ideal spaces occupied by tiny Attica and cramped England. At the same time, our critics somewhat too easily forgot that material must make ready the foundation for ideal triumphs, that the arts have no chance in poor countries. And it must be allowed that democracy stood for a great deal in our shortcoming. Perhaps it is the collective, not the individual, humanity that is to have a chance of nobler development among us. We shall see. We have a vast amount of imported ignorance, and, still worse, of native ready-made knowledge, to digest before even the preliminaries of such a consummation can be arranged. We have got to learn that statesmanship is the most complicated of all arts, and to come back to the apprenticeship-system too hastily abandoned.

But whatever we might do or leave undone, we were not genteel, and it was uncomfortable to be continually reminded that, though we should boast that we were the Great West till we were black in the face, it did not bring us an inch nearer to the world's West-End. That sacred in-closure of respectability was tabooed to us. The Holy Alliance did not inscribe us on its visiting-list. The Old World of wigs and orders and liv-eries would shop with us, but we must ring at the area-bell, and not venture to awaken the more august clamors of the knocker. Our manners, it must be granted, had none of those graces that stamp the caste of Vere de Vere, in whatever mu-seum of British antiquities they may be hidden. In short, we were vulgar.

This was one of those horribly vague accusa-tions, the victim of which has no defense. An um-brella is of no avail against a Scotch mist. It en-velops you, it penetrates at every pore, it wets you through without seeming to wet you at all. Vulgarity is an eighth deadly sin, added to the list in these latter days, and worse than all the others put together, since it perils your salvation in *this* world,—far the more important of the two in the minds of most men. It profits nothing to draw nice distinctions between essential and conventional, for the convention in this case *is* the essence, and you may break every command of the decalogue with perfect good-breeding, nay, if you are adroit, without losing caste. We, indeed, had it not to lose, for we had never gained it. We were as clean,—so far as my observation goes, I think we were cleaner, morally and physically, than the English, and therefore, of course, than everybody else. But we did not pronounce the diphthong *ou* as they did, and we said *eether* and not *eyther*, following therein the fashion of our ancestors, who unhappily could bring over no English better than Shakespeare's; and we did not stammer as they had learned to do from the courtiers, who in this way flattered the Hanoverian king, a foreigner among the people he had come to reign over. Worse than all, we might have the noblest ideas and the finest sentiments in the world, but we vented them through that organ by which men are led rather than leaders, though some physiologists would persuade us that Nature furnishes her captains with a fine handle to their faces that Opportunity may get a good purchase on them for dragging them to the front.

This state of things was so painful that excellent people were not wanting who gave their whole genius to reproducing here the original Bull, whether by gaiters, the cut of their whiskers, by a factitious brutality in their tone,

or by an accent that was forever tripping and
falling flat over the tangled roots of our common
tongue. Martyrs to a false ideal, it never occurred
to them that nothing is more hateful to gods and
men than a second-rate Englishman. If we could
contrive to be not too unobtrusively our simple
selves, we should be the most delightful of human
beings, and the most original; whereas, when the
plating of Anglicism rubs off, as it always will in
points that come to much wear, we are liable to
very unpleasing conjectures about the quality of
the metal underneath. Perhaps one reason why
the average Briton spreads himself here with such
an easy air of superiority may be owing to the
fact that he meets with so many bad imitations as
to conclude himself the only real thing in a wilderness of shams. Among genuine things, I know
nothing more genuine than the better men whose
limbs were made in England. So manly-tender, so
brave, so true, so warranted to wear, they make
us proud to feel that blood is thicker than water.

But it is not merely the Englishman; every
European candidly admits in himself some right
of primogeniture in respect of us, and pats this
shaggy continent on the back with a lively sense
of generous unbending. The German who plays
the bass-viol has a well-founded contempt, which
he is not always nice in concealing, for a country
so few of whose children ever take that noble instrument between their knees. The Frenchman
feels an easy mastery in speaking his mother

tongue, and attributes it to some native superiority of parts that lifts him high above us barbarians of the West. The Italian *prima donna* sweeps a curtsy of careless pity to the over-facile pit which unsexes her with the *bravo!* [7] innocently meant to show a familiarity with foreign usage. But all without exception make no secret of regarding us as the goose bound to deliver them a golden egg in return for *their* cackle. Is it in the climate? Either I have a false notion of European manners, or else the atmosphere affects them strangely when exported hither. Perhaps they suffer from the sea-voyage like some of the more delicate wines.

The fine old Tory aversion of former times was not hard to bear. There was something even refreshing in it, as in a northeaster to a hardy temperament. When a British parson, traveling in Newfoundland while the slash of our separation was still raw, after prophesying a glorious future for an island that continued to dry its fish under the ægis of Saint George, glances disdainfully over his spectacles in parting at the U. S. A., and forebodes for them a "speedy relapse into barbarism," now that they have madly cut themselves off from the humanizing influences of Britain, I smile with barbarian self-conceit. But this kind of thing became by degrees an unpleasant anachronism. For meanwhile the young giant was growing, was beginning indeed to feel tight in his clothes, was obliged to let in a gore here and there

in Texas, in California, in New Mexico, in
Alaska, and had the scissors and needle and
thread ready for Canada when the time came.
His shadow loomed over against Europe,—the
shadow of what they were coming to, that was the
unpleasant part of it. Even in such misty image
as they had of him, it was painfully evident that
his clothes were not of any cut hitherto fashionable, nor conceivable by a Bond Street tailor,—
and this in an age, too, when everything depends
upon clothes. From this moment the young giant
assumed the respectable aspect of a phenomenon,
to be got rid of if possible, but at any rate as
legitimate a subject of human study as the glacial
period.

It was something to have advanced even to the
dignity of a phenomenon, and yet I do not know
that the relation of the individual American to the
individual European was bettered by it; and that,
after all, must adjust itself comfortably before
there can be a right understanding between the
two. We had been a desert; we became a museum.
People came hither for scientific and not social
ends. The very cockney could not complete his
education without taking a vacant stare at us in
passing. But the sociologists (I think they call
themselves so) were the hardest to bear. There
was no escape. I have even known a professor of
this fearful science to come disguised in petticoats. We were cross-examined as a chemist cross-
examines a new substance. Human? Yes, all the

elements are present, though abnormally combined. Civilized? Hm! that needs a stricter assay. No entomologist could take a more friendly interest in a strange bug. After a few such experiences, I, for one, have felt as if I were merely one of those horrid things preserved in spirits (and very bad spirits, too) in a cabinet. I was not the fellow-being of these explorers: I was a curiosity; I was a *specimen*. Hath not an American organs, dimensions, senses, affections, passions even as a European hath? If you prick us, do we not bleed? If you tickle us, do we not laugh? I will not keep on with Shylock to his next question but one.

Till after our Civil War it never seemed to enter the head of any foreigner, especially of any Englishman, that an American had what could be called a country, except as a place to eat, sleep, and trade in. Then it seemed to strike them suddenly. "By Jove, you know, fellahs don't fight like that for a shop-till!" No, I rather think not. To Americans, America is something more than a promise and an expectation. It has a past and traditions of its own. A descent from men who sacrificed everything and came hither, not to better their fortunes, but to plant their idea in virgin soil, should be a good pedigree. There was never colony, save this, that went forth, not to seek gold, but God. Is it not as well to have sprung from such as these as from some burly beggar who came over with Wilhelmus Conquestor, unless, indeed, a line grow better as it runs farther away from stalwart ancestors? And for our history, it is dry enough, no doubt, in the books, but, for all that, is of a kind that tells in the blood.

Before our war we were to Europe but a huge mob of adventurers and shopkeepers. Leigh Hunt expressed it well enough when he said that he could never think of America without seeing a gigantic counter stretched all along the seaboard. Feudalism had by degrees made commerce, the great civilizer, contemptible. But a tradesman with sword on thigh and very prompt of stroke was not only redoubtable; he had become respectable also. A democracy that could fight for an abstraction, whose members held life and goods cheap compared with that larger life which we call country, was not merely unheard of, but portentous. The young giant had certainly got out of long-clothes. He had become the *enfant terrible* of the human household. It was not and will not be easy for the world (especially for our British cousins) to look upon us as grown up. The youngest of nations, its people must also be young and to be treated accordingly, was the syllogism. Youth has its good qualities, as people feel who are losing it, but boyishness is another thing. We had been somewhat boyish as a nation, a little loud, a little pushing, a little braggart. But might it not partly have been because we felt that we had certain claims to respect that were not admitted? The war which established our position as a vigorous nationality has also sobered us. A

nation, like a man, cannot look death in the eye
for four years without some strange reflections,
without arriving at some clearer consciousness of
the stuff it is made of, without some great moral
change. Such a change, or the beginning of it, no
observant person can fail to see here. Our thought
and our politics, our bearing as a people, are assuming a manlier tone. We have been compelled
to see what was weak in democracy as well as
what was strong. We have begun obscurely to recognize that things do not go of themselves, and
that popular government is not in itself a pana-
cea, is no better than any other form except as
the virtue and wisdom of the people make it so,
and that when men undertake to do their own
kingship, they enter upon the dangers and responsibilities as well as the privileges of the function. Above all, it looks as if we were on the way
to be persuaded that no government can be carried on by declamation. It is noticeable also that
facility of communication has made the best English and French thought far more directly opera-
tive here than ever before. Without being Euro-
peanized, our discussion of important questions
in statesmanship, in political economy, in æsthet-
ics, is taking a broader scope and a higher tone.
It had certainly been provincial, one might almost
say local, to a very unpleasant extent. Perhaps
our experience in soldiership has taught us to
value training more than we have been popularly
wont. We may possibly come to the conclusion,

one of these days, that self-made men may not be
always equally skillful in the manufacture of wisdom, may not be divinely commissioned to fabricate the higher qualities of opinion on all possible
topics of human interest.

So long as we continue to be the most common-
schooled and the least cultivated people in the
world, I suppose we must consent to endure this
condescending manner of foreigners toward us.
The more friendly they mean to be, the more ludi-
crously prominent it becomes. They can never
appreciate the immense amount of silent work
that has been done here, making this continent
slowly fit for the abode of man, and which will
demonstrate itself, let us hope, in the character of
the people. Outsiders can only be expected to judge
a nation by the amount it has contributed to the
civilization of the world; the amount, that is, that
can be seen and handled. A great place in history
can only be achieved by competitive examinations, nay, by a long course of them. How much
new thought have we contributed to the common
stock? Till that question can be triumphantly answered, or needs no answer, we must continue to
be simply interesting as an experiment, to be
studied as a problem, and not respected as an attained result or an accomplished solution.

It will take England a great while to get over
her airs of patronage toward us, or even passably
to conceal them. She cannot help confounding the
people with the country, and regarding us as

lusty juveniles. She has a conviction that whatever good there is in us is wholly English, when the truth is that we are worth nothing except so far as we have disinfected ourselves of Anglicism. The only sure way of bringing about a healthy relation between the two countries is for Englishmen to clear their minds of the notion that we are always to be treated as a kind of inferior and deported Englishman whose nature they perfectly understand, and whose back they accordingly stroke the wrong way of the fur with amazing perseverance. Let them learn to treat us naturally in our merits as human beings, as they would a German or a Frenchman, and not as if we were a kind of counterfeit Briton whose crime appeared in every shade of difference, and before long there would come that right feeling which we naturally call a good understanding. The common blood, and still more the common language, are fatal instruments of misapprehension. Let them give up *trying* to understand us, still more thinking that they do, and acting in various absurd ways as the necessary consequence, for they will never arrive at that devoutly-to-be-wished consummation, till they learn to look at us as we are and not as they suppose us to be. Dear old long-estranged mother-in-law, it is a great many years since we parted. Since 1660, when you married again, you have been a stepmother to us. Put on your spectacles, dear madam. Yes, we *have* grown, and changed likewise. You would not let us darken your doors, if you could help it. We know that perfectly well. But pray, when we look to be treated as men, don't shake that rattle in our faces, nor talk baby to us any longer.

NOTES

[1] upstarts who have climbed above their station in life through sudden riches.

[2] a system of landholding, peculiar to Kent, England, whereby property was divided among all the sons or among other male relatives.

[3] This refers to the mineral baths at this famous resort.

[4] Jonathan Wild, notorious swindler and thief; hero of Henry Fielding's novel of that name.

[5] Is it possible for a German to be a really fine spirit?

[6] John Lothrop Motley (1814–1877), American historian.

[7] *Bravo* is masculine; *brava*, the feminine form, would be more precise here.

QUESTIONS

1. What evidence of condescension toward Americans is apparent today? In whom?

2. How much of the foreign criticism referred to here was justifiable? How much is justifiable today?

3. What are the stronger qualities of a young nation? In what respects do older nations excel younger?

4. What does Lowell reveal about his own character by his manner of meeting the criticism of foreigners?

ON A CERTAIN CONDESCENSION IN
AMERICANS *

AGNES REPPLIER

AGNES REPPLIER began writing essays at the suggestion
of an editor of *The Catholic World,* to whom she had sub-
mitted short stories. His criticism of her fiction might well
have been applied to Montaigne's and Bacon's earliest essays: "transcripts of other people's books." That natural
tendency to draw pointed illustrations from the works of
others, much as the early writers of the *leçons morales,*
has characterized her thirteen volumes of essays; she
brings to the essay a rare combination of informality and
a respect for strictness of form. One is not always conscious, in reading her essays, of the underlying disciplined
progression of thought; her illustrations, while pointing
her own observations, always suggest by-paths. For years
readers of the *Atlantic Monthly* have considered Miss
Repplier's essays milestones in their reading. Born in
Philadelphia in 1858, of French parents, she was educated by French nuns at the Sacred Heart Convent of
Torresdale, Pennsylvania. *Our Convent Days* (1905), *Père
Marquette* (1929), and *Mère Marie of the Ursulines*
(1931) reflect her admiration for the forces that contributed to her early training. She is keenly interested in affairs of the day, and is always alert to detect and to decry false standards of thought and action. Miss Repplier

* Reprinted by permission of and special arrangement with
Houghton Mifflin Company, publishers.

has sometimes been called the foremost of living American essayists. "On a Certain Condescension in Americans" appeared in the *Atlantic Monthly* of May, 1926.

FIFTY-SEVEN years ago Mr. James Russell Lowell published in the *Atlantic Monthly* an urbanely caustic essay, "On a Certain Condescension in Foreigners." Despite discursiveness (it was a leisurely age), this *Apologia pro patria sua* [1] is a model of good temper, good taste, and good feeling. Its author regretted England's dislike for our accent, France's distaste for our food, and Germany's contempt for our music; but he did not suffer himself to be cast down. With a modesty past all praise, he even admitted, what no good American will admit to-day, that popular government "is no better than any other form except as the virtue and wisdom of the people make it so"; and that self-made men "may not be divinely commissioned to fabricate the higher qualities of opinion on all possible topics of human interest." Nevertheless he found both purpose and principle in the young nation, hammered into shape by four years of civil war. "One might be worse off than even in America," mused this son of Massachusetts; and we are instantly reminded of William James' softly breathed assurance: "A Yankee is also, in the last analysis, one of God's creatures."

Fifty-seven years are but a small fragment of time. Not long enough surely for the civilizations of Europe to decay, and the civilizations of the

United States to reach a pinnacle of splendor. Yet the condescension which Mr. Lowell deprecated, and which was based upon superiority of culture, seems like respectful flattery compared to the condescension which Americans now daily display, and which is based upon superiority of wealth. There has been no startling decline of European institutions, no magnificent upbuilding of our own; only a flow of gold from the treasuries of London, Paris, and Rome into the treasury of Washington. Germany's atavistic belief in the economic value of war, fruit of the evil seed sown in 1870, has been realized in a fashion which Germans least expected. England is impoverished in money and men. The casualties in the British army were over three million; the killed number six hundred and fifty-eight thousand. France is impoverished in money, men, and resources. A conscientious destruction of everything that might prove profitable if spared marked the progress of the invading Teutons. But the tide of wealth did not flow to Berlin. It leaped the sea, and filled the coffers of the nation that had provided the sinews of war, and that had turned the tide of victory.

Under these circumstances, the deep exhaustion of countries that have been struggling for life as a drowning man struggles for breath is hardly a matter of surprise. Cause and effect are too closely linked to need elucidation. When an American newspaper syndicate tells us that "Dr. Frank Crane [2] Explains Europe," we wonder how he comes to know more than the rest of us about it, until we find he doesn't.

"There is only one thing the matter with Europe," says "the man with a million friends"; "one root trouble from which all its difficulties spring. And the matter with Europe is that it has not yet learned to work and to love work. Europeans still idealize idleness. . . . What is happening now is that the people who are coming into power under the influence of democracy are getting tired of this sort of thing."

My only excuse for quoting these words is that they were written by an American adult, syndicated by American adults, and read by American adults, and that they may therefore be taken as representing one layer of the American adult mind. Now it is all very well for an ironical scientist, like Dr. Joseph Collins,[3] to intimate that there is no such thing as an American adult mind, and that the great body of the people think like children until they reach senility and cease thinking at all. The fact remains that nobody but a moron has any right to think like a child after he has ceased to be one. He goes on doing it because it is an easy, pleasant, and vastly self-sufficient thing for him to do. But the value of our thinking is the test of our civilization. If we apprehend the exact nature of our offering to the great depositories of human thought, we know where we stand in the orderly progress of the ages.

There does not seem to be much doubt on this

score in the mind (I must continue to use the word) of the average American. The *Atlantic Monthly* published, in February 1924, a paper by Mr. Langdon Mitchell on "The American Malady." The writer quoted a few lines from an editorial in the *Ladies' Home Journal,* August 1923. "There is only one first-class civilization in the world to-day. It is right here in the United States and the Dominion of Canada. Europe's is hardly second-class, and Asia's is about fourth- to sixth-class." I verified this quotation, finding it a little difficult to credit, and borrowed it for a lecture I was giving in New York. My audience took it at its face value, and cheerfully, I might say enthusiastically, applauded the sentiment. It was evident that to them it was a modest statement of an incontrovertible fact, and they registered their cordial agreement. They seemed—so far as I could apprehend them—to believe that we were, like the Jews, a chosen people, that our mission was the "uplift" of the human race, and that it behooved those who were to be uplifted to recognize their inferior altitude.

Is this an unusual frame of mind among educated Americans? Is it confined to Main Street,[4] or to those who cater with shameless solicitude to our national self-esteem? Where can we find a better spokesman for the race than Mr. Walter Hines Page,[5] a man to whom was given a hard and heartrending job, who did it superlatively well (even the animadversions of his critics are based upon the success of his activities), and who died in the doing of it, worn out, body and soul and mind, as if he had been shot to pieces in the trenches? Yet this able and representative American thought and said that Latin civilization was a negligible asset to the world. He could see little good in people who did not speak English, and no good at all in people who did not speak English or French. "Except the British and the French," he wrote to his son, Arthur Page, in December 1917, "there's no nation in Europe worth a tinker's damn when you come to the real scratch. The whole continent is rotten, or tyrannical, or yellow dog. I wouldn't give Long Island or Moore County for the whole of continental Europe."

It was a curious estimate of values. Long Island is a charming place, and very rich. Moore County is, I doubt not, one of the most beautiful tracts in a supremely beautiful state. Nevertheless, there are those who would think them dearly bought at the price of Rome. No one can truly say that Switzerland, Denmark, and Holland are rotten, or tyrannical, or yellow dog. Indeed Mr. Page admitted that the Danes were a free people, and that Switzerland was a true republic, but too small to count—a typically American ʻpoint of view. To interpret life in terms of size and numbers rather than in terms of intellect, beauty, and goodness is natural for a patriot who has more than three million square miles of country, and

over a hundred million countrymen. As Walt
Whitman lustily sang:—

> "I dote on myself—there is that lot of me, and
> all so luscious."

That Mr. Page clearly foresaw the wealth and
strength that would accrue to the United States
from the World War proves the keenness of his
vision. In 1914 he wrote to President Wilson:
"From an economic point of view, we *are* the
world; and from a political point of view also."
That he was sure this wealth and strength were
well placed proves the staunchness of his civic
pride. "In all the humanities, we are a thousand
years ahead of any people here," was his sum-
ming-up in a letter to Mr. Frank Doubleday,
1916. Even our reluctance to credit Prussia with
militarism showed the immaculate innocence of
our hearts. "There could be no better measure of
the moral advance that the United States has
made over Europe than the incredulity of our
people." Finally, in a burst of enthusiasm, or
sentiment, or perhaps homesickness, comes a
magnificent affirmation and elucidation of our
august pre-eminence: "God has yet made nothing
or anybody equal to the American people; and I
don't think He ever will or can." Which is a trifle
fettering to omnipotence.

Mr. Page's Americanism being what it was, I
cannot help thinking that his countrymen might
have more readily forgiven his admiration for the

admittedly inferior qualities of Great Britain. His regard for England was not wholly unlike the regard of the English for the United States in Mr. Lowell's day: a friendly feeling made friendlier by a definite and delightful consciousness of superiority. Ten months before the war, he wrote to President Wilson: "The future of the world belongs to us. . . . Now what are we going to do with this leadership when it falls into our hands? And how can we use the English for the highest uses of democracy?" [6]

The last sentence is a faultless expression of national condescension. It would have given Mr. Lowell as much entertainment as did the comments of his British acquaintances. I know nothing to put by its side, because it is so kindly meant. Our lordliness is, as a rule, a trifle more severe, tinged with reproof rather than sweetened with patronage. When the Locarno Conference progressed to its satisfactory conclusion without our help or hindrance, a leading American newspaper seized the opportunity (which was not a good opportunity) to assert our domination over Europe, and to remind her of the finality of our verdicts. If our President urged "international agreements," his words must be received outside the United States as "a warning that this government, as represented by Mr. Coolidge, will accept no excuse for war anywhere."

But why, in Heaven's name, should any European nation offer an excuse to Mr. Coolidge for anything it feels disposed to do? If it belongs to the League of Nations, and undertakes, however lamely, to go to war on its own account, excuses are in order, but not to Washington. Even in the World Court we share our rights and responsibilities with other Governments, and accept or reject excuses in accordance with the will of the majority.

II

The Locarno Treaty has, in fact, given us food for thought. It does not in any way impair our safety or our interests. We are as big and as strong and as rich as we were before. But it does show us that something can be accomplished without our controlling influence. Our help is needed in the reconstruction of battered Europe; but, while we can withhold it at pleasure, giving it does not warrant too sharp a tone of authority. A little boy, who has since grown into a distinguished man of letters, once stepped with deliberation into a pond and stood there, to the detriment of his health and of his shoes. An indignant aunt summoned him to dry land. The little boy, being well out of reach, remained water-logged and defiant. The aunt, indisposed to pursuit, said sternly: "Do you know what I do when youngsters refuse to obey me? I whip them." The little boy, aware of moral as well as of physical immunity, replied with decision:

"You don't vip other people's children, I presume." And neither, when it comes to the point, does the United States.

It is natural, though regrettable, that inferior nations, crowded together in Europe, which they have somehow contrived to make glorious and beautiful ("Thank God," cried Henry James, "for a world which holds so rich an England, so rare an Italy!"), should resent our presenting ourselves to them as an example. They have troubles and traditions of their own, inheritances great and grievous which reach back to

> . . . . old, unhappy, far-off things,
> And battles long ago.

They cannot wipe the slate clean, and begin afresh after a new and improved model. We keep on telling them (I quote now from recent American utterances) that our "accumulated heritage of spiritual blessings" is theirs to command; that our idealism "has made itself felt as a great contributory force to the advancement of mankind," and that "the Stars and Stripes are a harbinger of a new and happier day for the lesser nations of the world." We explain to them that we demand payment of their debts in order to maintain "the principle of the integrity of international obligations"; and that our connection with a World Court is in the nature of a public notice "that the enormous influences of our country are to be cast on the side of the enlightened processes of civilization." "Lord, gie us a guid conceit o' ourselves" is about the only prayer which the American has no need to utter.

If Europeans pay insufficient regard to our carefully catalogued virtues, Americans are far too deeply impressed by them. It is as demoralizing for a nation to feel itself an ethical exhibit as it is demoralizing for a young woman to win a beauty prize—by virtue of her nakedness—in an Atlantic City contest. The insult offered to our country by calling such a prize-winner "Miss America" is not greater than the insult offered to our country by calling every expansive wave of self-esteem "Americanism." If our civilization be "infinitely the best so far developed in the ages," we have all the less need to say so. If we are giving to the world "supreme grandeur in service," we can afford to be modest in calling attention to the fact. If we are, by virtue of precept and example, "working great changes in the spirit of international morality," it would be more self-respecting to give other nations a chance to express their unprodded appreciation and gratitude.

America has invested her religion as well as her morality in sound income-paying securities. She has adopted the unassailable position of a nation blessed because it deserves to be blessed; and her sons, whatever other theologies they may affect or disregard, subscribe unreservedly to this national creed. Scholars, men of letters, and the clergy lend it their seasonable support. Professor

Thomas Nixon Carver of Harvard, who has written a clear, forceful, and eminently readable book on *The Present Economic Revolution,* seems to have no shadow of doubt that our good fortune is due to our good behavior. "Prosperity is coming to us," he says, "precisely because our ideals are not materialistic. It is coming to us because we are pursuing the exalted ideal of equality under liberty, as it must of necessity come to any nation that pursues that ideal whole-heartedly and enthusiastically. . . . All these things are being added to us precisely because we are seeking the Kingdom of God and His righteousness, as they are always added, and must of logical necessity always be added, unto any nation that seeks those ideals of justice which are the very essence of the Kingdom of God."

I wonder if righteousness can be linked so securely to the elements of success; and if food and raiment—all that is promised in the Gospel—can be magnified into the colossal fortunes of America. The American may not be materialistic; but he has certainly hallowed commercialism, and made of it both a romantic and a moral adventure. He sings its saga at banquets, and he relates its conquests to his sons in magazines and in much-read books. There is great satisfaction in doing this, and we are told it is well done. If something be lacking in such a philosophy, that something is not missed. It is easy to count up the value of the proprieties in a watchful world;

but exceedingly hard to put the spiritual life on a paying basis. The Old Testament consistently taught that goodness and piety were rewarded with material well-being; but Christianity has committed itself to no such untenable proposition. "He that findeth his life shall lose it" sounds inconceivably remote from the contemplation of well-merited affluence.

III

A point of difference between the condescension of foreigners in 1869 and the condescension of Americans in 1926 is that the magniloquence which amused and ruffled Mr. Lowell was mainly spoken (he was in a position to hear it both at home and abroad), and the magniloquence which to-day ruffles without amusing sensitive foreigners and Americans is, as I have shown by liberal quotations, printed for all the reading world to see. An editorial in *Current Opinion* modestly suggests that "Europeans might learn a good deal if they would come over here, study the history of America since the war, and try to imitate our example. . . . We may be crass and uncultured; but at least we have been good sports, and have been honest enough, farsighted enough, and sagacious enough to render the United States the soundest and healthiest nation in the world to-day."

A "good sport" recognizes handicaps. He knows and he admits that poverty is not the equivalent of wealth, that dead men are not equal to live men, that ruined towns are less habitable than sound ones. A "good sport" may honestly believe that the one hope for mankind is "the Americanization of the world"; but he does not coarsely call on Europe to "clean up·and pay up"; he does not write with comprehensive ignorance: "Europeans will have to abandon their national vanities, and get together, before they can expect to get together with us"; he does not second the Congressman from Ohio who informed the American Chamber of Commerce in London that "right now the United States wants to see Europe do some housecleaning without delay." He may even venture a doubt when the Honorable David F. Houston,[7] writing ably and reasonably in *Harper's Magazine,* June 1924, affirms our superior spotlessness. "The United States," says Mr. Houston, "is in a position of leadership in all the fundamental idealistic, moral, and spiritual forces which make a nation great, and constitute a worthy civilization. It seeks as its highest aim to have a clean national household from cellar to attic."

Seeks it, yes. All civilized countries seek political integrity and justice in the administration of law. Sufficiency, security, and freedom are not the exclusive ideals of the United States. We may be as good as we are great, but our distaste for sincere and searching criticism blurs our national vision. A blustering, filibustering, narrow-minded Senate is not a source of legitimate pride. To lead the world in crime should be a source of legitimate humiliation. President Coolidge called the attention of the State Governors last January to the fact that twenty-four thousand persons had met their deaths by highway fatalities within twelve months. He said it was too many for one country in one year, and he was right. Yet twenty-four thousand deaths by accidents—are less appalling than eleven thousand deaths by violence in the same length of time. The combined numbers are worth the consideration of peace-loving Americans who write eloquently about the sacredness of life.

The crime waves in every State of the Union have now reached a stage of permanent inundation; and the ever-increasing youthfulness of criminals (the American Bar Association has called our attention to this point) promises more complete submersion in the future. It is gratifying to know that twenty-five million American children go to school every day; but some of them appear to spare time from their studies for the more exciting pursuits of robbery, housebreaking, and pathetically premature attempts at banditry, to say nothing of such higher flights as firing their schools and murdering their grandmothers. The *Ladies' Home Journal* has recently told us that "everywhere in Europe the ambitious youngsters of the new generation are learning English, and studying American geography and political history. They want to get the spirit of what American Democracy really is." We can but hope that these innocent offspring of effete civilizations will not extend their studies to American newspapers. If they do, they may give their backward countries an unexpected lesson in progress. In 1923, Scotland, with a population of five millions, had only eleven murders, while Massachusetts, with a population of four millions, could boast of one hundred and seven. It almost seems as if we could do a little housecleaning of our own.

The superiority complex is, however, as impervious to fact as to feeling. It denies the practical, it denies the intellectual, and it denies the spiritual. The Sorbonne and the Institut Pasteur make no more appeal to it than does the girl Jeanne d'Arc, or the defenders of Verdun. France as the inspiration of the artist, the stimulus of the thinker, the home of those who seek to breathe the keen air of human intelligence, is lost in the France that cannot stabilize the franc, or keep the peace in Syria. She is, in our eyes, a nation reprehensible because she demands the security which two oceans guarantee to us, and contemptible because she has failed to readjust herself after such calamities as we have never known.

What the American likes and respects is what he is happy enough to possess: efficiency, moral

uniformity, and a fairly good brand of standard-
ized thought. Conventions are the life and soul
of the country, and there is nothing like a convention (except perhaps a political campaign) for
making us think well of ourselves. The importunate virtues of small communities are nourished
by oratory, and by uplift-mongers on platforms,
and in the editorial columns of widely circulated
periodicals. Uplifting has become a vocation, and
its practitioners enjoy the esteem and gratitude
of the public. There is a poignantly funny description in one of William James' letters of a
lady, the wife of a Methodist minister, whom he
met at Chautauqua, who told him she had his
portrait hanging in her bedroom, and underneath
these words: "I want to bring balm to human
lives." "Supposed," said the horrified—and modest—philosopher, "to be a quotation from *me*."

Americanism has been defined as "the more or
less perfect expression of the common belief that
American ideals realize themselves in American
society." This belief is wholly disassociated from
the austere creed of the patriot. It was not patriotism which made foreigners in Mr. Lowell's day
so sure that they were conferring a favor on the
United States by visiting our shores. It is not
patriotism which makes Americans to-day so sure
that they are conferring a benefit on Europe by
advice and admonition, by bidding her study our
methods and imitate our example. There is an intellectual humility which is another name for

understanding. It enables us to measure the
depths of tragedies which have brought us no
personal pain, and the height of supremacies
which have failed to arouse our ambitions. It is
the key to history, and the open-sesame to the
hearts of men. It may even come as close to de-
ciphering the mysterious ways of God as the complete assurance that we are His deservedly
favorite children.

It takes a great deal to make an enjoyable
world. It takes all we have to give to make a
world morally worthy of man. Efficiency is an
asset; but, without a well-balanced emotional life,
it gets us no further than the door of human happiness. Peace and wealth are serviceable possessions; but only intense personalities can create
art and letters. Good-will, which Santayana [8] says
is the great American virtue, shines like a lamp;
but even good-will must be intelligently directed
if it is to light up the dark places of the earth;
and the dark places of the earth are not confined
to other continents than ours. The desire to taste
the pleasure of contrast—which is a cruel delight
—has disposed us to ignore those things which
may be conceived as lowering us to our neighbor's level. "In judging others," says the wise and
singularly ironic a-Kempis,[9] "a man usually toileth
in vain. For the most part he is mistaken, and he
easily sinneth. But in judging and scrutinizing
himself he always laboureth with profit."

Notes

[1] Apology for his country.

[2] Frank Crane's editorials were syndicated in all the newspapers owned or controlled by William Randolph Hearst.

[3] Author of *A Doctor Looks at Literature, A Doctor Looks at Biography,* etc.; writes about cultural subjects from a scientist's point of view.

[4] *Main Street,* a study of small-town life, by Sinclair Lewis, is one of the landmarks in American fiction. Lewis has been a storm center for years because of his criticism of American folk ways, and has exerted a powerful influence on contemporary thought.

[5] American Ambassador to England during the war. His published letters, edited by Burton J. Hendrick, were a best seller.

[6] See Gilbert Murray's essay "Satanism and the World Order" for the English point of view on this subject.

[7] Formerly professor of political science at Harvard University, President of the University of Texas, Secretary of Agriculture and, later, of the Treasury in the Cabinet of President Wilson.

[8] George Santayana, former professor of philosophy at Harvard University, and a poet of distinction.

[9] Thomas à Kempis (1380–1471), author of *The Imitation of Christ.*

Questions

1. How would you compare Miss Repplier's judgment of Americans with that of James Truslow Adams?

2. How much of this national weakness can be traced to the attitudes of individuals like ourselves?

3. Point out the relation between Miss Repplier's reference to James Russell Lowell's essay "On a Certain Condescension in Foreigners" and Montaigne's use of the old *leçon morale*.

4. What parts of this essay reflect Miss Repplier's reading?

5. What elements has this essay in common with James Truslow Adams' "The Mucker Pose"?

6. What, according to Miss Repplier, are the virtues of Americans? What are the shortcomings?

CULTURE AT DINNER *

STARK YOUNG

Through a curious mischance in the animal kingdom, STARK YOUNG graduated from college earlier than he expected. When he was fourteen, the well at the little school in Como, Mississippi, where he was born in 1881, became contaminated through a pig's falling into it. The school was forthwith closed, and those students who could pass the entrance requirements at the University of Mississippi without further study were allowed to do so. Stark Young did it. Graduated from the University in 1901, he studied further at Columbia University and taught in several schools in the South, traveling to Italy summers until the Great War broke out. His *The Three Fountains*, inimitable sketches of life and travel in Italy, is a by-product of these annual pilgrimages. For six years he taught English at Amherst College and in 1921 joined the staff of *The New Republic*, to which he has since contributed articles on the drama and kindred subjects. His *The Flower in Drama* is perhaps the nearest to a classic among modern books on the current theater and drama. To date, Young has written one volume of poems, four volumes of essays, three plays, three novels, and one volume of short stories. "Culture at Dinner", here presented, is representative of his treatment of the personal essay with its gentle reflection of the personality of others, as well as of his own.

---

* From *The Three Fountains;* copyright 1924, by Charles Scribner's Sons. By the permission of the publishers.

IT WAS early twilight just before the dinner hour when I went into the garden and saw him there. He was standing by the wall, with one hand resting on it, looking out across the Fontebranda at the Duomo,[1] whose black and white spaces now were buried in shadow and golden light. He was a young man, twenty perhaps, almost tall, fair, with a white, sensitive face that had long been beautiful with an intense ideal of living. I could see that as I stood in the doorway looking at him. And I could see also a hint of confusion somewhere about the eyes, a kind of glorious blur, a touch of the vagueness that might be in the face of a sort of academic young saint. He looked strong, athletic; but one of those strong Anglo-Saxon bodies that any fine dream can blow away. Plato, Francis Thompson, I figured, and perhaps the choruses of Aeschylus, would be his favorite reading.

He told me, when we fell into a conversation, that he had finished college, Yale, great old place, that spring. And now travelling? Yes, with rather a definite purpose. He had felt the limitations of his education; he felt that he needed more horizon. That he had talked and studied and been lectured to about so many things that were still all in his head and meant nothing as a part of his real development. He wanted an international quality added to what he had. Not so much study and art perhaps, but seeing people, social contacts. And to see the things of Europe through the eyes of people, of men and women. And so he thought it would be a good thing to come to a *pension* [2] like this, where he might be on more direct terms with a group of people that hailed from all parts of the world. In a hotel it might take longer or never happen. He meant to visit in this way a number of *pensions*.

He had what he meant clear at least. I stood there listening with a sinking heart, for I was going over the list of guests who sat at our board just then. Perhaps this young seeker after culture had his own vision that he had brought with him and was ready to throw it over anything. But in case he had not, what then? The people who were to be at the table began to pass before me in the light of those young eyes I looked into.

The best of the lot was Signorina dell'Orto, and even at that my young friend would have to learn to know her. She was a new note ahead of him, that was true; but he would have to stretch for it. Signorina dell'Orto was a short little woman of fifty, who wore a short plain skirt, a man's collar and coat and cravat, and pulled her hair straight back. After meals in the drawing-room she smoked a cheroot. She was very intelligent, and had been the tutor for the Czarina and for German and aristocratic families for twenty years before the war. She had been interned in Italy for a year on account of her free speech on the subject of the Allies. And for a Florentine she was unusually abrupt.

With her was her friend, a Miss Holtz, of twenty years' standing, as Miss Holtz loved to say, very German, long, tall, with prominent teeth. Between forty and fifty. Musical, rather maidenly, and flat.

At the head of the table sat a New York artist, with clear sharp features and white hair, alert, cool, like a cameo steeped in vinegar. Besides her were two Englishwomen in shirt waists who never said anything. Next to them came the young scion of a very old Roman house; but though he dressed very smartly, he had at the time a cracked head in a bandage, where a Socialista had hit him with a stone during the last riot. He too said nothing, but ate in silence. At the Roman's right sat Miss Ross from Birmingham, who ate almost nothing but biscuits which she brought with her to the table. She was one of those English daughters who have been slaves to noble, aged fathers; but he was dead now and she was left with an income, a dozen photographs of him, and several rings that he had given her on occasions. If she had been a little less simple and dull and crotchety, one might have blamed the father more for having blotted her out so completely. But she was a gentle creature who was always trying to divide her English jam and tea with someone whether it was wanted or not. There was, besides, an Italian doctor who was about to marry, and who had such strict views on the position of women that he had engaged an extra room upstairs where he and his wife were to dine apart from the men at the table. He believed on the whole in the harem system more or less, and said that women should be locked in, which enraged the New York artist and the English ladies to outbursts that were fortunately beyond their supply of Italian.

And finally, all the way round the table, at the artist's left, came Professor and Mrs. Jurden, from one of the two great universities of England. Professor Jurden was a very tall man, sallow, and very hesitant in his speech. He spoke so slowly in fact that his wife used to tap him on the back to get him through it, in spite of his saying always, "Darling, how often have I asked you not to do that?" He had served in India in some sort of forestry work, and during the war in South France hospitals, where he had won a number of small bronze medals, but had completely ruined his health. He spoke in a smothered voice with very impure vowels, and always as if his teeth were sagging and he feared to lose them if he left off holding down his upper lip. His wife was tall, thin, and wore her hair with a front of curls. She spoke in a voice that she considered to be very soft and elegant, though as a matter of fact it had lost all its bottom tone and sounded all breath. She and her husband disapproved of Italian cooking, exactly as they regarded Italians as cheats and liars, and went in for a vegetarian diet. At every meal she appeared at the table bringing cheese and a quantity of green stuff, lettuce, parsley, cress, and so on. Outside their rooms I used to see sometimes in the morning a waste paper basket filled with strange leaves and stalks for the maid to carry away, as if they kept asses or goats privately in their quarters, or were some secret creatures that browsed at night on plants and herbs.

I passed these guests of the *pension* through my mind in review as I stood listening to that boy from Yale with his beautiful face and fine dreams. I wondered what the dinner might be, as I thought of what it had too often been.

A long golden shaft of light was falling on the wall of the room when we took our seats at the table. It struck the old faded walls and touched the yellow hair of the new-comer, who had been assigned a place between Miss Ross and the Roman. But the golden sunbeam proved no good augury, as I had hoped; for the dinner began impossibly from the first course. Spinach and eggs, but not enough of it. There was never quite enough of anything, which was the incentive that kept us all exact in our knowledge of what every-one there ate. The artist, out of pure vexation at the sight of the small quantity of food, took twice as much as she wanted. The Roman, when his turn came, emptied the dish. "Was there more?" Mrs. Jurden asked. Maria, the maid, who was stupid and afraid of her mistress too, said that she did not know. Complaints arose. Maria returned with another platter one-fourth full. She brought a dish of sliced salami [3] to patch out. Dell'Orto said scathing things, for she knew the *padrona's* [4] wiles. To change the tone of the occasion, for my countryman's sake, I asked Professor Jurden how his Italian lessons were coming.

"But I am not taking lessons," he replied. "My wife is having them. I have a method I have devised for myself."

"What is that?" I asked, for I was having strenuous discipline under a priest, the author of a grammar.

"I am translating Shakespeare into Italian. I figure that way I'll get a good vocabulary as well as learning the language in my own way."

"To begin with Shakespeare without knowing any Italian!" I exclaimed, astonished. I asked only, "And are you putting it into verse also?"

"How do you mean?"

"I mean, are you trying to reproduce the verse of the original?"

Professor Jurden looked at me puzzled for a moment. His wife tapped his back.

"Darling, I asked you not to do that. Why, is the original in verse?" he asked, turning to me.

"Why, yes," I answered, "how do you mean?" I thought that there must be something that I had missed in his question.

"I didn't know that Shakespeare's plays were in verse."

"But of course not *all* of it is in verse," I helped

out, like a foolish, good American; "a good many of the speeches are in prose."

"Ah, that's probably why I never noticed it."

I looked at my idealist; he kept his eyes on his plate.

"I find Italian exceedingly easy," Mrs. Jurden observed; "I regard my progress as most encouraging."

At this the Signorina dell'Orto, who hated the Jurdens, turned to them. She understood some English but could not speak a word.

"*Cosa dice?*" [5] she asked encouragingly.

Mrs. Jurden undertook to put into Italian her ideas about the easy progress one made in the language. Her remarks were, in the main, pauses and incredible mistakes, but the Signorina was able to gather the general idea. Her face flushed red.

"Oh yes," she began in a great, man's voice, "the Italians will tell you that you are speaking very well. Don't believe them. I am always bored at these lies. A foreigner murders our language; but an Italian will say, 'Ah, you speak very well; you speak very well.'" She imitated the tone. "Well, I don't do it, I assure you. You just let an Italian go to England or Germany and you'll see. If he tries to ask a question in English, they're so stupid they don't understand a word of it. They just look and say Baa, like fools." The Signorina made a sound like a sheep and twisted her head to one side. "Italians are too polite. It makes me furious."

"What a temper they have!" Mrs. Jurden said to the New Yorker.

"Well," I thought, with my young dreamer in my heart, "he is learning. So much for cosmopolitan culture and politeness."

The Signorina dell'Orto was cooling somewhat now, for Mrs. Jurden began to make conciliations and to smile down from under that front of faded curls, but the Signorina had not yet finished what she had to say.

"The difficulty in English is the pronunciation, which is so unintelligent. There is no way of learning it except as one does in a nursery, by hearing it. No rules, no anything but individual cases. How does one use one's mind in such an affair? And the grammar, well it's simple enough for a child in arms. Italian has a grammar. Difficult, yes; but intelligent. It demands intelligence to create and to use Italian grammar. You have no grammar in English."

Miss Ross looked up with no little asperity, for her.

"I'm sure I don't know what she means by that," she said sharply, "I had a very good grammar."

The nature of this remark was so weak that even Mrs. Jurden saw it. A silence fell and lasted through the salad. Finally the New York artist, to improve the quality of the occasion, spoke to the young man.

"I'm sure you will find many delightful walks around Siena," she said. "Only this morning I was at San Francesco. The altar piece there is very interesting."

"I expect to find Siena very interesting," he replied in a conventional tone.

"And," Miss Ross added, gently, "there are two charming walks, one near Fontebranda and one toward Girasole. They are quite my favorites. I always take them. They are so like English lanes. Really Italy is lovely, isn't it?"

I had no wish to look into the eyes of the Yale lad; but I stole a glance as we rose from the table. He was smiling bravely, trying to find his way through this new cosmopolitan world that he had been dreaming such fine things about. The Signorina had taken out her cheroot and led the way to the drawing-room. I lingered a moment over my Vin Santo and then stole away up the little side stair to my room.

Through the closed shutters I could see the boy standing again by the wall. His hand rested on it and his face was turned toward the Cathedral, on which one last light rested now, at the very top. I had not enough courage to join him. But I stood there hoping that he was one of those impenetrable idealists on whom the world makes no dents, who are never willing to believe that the actual can be true. Still the fact remained that the international culture at that dinner-table had been rather actual. But, I thought, with Francis Thompson in my mind, the chambers in the house of dreams are filled with so divine an air that it would be a pity for these moths, however cosmopolitan, to get in. Or at least the first lesson might have been less stringent and wholesale. *L'idéal n'est que la vérité à distance*,[6] I knew from Lamartine. But how far? At how far distant must the ideal be?

But as I stood there with my head against the shutter, meditating, I saw Mrs. Jurden appear and engage him in conversation.

"Look, just look, do you see?" she said. "The light on the Duomo, how charming it is. I should call it yellow, would you? No, not exactly yellow. Well, orange. A sort of greyish orange. There, just at the top, do you see? How romantic Italy is! Are you going to stay long? Of course one longs for England. But we must have the change of climate. Look, do you see? I can't say I like the stripes in the Duomo, do you?"

Mrs. Jurden had fallen into that particular brand of scenic monologue that English ladies sometimes indulge. I saw the face of the boy turned quietly toward the Cathedral above the shadows of the Fontebranda. He was getting architecture through her eyes.

NOTES

[1] Duomo, the cathedral.
[2] pension—a private boarding-house.

³ salami—sausage.
⁴ padrona—the woman keeping the boarding-house.
⁵ Cosa dice—"Say something"—or "Shall we talk?"
⁶ The ideal is only the real seen from a distance.

QUESTIONS

1. What connection have some of these characters with Crothers' "Every Man's Natural Desire to Be Somebody Else"?
2. Who do you think gets the more out of life—the idealist or the realist?
3. Link this essay with Hazlitt's "On Going a Journey."

THE PRECEPT OF PEACE

Louise Imogen Guiney

LOUISE IMOGEN GUINEY, one of the most brilliant of American poets and essayists, was born in Roxbury, Massachusetts in 1861. Her earliest recollections were centered about the Civil War, in which her father served as a Colonel and later as General. At the age of five she visited him at his headquarters in the Union lines. Her early schooling was forced upon her; her abhorrence of it was so great that her teachers sometimes had to tie her to her chair. At eleven she was sent to Elmhurst, Providence, Rhode Island, to the Convent of the Sacred Heart. Determined not to like convents any better than public schools, she went equipped with a toy gun and a plentiful supply of agate marbles for ammunition. Mother Samuella Shaw soon won her over, however, by her sincerity and naturalness, and made her six years' stay in the school among the most contented of her life. Throughout her stay Louise Guiney was the leader of games and the editor of the school literary magazine. Later, while Postmistress at Auburndale, Massachusetts, working to support her widowed mother, she won a reputation as poet and essayist, and enjoyed the company and friendship of Longfellow, Emerson, Hawthorne, Holmes, Whittier, and other literary figures of the day. A growing interest in seventeenth-century English poets led to her leaving America for intensive scholastic work at Oxford. There she won an equally brilliant and select group of literary friends. Miss Guiney died in Oxford, in 1924. The biographies of her by Alice

Brown and by E. M. Tenison throw interesting light upon one of the rarest spirits in American literature. "The Precept of Peace" is taken from *Patrins,* which appeared in 1897.

A CERTAIN sort of voluntary abstraction is the oldest and choicest of social attitudes. In France, where all esthetic discoveries are made, it was crowned long ago: *la sainte indifférence* [1] is, or may be, a cult, and *le saint indifférent* an articled practitioner. For the Gallic mind, brought up at the knee of a consistent paradox, has found that not to appear concerned about a desired good is the only method to possess it; full happiness is given, in other words, to the very man who will never sue for it. This is a secret neat as that of the Sphinx: to "go softly" among events, yet domineer them. Without fear: not because we are brave, but because we are exempt; we bear so charmed a life that not even Baldur's mistletoe [2] can touch us to harm us. Without solicitude: for the essential thing is trained, falcon-like, to light from above upon our wrists, and it has become with us an automatic motion to open the hand, and drop what appertains to us no longer. Be it renown or a new hat, the shorter stick of celery, or

> "The friends to whom we had no natural right,
>   The homes that were not destined to be ours,"

it is all one: let it fall away! since only so, by depletions, can we buy serenity and a blithe mien.

It is diverting to study, at the feet of Antisthenes and of Socrates [3] his master, how many indispensables man can live without; or how many he can gather together, make over into luxuries, and so abrogate them. Thoreau [4] somewhere expresses himself as full of divine pity for the "mover" who on May-Day clouds city streets with his melancholy household caravans: fatal *impedimenta* [5] for an immortal. No: furniture is clearly a superstition. "I have little, I want nothing; all my treasure is in Minerva's tower." Not that the novice may not accumulate. Rather, let him collect beetles and Venetian interrogation-marks; if so be that he may distinguish what is truly extrinsic to him, and bestow these toys, eventually, on the children of Satan who clamor at the monastery gate. Of all his store, unconsciously increased, he can always part with sixteen-seventeenths, by way of concession to his individuality, and think the subtraction so much concealing marble chipped from the heroic figure of himself. He would be a donor from the beginning; before he can be seen to own, he will disencumber, and divide. Strange and fearful is his discovery, amid the bric-a-brac of the world, that this knowledge, or this material benefit, is for him alone. He would fain beg off from the acquisition, and shake the touch of the tangible from his imperious wings. It is not enough to cease to strive for personal favor; your true *indifférent* is Early Franciscan: caring not to have, he fears to hold.

Things useful need never become to him things desirable. Towards all commonly-accounted sine-cures, he bears the coldest front in Nature, like a magician walking a maze, and scornful of its flower-bordered detentions. "I enjoy life," says Seneca,[6] "because I am ready to leave it." Meanwhile, they who act with too jealous respect for their morrow of civilized comfort, reap only indigestion, and crow's-foot traceries for their deluded eye-corners.

Now nothing is farther from *le saint indifférent* than cheap indifferentism, so-called: the sickness of sophomores. His business is to hide, not to display, his lack of interest in fripperies. It is not he who looks languid, and twiddles his thumbs for sick misplacedness, like Achilles among girls. On the contrary, he is a smiling industrious elf, monstrous attentive to the canons of polite society. In relation to others, he shows what passes for animation and enthusiasm: for at all times his character is founded on control of these qualities, not on the absence of them. It flatters his sense of superiority that he may thus pull wool about the ears of joint and several. He has so strong a will that it can be crossed and counter-crossed, as by himself, so by a dozen outsiders, without a break in his apparent phlegm. He has gone through volition, and come out at the other side of it; everything with him is a specific act: he has no habits. *Le saint indifférent* is a dramatic wight: he loves to refuse your proffered six per cent, when, by a little haggling, he may obtain three-and-a-half. For so he gets away with his own mental processes virgin: it is inconceivable to you that, being sane, he should so comport himself. Amiable, perhaps, only by painful propulsions and sore vigilance, let him appear the mere inheritor of easy good-nature. Unselfish out of sheer pride, and ever eager to claim the slippery side of the pavement, or the end cut of the roast (on the secret ground, be it understood, that he is not as Capuan men, who wince at trifles), let him have his ironic reward in passing for one whose physical connoisseurship is yet in the raw. That sympathy which his rule forbids his devoting to the usual objects, he expends, with some bravado, upon their opposites; for he would fain seem a decent partizan of some sort, not what he is, a bivalve intelligence, Tros Tyriusque.[7] He is known here and there, for instance, as valorous in talk; yet he is by nature a solitary, and, for the most part, somewhat less communicative than

> "The wind that sings to himself as he makes stride,
> Lonely and terrible, on the Andean height."

Imagining nothing idler than words in the face of grave events, he condoles and congratulates with the genteelest air in the world. In short, while there is anything expected of him, while there are spectators to be fooled, the stratagems of the fellow prove inexhaustible. It is only when he is

quite alone that he drops his jaw, and stretches
his legs; then heigho! arises like a smoke, and
envelopes him becomingly, the beautiful native
well-bred torpidity of the gods, of poetic bore-
dom, of "the Oxford manner."

"How weary, stale, flat, and unprofitable!"
sighed Hamlet of this mortal outlook. As it came
from him in the beginning, that plaint, in its sincerity, can come only from the man of culture,
who feels about him vast mental spaces and
depths, and to whom the face of creation is but
comparative and symbolic. Nor will he breathe
it in the common ear, where it may woo misap-
prehensions, and breed ignorant rebellion. The
unlettered must ever love or hate what is nearest
him, and, for lack of perspective, think his own
fist the size of the sun. The social prizes, which,
with mellowed observers, rank as twelfth or thirteenth in order of desirability, such as wealth and
a foothold in affairs, seem to him first and sole;
and to them he clings like a barnacle. But to our
indifférent, nothing is so vulgar as close suction.
He will never tighten his fingers on loaned opportunity; he is a gentleman, the hero of the habitually relaxed grasp. A light unprejudiced hold on
his profits strikes him as decent and comely,
though his true artistic pleasure is still in "fallings
from us, vanishings." It costs him little to loose
and to forego, to unlace his tentacles, and from
the many who push hard behind, to retire, as it
were, on a never-guessed-at competency, "richer

than untempted kings." He would not be a life-
prisoner, in ever so charming a bower. While the
tranquil Sabine Farm [8] is his delight, well he
knows that on the dark trail ahead of him, even
Sabine Farms are not sequacious. Thus he learns
betimes to play the guest under his own cedars,
and, with disciplinary intent, goes often from
them; and, hearing his heart-strings snap the
third night he is away, rejoices that he is again
a freedman. Where his foot is planted (though it
root not anywhere), he calls that spot home. No
Unitarian in locality, it follows that he is the best
of travelers, tangential merely, and pleased with
each new vista of the human Past. He sometimes
wishes his understanding less, that he might itch
deliciously with a prejudice. With cosmic con-
gruities, great and general forces, he keeps, all
along, a tacit understanding, such as one has with
beloved relatives at a distance; and his finger,
airily inserted in his outer pocket, is really upon
the pulse of eternity. His vocation, however, is
to bury himself in the minor and immediate task;
and from his intent manner, he gets confounded,
promptly and permanently, with the victims of
commercial ambition.

The true use of the much-praised Lucius Cary,
Viscount Falkland,[9] has hardly been appre-
hended: he is simply the patron saint of *indiffér-
ents*. From first to last, almost alone in that discordant time, he seems to have heard far-off
resolving harmonies, and to have been rapt away

with foreknowledge. Battle, to which all knights were bred, was penitential to him. It was but a childish means: and to what end? He meanwhile —and no man carried his will in better abeyance to the scheme of the universe—wanted no diligence in camp or council. Cares sat handsomely on him who cared not at all, who won small comfort from the cause which his conscience finally espoused. He labored to be a doer, to stand well with observers; and none save his intimate friends read his agitation and profound weariness. "I am so much taken notice of," he writes, "for an impatient desire for peace, that it is necessary I should likewise make it appear how it is not out of fear for the utmost hazard of war." And so, driven from the ardor he had to the simulation of the ardor he lacked, loyally daring, a sacrifice to one of two transient opinions, and inly impartial as a star, Lord Falkland fell: the young never-to-be-forgotten martyr of Newburg field. The imminent deed he made a work of art; and the station of the moment the only post of honor. Life and death may be all one to such a man: but he will at least take the noblest pains to discriminate between Tweedledum and Tweedledee, if he has to write a book about the variations of their antennae. And like the Carolian exemplar is the disciple. The *indifférent* is a good thinker, or a good fighter. He is no "immartial minion," as dear old Chapman [10] suffers Hector to call Tydides. Nevertheless, his sign-manual is content with humble and stagnant conditions. Talk of scaling the Himalayas of life affects him, very palpably, as "tall talk." He deals not with things, but with the impressions and analogies of things. The material counts for nothing with him; he has moulted it away. Not so sure of the identity of the higher course of action as he is of his consecrating dispositions, he feels that he may make heaven again, out of sundries, as he goes. Shall not a beggarly duty, discharged with perfect temper, land him in "the out-courts of Glory," quite as successfully as a grand Sunday-school excursion to front the cruel Paynim foe? He thinks so. Experts have thought so before him. Francis Drake,[11] with the national alarum instant in his ears, desired first to win at bowls, on the Devon sward, "and afterwards to settle with the Don." No one will claim a buccaneering hero for an *indifférent,* however. The Jesuit novices were ball-playing almost at that very time, three hundred years ago, when some too speculative companion, figuring the end of the world in a few moments (with just leisure enough, between, to be shriven in chapel, according to his own thrifty mind), asked Louis of Gonzaga [12] how he, on his part, should employ the precious interval. "I should go on with the game," said the most innocent and most ascetic youth among them. But to cite the behavior of any of the saints is to step over the playful line allotted. Indifference of the mundane brand is not to be confounded with their detachment, which is emancipation wrought in the soul, and the ineffable efflorescence of the Christian spirit. Like most supernatural virtues, it has a laic shadow; the counsel to abstain, and to be unsolicitous, is one not only of perfection, but also of polity. A very little nonadhesion to common affairs, a little reserve of unconcern, and the gay spirit of sacrifice, provide the moral immunity which is the only real estate. The *indifférent* believes in storms: since tales of shipwreck encompass him. But once among his own kind, he wonders that folk should be circumvented by merely extraneous powers! His favorite catch, woven in among escaped dangers, rises through the roughest weather, and daunts it:

> "Now strike your sailes, ye jolly mariners,
>   For we be come into a quiet rode."

No slave to any vicissitude, his imagination is, on the contrary, the cheerful obstinate tyrant of all that is. He lives, as Keats once said of himself, "in a thousand worlds," withdrawing at will from one to another, often curtailing his circumference to enlarge his liberty. His universe is a universe of balls, like those which the cunning Oriental carvers make out of ivory; each entire surface perforated with the same delicate pattern, each moving prettily and inextricably within the other, and all but the outer one impossible to handle. In some such innermost asylum the right sort of dare-devil sits smiling, while men rage or weep.

NOTES

¹ saintly indifference; so called, probably, because those who have become Saints were notably indifferent to saintliness, and thought only of serving others.

² Baldur, or Balder, son of Odin in the old Norse Mythology. He was killed by a shaft of mistletoe, the only thing on earth by which he could be harmed. For the story of Baldur see Frazer's *The Golden Bough*.

³ Antisthenes (about 400 B.C.), was an Athenian cynic, a pupil of Socrates (469–399 B.C.), the philosopher and teacher whose influence dominated Greek thought for centuries.

⁴ Henry David Thoreau (1817–1862), member of the Concord, Massachusetts, group of philosophers, essayists, and poets, and advocate of the return to simple living. See page 513.

⁵ *impedimenta*—baggage.

⁶ Seneca (died A.D. 65), was a Stoic philosopher and playwright.

⁷ Trojan and Tyrian both.

⁸ A Sabine Farm was the retreat of Quintus Horatius Flaccus, Latin satirical poet, who celebrated it in his poetry.

⁹ Lucius Cary, Viscount Falkland (1610–1643), an English gentleman-warrior whose life was typical of the ideal *saint indifférent*.

¹⁰ George Chapman (1559?–1634), English poet and translator of Homer's *Iliad* and *Odyssey*.

¹¹ Francis Drake (1540–1596), English admiral who scourged the Spanish Armada for Queen Elizabeth.

¹² Louis of Gonzaga, one of the younger sons of a princely Italian family named after the town where they lived. Unlike the older brothers, who followed business and politics, Louis chose the more peaceful life of the Church.

QUESTIONS

1. How does Miss Guiney differ from Montaigne, Bacon, Agnes Repplier in the use of her reading? How does her essay differ from the old *leçon morale?*

2. What is the distinction between indifference and *in-différence?*

3. How far may this precept of peace be applied to other desired ends?

4. Summarize the precept of peace briefly in one sentence.

FIVE INCHES *

A. P. HERBERT

A. P. HERBERT is far from being merely the editor of the humorous London *Punch*. His interest in economic and social questions has made him one of the outstanding periodical writers in England today. In his novel *The Secret Battle* he presents a bitter arraignment of stupidity in high military circles as well as a harrowing tale of a friend who lost the secret battle between bravery and fear. This essay, from his *Little Rays of Moonshine*, is characteristic of the more serious side of one who is undeniably one of England's best humorists.

THEY came and split a turkey with us on Boxing Day,[1] ten old soldiers, all out of a job, and only ten legs between them. At least there were only ten real legs; two of them had admirable imitation ones, and there were sixteen excellent crutches. One of them was a miner—*was*, of course; just now he is not mining much; perhaps that is why he seemed such a decent fellow, not at all violent or unpleasant, as one knows those practising miners are. In fact he reminded one of the miners one used to have in one's platoon. Per-

---

* Reprinted from *Little Rays of Moonshine* by A. P. Herbert by permission of and special arrangement with Alfred A. Knopf, Inc., authorized publishers.

sonally I had the honour to have a whole platoon of them. Odd, isn't it, what capital fellows they were then, and how sadly they deteriorate when they get back to the mines? And it was odd, too, to hear this fellow say that he wished he could be back in the pits; I thought it was such a hateful and dangerous occupation.

Yes, he was a nice miner, and so were the rest of them, very cheerful and respectful. But they didn't talk much—at first. It was strangely difficult to find a safe subject. A few years ago there would have been no difficulty; one would have talked war-shop. "Were you ever at Ypres?" "I was on Gallipoli." "Did you know Captain ——?" and so on. We did a little of this, but it didn't go very well.

In the dining-room I keep a large coloured photograph of the top of the Vimy Ridge on the day of a battle—you know the sort of thing, a hideous expanse of broken brown earth, that dreadful endless brown, with walls of smoke all round the horizon, shells bursting in the middle distance, a battered trench in the foreground, with a few scattered men climbing out of it, gazing at the camera with expressionless faces, stretcher-bearers stooping on the parapet with their stretchers on their shoulders, odd men straying everywhere like lost sheep across the chocolate wilderness, looking aimless, looking small.

Our guests were interested in that picture; it was wonderfully *like*, they said; but I felt that my usual remark about it was hardly suitable. Usually I tell my guests, and it is true, that I keep the picture as a kind of chastener, so that, when I am moved to complain at the troubles of this world, I can look at the picture and think, "At any rate life is better than it was then—" It was on the tip of my tongue to say so to the one-legged men when it came to me that for them, perhaps, at the moment, it wasn't true.

After the turkey and the pudding and the crackers, and of course the beer, there was a slight thaw, but it was still very difficult. We tried to get them to sing. Only a few years ago how easy it was. There was "Tipperary" and many another rousing chorus. One was familiar in those times with the popular songs of the day. Unfortunately these were the only songs we could produce now. And they didn't suit. "Keep the Home-fires Burning," for instance—one didn't like to suggest that. The chief minstrel of the one-legged men, who was also the chief comedian, disinterred from a heap of old music, "Your King and Country Need You." "How would that go, Bert?" he said. He said it without bitterness, I don't know why; and Bert's answer was a silent grin, and one felt that Bert was right. "Pack up your Troubles in your old Kit-bag," "Till the Boys Come Home"—all the old titles had a certain ironic underlining in that company.

So we abandoned singing and we sat rather silent. There was some desultory conversation

about the various "trades" to which a grateful
State had trained them, and left it at that; there
was some mild chaff of Bill, who had been too
old (at thirty-five) to be trained at all, though
not too old to learn musketry and lose a leg; but
socially one felt the "party" was drifting to
disaster.

It was saved, like many parties, by "shop,"
and not war-shop, at least not exactly. What sort
of shop will amuse ten one-legged men? Why,
one-legged shop, of course. Somebody said, "Is
your leg comfortable?" and that set the ball rolling. All the tongues wagged gleefully at once; all
the technical details of one-leggedness, all the
points of the various kind of "legs", were brought
out and tossed about and hotly contested as if we
had been a number of golfers arguing the merits
of different makes of putters. Some of us wear
"stump-socks"; some of us can't stand the things.
Some of us have "buckets" (graphically described) which we can comfortably pad, and some
of us have something else not nearly so good.
Some of us are excited about the new "aluminum"
legs, four pounds lighter, which are soon to be
available, though we think it a terrible waste of
money now that we have most of us got wooden
ones. Here is a chance for the "economising" cam-
paigners! Now then, Lord Rothermere,[2] "No
Aluminum Legs!" What a war-cry! Altogether it
is an enthralling topic; there is no more awkwardness. . . .

And it is so amusing. Gad, how we laughed! There was the story of the man on the Underground,[3] a friend of ours. Someone trod on his false foot in the crowded train and, scrambling out in a hurry at a station, he found himself footless on the platform, while the train slid away with the other fellow still standing on his foot. Ha, ha! how we laughed.

But most of us are "above the knee," and that provides the best joke of all. You see it all depends on the length of your stump (or "stoomp"). If you have five inches left, you get an eighty per cent pension; if you have more, you get less— even if it is only five and a quarter. That quarter of an inch makes all the difference, financially, though practically it isn't a great deal of use. How much have *you* got? Ah, you're unlucky. I'm four and three-quarters—a near thing, eh? Peals of laughter. "You go back and have another inch off. Ho, ho, ho!" We roll about in our chairs.

Well, well, it's a queer world; but the party was a great success after all.

NOTES

[1] Boxing Day, the day after Christmas; in England a legal holiday on which Christmas boxes, or gifts, or annual tips are given to postmen, errand boys, dustmen (ash removers), etc.

[2] Harold Sidney Harmsworth (1868–   ), Air Minister during the War, and owner of the *London Daily Mail* and allied chains of newspapers in England.

[3] Underground—the subway. See H. L. Mencken's essay on "The General Character of the American Lan-

guage" for further differences between usage here and in England.

QUESTIONS

1. What is gained by presenting humor and sorrow so closely together?
2. What is the general tone of this essay? How gained?

SATANISM AND THE WORLD ORDER *

Gilbert Murray

There have been few persons more devoted to the cause of international friendship than Gilbert Murray. For years before the World War he seized every opportunity to decry the growing sentiment for war. He assisted in the drafting of the League of Nations Covenant and has been connected with the League in various capacities since. Naturally he has a loyalty to it, not so much as a perfect institution, as the best instrument so far available to bring about international accord. Murray was born in Sydney, New South Wales, in 1866, and left Australia at the age of eleven for his education at Merchant Tailors', London, and St. John's College, Oxford, where he won all sorts of prizes and scholarships for his excellence in the Classics. After his graduation from Oxford, he taught Greek at New College, Oxford, and at Glasgow University. In 1908 he was appointed Regius Professor of Greek at Oxford. Long known as the outstanding classical scholar of England, Gilbert Murray has recently earned a reputation as a Liberal in politics.

IN AN old novel,[1] still famous and once widely popular, the writer, oppressed with the burden of evil in the world, gives to her heroine the name Consuelo, "Consolation," and makes her half-mad

---

* Reprinted by permission of and special arrangement with Houghton Mifflin Co., publishers.

hero a descendant of a strange sect. He is one of those Bohemian Lollards who, despairing of any sympathy from God, threw themselves into the protecting arms of their fellow-outcast, fellow-sufferer, fellow-victim of persecution and slander, the Devil. Their word of salutation was: "The Injured One give you greeting," or "The Injured One give you blessing." And they made of the Injured One a figure rather resembling the suffering Christ, a champion of the poor and lowly, a Being more than persecuted, more than crucified, but differing from Christ inasmuch as he was no friend of Pope, priest or Emperor, and therefore presumably no friend of God; he was still unconquered and unreconciled. If the belief seems to us bizarre or even depraved, it can only be for a moment. The clue to it is that it is a belief of the persecuted and helpless, who know their own innocence and deduce the wickedness of their rulers. To these pious and simple mountain peasants, followers first of John Huss and Zyska, and then of leaders more ignorant and fiery, the world became gradually a place dominated by enemies. Every person in authority met them with rack and sword, cursed their religious leaders as emissaries of the Devil, and punished them for all the things which they considered holy. The earth was the Lord's, and the Pope and Emperor were the vicegerents of God upon the earth. So they were told; and in time they accepted the statement. That was the division of the world. On one side

God, Pope and Emperor and the army of per-
secutors; on the other themselves, downtrodden
and poor, their saintly leaders hunted like beasts,
and, above all, their eternal comforter and fellow-
rebel, that exiled Star of the Morning, cast into
darkness and torment like his innocent children.
Let them be true to him, and surely his day must
come!

Satanism in this sense is perfectly intelligible,
and may be strongly sympathetic. We need pay
no attention to the mere name of Satan or Lucifer; the name is a mythological accident. The
essence of the belief is that the World Order is
evil and a lie; goodness and truth are persecuted
rebels. In other forms the belief has been held by
many Christian saints and martyrs, and notably
by the author of the Apocalypse. But we should
notice that it is diametrically opposed to the
teaching of almost all the great moral philosophers. Plato, Aristotle and the Stoics, St. Augustine and Thomas Aquinas, Kant and J. S. Mill,
and Comte and T. H. Green, all argue or assume
that there exists in some sense a Cosmos or Divine
Order; that what is good is in harmony with this
Order, and what is bad is in discord against it.
I notice that one of the Gnostic schools in Hippo-
lytus the Church Father actually defines Satan
as "The spirit who works against the Cosmic
Powers"; the rebel or protestant who counteracts
the will of the whole, and tries to thwart the
community of which he is a member. Ancient

philosophers are particularly strong on this conception of evil, and on the corresponding conception of human goodness as being the quality of a good citizen. The world or the universe is one community, or, as they call it, one city; all men, or perhaps all living things, are citizens of that city, and human goodness consists in living for its good. God's providence or foresight consists in providing the future Good of the Universe; and it is our business to be to the best of our powers servants or ministers of the divine foresight. Thus goodness becomes identical with loyalty, or with what some of the persecuted Christians called faithfulness. There is an army of God, and there is an enemy. And the essential sin is rebellion or treason.

Loyalty is thus the central and typical virtue; but loyalty to what? So far we can only say it is loyalty to the Cosmic Process, or the Purpose of God, or the good of the whole, as representing that purpose. But in practice, for the ordinary human being who has no oddities or idiosyncrasies of belief, this central virtue takes the form of loyalty towards the most important active whole of which he is a member.

In practice, the good of any large society is accepted as sufficiently near to the Good of the Universe to justify a man's devotion to it. A man whose life was really devoted to the welfare of New York, assuming, of course, that his idea of the welfare of New York was reasonably adequate and sensible, would certainly count as a good man. It is speculatively possible that the good of the universe may demand the misery and degradation of the inhabitants of New York, but it is one of those possibilities which need not, in ordinary opinion, be taken seriously. *A fortiori,*[2] a man who really devoted his life to the welfare of all the inhabitants of America or of the British Empire, or all the inhabitants of the German Empire, or, still more, the inhabitants of the ancient Roman Empire, would be accepted as a good man leading a good life by all but the eccentric or prejudiced. If a person of this type is blamed— such as Cecil Rhodes or Bismarck, or William II or Augustus—there is always an implication that his conception of what constituted the welfare of his whole was wrong. He professed, and perhaps thought, that he was promoting the welfare of his great society, whereas he was really doing something quite different: inflaming its ambitions, or flattering its vices, or the like.

The clearest, and perhaps the most tragic, case is that of the Roman Empire. If we try to enter into the mind of a good Roman official, like Pliny, for instance, as shown in his letters to Trajan, he seems to feel that the service of Rome was for him the nearest approach possible to the service of God, or the helping of the human race as a whole. Rome, he would say, had doubtless her imperfections; and not all Roman proconsuls were worthy of their high calling. But, when all deductions were made,

the Roman Empire meant peace throughout the
known world; it meant decent and fairly disinterested government; it protected honest men from
thieves and robbers; it punished wrongdoers; it
gave effective help to towns wrecked by blizzards
or earthquakes, or to provinces where the crops had
failed. It spread education and civilized habits;
it put down the worst practices of savage superstition. And, if any improvement in the practice
of governing human beings could be pointed out,
on the whole a good Roman governor was willing
to consider it. If Pliny had been asked what was
the greatest calamity that could befall the human
race, he would probably have answered, "The
overthrow of the Roman Empire"; and it would
have been hard to contradict him. One might have
argued that, in nation after nation, Rome had
crushed a native art and culture, and put in its
place a very dull and mechanical civilization, with
little life, or beauty, or power of growth; that it
took the heart out of the local religions, and put
in their place a dead official ceremonial. But such
arguments would have been met with an incredu-
lous smile, as similar arguments are met nowadays. Pliny would answer, very justly, that if the
various subject nations all preferred Roman culture to their own, surely that must be because
Roman culture was obviously superior. If they
accepted the Roman official religion, it must be
for the same reason. As a matter of fact, he would
add, the religion of *Roma Dea*, the acceptance of

the spirit of the Roman Empire as something to be regarded with awe and love and worship, was the nearest approach to a truly philosophical religion that uncultured men could assimilate; and, after all, Rome never suppressed or injured any local religion that was not criminal in its practices. All that Rome asked was the recognition of a common brotherhood, a common loyalty, expressed in the simplest and most human way, by an offering of incense and prayer at the altar of *Roma Dea*, Rome the Divine Mother, or sometimes at that of the existing head of the State.

And then, as we know, certain odd people would not do it. It seems curious that so simple a point of difference could not be got over. I do not see why Jews or Christians need have refused to pray for the welfare of Rome, provided they did so at their own altars, nor why the magistrates should have made a difficulty about the particular altar used. But evidently the affair was badly managed at the beginning. And by the time we have any detailed evidence we find the Christians uttering curses and incantations against the Empire in place of prayers, and the Roman working classes trying by pogroms to stamp out such incredible wickedness. When people met secretly and prayed to an alien and hostile God to do ill to the whole Empire; when they called our holy Mother Rome a harlot riding on a wild beast and drunken with the blood of the saints; when they saw visions and uttered incantations fraught with the most appalling afflictions upon mankind that any mind can conceive, seals and bowls of poisoned blood, and Riders upon strange horses, who should eventually trample the whole Roman world beneath their feet until the blood of that wine-pressing should wash the horses' bridles, while the Christians receive rich rewards and sing for joy —by that time the average working man or peasant began to look about him for clubs and stones, and the worried magistrate to decide that this new Jewish sect must be registered as an illegal society.

The mental attitude of the Book of Revelation is almost exactly like that of the persecuted Bohemian sectaries in *Consuelo*. The world and the rulers of the world are absolutely evil—not faulty men who make mistakes, but evil powers, hating all that is good and acting on earth as the representatives of evil gods: the earthly Cosmos is evil, and all that the righteous can desire is its utter destruction. . . . But of that later: the point which I wish to lay stress on at this moment is a different one. It is that, unless I am mistaken, in every single case the man who believes that the order in which he lives is evil provides himself, either in this life or the next, with another order in which all is redeemed.

The writer of the Apocalypse looks forward, after the utter destruction of the hostile order of Rome, to a millennium upon earth, in which all the posts of authority are occupied by the faithful. Plato's righteous man, though in discord with the society which tortures him, is in harmony all the time with the true nature of things. Prometheus himself ultimately gains his point, and is reconciled to Zeus. The overpowering strength of this impulse in the persecuted, or unhappy, to project out of their own desires an imaginary order in which the injustices of the present order are corrected, a special Heaven in which the righteous are consoled, together with a special Hell in which the enemies of the righteous meet their deserts, is illustrated vividly in the apocalyptic literature of all persecuted faiths, both Christian and pagan. Persecution always generates vivid descriptions of Hell, the projection of righteous revenge unsatisfied. One of the most pathetic and amiable of these attempts to justify by imagination that which cannot be justified by the evidence is the theoretic optimism of the Neo-Platonic and Neo-Pythagorean communities. They had not suffered much. They did not revel in visions of revenge or recompense: they merely argued *in vacuo*.[3] Their fundamental doctrine was that the Cosmos, the Universe, was good. If it was not good, all their system reeled into ruins. But the world, as they actually saw it and lived in it, seemed to them a mere mass of gross matter, rolling in error and delusion, and wisdom could only be attained by abstention from it. How can these positions be reconciled? By a method so simple that it leaves one almost awed at the child-like power of living in dreams by which the human mind protects itself against the thorns of life. "True," said these philosophers, "all of the world that we see is bad, all steeped in matter and in error. But what about the parts we do not see? If you could once get above the moon, you would find it absolutely different. All those parts of the Universe about which we have no information are so extraordinarily and infinitely good, that the badness of the parts we do happen to know sinks into insignificance." It is as though a judge had to try a number of accused people, of whom some could not be caught; all those who were brought into court were found guilty of various crimes, but the judge has such a strong inward conviction of the saintliness of those whom the police could not lay hands upon that he acquits the whole gang, and they leave the court without a stain on their character.

Quite absurd, I venture to say. And yet I think it is in essentials what I believe myself, and what we all believe. And I very much doubt whether human beings can go on living without some such belief. It is a matter of human psychology. But perhaps we do wrong in using the words "good" and "bad"; we really mean "friend or enemy," on our side or against us. The division between "friend" and "enemy" goes far deeper down into human nature than that between good and bad. If you read the sort of literature that I have been treating, the ancient apocryphal or pagan apocalypses and descriptions of Hell, you will not find on the whole that Hell is primarily the place for people who do not come up to the received moral standard; it is the place for the enemy. It is the place for him who now persecutes us, robs us, hangs us, burns us, makes us fight with wild beasts, and laughs the while. Let him wait and he will be made to laugh on the other side of his mouth! And if a third person explains that a particular enemy is a decent and sober person, a good husband and father, the statement is almost irrelevant, as well as almost unbelievable. You may hate a man because he is wicked; or you may think him wicked because you hate him. You may love a man because you think him good, or you may feel him to be, with all his faults, a splendid fellow because he likes you. But in either case the psychological ground fact is not a moral judgment, good or bad, but an instinctive gesture, Friend or Enemy.

And as soon as we see this, we see also how it is almost impossible not to believe that ultimately in the real battle of life the Cosmos is with us. You cannot belong whole-heartedly to the Labour Party, or the Jesuits, as the case may be, without believing that God is on the side of the Labour Party or the Jesuits. You cannot belong to Islam without believing that God is on the side of Islam. In the main, whatever majority may be against you now, and however hostile you may find the present World Order, you cannot help believing in your heart that there is a better order which is on your side, and perhaps even that, as they say in melodrama, "a time will come . . ."

I once in my youth met the celebrated Nihilist, Bakunin, the unsuccessful Lenin of his day, who was credited with the doctrine that every act of destruction or violence is good; because either it does good directly, by destroying a person or thing which is objectionable, or else it does good indirectly by making an already intolerable world worse than before, and so bringing the Social Revolution nearer. Since he and his followers had no constructive scheme for this so-called Social Revolution, the theory is for practical purposes indistinguishable from true Satanism or hatred of the world. One of the deductions made from it was that, in the ordinary workaday business of political assassinations, it was far more desirable to murder innocent and even good persons than guilty or wicked ones. For two reasons: the wicked were some use, if left alive, in furthering the Revolution; and, also, to kill the wicked implied no really valuable criticism of the existing social order. If you kill an unjust judge, you may be understood to mean merely that you think judges ought to be just. But if you go out of your way to kill a just judge, it is clear that you object to judges altogether. If a son kills a bad father, the act, though meritorious in its humble way, does not take us much further. But if he kills a good father, it cuts at the root of all that pestilent system of family affection and loving kindness and gratitude on which the present world is largely based.

Let us become sane again and see where we are. What do we most of us, as a matter of fact, think about the existing World Order? I am thinking of all ordinary sensible people, whatever their politics, excluding only those who are prejudiced against the world by some intolerable private wrong, or in its favour by some sudden and delightful success. Strictly speaking, the world as a whole cannot be called good or bad, any more than the spectrum as a whole can be called light or dark. The world contains all the things we call good and all that we call bad: and since by the laws of language you call things bad if they are worse than you expect, and good if they are better than you expect, and your expectation itself is formed by your experience, you cannot apply any word of blame or praise to the whole. But when people speak of the world or the existing order, they are of course thinking of the part in which they are most interested: and that, for various reasons, is usually the part that depends on human society and human effort. And I shall feel a little disappointed if every one of my readers does not agree with me in thinking that on the whole, and allowing for exceptions, when people try to do something, and pay attention, they come nearer to doing it than if they did not try at all. Normally, therefore, that systematic organization of human effort which we call a civilized society, does on the whole succeed in being a good thing, just as the Roman Empire did. Doctors, on the whole, prolong human life rather than shorten it. Lawyers and judges, on the whole, bring about more justice than injustice. Even in a department of life so very imperfectly civilized as economics, on the whole, if you know of a young man who is hard-working, intelligent and honest, you do expect him to get on better than one who is lazy, stupid and a thief. This lands us in the belief, which any minute study of social history corroborates in letters of blood, that almost any Government is better than no government, and almost any law better than no law. And I think we may safely go further. If we take any of those cases where a civilized society obviously shows itself evil, where it rewards vice and punishes virtue, produces misery and slays happiness; when it appoints unjust tribunals, when it bribes witnesses to tell lies, when it treats its own members or subjects as enemies and tries to injure them instead of serving them; when it does these things it is not really carrying out its principles, but failing. It is not a machine meant for doing these bad things; it is a very imperfectly designed machine for doing just the opposite, at any rate inside its own boundaries.

If we accept this position, we see that the organized life of mankind is on the whole organized for good, and that the great pilgrimage of the

spirit of man from the beginnings of history onward has been on the whole not only a movement
from ignorance to knowlege, from collective im-
potence to collective power, from poverty of life
to richness of life, but also in some profound
sense of pilgrimage from lower to higher. And it
will follow, in spite of constant lapses and false
routes, which have to be corrected, that the road
of progress is in the main a road onward in the
same general direction; that the better order
which a reformer wishes to substitute for the
present order must be a fuller realization of the
spirit of the existing order itself. This belief does
not rule out changes which many people would
call extreme or revolutionary; to the eye of the
historian most revolutions are little more than a
ruffling of the surface of life. But it does mean
that a change which violates the consciences of
men, a change which aims at less justice and more
violence, at more hatred and less friendliness, at
more cruelty and less freedom, has the proba-
bilities heavily against its ultimate success.

The instinct of the average man is apt to be
shrewdly right on this point. We do instinctively
judge men and movements, not by the amount of
suffering or bloodshed they cause, but by the
quality of human behaviour which they represent.
For a general to cause a thousand deaths by an
unsuccessful attack is a much slighter disturbance
of the World Order than if, for example, he were
to cause one innocent man to be condemned to

death by forging false documents. The first would be a disaster and perhaps deserving of blame; the second would imply a shattering of the very foundations on which the World Order rests.

We seem to be led to a profound and almost complacent conservatism, but I think there has been one flaw in this justification of ordinary organized societies. It is the same as lurked in Pliny's arguments above, justifying *Roma Dea* to the rebellious Christian or Jew. It justifies them so far as they really represent, however imperfectly, the World Order; so far as they *are* organizations for justice and freedom. That is, the argument applies only to the action of the organized society within its own borders, and utterly fails to touch the relation of the state or society to those outside. On the inside a state is an organization for good government and mutual help; and it has a machinery, elaborate and well thought out, by which it can improve its powers and correct its errors. And only in cases of extreme failure are its own members its enemies. But towards other states or societies it is something utterly different; just as a tigress to her own cubs is a clever and delightful mother, but to strangers nothing of the kind. Seen from the outside, a state is mainly a fighting power, organized for the use of force. It is represented by diplomacy in its better moments and by war in its worse. And towards subject societies, if it has them, its relation is ambiguous; in favourable conditions, they are mem-

bers of the whole and in accord with it; in un-
favourable conditions, they approach more and
more nearly to rebels and half-conquered enemies.
The relation of empires to subject communities is,
in fact, the great seed-ground for those states of
mind which I have grouped under the name of
Satanism.

An appalling literature of hatred is in existence,
dating at least from the eighth century B.C., in
which unwilling subjects have sung and exulted
over the downfall of the various great empires, or
at least poured out the delirious, though often
beautiful, visions of their long-deferred hope. The
Burden of Nineveh, the Burden of Tyre, the Burden of Babylon: these are recorded in some of the
finest poetry of the world. The Fall of Rome, the
rise of her own vile sons against her, the plunging
of the Scarlet Woman in the lake of eternal torture and the slaying of the three-quarters of mankind who bowed down to her, form one of the
most eloquent and imaginative parts of the ca-
nonical Apocalypse. The cry of oppressed peoples
against the Turk and the Russian is written in
many languages and renewed in many centuries.
What makes this sort of literature so appalling is,
first, that it is inspired by hatred; and next that
the hatred is at least in part just; and thirdly, the
knowledge that we ourselves are now sitting in
the throne once occupied by the objects of these
execrations. Perhaps most of us are so accustomed
to think of Babylon and Nineveh and Tyre, and

even Rome, as seats of mere tyranny and corruption, that we miss the real meaning and warning of their history. These imperial cities mostly rose to empire not because of their faults, but because of their virtues; because they were strong and competent and trustworthy, and, within their borders and among their own people, were mostly models of effective justice. And we think of them as mere types of corruption! The hate they inspired among their subjects has so utterly swamped, in the memory of mankind, the benefits of their good government, or the contented and peaceful lives which they made possible to their own peoples. It is an awe-inspiring thought for us who now sit in their place.

The spirit that I have called Satanism, the spirit of unmixed hatred towards the existing World Order, the spirit which rejoices in any widespread disaster which is also a disaster to the world's rulers, is perhaps more rife to-day than it has been for over a thousand years. It is felt to some extent against all ordered Governments, but chiefly against all imperial Governments; and it is directed more widely and intensely against Great Britain than against any other Power. I think we may add that, while everywhere dangerous, it is capable of more profound world-wreckage by its action against us than by any other form that it is now taking. A few years ago probably the most prosperous and contented and certainly in many ways the most advanced region of

the whole world was Central Europe. As a result
of the War and the policy of the victors after the
War, Central Europe is now an economic wreck,
and large parts of it a prey to famine. A vast volume of hatred, just and unjust, partly social,
partly nationalist, partly the mere reaction of intolerable misery, is rolling up there against what
they call the Hungerherren, or Hunger-Lords.
The millions of Russia are torn.by civil war; but
one side thinks of us as the people who, taking no
risks ourselves, sent tanks and poison-gas to destroy masses of helpless peasants; and the other
side thinks of us as the foreigners who encouraged
them to make civil war and then deserted them.
All through the Turkish Empire, through great
parts of Persia and Afghanistan, from one end of
the Moslem world to the other, there are *Mullahs,*
holy men, seeing visions and uttering oracles
about the downfall of another Scarlet Woman
who has filled the world with the wine of her
abominations, and who is our own *Roma Dea,*
our British Commonwealth, whom we look upon
as the great agent of peace and freedom for mankind. Scattered among our own fellow-subjects in
India the same prophecies are current; they are
ringing through Egypt. Men in many parts of the
world—some even as close to us as Ireland—are
daily giving up their lives to the sacred cause of
hatred, even a hopeless hatred, against us, and the
World Order which we embody. I have read lately
two long memoranda about Africa, written inde-

pendently by two people of great experience, but of utterly different political opinions and habits of thought; both agreed that symptoms in Africa pointed towards a movement of union among all the native races against their white governors; and both agreed that, apart from particular oppressions and grievances, the uniting forces were the two great religions, Christianity and Islam, because both religions taught a doctrine utterly at variance with the whole method and spirit of the European dominion—the doctrine that men are immortal beings and their souls equal in the sight of God.

This state of things is in part the creation of the War. In part it consists of previously latent tendencies brought out and made conspicuous by the War. In part the War has suggested to susceptible minds its own primitive method, the method of healing all wrong by killing or hitting somebody. And for us British in particular, the War has left us, or revealed us, as the supreme type and example of the determination of the white man to rule men of all other breeds, on the ground that he is their superior. Here and there peoples who have experience know that the British are better masters than most; but masters they are, and masters are apt to be hated.

There is a memorable chapter in Thucydides, beginning with the words: *Not now for the first time have I seen that it is impossible for a Democracy to govern an Empire.* It may not be impossible, but it is extraordinarily difficult. It is so difficult to assert—in uncritical and unmeasured language—the sanctity of freedom at home, and systematically to modify or regulate freedom abroad. It is so difficult to make the government at home constantly more sympathetic, more humane, more scrupulous in avoiding the infliction of injustice or even inconvenience upon the governed British voters at home, and to tolerate the sort of incident that—especially in the atmosphere of war—is apt to occur in the government of voteless subjects abroad. When I read letters from friends of my own who are engaged in this work of world-government, I sometimes feel that it brings out in good men a disinterested heroism, a sort of inspired and indefatigable kindness, which is equalled by no other profession. And I think that many English people, knowing as they do the immense extent of hard work, high training and noble intention, on which our particular share in the World Order is based, feel it an almost insane thing that our subjects should ever hate us. Yet we must understand if we are to govern. And it is not hard to understand. We have seen lately in Amritsar a situation arising between governors and governed so acutely hostile that a British officer, apparently a good soldier, thought it right to shoot down without warning some hundreds of unarmed men. In Mesopotamia, since the War, it is said that certain villages which did not pay their taxes, and were thought to be setting a bad example, were actually bombed from the air at night, when all the population was crowded together in the enclosures. In Ceylon, in 1915, large numbers of innocent people were either shot or flogged, and many more imprisoned, owing to a panic in the Government. In Ireland prisoners have been tortured to obtain evidence and, it is alleged, innocent men murdered to suppress it. In Rhodesia a few weeks ago a boy of sixteen, who shot a native dead for fun, was let off with eight strokes of the birch.

I wish to pass no harsh judgment on the men who did any of these things. I give full value to the argument that those of us who sit at home in safety have no right to pour denunciation on the errors of overworked and overstrained men in crises of great peril and difficulty. I mention these incidents only to illustrate how natural it is for imperial races to be hated. The people who suffer such things as these do not excuse them, and do not forget them. The stories are repeated, and do not lose in the telling. And many a boy and girl in the East will think of the English simply and solely as the unbelievers who habitually flog and shoot good people, just as the Jews felt about the Romans, or the Manichæans about the Orthodox. Now my own view is that all these actions in their different degrees were wrong; all were blunders; also, all were really exceptional and not typical; and, further, that no action like them, or remotely approaching them, is normally necessary for the

maintenance of the Empire. I am too confirmed a
Liberal to take the opposite view. But suppose we
had to take it. Suppose we were convinced by
argument that all these actions were wise and
necessary, and that violence and injustice of this
sort are part of the natural machinery by which
Empire is maintained; that the rule of the white
man over the coloured man, the Christian over
the "heathen," the civilized over the uncivilized,
cannot be carried on except at the cost of these
bloody incidents and the world-wide passion of
hatred which they involve, I think the conclusion
would be inevitable, not that such acts were right
—for they cannot be right—but simply that humanity will not for very long endure the contin-
uance of this form of World Order.

William Morris used to say that no man was
good enough to be another man's master. If that
were true of individuals, it would, as great authorities have pointed out, be much more true of
nations. No nation certainly is as trustworthy as
its own best men. But I do not think it is true,
unless, indeed, you imply in the word "master"
some uncontrolled despotism. Surely there is
something wrong in that whole conception of human life which implies that each man should be a
masterless, unattached and independent being. It
would be almost truer to say that no man is happy
until he has a master, or at least a leader, to admire and serve and follow. That is the way in

which all societies naturally organize themselves, from boys at school to political parties and social groups. As far as I can see, it is the only principle on which brotherhood can be based among beings who differ so widely as human beings do in intellect, in will-power or in strength. I do not think it is true that no nation is good enough in this qualified sense to be another's master. The World Order does imply leaders and led, governors and governed; in extreme cases it does imply the use of force. It does involve, amid a great mass of other feelings, the risk of a certain amount of anger, and even hatred, from the governed against the governor. A World Order which shirked all unpopularity would be an absurdity.

I sometimes think, in comparing the ancient world with the modern, that one of the greatest distinguishing characteristics of modern civilization is an unconscious hypocrisy. The ancients shock us by their callousness; I think we should sometimes startle them by the contrast between our very human conduct and our absolutely angelic professions. If you ask me what possible remedy I see, from the point of view of the British Commonwealth, against these evils I have described, I would answer simply that we must first think carefully what our principles are and not overstate them; next, we must sincerely carry them out. These principles are not unknown things. They have been laid down by the great men of the last century, by Cobden and Macaulay and John Stuart Mill, even to a great extent by Lord Salisbury and Gladstone. We hold our Empire as a trust for the governed, not as an estate to be exploited. We govern backward races that they may be able to govern themselves; we do not hold them down for our own profit, nor in order to use them as food for cannon. Above all, in our government and our administration of justice, we try to act without fear or favour, treating the poor man with as much respect as the rich man, the coloured man as the white, the alien as the Englishman. We have had the principles laid down again and again; they are all embodied in the Covenant of the League of Nations, which we have signed, and which is on sale everywhere for a penny.

It was a belief of the ancient Greeks that when a man had shed kindred blood he had to be purified; and until he was purified the bloodstain worked like a seed of madness within him, and his thoughts could never rest in peace or truth. The blood, I fear, is still upon the hands of all of us, and some of the madness still in our veins. The first thing we must do is to get back to our prewar standard. Then, from that basis, we must rise higher.

The War has filled not only Russia, but most of Eastern Europe and Western Asia with the spirit that I have called Satanism; the spirit which hates the World Order wherever it exists and seeks to vent its hate without further plan. That is wrong. But this spirit would not have got abroad; it would not have broken loose and grown like seed and spread like pestilence, had not the World Order itself betrayed itself and been false to its principles, and acted towards enemies and subjects in ways which seem to them what the ways of Nero or Domitian seemed to St. John on Patmos. I do not know whether it is possible for a nation to repent. Penitence in a nation, as a rule, means nothing but giving a majority to a different political party. But I think it is possible for individual human beings, even for millions of them. I see few signs so far of a change of heart in the public action of any nation in the world; few signs of any rise in the standard of public life, and a great many signs of its lowering. Some actions of great blindness and wickedness, the sort of actions which leave one wondering whether modern civilization has any spiritual content at all to differentiate us from savages, have been done, not during the War, but since the War was over. Yet I am convinced that, though it has not yet prevailed in places of power, there is a real desire for change of heart in the minds of millions. This desire is an enthusiasm, and is exposed to all the dangers of enthusiasm. It is often ignorant; it is touched with folly and misplaced passion and injustice. It is even exploited by interested persons. These are serious faults, and must be guarded against; but I believe the desire for a change of heart is a genuine longing, and, furthermore, I believe firmly that unless the World Order is affected by this change of heart, the World Order is doomed. Unless it abstains utterly from war and the causes of war, the next great war will destroy it. Unless it can seek earnestly the spirit of brotherhood and sobriety at home, Bolshevism will destroy it. Unless it can keep its rule over subject peoples quite free from the spirit of commercial exploitation and the spirit of slavery, and make it like the rule of a good citizen over his fellows, it will be shattered by the widespread hatred of those whom it rules.

The present World Order, if it survives the present economic crisis, has a wonderful opportunity, such an opportunity as has never been granted to any previous order in the history of recorded time. Our material wealth, our organization, our store of knowledge, our engines of locomotion and destruction, are utterly unprecedented, and surpass even our own understanding. Furthermore, on the whole, we know what we ought to do. We have, what no previous Empire or collection of ruling states ever had, clear schemes set before us of the road ahead which will lead out of these dangers into regions of safety; the League of Nations, with the spirit which it implies; the reconcilement and economic re-integration of European society; and the system of Mandate for the administration of backward territories. We have the power, and we know the course. Almost every element necessary to success has been put into the hands of those now governing the world except, as an old Stoic would say, the things that we must provide ourselves. We have been given everything, except, it would seem, the resolute and sincere will. Just at present that seems lacking; the peoples blame their rulers for the lack of it, and the rulers explain that they dare not offend their peoples. It may be recovered. We have had it in the past in abundance, and we probably have the material for it even now. If not, if for any reason the great democracies permanently prefer to follow low motives and to be governed by inferior men, it looks as if not the British Empire only, but the whole World Order established by the end of the War and summarized roughly in the League of Nations, may pass from history under the same fatal sentence as the great empires of the past—that the world which it ruled hated it and risked all to compass its overthrow.

NOTES

[1] *Consuelo*, by George Sand.
[2] Thus, for a stronger reason.
[3] in a vacuum.

QUESTIONS

1. Upon what are our definitions of good and bad based?
2. How, under the present world system, is war constantly made possible?

3. What is Murray's solution to the problem of future world peace?

4. Give reasons based upon your own observation to support Murray's assertion that organization is natural and inevitable.

5. How does Gilbert Murray account for the growing Satanism against Great Britain?

WHAT I DEMAND OF LIFE *

Frank Swinnerton

Severe illness caused FRANK SWINNERTON, the English novelist, to forego the usual pursuits of boyhood and to limit his schooling. His love of reading, however, contributed more to his knowledge and love of books than the best of schooling frequently contributes to those who are less inclined to get ahead. At twenty-five he had written and destroyed three novels, had published one, and was making a place for himself in the well-established publishing house of Chatto and Windus. His novels, outstanding among which is *Nocturne* (1917), show deep insight into the lives of the working classes of England without being excessively psychological. His two critical studies, *George Gissing* (1912) and *R. L. Stevenson* (1914), are authoritative in their fields. The latter, which stirred up Stevensonians both here and abroad, did much to dispel "the Stevenson myth", that Stevenson was essentially the writer of poems and romances for children. After spending nineteen years as literary adviser of Chatto and Windus, Mr. Swinnerton recently resigned and now devotes his time to writing and gardening at his country home, a sixteenth-century stone cottage in Old Tokefield, Surrey. His one volume of essays, *Tokefield Papers*, from which this essay is taken, was published in 1927. Swinnerton was born in Wood Green, a suburb of London, in 1884.

* Reprinted by permission of Doubleday, Doran Co., publishers, and James B. Pinker and Son, Inc.

HAVING lately reached the age of forty, I believe that I may fairly consider myself settled in character. This is not the place to bewail the fact, although few of us are satisfied of our own perfection. We may seem so, and may even inspire hatred in others because of our ability to seem so; but in fact we are none of us satisfied. If we *were* satisfied, we should be spiritually dead. This would be a pity.

But—still dissatisfied—I have been taking stock of the last forty years, and imagining the next—how many years? It is what Mr. Arnold Bennett would call "a solemnising thought" that I have lived possibly two-thirds of my life, that I know what I want for the future, and that there is a chance of my getting a fair proportion of what I want.

Few people get what they believe themselves most to desire; but that is because they make one great mistake in youth. They want to *be* something, instead of to *do* something. And their instincts lead them one way, while their judgment leads them another. In such cases instincts often win—more often than not.

And here let me say one hard thing. I have heard many complaints of circumstance from those who have not done as they wished. In all such cases it has been easy to discover an explanation. While the man who fails because he has aimed too high is to be revered, he is a rarity. Such men do not regard their failures. They look forward to further adventure. Their optimism is inexhaustible. But they are not—as some sentimentalists would have us think—the only failures. There is a more common kind of failure, much more often to be met with. The man who fails because he aims astray or because he does not aim at all is to be found everywhere. He demands our sympathy without shame. He complains freely. He borrows from us the wherewithal to live. He saps our energy with his parasitism. Such a man is merely to be pitied. Nothing can help him, or could ever have helped him, for the reason that he is fundamentally unstable or incapable of helping himself. Such men are as the wild convolvulus. They must cling to others for support of their strangling growths.

Let us pity our failures, but do not let us suppose them to be (as one was once in my hearing extolled for being) failures because they lack alloy, because they are pure gold. They are failures in what they have desired because they have not sincerely desired it, or because they have desired something else more. Or, as I have said, because they are born parasites.

I do not mean to suggest that there is no such thing as luck. On the contrary.

This explanation made, I should like to tabulate some few of the things I do *not* want. There are many others, but these will do.

I do not want money.

I do not want fame.

I do not want a life of gaiety.

I do not want possessions, in the sense of jewels, motor-cars, villas on the Riviera and town houses, slaves, or gold and silver plate.

I do not want innumerable acquaintances.

I do not want contentment.

I do not want "For he's a jolly good fellow" to be sung when I rise to my feet.

These, I say, are a few of the things I do not want. Other people want such things. To many, these are the prizes of life. Very well, if that is so, we shall know how to distribute such prizes; for if they want them steadfastly enough, these people will get them all. But as far as I am concerned, others may have every one of the blessings I do not need.

Some like to find themselves in a theatre, on a first night, surrounded by folk they know. When I go to the theatre it is to see a play; and when the play is over I like to go home to bed. Not for me is the theatre-supper, the after-supper dance, the carouse. Some need these things as stimulants. They wish to have gaiety, excitement. They are incessantly in search of diversion. In return for some imaginary contributions to the credit side of their account with life, they demand quick and frequent settlements. They give little or nothing except their company, but they must have entertainment at any cost.

Others want what they call "a quiet life." They want to vegetate. They want to lose interest in everything but their own comfort. I hope I shall never be as they. There are human beings who wish the visible trappings of success, the automobiles, the applause, the servility of hotel employees, the consciousness of opulence and distinction in the world's eyes. How short-sighted are these people! They may have all these blessings, may carry them everywhere, but they may never know the love and respect of their fellow-creatures. As soon as their backs are turned they may be forgotten. As soon as their purses are empty they may lack even hospitality. They may have toadies, but they may never have friends. What a world to live in!

The reason I do not want wealth is that money is only useful in so far as it buys ease and comfort and the regard of those whose regard is not worth having. As for ease and comfort—once one has attained a reasonable degree of comfort, the rest is a superfluity. Luxury is good for nobody except the manufacturer of luxuries. And habitual luxury is a bore, for it kills enjoyment of the occasional rare treat.

Wealth has no value in itself. It has no real value as the means of helping others, because sporadic charity is one of the most uncertain of all benefits to the unfortunate. I have known some rich men, some "successful" men, and I have been shocked by the sight of their friends and beneficiaries. These friends and beneficiaries are deferential, flattering, even boastful of acquaintance with the great; but this is not the friendship I covet. I will explain in a little while what I require of friendship. It is certainly not deference or flattery. I can say at once that I have never enjoyed deference or flattery, except from strangers. My own friends are the reverse of flattering or deferential. They would not understand any suggestion that they should behave otherwise than naturally. Most of them are extremely caustic. I need say no more.

And I do not want fame. Of what use is it? It may tickle the vanity for a time, but it becomes an intolerable nuisance. The film star is probably the most famous kind of person now living; and the film star—like a royal personage—has no private life to speak of. There is no privacy for the famous. Every action of theirs is seen and judged; together with some actions which have been only rumoured, invented by some gossip as a topic of sterile conversation. As one famous man once said to me, "Much worse than the worst is known of me." The benefits to be derived from obscurity are incalculable. Only the very young believe that it is pleasant to be stared at. I do not think any distress can exceed that of being pointed out in the street or in a restaurant or theatre. The famous person shares such distinction with the infamous.

There is the question of "influence." I am told that when one is rich and famous one has great power to do good to the world. Is that the reason

men seek fame and fortune? I think not. I think
the real motive power is ambition, the ambition
to be rich and famous and powerful for the sake
of being rich and famous and powerful. I have
never had such ambition. It takes all sorts of men
to make up humankind, and I do not grudge the
men who desire wealth and position the attainment of their object. But this kind of ambition
affects most of the more solemn kind of men. In
its meanest form this ambition creates the petty
domestic tyrant, the shining light of the small debating society, the pompous town councillor, the
frog who bursts himself in trying to seem to be a
bull.

When I was very young indeed I lived in such
poverty that sometimes a whole day would pass
without a meal. I had poor clothes. I was ill, often
so sick with hunger and fatigue that I could
hardly raise my head. My mother, father, and
brother shared those wretched days. We starved
for weeks and years, living from day to day on
chance earnings, and, when we had nothing to
eat, laughing at our own distresses. This laughter was not what is called "plucky." It was not
deliberate cheerfulness. It arose from natural
buoyancy of spirit. We laughed because it was
our nature to laugh. We did not grow bitter, or
rage against the capitalist, or steal, or do any desperate thing. We laughed. Very poor people have
to have good spirits, or they could not live.

Some time during this period I realised that I

wanted to be a journalist. I have always wanted
to be a journalist, and, although I have contributed articles, reviews, theatrical criticism,
stories, and even odd nondescript paragraphs to
periodicals since I was fifteen years old, I have
never been a journalist. In that respect I have been
thwarted by circumstance. The change in direction—for to be a novelist and the writer of two
critical studies is only to vary a direction—arose
from the fact that at the age of sixteen I went
into the trade of book publishing. A friend
(whom at that time I knew almost exclusively by
correspondence) was good enough to introduce
me to Mr. Hugh Dent, of Messrs. J. M. Dent &
Co., and I became a reception clerk in the office
of that firm.

It was my duty to encounter every caller, as-
certain his business, and attend to his wants. As
a groundwork for my ultimate occupation the experience gained was invaluable. Mr. Dent was
always a very difficult man to see, and I had to
tackle all sorts of visitors, from those who
brought masterpieces to those who wished to borrow half-crowns. It was necessary to decide at
sight whether Mr. Dent might wish or be willing
to see each man or woman, or whether the caller
must be manoeuvred out of the building, without
offence, without an interview. It will be seen at
once how such a task formed a training in the
summary estimate of character, which must always play an important part in the novelist's

equipment. It will also be seen how such work influences ambition.

At the age of eighteen, accordingly, I formed the ambition that has remained constant ever since. I wanted to write a novel about human beings. From that moment human beings became my absorbing study. I wrote a novel about human beings. It was not published, but it was written to the bitter end. I wanted at that time to write goodish novels, and to read everything. I wanted to live in a little old-fashioned cottage in the country, to write goodish novels, and to marry for love. It was never my ambition to write great novels—I recognised perfectly that, although I had talent, I was not a genius. But I wanted to do the best I could, to live by the work of my pen, and to be happy.

This last item was a superfluous ambition, because it is very difficult for me to be unhappy. "Cheerfulness," as the would-be philosopher once said, "will keep breaking in." [1] In the matter of writing I have always done the best I could do at the given moment, and I do not feel that what I have written has ever been more than "goodish." As for the rest, I have married for love, and I live in a little Elizabethan or Jacobean cottage in a charming countryside. And anything human is dearer to me than all the wealth of all the world.

As to friends, I have always found it easy to make them. My manners are affable and inoffensive. I have a sharp, but not a venomous tongue;

and my friends do not greatly fear it. Moreover, I have a considerable capacity for interest and affection. This capacity is not claimed as a virtue; but it is admitted by those who should know best. My friends are all friends worth having. Most of them are not especially wealthy or famous, but they are loyal, humorous, trustworthy, and beautifully simple. Nobody has ever had better friends than I. And no person is my friend who is not also my superior.

If I had a great deal of money I should not work. But that does not mean that I want to try starvation a second time. I used to want three hundred pounds a year. I thought that if I could make three hundred pounds a year, and live with my wife in a country cottage, I would write the books I liked and read everything.

Well, I now want more than three hundred pounds a year (to some extent because the purchasing power of the pound has diminished, but also because others are dependent upon me); but I have the cottage, and have had a great piece of luck. Although my novels have been only "goodish," they have secured for me a small body of friendly readers in both America and England. These readers are so few compared with the numbers of which I see other authors and their publishers boasting, that they do not suffice to make me opulent. But they are constant. Therefore I do not feel bound, as the writers of very successful books may feel bound, to write every book according to the pattern of the last. I write what I want to write. I can earn enough by this means to keep me fed and clothed, and to keep fed and clothed those who belong to me. I have leisure and tranquillity. I have not only attained all the ambitions of my youth (saving only that one which had journalism as its objective), but I have surpassed them. There remains the future.

What do I demand of life? First, health. Second, privacy. Third, a moderate degree of security. Fourth, the continued affection of those who are dear to me. Fifth, a modicum of leisure, during which I may indulge my vice of laziness and read the books I want to read, play the games I want to play, see the places I want to see. These things are all possible of attainment, providing the first—health—is vouchsafed to me. Privacy is a benefit which determination can secure. In the outdoor studio of my cottage, which has no telephone and no wireless apparatus, I can "sport my oak" [2] as firmly as any working undergraduate. By means of privacy and the consequent favourable circumstances for work I can write the books I want to write, and obtain such security as any man can enjoy in this modern world of change and passion. Even if the restraints of civilisation were to fall to powder, I should still be no worse off than my fellows; and I do not yet visualise chaos.

And as long as I work in this way I shall have the leisure I require. It need not be stolen, because only that man is denied leisure who is so bent upon prosperity that he must not leave his work for a day lest it perish or cease to produce those monetary profits which are his only touchstone of well-being.

Finally, there is the question of affection. I think that any man can endure if he has good friends. And I have proved my friends. In ordinary life they may regard me with great irony. They may find me facetious and voluble, and even tiresome. But when I have ever been in trouble I have found my friends constant and inexhaustible in patience. I should desire them always to remain so. If they were to fall away, I should indeed be desolate. They will not so fall away as long as they and I remain unchanged.

As to comfort, I have enough of it. A roof to my head, chairs, books, and a bed; a warm fire in the evening. It is ample. It is more than ample. It is ideal. I do not want to live in great hotels or to have many servants at my beck and call. And I do not want anything that will cause me to vegetate, because in return for the benefits I claim from life, it is my desire to write one novel that is more than "goodish."

That is the whole point. No man can be satisfied with his attainment, although he may be satisfied with his circumstances. In all the foregoing remarks, if I have given any suggestion that I am satisfied with what I have *done*, the suggestion is due to clumsy expression. I have been returning thanks to good fortune. I have been betraying, perhaps, a readiness to be pleased with small results. But I have not been patting myself upon the back. Something more is needed. A philosopher once said to me, "The man who is satisfied has no future but the dust-bin."

Moreover, I am quite aware that it is not the highest type of man who has moderate ambitions. The really great man is immoderate in his claims upon life; but that is because he is conscious of his power to give to life in return incomparable services. His mind works upon a different plane from mine. His conceptions of life are lofty and incalculable. He may be serene, as Shakespeare must have been serene; but he dwells apart, wrapt in the inscrutable majesty of power. My own lot in life is less exalted. I have wanted only to understand human nature. I have not wanted to improve it, or to change the face of the world. There are such idealists, men as far above their fellows as spirit is above animalism. They are bringers of glad tidings to the suffering, the creators of a new era. They are men of destiny. I admire, I reverence them. But my impulses lie more upon the surface. I cannot too strongly emphasise the fact that I am agnostic even as regards the destiny of mankind. The stars fascinate and bewilder me; the beauty of the earth is a mystery to my heart. I love the earth, and a great many of those who dwell upon it; but I have never experienced revelation, and I remain merely a mar-

velling student of the wonder of the universe and
of life itself.

For this reason I look forward to the remainder
of my earthly existence as the culmination of all
that I am likely ever to know. Having seen and
experienced earthly hardship, I demand henceforward immunity from such hardship. I demand
tranquillity and the beauty of human affection.
But I do not insist that the miracle of life should
be explained to me. Having been born ignorant
and curious, I expect (with equanimity) to die almost as ignorant and curious as I was born. My
ancestors and my environment have given me a
not very vigorous body, an extremely buoyant
temperament, a modest talent, and considerable
facility. To the exercise of these possessions in
the future I look forward. I do not demand to be
happy, because I expect—on a basis of experience
—to be happy. Is not happiness the most satisfactory of all possessions? I think it is. Others
may demand wisdom, may demand eternity, or
the salvation of the human race. I do not demand
these things. If there are those among my readers
who despise such an attitude as the one I have
outlined in this article, I would remind them that
when I come to die I shall be able—in spirit at
least—to repeat the memorable last words of William Hazlitt. Hazlitt, as he lay dying, said, "Well,
I've had a happy life." Which of us—uncertain
travellers as we are upon uncharted ways—can
ask to say more? Not I.

NOTES

[1] See E. V. Lucas' "A Philosopher That Failed."
[2] English university slang—meaning to exclude visitors by closing one's outer or oaken door.

QUESTIONS

1. Do you agree that youth generally aspires to *be* something rather than to *do* something? What are your reasons? Compare this with Crothers' essay, "Every Man's Natural Desire to Be Somebody Else."

2. Wherein does Swinnerton differ from Thoreau, Jacks, and other essayists you have read? Wherein does he agree with them?

3. Were you to base a character sketch of Swinnerton on this essay, what qualities would you ascribe to him?

WHEN I LEFT BUSINESS FOR
LITERATURE *

SHERWOOD ANDERSON

SHERWOOD ANDERSON, one of the most interesting personalities in contemporary American literature, was born in Camden, Ohio, in 1876, of Scotch-Irish and Italian-American descent. The father being a rover, Sherwood's early education was acquired on the run until, at 12, he went to work to help support the family of five boys and three girls. After the death of his mother, two years later, Anderson worked in various factories for three years and then joined an older brother in Chicago. After serving in the Spanish-American War, he returned to Ohio, married, and became the manager of a paint factory in Elyria. Through the interest of H. L. Mencken of the *Smart Set*, Anderson's first book *Windy McPherson's Son* was published in 1916. The same year Anderson was forced, for reasons of health, to take a cabin in the Ozark Mountains. Returning to the East the next year with the manuscript of another novel, he suddenly became disgusted with his work and threw the entire manuscript out the car window. Later works of Anderson include *Winesburg, Ohio, A Story Teller's Story,* and *Dark Laughter.* Of recent years Mr. Anderson has owned and edited two weekly newspapers in Marion, Virginia: one, Democratic; the other, Republican. In January, 1932, he sold the controlling interest in the two papers to his son, Robert Lane Anderson. The

---

* Reprinted by permission of the author.

story of his sudden change from business to literature is found in this essay.

ON AN evening of the late summer I got off a train at a growing industrial Ohio town where I had once lived. I was rapidly becoming a middle-aged man. Two years before I had left the place in disgrace. There I had tried to be a manufacturer, a money-maker, and had failed. Some thousands of dollars had been lost for others. An effort to conform to the standard dreams of the men of my times had failed, and in the midst of my disgrace and generally hopeless outlook as regards making a living I had been filled with joy at coming to the end of it all. One morning I had left the place afoot, leaving my poor little factory, like an illegitimate child, on another man's doorstep. I had left, merely taking what money was in my pocket, some eight or ten dollars.

What a moment that leaving had been! To one of the European artists I afterward came to know, the situation would have been unbelievably grotesque. Such a man could not have believed in my earnestness about it all and would have thought my feelings at the moment a worked-up thing. I can in fancy hear one of the Frenchmen, Italians, or Russians I later knew laughing at me.

"Well, but why get so worked up? A factory is a factory, is it not? Why may not one break it like an empty bottle? You have lost some money for others? See the light on that field over there.

These others, for whom you lost money, were they compelled to beg in the streets, were their children torn by wolves? What is it you Americans get so excited about when a little money is lost?"

A European artist may not understand, but an American will understand. The devil! it is not a question of money. No men are so careless and free with money as the Americans. There is another matter involved.

It strikes rather deep at the roots of our beings. Childish as it all may have seemed to an older and more sophisticated world, we Americans, from the beginning, have been up to something, or we have wanted to think we were up to something. We came here, or our fathers or grandfathers came here, from a hundred diverse places, and you may be sure it was not the artists who came. Artists do not want to cut down trees, root stumps out of the ground, build towns and railroads. The artist wants to sit with a strip of canvas before him, face an open space on a wall, carve a bit of wood, make combinations of words and sentences, as I am doing now, trying to express to others some thought or feeling of his own. He wants to dream of color, to lay hold of form, free the sensual in himself, live more fully and freely in his contact with the materials before him than he can possibly live in life. He seeks a kind of controlled ecstasy and is a man with a passion, a "nut," as we love to say in

America. And very often, when he is not in actual contact with his materials, he is a much more vain and disagreeable ass than any man not an artist could possibly be. As a living man he is almost always a pest. It is only when dead he begins to have value.

The simple truth is that in a European country the artist is more freely accepted than he is among us, and only because he has been longer about. They know how harmless he really is, or, rather, do not know how subtly dangerous he can be, and accept him only as one might accept a hybrid cross between a dog and a cat that went growling, mewing, barking, and spitting about the house. One might want to kill the first of such strange beasts he sees about, but after he has seen a dozen and has realized that, like the mule, they cannot breed their own kind, he laughs, and lets them live, paying no more attention to them than modern France, for example, pays to its artists.

But in America things are somewhat different. Here something went wrong in the beginning. We pretended to so much and were going to do such great things here. This vast land was to be a refuge for all the outlawed brave, foolish folk of the world. The declaration of the rights of man was to have a new hearing in a new place. The devil! we did get ourselves into a bad hole! We were going to be superhuman, and it turned out we were sons of men who were not such devilish fellows after all. You cannot blame us that we were somewhat reluctant about finding out the very human things concerning ourselves. One does so hate to come down off the perch!

We are now losing our former feeling of inherent virtue, are permitting ourselves to laugh occasionally at ourselves for our pretensions; but there was a time here when we were sincerely in earnest about all this American business, the land for the free and the home for the brave. We actually meant it, and no one will ever understand present-day America or Americans, who does not concede that we meant it and that while we were building all of our big, ugly, hurriedly thrown-together towns, creating our great industrial system, growing always more huge and prosperous, we were as much in earnest about what we thought we were up to as were the French of the thirteenth century when they built the Cathedral of Chartres to the glory of God.

They built the Cathedral of Chartres to the glory of God, and we really intended building here a land to the glory of man and thought we were doing it, too. That was our intention, and the affair only blew up in the process, or got perverted, because man, even the brave and the free man, is somewhat a less worthy object of glorification than God. This we might have found out long ago, but we did not know one another. We came from too many different places to know one another, had been promised too much, wanted too much. We were afraid to know one another.

Oh, how Americans have wanted heroes, wanted brave, simple, fine men! And how sincerely and deeply we Americans have been afraid to understand and love one another, fearing to find ourselves at the end no more brave, heroic, and fine than the people of almost any other part of the world!

I, however, disagree. What I am trying to do is to give the processes of my own mind at two distinct moments of my own life. First, the moment when, after many years of effort to conform to an unstated and but dimly understood American dream by making myself a successful man in the material world, I threw all overboard; and then, at another moment, when having come back to the same spot where I passed through the first moment, I attempted to confront myself with myself in a somewhat changed point of view.

II

As for the first of these moments, it was melodramatic and even silly enough. The struggle centered itself, at the last, within the walls of a particular moment and within the walls of a particular room.

I sat in the room with a woman who was my secretary. For several years I had been sitting there, dictating to her regarding the goods I had

made in my factory and that I was attempting to
sell. The attempt to sell the goods had become a
sort of madness in me. There were certain thousands, or perhaps hundreds of thousands of men,
living in towns or on farms in many States of my
country who might possibly buy the goods I had
made rather than the goods made in another factory by another man. How I had wheedled! How
I had schemed! In some years I gave myself quite
fully to the matter in hand, and the dollars
trickled in. Well, I was about to become rich. It
was a possibility. After a good day or week, when
many dollars had come, I went to walk; and when
I had got into a quiet place where I was unobserved, I threw back my shoulders and strutted.
During the year I had made for myself so many
dollars. Next year I would make so many more,
and the next year so many more. But my thoughts
of the matter did not express themselves in the
dollars. It never does to the American man. Who
calls the American a dollar-lover is a fool. My
factory was of a certain size,—it was in reality a
poor haphazard-enough-run place,—but after a
time I would build a great factory and after that
a greater and greater Like a true American, I
thought in size.

My fancy played with the matter of factories
as a child would play with a toy. There would be
a great factory with walls going up and up, and
a little open place for a lawn at the front, shower-
baths for the workers, with perhaps a fountain

playing on a lawn, and up before the door of this place I would drive in a large automobile.

Oh, how I would be respected by all, how I would be looked up to by all! I walked in a little dark street, throwing back my shoulders. How grand and glorious I felt!

The houses along the street in which I walked were small and ugly, and dirty-faced children played in the yards. I wondered. Having walked, dreaming my dream for a long time, I returned to the neighborhood of my factory and, opening my office, went in to sit at my desk, smoking a cigarette. The night watchman came in. He was an old man who had once been a school teacher; but, as he said, his eyes had gone back on him.

When I had walked alone, I had been able to make myself feel somewhat as I fancied a prince might have felt; but when any one came near me, something exploded inside. I was a deflated balloon. Well, in fancy, I had a thousand workmen under me. They were children, and I was their father and would look out for them. Perhaps I would build them model houses to live in, a town of model houses, built about my great factory, eh. The workmen would be my children, and I would look out for my children. "Land of the free, home of the brave."

But I was back in my factory now, and the night watchman sat smoking with me. Sometimes we talked far in the night. The devil! He was a fellow like myself, having the same problems as myself. How could I be his father? The thought was absurd. Once, when he was a younger man, he had dreamed of being a scholar, but his eyes had gone back on him. What had he wanted to do? He spoke of it for a time. He had wanted to be a scholar, and I myself had spent those earlier years eagerly reading books.

"I would really like to have been a learned monk, one of those fellows such as appeared in the Middle Ages, one of the fellows who went off and lived by himself and gave himself up wholly to learning, one who believed in learning, who spent his life humbly seeking new truths; but I got married, and my wife had kids, and then, you see, my eyes went back on me."

He spoke of the matter philosophically. One did not let oneself get too much excited. After a time one got over any feeling of bitterness. The night watchman had a boy, a lad of fifteen, who also loved books.

"He is pretty lucky, can get all the books he wants at the public library. In the afternoon after school is out and before I come down here to my job, he reads aloud to me."

III

Men and women! Many men and women! There were men and women working in my factory, men and women walking in streets with me, many men and women scattered far and wide over the country to whom I wanted to sell my goods. I sent men, salesmen, to see them: I wrote letters, how many thousands of letters, all to the same purpose. "Will you buy my goods?" And again, "Will you buy my goods?"

What were the other men thinking about? What was I myself thinking about? Suppose it were possible to know something of the men and women, to know something of oneself, too. The devil! these were not thoughts that would help me to sell my goods to all the others. What were all the others like? What was I myself like? Did I want a large factory with a little lawn and a fountain in front and with a model town built about it?

Days of endlessly writing letters to men, nights of walking in strange, quiet streets—what had happened to me? "I shall go get drunk," I said to myself, and I did go and get drunk. Taking a train to a near-by city I drank until a kind of joy came to me and, with some man I had found and who had joined in my carousal, I walked in streets, shouting at other men, singing songs, going sometimes into strange houses to laugh with people, talk with people I found there.

Here was something I liked, and something the others liked, too. When I had come to people in strange houses half drunk, released, they were not afraid of me. "Well, he wants to talk," they seemed to be saying to themselves. "That's fine!" There was something broken down between us, a

wall broken down. We talked of outlandish things
for Anglo-Saxon trained people to speak of, of
love between men and women, of what children's
coming meant. Food was brought forth. Often in
a single evening of this sort I got more from people
than I could get from weeks of ordinary intercourse. The people were a little excited by the
strangeness of two unknown men in their houses.
With my companion I went boldly to the door
and knocked. Laughter, "Hello, the house!" It
might be the house of a laborer or that of a well-
to-do merchant. I had hold of my newfound
friend's arm and explained our presence as well
as I could. "We are a little drunk and we are
travelers. We just want to sit and visit with you a
while."

There was a kind of terror in people's eyes and
a kind of gladness, too. An old workman showed
us a relic he had brought home with him from the
Civil War, while his wife ran into a bedroom and
changed her dress. Then a child awoke in a
near-by room and began to cry and was permitted
to come in in her nightgown and lie in my arms or
in the arms of the newfound friend who had got
drunk with me. The talk swept over strange, intimate subjects. What were men up to? What were
women up to? There was a kind of deep taking of
breath, as though we had all been holding something back from one another and had suddenly
decided to let go. Once or twice we stayed all
night in the house to which we had gone.

And then back to the writing of letters to sell my goods. In the city to which I had gone to carouse I had seen many women of the streets, standing at corners, looking furtively about.

What thoughts in the mind! There was a note due and payable at the bank. "Now, here, you man, attend to your affairs. You have induced others to put money into your enterprises. If you are to build a great enterprise here, you must be up and at it."

How often in after years I have laughed at myself for the thoughts and emotions of that time. There is a thought I have had that is very delicious. It is this, and I dare say it will be an unwelcome thought to many. "I am the American man. I think there is no doubt of it. I am just the mixture, the cold, moral man of the North, into whose body has come the warm pagan blood of the South. I love and am afraid to love. Behold in me the American man striving to become an artist, to become conscious of himself, filled with wonder concerning himself and others, trying to have a good time and not fake a good time. I am not English, Italian, Jew, German, Frenchman, Russian. What am I? I am tremendously serious about it all, but at the same time I laugh constantly at myself for my own seriousness. Like all real American men of our day, I wander constantly from place to place, striving to put down roots into the American soil and not quite doing it. If you say the real American man is not yet born, you lie. I am the type of the fellow.

This is somewhat of a joke on me, but it is a greater joke on you readers, too. As respectable and conventional a man as President Coolidge has me in him, and I have him in myself. Do not doubt it. I have him in me, and Eugene Debs [1] in me, and the crazy political idealists of the Western States, and Mr. Gary [2] of the Steel Trust, and the whole crew. I accept them all as a part of myself. Would to God they would thus accept me!

IV

And being this thing I have tried to describe, I return now to myself sitting between the walls of a certain room and between the walls of a certain moment, too. Just why was that moment so pregnant? I will never quite know.

It came with a rush, the feeling that I must quit buying and selling, the overwhelming feeling of uncleanliness. I was in my whole nature a tale-teller. My father had been one, and his not knowing had destroyed him. The tale-teller cannot bother with buying and selling. To do so will destroy him. No class of men I have ever known are so dull and cheerless as the writers of glad, pretty pictures. The corrupt, unspeakable thing that had happened to tale-telling in America was all concerned with this matter of buying and selling. The horse cannot sing like a canary bird, or the canary bird pull a plow like a horse, and either of them attempting it becomes something ridiculous.

There was a door leading out from my office to the street. How many steps to the door? I counted them, "five, six, seven." "Suppose," I asked myself, "I could take those five, six, seven steps to the door, pass out at the door, go along that railroad track out there, disappear into the far horizon beyond." Where was I to go? In the town where my factory was located I had still the reputation of being a bright young business man. In my first years there I had been filled with shrewd, vast schemes. I had been admired, looked up to. Since that time I had gone down and down as a bright young man, but no one yet knew how far I had gone. I was still respected in the town, my word was still good at the bank. I was a respectable man.

Did I want to do something not respectable, not decent? I am trying to give you the history of a moment, and, as a tale-teller, I have come to think that the true history of life is but a history of moments. It is only at rare moments we live. I wanted to walk out at a door and go away into the distance. The American is still a wanderer, a migrating bird not yet ready to build a nest. All of our cities are built temporarily, as are the houses in which we live. We are on the way— toward what? There have been other times in the history of the world when many strange peoples came together in a new strange land. To assume that we have made an America, even materially, seems to me now but telling ourselves fairy-tales in the night. We have not even made it materially yet, and the American man has only gone in for money-making on a large scale to quiet his own restlessness, as the monk of old days was given the *Regula* [3] of Augustine to quiet him and still the lusts in himself. For the monk, kept occupied with the saying of prayers and the doing of many little sacred offices, there was no time for the lusts of the world to enter in, and for the American to be perpetually busy with his affairs, with his automobiles, with his movies, there is no time for unquiet thoughts.

On that day in the office at my factory I looked at myself and laughed. The whole struggle I am trying to describe, and that I am confident will be closer to the understanding of most Americans than anything else I have ever written, was accompanied by a kind of mocking laughter at myself and my own seriousness about it all.

Very well, then, I wanted to go out of the door and never come back. How many Americans want to go! But where do they want to go? I wanted to accept for myself all of the little restless thoughts of which I and the others had been so afraid, and you, who are Americans, will understand the necessity of my continually laughing at myself and at all things dear to me. I must laugh at the thing I love the more intensely because of my love. Any American will understand that.

It was a trying moment for me. There was the woman, my Secretary, now looking at me. What did she represent? Would I dare be honest with her? It was quite apparent to me I would not. I had got to my feet, and we stood looking at each other. "It is now or never," I said to myself, and I remember that I kept smiling. I had stopped dictating to her in the midst of a sentence. "The goods about which you have inquired are the best of their kind made in the——"

I stood, and she sat, and we were looking at each other intently.

"What's the matter?" she asked. She was an intelligent woman, more intelligent, I am sure, than I, just because she was a woman and good, while I have never been good, do not know how to be good. Could I explain all to her? The words of a fancied explanation marched through my mind.

"My dear young woman, it is all very silly, but I have decided no longer to concern myself with this buying and selling. It may be all right for others, but for me it is poison. There is this factory. You may have it, if it pleases you. It is of little value, I dare say. Perhaps it is money ahead, and then again it may well be it is money behind. I am uncertain about it all, and now I am going away. Now, at this moment, with the letter I have been dictating, with the very sentence you

have been writing left unfinished, I am going out
that door and never come back. What am I going
to do? Well, now, that I don't know. I am going
to wander about. I am going to sit with people,
listen to words, tell tales of people, what they are
thinking, what they are feeling. The devil! it may
even be I am going forth in search of myself."

The woman was looking into my eyes the while
I looked into hers. Perhaps I had grown a little
pale, and now she grew pale. "You're sick," she
said, and her words gave me an idea. There was
wanted a justification of myself not to myself, but
to the others. A crafty thought came. Was the
thought crafty or was I at the moment a little
insane, a "nut," as every American so loves to
say of every man who does something a little out
of the groove.

I had grown pale, and it may be I was ill; but
nevertheless I was laughing, the American laugh.
Had I suddenly become a little insane? What a
comfort that thought would be, not to myself, but
to the others! My leaving the place I was then
in would tear up roots that had gone down a little
into the ground. The ground I did not think
would support the tree that was myself and that
I thought wanted to grow.

My mind dwelt on the matter of roots, and I
looked at my feet. The whole question with which
I was at the moment concerned became a matter
of feet. I had two feet that could take me out of
the life I was then in and that, to do so, would

need but take three or four steps to a door. When I had reached the door and had stepped out of my little factory office, everything would be quite simplified, I was sure. I had to lift myself out. Others would have to tackle the job of getting me back once I had stepped over that threshold.

Whether at the moment I merely became shrewd and crafty, or whether I really became temporarily insane, I shall never quite know. What I did was to step very close to the woman and, looking directly into her eyes, I laughed gaily. Others beside herself would, I knew, hear the words I was now speaking. I looked at my feet.

"I have been wading in a long river, and my feet are wet," I said.

Again I laughed as I walked lightly toward the door and out of a long and tangled phase of my life, out of the door of buying and selling, out of the door of affairs.

"They want me to be a 'nut,' will love to think of me as a 'nut', and why not? It may just be that's what I am," I thought gaily, and at the same time turned and said a final confusing sentence to the woman, who now stared at me in speechless amazement. "My feet are cold, wet, and heavy from long wading in a river. Now I shall go walk on dry land," I said, and as I passed out at the door a delicious thought came. "Oh, you little tricky words, you are my brothers. It is you, not myself, have lifted me over this threshold. It is you who have dared give me a hand. For the rest of my life I will be a servant to you," I whispered to myself, as I went along a spur of railroad track, over a bridge, out of a town, and out of that phase of my life.

Notes

[1] Former leader of the Socialist Party, imprisoned for political offenses.

[2] Judge Elbert Gary, former head of the United States Steel Corporation.

[3] *The Regula,* a book by St. Augustine outlining the rules for monastic living.

Questions

1. Why did Mr. Anderson expect Americans, more than others, to understand his breaking away from business?

2. Why did he laugh at his plight? Of what does the true sense of humor consist?

3. What did Mr. Anderson mean by "The true history of life is but a history of moments"?

Windfalls of Observation ... Patagonians.

THE TYRANNY OF THINGS *

Edward Sandford Martin

Edward Sandford Martin, best known to American readers as the writer of the *Editor's Easy Chair* in *Harper's Magazine,* was born in Owasco, New York, in 1856. He is a graduate of Harvard University (1877) and a member of the New York State Bar. In addition to his interpretations of current history, Martin has written familiar essays which rank with those of some of the classical masters of the essay form. Whether he writes of international or domestic political problems, or of the amenities of more personal living, such as *The Courtship of a Careful Man,* he writes with a penetrative insight that makes for simplicity. "The Tyranny of Things" is from his volume *Windfalls of Observation.*

A TRAVELER newly returned from the Pacific Ocean tells pleasant stories of the Patagonians. As the steamer he was in was passing through Magellan's Straits some natives came out to her in boats. They wore no clothes at all, though there was snow in the air. A baby that came along with them made some demonstration that displeased its mother, who took it by the foot, as Thetis took

Achilles,[1] and soused it over the side of the boat into the cold sea-water. When she pulled it in, it lay a moment whimpering in the bottom of the boat, and then curled up and went to sleep. The missionaries there have tried to teach the natives to wear clothes, and to sleep in huts; but, so far, the traveler says, with very limited success. The most shelter a Patagonian can endure is a little heap of rocks or a log to the windward of him; as for clothes, he despises them, and he is indifferent to ornament.

To many of us, groaning under the oppression of modern conveniences, it seems lamentably meddlesome to undermine the simplicity of such people, and enervate them with the luxuries of civilization. To be able to sleep out-o-doors, and go naked, and take sea-baths on wintry days with impunity, would seem a most alluring emancipation. No rent to pay, no tailor, no plumber, no newspaper to be read on pain of getting behind the times; no regularity in anything, not even meals; nothing to do except to find food, and no expense for undertakers or physicians, even if we fail; what a fine, untrammeled life it would be! It takes occasional contact with such people as the Patagonians to keep us in mind that civilization is the mere cultivation of our wants, and that the higher it is the more our necessities are multiplied, until, if we are rich enough, we get enervated by luxury, and the young men come in and carry us out.

We want so many, many things, it seems a pity that those simple Patagonians could not send missionaries to us to show us how to do without. The comforts of life, at the rate they are increasing, bid fair to bury us soon, as Tarpeia was buried under the shields of her friends the Sabines. Mr. Hamerton,[2] in speaking of the increase of comfort in England, groans at the "trying strain of expense to which our extremely high standard of living subjects all except the rich." It makes each individual of us very costly to keep, and constantly tempts people to concentrate on the maintenance of fewer individuals' means that would in simpler times be divided among many. "My grandfather," said a modern the other day, "left $200,000. He was considered a rich man in those days; but, dear me! he supported four or five families—all his needy relations and all my grandmother's." Think of an income of $10,000 a year being equal to such a strain, and providing suitably for a rich man's large family in the bargain! It wouldn't go so far now, and yet most of the reasonable necessaries of life cost less to-day than they did two generations ago. The difference is that we need so very many comforts that were not invented in our grandfather's time.

There is a hospital, in a city large enough to keep a large hospital busy, that is in straits for money. Its income from contributions last year was larger by nearly a third than its income ten years ago, but its expenses were nearly double

its income. There were some satisfactory reasons
for the discrepancy—the city had grown, the
number of patients had increased, extraordinary
repairs had been made—but at the bottom a very
large expenditure seemed to be due to the struggle
of the managers to keep the institution up to
modern standards. The patients are better cared
for than they used to be; the nurses are better
taught and more skillful; "conveniences" have
been greatly multiplied; the heating and cooking
and laundry work is all done in the best manner
with the most approved apparatus; the plumbing
is as safe as sanitary engineering can make it; the
appliances for antiseptic surgery are fit for a
fight for life; there are detached buildings for
contagious diseases, and an out-patient department, and the whole concern is administered with
wisdom and economy. There is only one distressing circumstance about this excellent charity, and
that is that its expenses exceed its income. And
yet its managers have not been extravagant; they
have only done what the enlightened experience
of the day has considered to be necessary. If the
hospital has to shut down and the patients must
be turned out, at least the receiver will find a
well-appointed institution of which the managers
have no reason to be ashamed.

The trouble seems to be with very many of us,
in contemporary private life as well as in institutions, that the enlightened experience of the day
invents more necessaries than we can get the

money to pay for. Our opulent friends are constantly demonstrating to us by example how indispensably convenient the modern necessaries are, and we keep having them until we either exceed our incomes or miss the higher concerns of life in the effort to maintain a complete outfit of its creature comforts.

And the saddest part of all is that it is in such great measure an American development. We Americans keep inventing new necessaries, and the people of the effete monarchies gradually adopt such of them as they can afford. When we go abroad we growl about the inconveniences of European life—the absence of gas in bedrooms, the scarcity and sluggishness of elevators, the primitive nature of the plumbing, and a long list of other things without which life seems to press unreasonably upon our endurance. Nevertheless, if the *res angustae domi* [3] get straiter than usual, we are always liable to send our families across the water to spend a season in the practice of economy in some land where it costs less to live.

Of course it all belongs to Progress, and no one is quite willing to have it stop, but it does a comfortable sufferer good to get his head out of his conveniences sometimes and complain.

There was a story in the newspapers the other day about a Massachusetts minister who resigned his charge because someone had given his parish a fine house, and his parishioners wanted him to live in it. His salary was too small, he said, to admit of his living in a big house, and he would not do it. He was even deaf to the proposal that he should share the proposed tenement with the sewing societies and clubs of his church, and when the matter came to a serious issue, he relinquished his charge and sought a new field of usefulness. The situation was an amusing instance of the embarrassment of riches. Let no one to whom restricted quarters may have grown irksome, and who covets larger dimensions of shelter, be too hasty in deciding that the minister was wrong. Did you ever see the house that Hawthorne lived in at Lenox? Did you ever see Emerson's house at Concord? They are good houses for Americans to know and remember. They permitted thought.

A big house is one of the greediest cormorants which can light upon a little income. Backs may go threadbare and stomachs may worry along on indifferent filling, but a house *will* have things, though its occupants go without. It is rarely complete, and constantly tempts the imagination to flights in brick and dreams in lath and plaster. It develops annual thirsts for paint and wallpaper, at least, if not for marble and woodcarving. The plumbing in it must be kept in order on pain of death. Whatever price is put on coal, it has to be heated in winter; and if it is rural or suburban, the grass about it must be cut even though funerals in the family have to be put off for the mowing. If the tenants are not rich enough to hire people to keep their house clean, they must do it themselves, for there is no excuse that will pass among housekeepers for a dirty house. The master of a house too big for him may expect to spend the leisure which might be made intellectually or spiritually profitable, in acquiring and putting into practice fag ends of the arts of the plumber, the bell-hanger, the locksmith, the gas-fitter, and the carpenter. Presently he will know how to do everything that can be done in the house, except enjoy himself. He will learn about taxes, too, and water-rates, and how such abominations as sewers or new pavements are always liable to accrue at his expense. As for the mistress, she will be a slave to carpets and curtains, wall-paper, painters, and women who come in by the day to clean. She will be lucky if she gets a chance to say her prayers, and thrice and four times happy when she can read a book or visit with her friends. To live in a big house may be a luxury, provided that one has a full set of money and an enthusiastic housekeeper in one's family; but to scrimp in a big house is a miserable business. Yet such is human folly, that for a man to refuse to live in a house because it is too big for him, is such an exceptional exhibition of sense that it becomes the favorite paragraph of a day in the newspapers.

An ideal of earthly comfort, so common that every reader must have seen it, is to get a house so big that it is burdensome to maintain, and fill it up so full of jimcracks that it is a constant occupation to keep it in order. Then, when the expense of living in it is so great that you can't afford to go away and rest from the burden of it, the situation is complete and boarding-houses and cemeteries begin to yawn for you. How many Americans, do you suppose, out of the droves that flock annually to Europe, are running away from oppressive houses?

When nature undertakes to provide a house, it fits the occupant. Animals, which build by instinct, build only what they need; but man's building instinct, if it gets a chance to spread itself at all, is boundless, just as all his instincts are. For it is man's peculiarity that nature has filled him with impulses to do things, and left it to his discretion when to stop. She never tells him when he has finished. And perhaps we ought not to be surprised that in so many cases it happens that he doesn't know, but just goes ahead as long as the materials last.

If another *man* tries to oppress him, he understands that and is ready to fight to death and sacrifice all he has, rather than submit; but the tyranny of *things* is so subtle, so gradual in its approach, and comes so masked with seeming benefits, that it has him hopelessly bound before he suspects his fetters. He says from day to day, "I will add thus to my house;" "I will have one or two more horses;" "I will make a little greenhouse in my garden;" "I will allow myself the luxury of another hired man;" and so he goes on having things and imagining that he is richer for them. Presently he begins to realize that it is the things that own him. He has piled them up on his shoulders, and there they sit like Sindbad's Old Man and drive him; and it becomes a daily question whether he can keep his trembling legs or not.

All of which is not meant to prove that property has no real value, or to rebut Charles Lamb's scornful denial that enough is as good as a feast. It is not meant to apply to the rich, who can have things comfortably, if they are philosophical; but to us poor, who have constant need to remind ourselves that where the verbs *to have* and *to be* cannot both be completely inflected, the verb *to be* is the one that best repays concentration.

Perhaps we would not be so prone to swamp ourselves with luxuries and vain possessions that we cannot afford, if it were not for our deep-lying propensity to associate with people who are better off than we are. It is usually the sight of their appliances that upsets our little stock of sense, and lures us into an improvident competition.

There is a proverb of Solomon's which prophesies financial wreck or ultimate misfortune of some sort of people who make gifts to the rich. Though not expressly stated, it is somehow implied that the proverb is intended not as a warning to the rich themselves, who may doubtless exchange presents with impunity, but for persons whose incomes rank somewhere between "moderate circumstances" and destitution. That such persons should need to be warned not to spend their substance on the rich seems odd, but when Solomon was busied with precept he could usually be trusted not to waste either words or wisdom. Poor people *are* constantly spending themselves upon the rich, not only because they like them, but often from an instinctive conviction that such expenditure is well invested. I wonder sometimes whether this is true.

To associate with the rich seems pleasant and profitable. They are apt to be agreeable and well informed, and it is good to play with them and enjoy the usufruct of all their pleasant apparatus; but, of course, you can neither hope nor wish to get anything for nothing. Of the cost of the practice, the expenditure of time still seems to be the item that is most serious. It takes a great deal of time to cultivate the rich successfully. If they are working people their time is so much more valuable than yours, that when you visit them it is apt to be your time that is sacrificed. If they are not working people it is worse yet. Their special outings, when they want your company, always come when you cannot get away from work except at some great sacrifice, which, under the stress of temptation, you are too apt to make.

Their pleasuring is on so large a scale that you cannot make it fit your times or necessities. You can't go yachting for half a day, nor will fifty dollars take you far on the way to shoot big game in Manitoba. You simply cannot play with them when they play, because you cannot *reach;* and when they work you cannot play with them, because their time then is worth so much a minute that you cannot bear to waste it. And you cannot play with them when you are working yourself and they are inactively at leisure, because, cheap as your time is, you can't spare it.

Charming and likeable as they are, and good to know, it must be admitted that there is a superior convenience about associating most of the time with people who want to do about what we want to do at about the same time, and whose abilities to do what they wish approximate to ours. It is not so much a matter of persons as of times and means. You cannot make your opportunities concur with the opportunities of people whose incomes are ten times greater than yours. When you play together it is at a sacrifice, and one which *you* have to make. Solomon was right. To associate with very rich people involves sacrifices. You cannot even be rich yourself without expense, and you may just as well give over trying. Count it, then, among the costs of a considerable income that in enlarging the range of your sports it inevitably contracts the circle of those who will find it profitable to share them.

Notes

[1] Thetis dipped her baby son Achilles in the river Styx to make him incapable of injury by man, unknowingly leaving him vulnerable in the heel by which she held him.

[2] Philip Gilbert Hamerton (1834–1894), art critic and man of letters, authority on French art and letters as well as English.

[3] Narrow circumstances at home; hence, need.

Questions

1. How would you link this essay with those of Thoreau, Stevenson, and Anderson?

2. How do they differ?

3. What other "things" besides material things can, and do, tyrannize men and women?

4. What means can people employ to shake off the domination of things?

AN APOLOGY FOR IDLERS

ROBERT LOUIS STEVENSON

From earliest boyhood, ROBERT LOUIS STEVENSON
(1850–1894) wanted to become a writer. His determined
efforts to acquire style and his desire to impress his authorship upon his friends, created considerable comment in
Edinburgh. Clothed in a velvet jacket, Byronic shirt open
at the neck, and flowing tie, with long straight hair to his
shoulders, the youthful Stevenson took every opportunity
to pose as a creative artist, and by so doing frequently
made himself the butt of ridicule. But Stevenson's father,
a successful lighthouse engineer, would have no author in
his family; Louis must study civil engineering or law, at
least. Accordingly, Stevenson studied enough law to enable
him to pass the Scottish Bar Examinations. For some time
"R. L. Stevenson, Advocate" was on the door plate of 17
Heriot Row, Edinburgh; but it is not known that Stevenson
ever practised law. Indeed, one story has it that Stevenson,
seeing a prospective client coming toward his door, stole
quickly out the back way, rather than face the necessity of
giving professional advice. More and more he devoted
himself to the cultivation of his writing, "playing the sedu-
lous ape" to De Quincey by copying out page after page of
De Quincey's essays in longhand, trying in this way to form
the habit of writing sentences like his. Stevenson never
mastered De Quincey's style, as a comparison of the two
will show; but he did master a style that had some of the
other's qualities and had enough distinction of its own to

make an important place for its creator in the ranks of the great English prose writers. While taking a cure at Fontainebleau, he met and immediately·fell in love with a Mrs. Osbourne, a Californian temporarily estranged from her husband. When she returned home the next year, Stevenson decided to follow and urge her to marry him. Parental disapproval only accentuated this determination and led to an open break with his father and the loss of his inheritance. Then followed his journey by immigrant boat and immigrant train to California and his subsequent battle with poverty and ill health. Nursed back to comparative health by Mrs. Osbourne, Stevenson then married her and set out in search of literary fame. Reconciliation with his father made possible his visiting Edinburgh and England and enough freedom to pursue his writing. *Treasure Island, Kidnapped,* and his essays enjoyed increasing popular support both here and in England. After an unsuccessful attempt to conquer tuberculosis at Saranac Lake, New York, Stevenson set off in a small sloop for the Tropics. After some wandering, he settled in Samoa, where his home, Vailima, soon became the resort of native chiefs and all sorts of wanderers who desired his friendly counsel or aid. The last four years of his life were spent there, devoted for the most part to the welfare of others. Perhaps this period is characteristic of the best in Stevenson. His masterful "Father Damien", a product of this period, is one of the strongest denunciations of hypocrisy ever written. Upon his death in 1894, native chieftains bore his body laboriously up a half-broken trail to the summit of a mountain overlooking Vailima, where they buried him with his own *Requiem* as his epitaph:

> Under the wide and starry sky
> Dig the grave and let me lie;
> Glad did I live and gladly die
> And I lay me down with a will.

This be the verse you grave for me:
Here he lies where he longed to be;
Home is the sailor, home from sea,
And the hunter home from the hill.

Boswell: *We grow weary when idle.*

Johnson: *That is, sir, because others being busy, we want company; but if we were idle, there would be no growing weary; we should all entertain one another.*

JUST now, when every one is bound, under pain of a decree in absence convicting him of lèse-respectability, to enter on some lucrative profession, and labor therein with something not far short of enthusiasm, a cry from the opposite party who are content when they have enough, and like to look on and enjoy in the meanwhile, savors a little of bravado and gasconade.[1] And yet this should not be. Idleness so-called, which does not consist of doing nothing, but in doing a great deal not recognized in the dogmatic formularies of the ruling class, has as good a right to state its position as industry itself. It is admitted that the presence of people who refuse to enter in the great handicap race for sixpenny pieces is at once an insult and a disenchantment for those who do. A fine fellow (as we see so many) takes his determination, votes for the sixpences, and, in the emphatic Americanism, "goes for" them. And while such an one is plowing distressfully up the road, it is not hard to understand his resentment, when he perceives cool persons in the meadows by the wayside, lying with a handkerchief over their ears and a glass at their elbow. Alexander is touched in a very delicate place by the disregard of Diogenes.[2] Where was the glory of having taken Rome for these tumultuous barbarians who poured into the Senate house and found the Fathers sitting silent and unmoved by their success? It is a sore thing to have labored along and scaled the arduous hilltops, and, when all is done, find humanity indifferent to your achievement. Hence physicists condemn the unphysical; financiers have only a superficial toleration for those who know little of stocks; literary persons despise the unlettered; and people of all pursuits combine to disparage those who have none.

But, though this is one difficulty of the subject, it is not the greatest. You could not be put in prison for speaking against industry, but you can be sent to Coventry [3] for speaking like a fool. The greatest difficulty with most subjects is to do them well; therefore, please to remember this is an apology. It is certain that much may be judiciously argued in favor of diligence; only there is something to be said against it, and that is what, on the present occasion, I have to say. To state one argument is not necessarily to be deaf to all others, and that a man has written a book of travels in Montenegro is no reason why he should never have been to Richmond.

It is surely beyond a doubt that people should be a good deal idle in youth. For though here and there a Lord Macaulay may escape from school honors with all his wits about him, most boys pay so dear for their medals that they never afterward have a shot in their locker, and begin the world bankrupt. And the same holds true during all the time a lad is educating himself, or suffering others to educate him. It must have been a very foolish old gentleman who addressed Johnson at Oxford in these words: "Young man, ply your book diligently now, and acquire a stock of knowledge; for when years come upon you, you will find that poring upon books will be an irksome task." The old gentleman seems to have been unaware that many other things besides reading grow irksome, and not a few become impossible by the time a man has to use spectacles and cannot walk without a stick. Books are good enough in their own way, but they are a mighty bloodless substitute for life. It seems a pity to sit, like the Lady of Shalott, peering into a mirror, with your back turned on all the bustle and glamour of reality. And if a man reads very hard, as the old anecdote reminds us, he will have little time for thoughts.

If you look back on your own education, I am sure it will not be the full, vivid, instructive hours of truantry that you regret; you would rather cancel some lack-luster periods between sleep and waking in the class. For my own part, I have attended a good many lectures in my time. I still remember that the spinning of a top is a case of

kinetic stability. I still remember that emphy-
teusis is not a disease, nor stillicide a crime. But,
though I would not willingly part with such
scraps of science, I do not set the same store by
them as by certain other odds and ends that I
came by in the open street while I was playing
truant. This is not the moment to dilate on that
mighty place of education, which was the favorite school of Dickens and of Balzac and turns out
yearly many inglorious masters in the Science of
the Aspects of Life. Suffice it to say this: if a lad
does not learn in the streets, it is because he has
no faculty of learning. Nor is the truant always
in the streets, for, if he prefers, he may go out
by the gardened suburbs into the country. He
may pitch on some tuft of lilacs over a burn and
smoke innumerable pipes to the tune of the water
on the stones. A bird will sing in the thicket. And
there he may fall into a vein of kindly thought
and see things in a new perspective. Why, if this
be not education, what is? We may conceive Mr.
Worldly Wiseman accosting such an one and the
conversation that should thereupon ensue:

"How now, young fellow, what dost thou
here?"

"Truly, sir, I take mine ease."

"Is not this the hour of the class? and shouldst
thou not be plying thy Book with diligence, to
the end thou mayest obtain knowledge?"

"Nay, but thus also I follow after Learning, by
your leave."

"Learning, quotha! After what fashion, I pray thee? Is it mathematics?"

"No, to be sure."

"Is it metaphysics?"

"Nor that."

"Is it some language?"

"Nay, it is no language."

"Is it a trade?"

"Nor a trade neither."

"Why, then, what is't?"

"Indeed, sir, as a time may soon come for me to go upon Pilgrimage, I am desirous to note what is commonly done by persons in my case, and where are the ugliest Sloughs and Thickets on the Road; as also, what manner of Staff is of the best service. Moreover, I lie here, by this water, to learn by root-of-heart a lesson which my master teaches me to call Peace, or Contentment."

Hereupon Mr. Worldly Wiseman was much commoved with passion, and, shaking his cane with a very threatful countenance, broke forth upon this wise: "Learning, quotha!" said he; "I would have all such rogues scourged by the Hangman!"

And so he would go his way, ruffling out his cravat with a crackle of starch, like a turkey when it spread its feathers.

Now this, of Mr. Wiseman's, is the common opinion. A fact is not called a fact, but a piece of gossip, as it does not fall into one of your scholastic categories. An inquiry must be in some ac-

knowledged direction, with a name to go by, or
else you are not inquiring at all, only lounging;
and the workhouse is too good for you. It is supposed that all knowledge is at the bottom of a
well or the far end of a telescope. Sainte-Beuve,[4]
as he grew older, came to regard all experience as
a single great book in which to study for a few
years ere we go hence; and it seemed all one to
him whether you should read in chapter XX,
which is the differential calculus, or in chapter
XXXIX, which is hearing the band play in the
gardens. As a matter of fact, an intelligent person,
looking out of his eyes and harkening in his ears,
with a smile on his face all the time, will get more
true education than many another in a life of
heroic vigils. There is certainly some chill and
arid knowledge to be found upon the summits of
formal and laborious science; but it is all round
about you, and for the trouble of looking, you will
acquire the warm and palpitating facts of life.
While others are filling their memory with a lumber of words, one-half of which they will forget
before the week be out, your truant may learn
some really useful art: to play the fiddle, to know
a good cigar, or to speak with ease and opportunity to all varieties of men. Many who have
"plied their book diligently" and know all about
some one branch or another of accepted lore come
out of the study with an ancient and owl-like de-
meanor and prove dry, stockish, and dyspeptic
in all the better and brighter parts of life. Many

make a large fortune, who remain underbred and pathetically stupid to the last. And meantime there goes the idler, who began life along with them—by your leave—a different picture. He has had time to take care of his health and his spirits; he has been a great deal in the open air, which is the most salutary of all things for both body and mind; and, if he has never read the great Book in very recondite places, he has dipped into it and skimmed it over to excellent purpose. Might not the student afford some Hebrew roots, and the business man some of his half-crowns, for a share of the idler's knowledge of life at large and Art of Living? Nay, and the idler has another and more important quality than these. I mean his wisdom. He who has much looked on at the childish satisfaction of other people in their hobbies will regard his own with only a very ironical indulgence. He will not be heard among the dogmatists. He will have a great and cool allowance for all sorts of people and opinions. If he finds no out-of-the-way truths, he will identify himself with no very burning falsehood. His way takes him along a by-road, not much frequented, but very even and pleasant, which is called Commonplace Lane and leads to the Belvedere of Common Sense. Thence he shall command an agreeable, if no very noble prospect; and while others behold the East and West, the Devil and the Sunrise, he will be contentedly aware of a sort of morning hour upon all sublunary things, with an army of shadows running speedily and in many different directions into the great daylight of Eternity. The shadows and the generations, the shrill doctors and the plangent wars, go by into ultimate silence and emptiness; but, underneath all this, a man may see out of the Belvedere windows much green and peaceful landscape; many firelit parlors; good people laughing, drinking, and making love as they did before the Flood or the French Revolution; and the old Shepherd telling his tale under the hawthorn.

Extreme busyness, whether at school or college, kirk or market, is a symptom of deficient vitality; and a faculty for idleness implies a catholic appetite and a strong sense of personal identity. There is a sort of dead-alive, hackneyed people about, who are scarcely conscious of living except in the exercise of some conventional occupation. Bring these fellows into the country, or set them aboard ship, and you will see how they pine for their desk or study. They have no curiosity; they cannot give themselves over to random provocations; they do not take pleasure in the exercise of their faculties for its own sake; and, unless Necessity lays about them with a stick, they will even stand still. It is no good speaking to such folk; they cannot be idle, their nature is not generous enough, and they pass those hours in a sort of coma which are not dedicated to furious moiling in the gold-mill. When they do not require to go to the office, when they are not hungry and have no mind to drink, the whole breathing world is a blank to them. If they have to wait an hour or so for a train, they fall into a stupid trance with their eyes open. To see them, you would suppose there was nothing to look at and no one to speak with; you would imagine they were paralyzed or alienated; and yet very possibly they are hard workers in their own way, and have good eyesight for a flaw in a deed or a turn of the market. They have been to school and college, but all the time they had their eye on the medal; they have gone about in the world and mixed with clever people, but all the time they were thinking of their own affairs. As if a man's soul were not too small to begin with, they have dwarfed and narrowed theirs by a life of all work and no play until here they are at forty, with a listless attention, a mind vacant of all material of amusement, and not one thought to rub against another, while they wait for the train. Before he was breeched he might have clambered on the boxes; when he was twenty he would have stared at the girls; but now the pipe is smoked out, the snuff-box empty, and my gentleman sits bolt upright upon a bench, with lamentable eyes. This does not appeal to me as being Success in Life.

But it is not only the person himself who suffers from his busy habits, but his wife and children, his friends and relations, and down to the very people he sits with in a railway carriage or

an omnibus. Perpetual devotion to what a man
calls his business is only to be sustained by perpetual neglect of many other things. And it is not
by any means certain that a man's business is the
most important thing he has to do. To an impartial estimate it will seem clear that many of the
wisest, most virtuous, and most beneficent parts
that are to be played upon the Theater of Life are
filled by gratuitous performers, and pass, among
the world at large, as phases of idleness. For in
that Theater not only the walking gentlemen,
singing chambermaids, and diligent fiddlers in
the orchestra, but those who look on and clap
their hands from the benches do really play a part
and fulfil important offices toward the general
result. You are no doubt very dependent on the
care of your lawyer and stockbroker, of the
guards and signalmen who convey you rapidly
from place to place, and the policemen who walk
the streets for your protection; but is there not
a thought of gratitude in your heart for certain
other benefactors who set you smiling when they
fall in your way, or season your dinner with good
company? Colonel Newcome helped to lose his
friend's money; Fred Bayham had an ugly trick
of borrowing shirts; and yet they were better
people to fall among than Mr. Barnes. And,
though Falstaff was neither sober nor very honest,
I think I could name one or two long-faced Bar-
abbases whom the world could better have done
without. Hazlitt mentions that he was more sen-

sible of obligation to Northcote, who had never done him anything he could call a service, than to his whole circle of ostentatious friends; for he thought a good companion emphatically the greatest benefactor. I know there are people in the world who cannot feel grateful unless the favor has been done them at the cost of pain and difficulty. But this is a churlish disposition. A man may send you six sheets of letter-paper covered with the most entertaining gossip, or you may pass half an hour pleasantly, perhaps, profitably, over an article of his; do you think the service would be greater if he had made the manuscript in his heart's blood, like a compact with the devil? Do you really fancy you should be more beholden to your correspondent if he had been damning you all the while for your importunity? Pleasures are more beneficial than duties because, like the quality of mercy, they are not strained, and they are twice blest. There must always be two to a kiss, and there may be a score in a jest; but wherever there is an element of sacrifice, the favor is conferred with pain, and, among generous people, received with confusion. There is no duty we so much underrate as the duty of being happy. By being happy, we sow anonymous benefits upon the world, which remain unknown even to ourselves, or, when they are disclosed, surprise nobody so much as the benefactor. The other day a ragged, barefoot boy ran down the street after a marble with so jolly an air that he set every one he passed into a good humor; one of these persons, who had been delivered from more than usually black thoughts, stopped the little fellow and gave him some money with this remark: "You see what sometimes comes of looking pleased." If he had looked pleased before, he had now to look both pleased and mystified. For my part, I justify this encouragement of smiling rather than tearful children; I do not wish to pay for tears anywhere but upon the stage; but I am prepared to deal largely in the opposite commodity. A happy man or woman is a better thing to find than a five-pound note. He or she is a radiating focus of good will; and their entrance into a room is as though another candle had been lighted. We need not care whether they could prove the forty-seventh proposition; they do a better thing than that—they practically demonstrate the great Theorem of the Livableness of Life. Consequently, if a person cannot be happy without remaining idle, idle he should remain. It is a revolutionary precept; but, thanks to hunger and the workhouse, one not easily to be abused; and, within practical limits, it is one of the most incontestable truths in the whole Body of Morality. Look at one of your industrious fellows for a moment, I beseech you. He sows hurry and reaps indigestion; he puts a vast deal of activity out to interest and receives a large measure of nervous derangement in return. Either he absents himself entirely from all fellowship, and lives a recluse in a garret, with carpet slippers and a leaden inkpot; or he comes among people swiftly and bitterly, in a contraction of his whole nervous system, to discharge some temper before he returns to work. I do not care how much or how well he works, this fellow is an evil creature in other people's lives. They would be happier if he were dead. They could easier do without his services in the Circumlocution Office than they can tolerate his fractious spirits. He poisons life at the well-head. It is better to be beggared out of hand by a scapegrace nephew than daily hag-ridden by a peevish uncle.

And what, in God's name, is all this pother about? For what cause do they embitter their own and other people's lives? That a man should publish three or thirty articles a year, that he should finish or not finish his great allegorical picture, are questions of little interest to the world. The ranks of life are full; and, although a thousand fall, there are always some to go into the breach. When they told Joan of Arc she should be at home minding women's work, she answered there were plenty to spin and wash. And so even with your own rare gift! When nature is "so careless of the single life," why should we coddle ourselves into the fancy that our own is of exceptional importance? Suppose Shakespeare had been knocked on the head some dark night in Sir Thomas Lucy's preserves, the world would have wagged on better or worse, the pitcher gone to

the well, the scythe to the corn, and the student
to his book; and no one been any the wiser of
the loss. There are not many works extant, if you
look the alternative all over, which are worth the
price of a pound of tobacco to a man of limited
means. This is a sobering reflection for the proud-
est of our earthly vanities. Even a tobacconist
may, upon consideration, find no great cause for
personal vainglory in the phrase; for, although tobacco is an admirable sedative, the qualities necessary for retailing it are neither rare nor precious in
themselves. Alas and alas! you may take it how
you will, but the services of no single individual
are indispensable. Atlas was just a gentleman
with a protracted nightmare! And yet you see
merchants who go and labor themselves into a
great fortune and thence into the bankruptcy
court; scribblers who keep scribbling at little
articles until their temper is a cross to all who
come about them, as though Pharaoh should set
the Israelites to make a pin instead of a pyramid;
and find young men who work themselves into a
decline, and are driven off in a hearse with white
plumes upon it. Would you not suppose these
persons had been whispered, by the Master of the
Ceremonies, the promise of some momentous destiny; and that this lukewarm bullet on which they
play their farces was the bull's-eye and center
point of all the universe? And yet it is not so.
The ends for which they give away their priceless
youth, for all they know, may be chimerical or

hurtful; the glory and riches they expect may never come, or may find them indifferent; and they and the world they inhabit are so inconsiderable that the mind freezes at the thought.

NOTES

[1] The natives of Gascony are considered by other Frenchmen to be prime boasters and braggarts. A notable Gascon in literature is Cyrano de Bergerac, immortalized by Edmond Rostand.

[2] Look up the life story of this Greek philosopher who made the celebrated hunt for an honest man.

[3] To be sent to Coventry is a common expression in England meaning to be banished from one's own circle of friends.

[4] Charles Augustin Sainte-Beuve, the brilliant French critic (1804–1869).

QUESTIONS

1. What is Stevenson's definition of idleness?
2. What are the fundamentally good things of life, according to Stevenson?
3. What connection has this essay with Martin's?

WHERE I LIVED, AND WHAT I LIVED FOR

Henry David Thoreau

Henry David Thoreau (1817–1862) was born in Concord, Massachusetts, of Scotch and French stock. At the age of sixteen, he entered Harvard University, and, soon after, through the intercession of Ralph Waldo Emerson received scholarship aid, though he was in no way a distinguished scholar. Upon his graduation, Thoreau taught school in Concord for two years, to the discomfort and indignation of the townspeople who considered as absurd and dangerous Thoreau's substitution of reasoning, or "talking morals," for the customary rod. The manufacture of lead pencils, his father's trade, came next; and to this Thoreau applied himself so diligently that he soon perfected a pencil which assured him success and fortune. But Thoreau, already different from his friends, declared he would never make another pencil, saying, "Why should I? I would not do again what I have done once." Next, came the study of nature, and when he was about twenty-eight years old, the two-year hermitage at Lake Walden, during which Thoreau earned the minimum wants of life by doing manual labor for his neighbors: building fences and boats, planting, grafting, and some surveying. "Where I Lived, and What I Lived For" was written during this self-imposed exile in the woods. A close friend of the Concord authors headed by Emerson, he derived more from them, seemingly, than his shyness would permit him to contribute. But his influence has steadily grown; Thoreau's essay on *Civil Disobedience* influenced Mahatma Gandhi so profoundly at the outset of his legal career that it has remained to this day a sort of sacred scripture by which Gandhi hopes to teach the natives of India the way toward the light.

AT A certain season of our life we are accustomed to consider every spot as the possible site of a house. I have thus surveyed the country on every side within a dozen miles of where I live. In imagination I have bought all the farms in succession, for all were to be bought, and I knew their price. I walked over each farmer's premises, tasted his wild apples, discoursed on husbandry with him, took his farm at his price, at any price, mortgaging it to him in my mind; even put a higher price on it,—took everything but a deed of it,—took his word for his deed, for I dearly love to talk,—cultivated it, and him too to some extent, I trust, and withdrew when I had enjoyed it long enough, leaving him to carry it on. This experience entitled me to be regarded as a sort of real-estate broker by my friends. Wherever I sat, there I might live, and the landscape radiated from me accordingly. What is a house but a *sedes*, a seat?—better if a country seat. I discovered many a site for a house not likely to be soon improved, which some might have thought too far from the village, but to my eyes the village was too far from it. Well, there I might live, I said; and there I did live, for an hour, a summer and a winter life; saw how I could let the years run off, buffet the winter through, and see the spring come in. The future inhabitants of this region, wherever they may place their houses, may be sure that they have been anticipated. An afternoon sufficed to lay out the land into orchard, woodlot, and pasture, and to decide what fine oaks or pines should be left to stand before the door, and whence each blasted tree could be seen to the best advantage; and then I let it lie, fallow perchance, for a man is rich in proportion to the number of things which he can afford to let alone.

My imagination carried me so far that I even had the refusal of several farms,—the refusal was all I wanted,—but I never got my fingers burned by actual possession. The nearest that I came to actual possession was when I bought the Hollowell place, and had begun to sort my seeds, and collected materials with which to make a wheelbarrow to carry it on or off with; but before the owner gave me a deed of it, his wife—every man has such a wife—changed her mind and wished to keep it, and he offered me ten dollars to release him. Now, to speak the truth, I had but ten cents in the world, and it surpassed my arithmetic to tell, if I was that man who had ten cents, or who had a farm, or ten dollars, or all together. However, I let him keep the ten dollars and the farm too, for I had carried it far enough; or rather, to be generous, I sold him the farm for just what I gave for it, and as he was not a rich man, made him a present of ten dollars, and still had my ten cents, and seeds, and materials for a wheelbarrow left. I found thus that I had been a rich man without any damage to my poverty. But I retained the landscape, and have since annually carried off what it yielded without a wheelbarrow. With respect to landscapes,—

> "I am monarch of all I *survey,*
> My right there is none to dispute."

I have frequently seen a poet withdraw, having enjoyed the most valuable part of a farm, while the crusty farmer supposed that he had got a few wild apples only. Why, the owner does not know it for many years when a poet has put his farm in rhyme, the most admirable kind of invisible fence, has fairly impounded it, milked it, skimmed it, and got all the cream, and left the farmer only the skimmed milk.

The real attractions of the Hollowell farm, to me, were: its complete retirement, being about two miles from the village, half a mile from the nearest neighbour, and separated from the highway by a broad field; its bounding on the river, which the owner said protected it by its fogs from frosts in the spring, though that was nothing to me; the grey colour and ruinous state of the house and barn, and the dilapidated fences, which put such an interval between me and the last occupant; the hollow and lichen-covered apple trees, gnawed by rabbits, showing what kind of neighbours I should have; but above all, the recollection I had of it from my earliest voyages up the river, when the house was concealed behind a dense grove of red maples, through which I heard the house-dog bark. I was in haste to buy it, before the proprietor finished getting out some rocks, cutting down the hollow apple trees, and grubbing up some young birches which had sprung up in the pasture, or, in short, had made any more of his improvements. To enjoy these advantages I was ready to carry it on; like Atlas, to take the world on my shoulders,—I have never heard what compensation he received for that,—and do all those things which had no other motive or excuse but that I might pay for it and be unmolested in my possession of it; for I knew all the while that it would yield the most abundant crop of the kind I wanted if I could only afford to let it alone. But it turned out as I have said.

All that I could say, then, with respect to farming on a large scale (I have always cultivated a garden), was, that I had had my seeds ready. Many think that seeds improve with age. I have no doubt that time discriminates between the good and the bad; and when at last I shall plant, I shall be less likely to be disappointed. But I would say to my fellows, once for all, as long as possible live free and uncommitted. It makes but little difference whether you are committed to a farm or the county jail.[1]

Old Cato,[2] whose "De Re Rustica" is my "Cultivator", says, and the only translation I have seen makes sheer nonsense of the passage, "When you think of getting a farm, turn it thus in your mind, not to buy greedily, nor spare your pains to look at it, and do not think it enough to go round it once. The oftener you go there the more it will please you, if it is good." I think I shall not buy greedily, but go round and round it as long as I live, and be buried in it first, that it may please me the more at last.

The present was my next experiment of this kind, which I purpose to describe more at length; for convenience, putting the experience of two years into one. As I have said, I do not propose to write an ode to dejection, but to brag as lustily as chanticleer in the morning, standing on his roost, if only to wake my neighbours up.

When first I took up my abode in the woods, that is, began to spend my nights as well as days there, which, by accident, was on Independence Day, on the 4th of July, 1845, my house was not finished for winter, but was merely a defence against the rain, without plastering or chimney, the walls being of rough weatherstained boards, with wide chinks, which made it cool at night.[3] The upright white hewn studs and freshly planed door and window-casings gave it a clean and airy look, especially in the morning, when its timbers were saturated with dew, so that I fancied that by noon some sweet gum would exude from them. To my imagination it retained throughout the day more or less of this auroral character, reminding me of a certain house on a mountain which I had visited the year before. This was an airy, an unplastered cabin, fit to entertain a travelling god, and where a goddess might trail her garments. The winds which passed over my dwelling were such as sweep over the ridges of mountains, bearing the broken strains, or celestial parts only, of terrestrial music. The morning wind forever blows, the poem of creation is uninterrupted; but few are the ears that hear it. Olympus is but the outside of the earth everywhere.

The only house I had been the owner of before, if I except a boat, was a tent, which I used occasionally when making excursions in the summer, and this is still rolled up in my garret; but the boat, after passing from hand to hand, has gone down the stream of time. With this more substantial shelter about me, I had made some progress toward settling in the world. This frame, so slightly clad, was a sort of crystallization around me, and reacted on the builder. It was suggestive somewhat as a picture in outlines. I did not need to go out doors to take the air, for the atmosphere within had lost none of its freshness. It was not so much within doors as behind a door where I sat, even in the rainiest weather. The Harivansa [4] says, "An abode without birds is like a meat without seasoning." Such was not my abode, for I found myself suddenly neighbour to the birds; not by having imprisoned one, but having caged myself near them. I was not only nearer to some of those which commonly frequent the garden and

the orchard, but to those wilder and more thrilling
songsters of the forest which never, or rarely,
serenade a villager,—the woodthrush, the veery,
the scarlet tanager, the field-sparrow, the whip-
poorwill, and many others.

I was seated by the shore of a small pond,[5]
about a mile and a half south of the village of
Concord and somewhat higher than it, in the
midst of an extensive wood between that town
and Lincoln, and about two miles south of that
our only field known to fame, Concord battle
ground; but I was so low in the woods that the
opposite shore, half a mile off, like the rest, covered with wood, was my most distant horizon.
For the first week, whenever I looked out on the
pond, it impressed me like a tarn high up on the
one side of a mountain, its bottom far above the
surface of other lakes, and, as the sun arose, I
saw it throwing off its nightly clothing of mist,
and here and there, by degrees, its soft ripples or
its smooth reflecting surface was revealed, while
the mists, like ghosts, were stealthily withdrawing
in every direction into the woods, as at the breaking up of some nocturnal conventicle. The very
dew seemed to hang upon the trees later into the
day than usual, as on the sides of mountains.

This small lake was of most value as a neighbour in the intervals of a gentle rain-storm in
August, when, both air and water being perfectly
still, but the sky overcast, mid-afternoon had all
the serenity of evening, and the woodthrush sang

around, and was heard from shore to shore. A lake like this is never smoother than at such a time; and the clear portion of the air above it being shallow and darkened by clouds, the water, full of light and reflections, becomes a lower heaven itself so much the more important. From a hill-top near by, where the wood had been recently cut off, there was a pleasing vista southward across the pond, through a wide indentation in the hills which form the shore there, where their opposite sides sloping toward each other suggested a stream flowing out in that direction through a wooded valley, but stream there was none. That way I looked between and over the near green hills to some distant and higher ones in the horizon, tinged with blue. Indeed, by standing on tip-toe I could catch a glimpse of some of the peaks of the still bluer and more distant mountain ranges in the north-west, those true-blue coins from heaven's own mint, and also of some portion of the village. But in other directions, even from this point, I could not see over or beyond the woods which surrounded me. It is well to have some water in your neighbourhood, to give buoyancy to and float the earth. One value even of the smallest well is, that when you look into it you see that earth is not continent but insular. This is as important as that it keeps butter cool. When I looked across the pond from this peak toward the Sudbury meadows, which in time of flood I distinguished elevated perhaps by a mirage in their seething valley, like a coin in a basin, all the earth beyond the pond appeared like a thin crust insulated and floated even by this small sheet of intervening water, and I was reminded that this on which I dwelt was but *dry land*.

Though the view from my door was still more contracted, I did not feel crowded or confined in the least. There was pasture enough for my imagination. The low shrub-oak plateau to which the opposite shore arose, stretched away toward the prairies of the West and the steppes of Tartary, affording ample room for all the roving families of men. "There are none happy in the world but beings who enjoy freely a vast horizon," said Damodara, when his herds required new and larger pastures.

Both place and time were changed, and I dwelt nearer to those parts of the universe and to those eras in history which had most attracted me. Where I lived was as far off as many a region viewed nightly by astronomers. We are wont to imagine rare and delectable places in some remote and more celestial corner of the system, behind the constellation of Cassiopeia's Chair, far from noise and disturbance. I discovered that my house actually had its site in such a withdrawn, but for ever new and unprofaned, part of the universe. If it were worth the while to settle in those parts near to the Pleiades or the Hyades, to Aldebaran or Altair, then I was really there, or at an equal remoteness from the life which I had left behind, dwindled and twinkling with as fine a ray to my nearest neighbour, and to be seen only in moon-less nights by him. Such was that part of creation where I had squatted—

> "There was a shepherd that did live,
>   And held his thoughts as high
> As were the mounts whereon his flocks
>   Did hourly feed him by."

What should we think of the shepherd's life if his flocks always wandered to higher pastures than his thoughts?

Every morning was a cheerful invitation to make my life of equal simplicity, and I may say innocence, with Nature herself. I have been as sincere a worshipper of Aurora as the Greeks. I got up early and bathed in the pond: that was a religious exercise, and one of the best things which I did. They say that characters were en-graven on the bathing tub of king Tching-thang to this effect: "Renew thyself completely each day; do it again and again, and forever again." I can understand that. Morning brings back the heroic ages. I was as much affected by the faint hum of a mosquito making its invisible and un-imaginable tour through my apartment at earliest dawn, when I was sitting with door and windows open, as I could be by any trumpet that ever sang of fame. It was Homer's [6] requiem; itself an Iliad and Odyssey in the air, singing its own wrath and wanderings. There was something cosmical about it; a standing advertisement, till forbidden, of the everlasting vigour and fertility of the world. The morning, which is the most memorable season of the day, is the awakening hour. Then there is least somnolence in us; and for an hour, at least, some part of us awakes which slumbers all the rest of the day and night. Little is to be expected of that day, if it can be called a day, to which we are not awakened by our Genius, but by the mechanical nudgings of some servitor, are not awakened by our own newly-acquired force and aspirations from within, accompanied by the undulations of celestial music, instead of factory bells, and a fragrance filling the air—to a higher life than we fell asleep from; and thus the darkness bears its fruit, and proves itself to be good, no less than the light. That man who does not believe that each day contains an earlier, more sacred, and auroral hour than he has yet profaned, has despaired of life, and is pursuing a descending and darkening way. After a partial cessation of his sensuous life, the soul of man, or its organs rather, are reinvigorated each day, and his Genius tries again what noble life it can make. All memorable events, I should say, transpire in morning time and in a morning atmosphere. The Vedas [7] say, "All intelligences awake with the morning." Poetry and art, and the fairest and most memorable of the actions of men, date from such an hour. All poets and heroes, like

Memnon, are the children of Aurora, and emit their music at sunrise. To him whose elastic and vigorous thought keeps pace with the sun, the day is a perpetual morning. It matters not what the clocks say or the attitudes and labours of men. Morning is when I am awake and there is a dawn in me. Moral reform is the effort to throw off sleep. Why is it that men give so poor an account of their day if they have not been slumbering? They are not such poor calculators. If they had not been overcome with drowsiness they would have performed something. The millions are awake enough for physical labour; but only one in a million is awake enough for effective intellectual exertion, only one in a hundred millions to a poetic or divine life. To be awake is to be alive. I have never yet met a man who was quite awake. How could I have looked him in the face?

We must learn to reawaken and keep ourselves awake, not by mechanical aids, but by an infinite expectation of the dawn, which does not forsake us in our soundest sleep. I know of no more encouraging fact than the unquestionable ability of man to elevate his life by a conscious endeavour. It is something to be able to paint a particular picture, or to carve a statue, and so to make a few objects beautiful; but it is far more glorious to carve and paint the very atmosphere and medium through which we look, which morally we can do. To affect the quality of the day, that is the highest of arts. Every man is tasked to make his life, even in its details, worthy of the contemplation of his most elevated and critical hour. If we refused, or rather used up, such paltry information as we get, the oracles would distinctly inform us how this might be done.

I went to the woods because I wished to live deliberately, to front only the essential facts of life, and see if I could not learn what it had to teach, and not, when I came to die, discover that I had not lived. I did not wish to live what was not life, living is so dear; nor did I wish to practise resignation, unless it was quite necessary. I wanted to live deep and suck out all the marrow of life, to live so sturdily and Spartan-like as to put to rout all that was not life, to cut a broad swath and shave close, to drive life into a corner, and reduce it to its lowest terms, and, if it proved to be mean, why then to get the whole and genuine meanness of it, and publish its meanness to the world; or if it were sublime, to know it by experience, and be able to give a true account of it in my next excursion. For most men, it appears to me, are in a strange uncertainty about it, whether it is of the devil or of God, and have *somewhat hastily* concluded that it is the chief end of man here to "glorify God and enjoy Him forever."

Still we live meanly, like ants; though the fable tells us that we were long ago changed into men; like pygmies we fight with cranes; it is error upon error, and clout upon clout, and our best virtue has for its occasion a superfluous and evitable wretchedness. Our life is frittered away by detail. An honest man has hardly need to count more than his ten fingers, or in extreme cases he may add his ten toes, and lump the rest. Simplicity, simplicity, simplicity! I say, let your affairs be as two or three, and not a hundred or a thousand; instead of a million count half-a-dozen, and keep your accounts on your thumbnail. In the midst of this chopping sea of civilised life, such are the clouds and storms and quicksands and thousand-and-one items to be allowed for, that a man has to live, if he would not founder and go to the bottom and not make his port at all, by dead reckoning, and he must be a great calculator indeed who succeeds. Simplify, simplify. Instead of three meals a-day, if it be necessary eat but one; instead of a hundred dishes, five; and reduce other things in proportion. Our life is like a German Confederacy, made up of petty states, with its boundary forever fluctuating, so that even a German cannot tell you how it is bounded at any moment. The nation itself, with all its so-called internal improvements, which, by the way, are all external and superficial, is just such an unwieldy and overgrown establishment, cluttered with furniture and tripped up by its own traps, ruined by luxury and heedless expense, by want of calculation and a worthy aim, as the million households in the land; and the only cure for it as for them is in a rigid economy, a stern and

more than Spartan simplicity of life and eleva-
tion of purpose. It lives too fast. Men think that
it is essential that the *Nation* have commerce, and
export ice, and talk through a telegraph, and ride
thirty miles an hour, without a doubt, whether
they do or not; but whether we should live like
baboons or like men, is a little uncertain. If we
do not get out sleepers, and forge rails, and devote days and nights to the work, but go to
tinkering upon our *lives* to improve *them*, who
will build railroads? And if railroads are not built,
how shall we get to heaven in season? But if we
stay at home and mind our business, who will
want railroads? We do not ride on the railroad;
it rides upon us. Did you ever think what those
sleepers are that underlie the railroad? Each one
is a man, an Irishman, or a Yankee man. The
rails are laid on them, and they are covered with
sand, and the cars run smoothly over them. They
are sound sleepers, I assure you. And every few
years a new lot is laid down and run over; so
that, if some have the pleasure of riding on a
rail, others have the misfortune to be ridden upon.
And when they run over a man that is walking
in his sleep, a supernumerary sleeper in the wrong
position, and wake him up, they suddenly stop
the cars, and make a hue and cry about it, as if
this were an exception. I am glad to know that it
takes a gang of men for every five miles to keep
the sleepers down and level in their beds as it is,

for this is a sign that they may sometime get up again.

Why should we live with such hurry and waste of life? We are determined to be starved before we are hungry. Men say that a stitch in time saves nine, and so they take a thousand stitches to-day to save nine to-morrow. As for *work*, we haven't any of any consequence. We have the Saint Vitus' dance, and cannot possibly keep our heads still. If I should only give a few pulls at the parish bell-rope, as for a fire, that is, without setting the bell, there is hardly a man on his farm in the outskirts of Concord, notwithstanding that press of engagements which was his excuse so many times this morning, nor a boy, nor a woman, I might almost say, but would forsake all and follow that sound, not mainly to save property from the flames, but, if we will confess the truth, much more to see it burn, since burn it must, and we, be it known, did not set it on fire,—or to see it put out, and have a hand in it, if that is done as handsomely; yes, even if it were the parish church itself. Hardly a man takes a half-hour's nap after dinner, but when he wakes he holds up his head and asks, "What's the news?" as if the rest of mankind had stood his sentinels. Some give directions to be waked every half hour, doubtless for no other purpose; and then to pay for it, they tell what they have dreamed. After a night's sleep the news is as indispensable as the breakfast. "Pray, tell me anything new that has happened to a man anywhere on this globe,"—and he reads it over his coffee and rolls, that a man has had his eyes gouged out this morning on the Wachito River; never dreaming the while that he lives in the dark unfathomed mammoth cave of this world, and has but the rudiment of an eye himself.

For my part, I could easily do without the post office. I think that there are very few important communications made through it. To speak critically, I never received more than one or two letters in my life—I wrote this some years ago—that were worth the postage. The penny-post is, commonly, an institution through which you seriously offer a man that penny for his thoughts which is so often safely offered in jest. And I am sure that I never read any memorable news in a newspaper. If we read of one man robbed, or murdered, or killed by accident, or one house burned, or one vessel wrecked, or one steamboat blown-up, or one cow run over on the Western Railroad, or one mad dog killed, or one lot of grasshoppers in the winter,—we never need read of another. One is enough. If you are acquainted with the principle, what do you care for a myriad instances and applications? To a philosopher all *news*, as it is called, is gossip, and they who edit and read it are old women over their tea. Yet not a few are greedy after this gossip. There was such a rush, as I hear, the other day at one of the offices to learn the foreign news by the last ar-

rival that several large squares of plate glass belonging to the establishment were broken by the
pressure,—news which I seriously think a ready
wit might write a twelvemonth or twelve years
beforehand with sufficient accuracy. As for Spain,
for instance, if you know how to throw in Don
Carlos and the Infanta, and Don Pedro and Se-
ville and Granada, from time to time in the right
proportions,—they may have changed the names
a little since I saw the papers,—and serve up a
bullfight when other entertainments fail, it will
be true to the letter, and give us as good an idea
of the exact state of ruin of things in Spain as
the most succinct and lucid reports under this
head in the newspapers: and as for England, almost the last significant scrap of news from that
quarter was the Revolution of 1649; and if you
have learned the history of her crops for an average year, you never need attend to that thing
again, unless your speculations are of a merely
pecuniary character. If one may judge who rarely
looks into the newspapers, nothing new does ever
happen in foreign parts, a French Revolution not
excepted.

What news! how much more important to
know what that is which was never old! "Kieou-
he-yu (great dignitary of the state of Wei) sent
a man to Khoung-tseu to know his news. Khoung-
tseu caused the messenger to be seated near him,
and questioned him in these terms: What is your
master doing? The messenger answered with re-

spect: My master desires to diminish the number of his faults, but he cannot come to the end of them. The messenger being gone, the philosopher remarked: What a worthy messenger! What a worthy messenger!" The preacher, instead of vexing the ears of drowsy farmers on their day of rest at the end of the week,—for Sunday is the fit conclusion of an ill-spent week, and not the fresh and brave beginning of a new one,—with this one other draggle-tail of a sermon, should shout with thundering voice,—"Pause! Avast! Why so seeming fast, but deadly slow?"

Shams and delusions are esteemed for soundest truths, while reality is fabulous. If men would steadily observe realities only, and not allow themselves to be deluded, life, to compare it with such things as we know, would be like a fairy tale and the Arabian Nights' Entertainments. If we respected only what is inevitable and has a right to be, music and poetry would resound along the streets. When we are unhurried and wise, we perceive that only great and worthy things have any permanent and absolute existence,—that petty fears and petty pleasures are but the shadow of the reality. This is always exhilarating and sublime. By closing the eyes and slumbering, and consenting to be deceived by shows, men establish and confirm their daily life of routine and habit everywhere, which still is built on purely illusory foundations. Children, who play life, discern its true law and relations more clearly than men, who fail to live it worthily, but who think that they are wiser by experience, that is, by failure. I have read in a Hindoo book, that "there was a king's son, who, being expelled in infancy from his native city, was brought up by a forester, and, growing up to maturity in that state, imagined himself to belong to the barbarous race with which he lived. One of his father's ministers having discovered him, revealed to him what he was, and the misconception of his character was removed, and he knew himself to be a prince. So the soul," continues the Hindoo philosopher, "from the circumstances in which it is placed, mistakes its own character, until the truth is revealed to it by some holy teacher, and then it knows itself to be *Brahme*." I perceive that we inhabitants of New England live this mean life that we do because our vision does not penetrate the surface of things. We think that that *is* which *appears* to be. If a man should walk through this town and see only the reality, where, think you, would the "Mill dam" go to? If he should give us an account of the realities he beheld there, we should not recognise the place in his description. Look at a meeting-house, or a court-house, or a jail, or a shop, or a dwelling-house, and say what that thing really is before a true gaze, and they would all go to pieces in your account of them. Men esteem truth remote, in the outskirts of the system, behind the farthest star, before Adam and after the last man. In eternity there is indeed something true and sublime. But all these times and places and occasions are now and here. God Himself culminates in the present moment, and will never be more divine in the lapse of all the ages. And we are enabled to apprehend at all what is· sublime and noble only by the perpetual instilling and drenching of the reality that surrounds us. The universe constantly and obediently answers to our conceptions; whether we travel fast or slow, the track is laid for us. Let us spend our lives in conceiving them. The poet or the artist never yet had so fair and noble a design but some of his posterity at least could accomplish it.

Let us spend one day as deliberately as Nature, and not be thrown off the track by every nutshell and mosquito's wing that falls on the rails. Let us rise early and fast, or break fast, gently and without perturbation; let company come and let company go, let the bells ring and the children cry,—determined to make a day of it. Why should we knock under and go with the stream? Let us not be upset and overwhelmed in that terrible rapid and whirlpool called a dinner, situated in the meridian shallows. Weather this danger and you are safe, for the rest of the way is down hill. With unrelaxed nerves, with morning vigour, sail by it, looking another way, tied to the mast like Ulysses.[8] If the engine whistles, let it whistle till it is hoarse for its pains. If the bell rings, why should we run? We will consider what kind of music they are like. Let us settle ourselves, and work and wedge our feet downward through the mud and slush of opinion, and prejudice, and tradition, and delusion, and appearance, that alluvion which covers the globe, through Paris and London, through New York and Boston and Concord, through church and state, through poetry and philosophy and religion, till we come to a hard bottom and rocks in place, which we can call *reality,* and say, This is, and no mistake; and then begin, having a *point d'appui,*[9] below freshet and frost and fire, a place where you might found a wall or a state, or set a lamp-post safely, or perhaps a gauge, not a Nilometer, but a "Realometer," [10] that future ages might know how deep a freshet of shams and appearances had gathered from time to time. If you stand right fronting and face to face to a fact, you will see the sun glimmer on both its surfaces, as if it were a scimitar, and feel its sweet edge dividing you through the heart and marrow, and so you will happily conclude your mortal career. Be it life or death, we crave only reality. If we are really dying, let us hear the rattle in our throats and feel cold in the extremities; if we are alive, let us go about our business.

Time is but the stream I go a-fishing in. I drink at it; but while I drink I see the sandy bottom and detect how shallow it is. Its thin current slides away, but eternity remains. I would drink deeper; fish in the sky, whose bottom is pebbly with stars. I cannot count one. I know not the first letter of the alphabet. I have always been regretting that I was not as wise as the day I was born. The intellect is a cleaver; it discerns and rifts its way into the secret of things. I do not wish to be any more busy with my hands than is necessary. My head is hands and feet. I feel all my best faculties concentrated in it. My instinct tells me that my head is an organ for burrowing, as some creatures use their snout and forepaws, and with it I would mine and burrow my way through these hills. I think that the richest vein is somewhere hereabouts; so by the divining rod and thin rising vapours I judge; and here I will begin to mine.

NOTES

[1] See E. S. Martin's "The Tyranny of Things" for an enlargement of this point.

[2] Cato the Elder, Roman statesman, 234–149 B.C., renowned for his wisdom.

[3] James Russell Lowell ridiculed the severity of Thoreau's living in solitude less than two miles from Concord. On hearing of the experiment, Stevenson, the author of "An Apology for Idlers," called Thoreau a skulker, but later retracted.

[4] The *Harivansa*, a Sanskrit epic devoted to the life and adventures of Krishna as an incarnation of the god Vishnu. Part three of the epic deals with future ages and the decadence of the world.

[5] Walden Pond.

[6] Homer, blind Greek poet of the 9th century B.C., reputed author of the epics *Iliad* and *Odyssey*.

[7] The Vedas:—The Sacred Books of the Hindus.

[8] Ulysses, hero of Homer's *Odyssey*.

⁹ *point d'appui:* base, fulcrum, point of support.
¹⁰ gauges of trivialities or nothing, and of essentials or reality.

Questions

1. What Hollowell houses have you lived in imaginatively?
2. What did Thoreau mean by "the essential facts of life"?
3. What, according to Thoreau, is the value of a healthy doubt?
4. Of what institutions today do you think Thoreau would disapprove? Why?
5. What arguments, do you suppose, have been opposed to these doctrines of Thoreau?

INTERLUDE: ON JARGON *

Sir Arthur Quiller-Couch

Sir Arthur Quiller-Couch is best known in America for his editing of the monumental anthology, *The Oxford Book of English Verse;* in England he is revered as one of the most scholarly of Cambridge dons, as the masterful "Q" of several literary magazines, and as an authority on the history of Cornish coast towns. Born in Fowey, Cornwall, in 1863 and educated at Newton Abbot, Clifton, and Trinity Colleges, Oxford, he remained at Oxford for a year after graduation as lecturer in the Classics. In 1887 he left university life to do critical writing for *The Speaker,* which was then being launched in London. His growing reputation as critic and scholar, his commission in 1897 to complete Stevenson's unfinished *St. Ives,* and his unsurpassed *Oxford Book of English Verse* led to his being knighted in 1910. Two years later he became Professor of English Literature at Cambridge University, and as such has contributed lectures *On the Art of Writing, Studies of Literature,* and *On the Art of Reading* which occupy authoritative positions in critical literature. Several of his novels deal with Cornwall coast towns, particularly Fowey, to which he returns from his lecturing at Cambridge. At seventy he is still slight and athletic-looking, interested in yachting and all sorts of smaller boats that haunt the Cornish coast, and combines the breeziness of an old salt

* Reprinted from *On the Art of Writing* by Sir Arthur Quiller-Couch by permission of G. P. Putnam's Sons, publishers.

with the scholar's air which he wears lightly. His lecture "On Jargon", from *On the Art of Writing* is already a classic and is regarded in literary circles as law.

WE PARTED, Gentlemen, upon a promise to discuss the capital difficulty of Prose, as we have discussed the capital difficulty of Verse. But, although we shall come to it, on second thoughts I ask leave to break the order of my argument and to interpose some words upon a kind of writing which, from a superficial likeness, commonly passes for prose in these days, and by lazy folk is commonly written for prose, yet actually is not prose at all; my excuse being the simple practical one that, by first clearing this sham prose out of the way, we shall the better deal with honest prose when we come to it. The proper difficulties of prose will remain; but we shall be agreed in understanding what it is, or at any rate what it is not, that we talk about. I remember to have heard somewhere of a religious body in the United States of America which had reason to suspect one of its churches of accepting spiritual consolation from a coloured preacher—an offence against the laws of the Synod—and despatched a Disciplinary Committee with power to act; and of the Committee's returning to report itself unable to take any action under its terms of reference, for that while a person undoubtedly coloured had undoubtedly occupied the pulpit and had audibly spoken from it in the Committee's presence, the performance could be brought within no defini-

tion of preaching known or discoverable. So it is
with that infirmity of speech—that flux, that determination of words to the mouth, or to the pen,
—which, though it be familiar to you in parliamentary debates, in newspapers, and as the staple
language of Blue Books, Committees, Official
Reports, I take leave to introduce to you as prose
which is not prose and under its real name of
Jargon.

You must not confuse this Jargon with what is
called Journalese. The two overlap, indeed, and
have a knack of assimilating each other's vices.
But Jargon finds, maybe, the most of its votaries
among good douce people who have never written
to or for a newspaper in their life, who would
never talk of "adverse climatic conditions" when
they mean "bad weather"; who have never trifled
with verbs such as "obsess," "recrudesce," "en-
visage," "adumbrate," or with phrases such as
"the psychological moment," "the true inward-
ness," "it gives furiously to think." It dallies with
Latinity—"sub silentio," "de die in diem," "cui
bono?" (always in the sense, unsuspected by
Cicero, of "What is the profit?")—but not for
the sake of style. Your journalist at the worst is
an artist in his way; he daubs paint of this kind
upon the lily with a professional zeal; the more
flagrant (or, to use his own word, arresting) the
pigment, the happier is his soul. Like the Babu
he is trying all the while to embellish our poor
language, to make it more floriferous, more poet-

ical—like the Babu for example who, reporting
his mother's death, wrote, "Regret to inform you,
the hand that rocked the cradle has kicked the
bucket."

There is metaphor; *there* is ornament; *there* **is**
a sense of poetry, though as yet groping in a
world unrealised. No such gusto marks—no such
zeal, artistic or professional, animates—the practitioners of Jargon, who are, most of them (I repeat), douce respectable persons. Caution is its
father; the instinct to save everything and especially trouble; its mother, Indolence. It looks precise, but is not. It is, in these times, *safe:* a thousand men have said it before and not one to your
knowledge had been prosecuted for it. And so,
like respectability in Chicago, Jargon stalks un-
checked in our midst. It is becoming the language
of Parliament; it has become the medium through
which Boards of Government, County Councils,
Syndicates, Committees, Commercial Firms, express the processes as well as the conclusions of
their thought and so voice the reason of their
being.

Has a Minister to say "No" in the House of
Commons? Some men are constitutionally incapable of saying no; but the Minister conveys it
thus: "The answer to the question is in the negative." That means "no." Can you discover it to
mean anything less, or anything more except that
the speaker is a pompous person?—which was no
part of the information demanded.

That is Jargon, and it happens to be accurate. But as a rule Jargon is by no means accurate, its method being to walk circumspectly around its target; and its faith, that having done so it has either hit the bull's-eye or at least achieved something equivalent, and safer.

Thus the clerk of a Board of Guardians will minute that—

In the case of John Jenkins deceased the coffin provided was of the usual character.

Now this is not accurate. "In the case of John Jenkins deceased," for whom a coffin was supplied, it is wholly superfluous to tell us that he is deceased. But actually John Jenkins never had more than one case, and that was the coffin. The clerk says he had two,—a coffin in a case; but I suspect the clerk to be mistaken, and I am sure he errs in telling us that the coffin was of the usual character; for coffins have no character, usual or unusual.

For another example (I shall not tell you whence derived)—

In the case of every candidate who is placed in the first class (So you see the lucky fellow gets a case as well as a first-class. He might be a stuffed animal: perhaps he is)— In the case of every candidate who is placed in the first class the class-list will show by some convenient mark (1) the Section or Sections for proficiency in which he is placed in the first class and (2) the Section or Sections (if any) in which he has passed with special distinction.

"The Section or Sections (if any)"—But how, if they are not any, could they be indicated by a mark however convenient?

The Examiners will have regard to the style and method of the candidate's answers, and will give credit for excellence in *these respects*.

Have you begun to detect the two main vices of Jargon? The first is that it uses circumlocution rather than short straight speech. It says: "In the case of John Jenkins deceased, the coffin" when it means "John Jenkins' coffin"; and its yea is not yea, neither is its nay nay; but its answer is in the affirmative or in the negative, as the foolish and superfluous "case" may be. The second vice is that it habitually chooses vague woolly abstract nouns rather than concrete ones. I shall have something to say by-and-by about the concrete noun, and how you should ever be struggling for it whether in prose or in verse. For the moment I content myself with advising you, if you would write masculine English, never to forget the old tag of your Latin Grammar—

> Masculine will only be
> Things that you can touch and see.

But since these lectures are meant to be a course in First Aid to writing, I will content myself with one or two extremely rough rules; yet I shall be disappointed if you do not find them serviceable.

The first is: Whenever in your reading you

come across one of these words, case, instance, character, nature, condition, persuasion, degree —whenever in writing your pen betrays you to one or another of them—pull yourself up and take thought. If it be "case" (I choose it as Jargon's dearest child—"in Heaven yclept Metonomy") turn to the dictionary, if you will, and seek out what meaning can be derived from casus, its Latin ancestor; then try how, with a little trouble, you can extricate yourself from that case. The odds are, you will feel like a butterfly who has discarded his chrysalis.

Here are some specimens to try your hand on:

(1) All those tears which inundated Lord Hugh Cecil's head were dry in the case of Mr. Harold Cox.

Poor Mr. Cox! left gasping in his aquarium!

(2) (From a cigar-merchant.) In any case, let us send you a case on approval.

(3) It is contended that Consols have fallen in consequence: but such is by no means the case.

"Such," by the way, is another spoilt child of Jargon, especially in Committee's Rules— "Coöpted members may be eligible as such; such members to continue to serve for such time as"— and so on.

(4) Even in the purely Celtic areas only in two or three cases do the Bishops bear Celtic names.

For "cases" read "dioceses."

Instance. In most instances the players were below their form.

But what were they playing at? Instances?

Character—Nature. There can be no doubt that the accident was caused through the dangerous nature of the spot, the hidden character of the by-road, and the utter absence of any warning or danger signal.

Mark the foggy wording of it all! And yet the man hit something and broke his neck! Contrast that explanation with the verdict of a coroner's jury in the west of England on a drowned post-man: "We find that deceased met his death by an act of God, caused by sudden overflowing of the river Walkham and helped out by the scandalous neglect of the way-wardens."

The Aintree course is notoriously of a trying nature.
On account of its light character, purity, and age, Usher's whiskey is a whiskey that will agree with you.
Order. The mésalliance was of a pronounced order.
Condition. He was conveyed to his place of residence in an intoxicated condition.

"He was carried home drunk."

Quality and *Section.* Mr. ——, exhibiting no less than five works, all of a superior quality, figures prominently in the oil section.

—This was written of an exhibition of pictures.

Degree. A singular degree of rarity prevails in the earlier editions of this romance.

That is Jargon. In prose it runs simply "The earlier editions of this romance are rare"—or "are very rare"—or even (if you believe what I take leave to doubt), "are singularly rare"; which should mean that they are rarer than the editions of any other work in the world.

Now what I ask you to consider about these quotations is that in each the writer was using Jargon to shirk prose, palming off periphrases upon us when with a little trouble he could have gone straight to the point. "A singular degree of rarity prevails," "the accident was caused through the dangerous nature of the spot," "but such is by no means the case." We may not be capable of much; but we can all write better than that, if we take a little trouble. In place of, "the Aintree course is of a trying nature" we can surely say "Aintree is a trying course" or "the Aintree course is a trying one"—just that and nothing more.

Next, having trained yourself to keep a look-out for these worst offenders (and you will be surprised to find how quickly you get into the way of it), proceed to push your suspicions out among the whole cloudy host of abstract terms. "How excellent a thing is sleep," sighed Sancho Panza; "it wraps a man round like a cloak" [1] an excellent example, by the way, of how to say a thing concretely; a Jargoneer would have said that "among the beneficent qualities of sleep its capacity for withdrawing the human consciousness from the contemplation of immediate circumstances may perhaps be accounted not the least remarkable." How vile a thing—shall we say?—is the abstract noun! It wraps a man's thoughts round like cotton wool.

Here is a pretty little nest of specimens, found in *The Times* newspaper by Messrs. H. W. and F. G. Fowler, authors of that capital little book *The King's English:*

> One of the most important reforms mentioned in the rescript is the unification of the organization of judicial institutions and the guarantee for all the tribunals of the independence necessary for securing to all classes of the community equality before the law.

I do not dwell on the cacophony; but, to convey a straightforward piece of news, might not the editor of *The Times* as well employ a man to write:

> One of the most important reforms is that of the Courts, which need a uniform system and to be made independent. In this way only can men be assured that all are equal before the law.

I think he might.

A day or two ago the musical critic of the *Standard* wrote this:

MR. LAMOND IN BEETHOVEN

Mr. Frederick Lamond, the Scottish pianist, as an interpreter of Beethoven has few rivals. At this second recital of the composer's works at Bechstein Hall on Saturday afternoon he again displayed a complete sympathy and understanding of his material that extracted the very essence of aesthetic and musical value from each selection he undertook. The delightful intimacy of his playing and his unusual force of individual expression are invaluable assets, which, allied to his technical brilliancy, enable him to achieve an artistic triumph. The two lengthy Variations in E flat major (Op. 35) [2] and in D major, the latter on the Turkish March from *The Ruins of Athens,* when included in the same programme, require a master hand to provide continuity of interest. *To say that Mr. Lamond successfully avoided moments that might at times, in these works, have inclined to comparative disinterestedness, would be but a moderate way of expressing the remarkable fascination with which his versatile playing endowed them,* but *at the same time* two of the sonatas given included a similar form of composition, and no matter how intellectually brilliant may be the interpretation, the extravagant use of a certain mode is bound in time to become somewhat ineffective. In the Three Sonatas, the E major (Op. 109), the A major (Op. 2), No. 2, and the C minor (Op. 111), Mr. Lamond signalized his perfect insight into the composer's varying moods.

Will you not agree with me that here is no writing, here is no prose, here is not even English, but merely a flux of words to the pen?

Here again is a string, a concatenation—say, rather, a tiara of gems of purest ray serene from the dark unfathomed caves of a Scottish newspaper:

The Chinese viewpoint, as indicated in this letter, may not be without interest to your readers, because it evidently is suggestive of more than an academic attempt to explain an unpleasant aspect of things which, if allowed to materialise, might suddenly culminate in disaster resembling the Chang-Sha riots. It also ventures to illustrate incidents having their inception in recent premature endeavours to accelerate the development of Protestant missions in China; but we would hope for the sake of the interests involved that what my correspondent describes as "the irresponsible ruffian element" may be known by their various religious designations only within very restricted areas.

Well, the Chinese have given it up, poor fellows! and are asking the Christians—as to-day's newspapers inform us—to pray for them. Do you wonder? But that is, or was, the Chinese "viewpoint," —and what a willow-pattern viewpoint! Observe its delicacy. It does not venture to interest or be interesting; merely "to be not without interest." But it does "venture to illustrate incidents"— which, for a viewpoint, is brave enough; and this illustration "is suggestive of something more than an academic attempt to explain an unpleasant aspect of things which, if allowed to materialise, might suddenly culminate." *What* materialises? The unpleasant aspect? or the things? Grammar says the "things," "things which if allowed to materialise." But things are materialised already, and as a condition of their being things. It must be the aspect, then, that materialises. But, if so, it is also the aspect that culminates, and an aspect, however unpleasant, can hardly do that, or at worst cannot culminate in anything resembling the Chang-Sha riots. . . . I give it up.

Let us turn to another trick of jargon; the

trick of Elegant Variation, so rampant in the sporting press that there, without needing to attend these lectures, the undergraduate detects it for laughter:—

Hayward and C. B. Fry now faced the bowling, which apparently had no terrors for the Surrey crack. The old Oxonian, however, took some time in settling to work. . . .

Yes, you all recognise it and laugh at it. But why do you practise it in your essays? An undergraduate brings me an essay on Byron. In an essay on Byron, Byron is (or ought to be) mentioned many times. I expect, nay exact, that Byron shall be mentioned again and again. But my undergraduate has a blushing sense that to call Byron Byron twice on one page is indelicate. So Byron, after starting bravely as Byron, in the second sentence turns into "that great but unequal poet" and thenceforward I have as much trouble with Byron as ever Telemachus with Proteus to hold and pin him back to his proper self. Half-way down the page he becomes "the gloomy master of Newstead"; overleaf he is reincarnated into "the meteoric darling of society"; and so proceeds through successive avatars—"this archrebel," "the author of *Childe Harold*," "the apostle of scorn," "the ex-Harrovian, proud, but abnormally sensitive of his club-foot," "the martyr of Missolonghi," "the pageant-monger of a bleeding heart." Now this again is jargon. It does not, as most jargon does, come of laziness; but it comes of timidity, which is worse. In literature as in life he makes himself felt who not only calls a spade a spade but has the pluck to double spades and redouble.

For another rule—just as rough and ready, but just as useful: Train your suspicions to bristle up whenever you come upon "as regards," "with regard to," "in respect of," "in connection with," "according as to whether," and the like. They are all dodges of jargon, circumlocutions for evading this or that simple statment; and I say that it is not enough to avoid them nine times out of ten, or nine-and-ninety times out of a hundred. You should never use them. That is positive enough, I hope? Though I cannot admire his style, I admire the man who wrote to me, "Re Tennyson—your remarks anent his *In Memoriam* make me sick"; for though *re* is not a preposition of the first water, and "anent" has enjoyed its day, the finish crowned the work. But here are a few specimens far, very far, worse:—

The special difficulty in Professor Minocelsi's case (our old friend "case" again) arose *in connexion with* the view he holds *relative* to the historical value of the opening pages of Genesis.

That is jargon. In prose, even taking the miserable sentence as it stands constructed, we should write "the difficulty arose over the views he holds about the historical value," etc. From a popular novelist:—

I was entirely indifferent *as to* the results of the game, caring nothing at all *as to* whether *I had losses or gains*——

Cut out the first "as" in "as to," and the second "as to" altogether, and the sentence begins to be prose—"I was indifferent to the results of the game, caring nothing whether I had losses or gains."

But why, like Dogberry, have "had losses"? Why not simply "lose." Let us try again. "I was entirely indifferent to the results of the game, caring nothing at all whether I won or lost."

Still the sentence remains absurd; for the second clause but repeats the first without adding one jot. For if you care not at all whether you win or lose, you must be entirely indifferent to the results of the game. So why not say, "I was careless if I won or lost," and have done with it?

A man of simple and charming character, he was fitly *associated with* the distinction of the Order of Merit.

I take this gem with some others from a collection made three years ago, by the *Oxford Magazine;* and I hope you admire it as one beyond price. "He was associated with the distinction of the Order of Merit" means "he was given the Order of Merit." If the members of that Order make a society then he was associated with them; but you cannot associate a man with a distinction. The inventor of such fine writing would doubtless have answered Canning's Needy Knife-grinder with:—

> I associate thee with sixpence! I will see thee in another association first!

But let us close our *florilegium* and attempt to illustrate jargon by the converse method of taking a famous piece of English (say Hamlet's soliloquy) and remoulding a few lines of it in this fashion:—

> To be, or the contrary? Whether the former or the latter be preferable would seem to admit of some difference of opinion; the answer in the present case being of an affirmative or of a negative character according as to whether one elects on the one hand to mentally suffer the disfavour of fortune, albeit in an extreme degree, or on the other to boldly envisage adverse conditions in the prospect of eventually bringing them to a conclusion. The condition of sleep is similar to, if not indistinguishable from that of death; and with the addition of finality the former might be considered identical with the latter: so that in this connection it might be argued with regard to sleep that, could the addition be effected, a termination would be put to the endurance of a multiplicity of inconveniences, not to mention a number of downright evils incidental to our fallen humanity, and thus a consummation achieved of a most gratifying nature.

That is jargon: and to write jargon is to be perpetually shuffling around in the fog and cotton-wool of abstract terms; to be for ever hearkening, like Ibsen's Peer Gynt, to the voice of the Boyg exhorting you to circumvent the difficulty, to beat the air because it is easier than to flesh your sword in the thing. The first virtue, the touchstone of masculine style, is its use of the active verb and the concrete noun. When you write in the active voice, "They gave him a silver teapot," you write as a man. When you write "He was made the recipient of a silver teapot," you write jargon. But at the beginning set even higher store on the concrete noun. Somebody—I think it was FitzGerald—once posited the question, "What would have become of Christianity if Jeremy Bentham had had the writing of the Parables?" Without pursuing that dreadful enquiry I ask you to note how carefully the Parables—those exquisite short stories—speak only of "things which you can touch and see"—"A sower went forth to sow," "The Kingdom of Heaven is like unto leaven, which a woman took,"—and not the Parables only, but the Sermon on the Mount and almost every verse of the Gospel. The Gospel does not, like my young essayist, fear to repeat a word, if the word be good. The Gospel says, "Render unto Caesar the things that are Caesar's"—not "Render unto Caesar the things that appertain to that potentate." The Gospel does not say "Consider the growth of the lilies," or even "Consider how the lilies grow." It says, "Consider the lilies, how they grow."

Or take Shakespeare. I wager you that no writer of English so constantly chooses the concrete word, in phrase after phrase forcing you to touch and see. No writer so insistently teaches the general through the particular. He does it even in *Venus and Adonis* (as Professor Wendell, of Harvard, pointed out in a brilliant little monograph on Shakespeare, published some ten years ago). Read any page of *Venus and Adonis* side by side with any page of Marlowe's [3] *Hero and Leander* and you cannot but mark the contrast: in Shakespeare the definite, particular, visualised image, in Marlowe the beautiful generalisation, the abstract term, the thing seen at a literary remove. Take the two openings, both of which start out with the sunrise. Marlowe begins:—

> Now had the Morn espied her lover's steeds:
> Whereat she starts, puts on her purple weeds,
> And, red for anger that he stay'd so long,
> All headlong throws herself the clouds among.

Shakespeare wastes no words on Aurora and her feelings, but gets to his hero and to business without ado:—

> Even as the sun with purple-colour'd face—

(You have the sun visualised at once),

> Even as the sun with purple-colour'd face
> Had ta'en his last leave of the weeping morn,
> Rose-cheek'd Adonis hied him to the chase;
> Hunting he loved, but love he laugh'd to scorn.

When Shakespeare has to describe a horse, mark how definite he is:—

> Round-hoof'd, short-jointed, fetlocks shag and long,
> Broad breast, full eye, small head and nostril wide,
> High crest, short ears, straight legs and passing strong,
> Thin mane, thick tail, broad buttock, tender hide.

Or again, in a casual simile, how definite:—

> Upon this promise did he raise his chin,
> Like a dive-dipper peering through a wave,
> Which, being look'd on, ducks as quickly in.

Or take, if you will, Marlowe's description of Hero's first meeting Leander:—

> It lies not in our power to love or hate,
> For will in us is over-ruled by fate . . .

and set against it Shakespeare's description of Venus' last meeting with Adonis, as she came on him lying in his blood:—

> Or as a snail whose tender horns being hit
> Shrinks backward in his shelly cave with pain,
> And there, all smother'd up, in shade doth sit,
> Long after fearing to creep forth again;
>   So, at his bloody view—

I do not deny Marlowe's lines (if you will study the whole passage) to be lovely. You may even judge Shakespeare's to be crude by comparison. But you cannot help noting that whereas Marlowe steadily deals in abstract, nebulous terms, Shakespeare constantly uses concrete ones, which later on he learned to pack into verse, such as:—

> Sleep that knits up the ravell'd sleeve of care.

Is it unfair to instance Marlowe, who died young? Then let us take Webster for the comparison; Webster,[4] a man of genius or of something very like it, and commonly praised by the critics for his mastery over definite, detailed, and what I may call *solidified sensation*. Let us take this admired passage from his *Duchess of Malfy:*—

Ferdinand.   How doth our sister Duchess bear herself
              In her imprisonment?

Basola.   Nobly: I'll describe her.
              She's sad as one long wed to 't, and she
                  seems
              Rather to welcome the end of misery
              Than shun it: a behaviour so noble
              As gives a majesty to adversity.*
              You may discern the shape of loveliness
              More perfect in her tears than in her
                  smiles;
              She will muse for hours together; † and
                  her silence
              Methinks expresseth more than if she
                  spake.

Now set against this the well-known passage from *Twelfth Night* where the Duke asks and Viola answers a question about someone unknown to him and invented by her—a mere phantasm, in short: yet note how much more definite is the language:—

---

* Note the abstract terms.
† Here we first come on the concrete: and beautiful it is.

Viola. My father had a daughter lov'd a man;
       As it might be, perhaps, were I a woman,
       I should your lordship.
Duke.   And what's her history?
Viola. A blank, my lord. She never told her love,
       But let concealment, like a worm i' the bud,
       Feed on her damask cheek; she pined in
           thought,
       And with a green and yellow melancholy
       She sat like Patience on a monument
       Smiling at grief. Was not this love indeed?

Observe (apart from the dramatic skill of it) how, when Shakespeare *has* to use the abstract noun "concealment," on an instant it turns into a visible worm "feeding" on the visible rose; how, having to use a second abstract word "patience," at once he solidifies it in tangible stone.

Turning to prose, you may easily assure yourselves that men who have written learnedly on the art agree in treating our maxim—to prefer the concrete term to the abstract, the particular to the general, the definite to the vague—as a canon of rhetoric. Whately has much to say on it. The late Mr. E. J. Payne, in one of his admirable prefaces to Burke (prefaces too little known and valued, as too often happens to scholarship hidden away in a schoolbook), illustrated the maxim by setting a passage from Burke's [5] speech *On Conciliation with America* alongside a passage of like purport from Lord Brougham's [6] *Inquiry into the Policy of the European Powers*. Here is the deadly parallel:—

BURKE.

BROUGHAM.

In large bodies the circulation of power must be less vigorous at the extremities. Nature has said it. The Turk cannot govern Ægypt and Arabia and Curdistan as he governs Thrace; nor has he the same dominion in Crimea and Algiers which he has in Brusa and Smyrna. Despotism itself is obliged to truck and huckster. The Sultan gets such obedience as he can. He governs with a loose rein, that he may govern at all; and the whole of the force and vigour of his authority in his centre is derived from a prudent relaxation in all his borders.

In all the despotisms of the East, it has been observed that the further any part of the empire is removed from the capital, the more do its inhabitants enjoy some sort of rights and privileges: the more inefficacious is the power of the monarch; and the more feeble and easily decayed is the organisation of the government.

You perceive that Brougham has transferred Burke's thought to his own page; but will you not also perceive how pitiably, by dissolving Burke's vivid particulars into smooth generalities, he has enervated its hold on the mind?

"This particularising style," comments Mr. Payne, "is the essence of poetry; and in prose it is impossible not to be struck with the energy it produces. Brougham's passage is excellent in its way; but it pales before the flashing lights of Burke's sentences." The best instances of this energy of style, he adds, are to be found in the classical writers of the seventeenth century. "When South [7] says, 'An Aristotle was but the rubbish of an Adam, and Athens but the rudiments of Paradise,' he communicates more effectually the notion of the difference between the intellect of fallen and of unfallen humanity than in all the philosophy of his sermons put together."

You may agree with me, or you may not, that South in this passage is expounding trash; but you will agree with Mr. Payne and me that he uttered it vividly.

Let me quote to you, as a final example of this vivid style of writing, a passage from Dr. John Donne [8] far beyond and above anything that ever lay within South's compass:—

The ashes of an Oak in the Chimney are no epitaph of that Oak, to tell me how high or how large that was; it tells me not what flocks it sheltered while it stood, nor what men it hurt when it fell. The dust of great persons' graves is speechless, too; it says nothing, it distinguishes nothing. As soon the dust of a wretch whom thou wouldest not, as of a prince whom thou couldest not look upon will trouble thine eyes if the wind blow it thither; and when a whirlewind hath blown the dust of the Churchyard into the Church, and the man sweep out the dust of the Church into the Churchyard, who will undertake to sift those dusts again and to pronounce, This is the Patrician, this is the noble flowre (flour), this the yeomanly, this the Plebeian bran? So is the death of *Iesabel* (*Iesabel* was a Queen) expressed. They shall not say *This is Iesabel;* not only not wonder that it is, nor pity that it should be; but they shall not say, they shall not know, *This is Iesabel.*

Carlyle noted of Goethe,[9] "his emblematic intellect, his never-failing tendency to transform into *shape*, into *life*, the feeling that may dwell in him. Everything has form, has visual excellence: the poet's imagination bodies forth the forms of things unseen, and his pen turns them into shape."

Perpend this, Gentlemen, and maybe you will not hereafter set it down to my reproach that I wasted an hour of a May morning in a denunciation of jargon, and in exhorting you upon a technical matter at first sight so trivial as the choice between abstract and definite words.

A lesson about writing your language may go deeper than language; for language (as in a former lecture I tried to preach to you) is your reason, your λόγος. So long as you prefer abstract words, which express other men's summarised concepts of things, to concrete ones which lie as near as can be reached to things themselves and are the first-hand material for your thoughts, you will remain, at the best, writers at second-hand. If your language be jargon, your intellect, if not your whole character, will almost certainly correspond. Where your mind should go straight, it will dodge: the difficulties it should approach with a fair front and grip with a firm hand it will be seeking to evade or circumvent. For the style is the man, and where a man's treasure is there his heart, and his brain, and his writing, will be also.

NOTES

[1] The student will do well to look up and read part of Cervantes' *Don Quixote* to become familiar with the romantic Don Quixote and the practical Sancho Panza.

[2] Opus 35, or his 35th composition.

[3] Christopher Marlowe (1564–1593), Elizabethan poet and dramatist.

[4] John Webster (1580?–1625?), Elizabethan dramatist, whose *Duchess of Malfy* is perhaps his best-known work.

[5] Edmund Burke (1729–1797), British statesman, had probably the best-informed mind in eighteenth-century England.

[6] Henry Peter Brougham (1778–1868), English jurist and author.

[7] Robert South (1634–1716), English divine, friend of Sacheverell, the famous Tory preacher whom Sam Johnson was taken to hear while still a very young boy.

[8] John Donne (1573–1631), English divine and poet, Dean of St. Paul's in London, whose poems have recently been brought back into a considerable vogue.

[9] Johann Wolfgang von Goethe (1749–1832), German poet and philosopher, author of *Faust,* and *Wilhelm Meister.*

QUESTIONS

1. What other examples of jargon can you name? Where do you find these most frequently?

2. Which is easier to write, jargon or clear, concise English? Why?

CONVALESCENCE AFTER NEWSPAPER *

A. R. ORAGE

A. R. ORAGE is comparatively unknown in America, but is steadily gaining prominence in English critical circles. Over the initials "R. H. C." and, occasionally, "Congreve", he contributed such startling and penetrating criticism to the London *New Age* that he won for that periodical a very lively dislike, and for himself the editorship, the respect of the English reading public, and repute as a writer of "brilliant commonsense." "Convalescence after Newspaper" is from his volume *Readers and Writers,* published in 1921. After a ten years' absence from the literary world of London, Mr. Orage returned in 1932 and started *The New English Review* through which he will continue the work he left so abruptly in 1922.

MATTHEW ARNOLD used to say that to get his feet wet spoiled his style for days. But there is a far worse enemy of style than natural damp; it is too much newspaper-reading. Too much newspaper not only spoils one's style; it takes off the edge of one's taste, so that I know not what grindstones are necessary to put it on again. Indulgent readers, I have been compelled for some weeks to

* Reprinted from *Readers and Writers* by A. R. Orage by permission of and special arrangement with Alfred A. Knopf, Inc., authorized publishers.

read too much newspaper, with the consequence that at the end of my task I was not only certain that my little of style was gone, but I was indifferent in my taste. The explanation of the *reductio ad absurdum* [1] to which an overdose of newspaper leads is to be found, I think, in the uniformity mass and collectivity of newspaper literature. The writing that fills the Press is neither individual nor does it aim at individuality. If a citizens' meeting, a jury, or the House of Commons were to perform the feat of making its voice heard, the style of their oracles would be perfect newspaper. But literature, I need not say, is not made after this fashion; nor is it inspired by such performances. Literature, like all art, is above everything, individual expression. *Gardez-vous!* [2] I do not mean that literature is a personal expression of the personal opinion of the writer. On the contrary, it is the rôle of newspaper to give common expression to personal opinions; but it is the function of literature to give personal expression to common opinions. And since it is only personal expression that provokes and inspires personal expression, from newspapers one can derive no stimulus to literature, but only the opposite, a disrelish and a distaste.

How to recover one's health after newspaper poisoning is a problem. To plunge back forthwith into books was for me an impossibility. It was necessary to begin again from the very beginning and gradually to accustom myself to the taste for

literature again. Re-arranging my books, and
throwing away the certainly-done-with was, I
found, as useful a preliminary tonic as any other
I could devise. In particular there is a satisfaction
in throwing out books which makes this medicine
as pleasant as it is tonic.[3] It visibly reduces the
amount left to be read; there is then not so much
on one's plate that the appetite revolts at the
prospect. And who can throw away a book without glancing into it to make sure that it will never
again be wanted? Picking and tasting in this in-
deliberate way, the invalid appetite is half coaxed
to sit up and take proper nourishment. This destruction and reconstruction I certainly found recovering, and I can, therefore, commend them to
be included in the pharmacopæias.

Another nourishing exercise when you are in
this state is the overhauling of your accumula-
tions of memoranda, cuttings and note-books. I
have sat for hours during the last few days, like
a beaver unbuilding its dam, turning out with a
view to destroying their contents, drawer after
drawer and shelf upon shelf. It is fatal to set
about the operation with any tenderness. Your
aim must be to destroy everything which does not
command you to spare it. The tragic recklessness
of the procedure is the virtue of the medicine. As
a matter of fact there is little or nothing now left
in my drawers for future use. Nearly all my
paper-boats have been burned, including some
three-decked galleons which were originally de-

signed to bring me fame. No matter; the Rubicon [4] is crossed, and to be on the other side of newspaper with no more than a thin portfolio of notes is to have escaped cheaply.

For the humour of it, however, I will record a careful exception. It appears, after all, that I was not so mad as I seemed. Perchance newspaper, being only a feigned literature, induces only a feigned madness. Be it as it may. I find that my current note-book, though as handy and tempting to be destroyed as any other, was nevertheless destroyed only after the cream of it had been whipped into the permanent book which I have kept through many rages for a good many years. The extracts are here before me as I write in convalescence. It is amusing to me to observe, moreover, that their cream is not very rich. Much better has gone into the bonfire. Why, then, did I save these and sacrifice those? Look at a few of them. "Nobody's anything always"—is there aught irrecoverable in that to have compelled me to spare it? "Lots of window, but no warehouse" —a remark, I fancy, intended to hit somebody or other very hard indeed—but *does* it? Is any of the present company fitted with a cap? "The judgment of the world is good, but few can put it into words." That is a premonitory symptom, you will observe, of a remark made a few lines above to the effect that literature is a personal expression of a common opinion or judgment. I have plainly remembered it. *Apropos* of the *New Age*,

I must have told somebody, and stolen home to write it down, that its career is that of a rocking-horse, all ups and downs but never any getting forward. It is too true to be wholly amusing; let me horse-laugh at it and pass it on. "A simple style is like sleep, it will not come by effort." Not altogether true, but true enough. The rest are not much worse or better, and the puzzle is to explain why those should be taken and these left.

Again *apropos,* may a physician who has healed himself offer this piece of advice? Read your own note-books often. I have known some people who have a library of note-books worth a dukedom, who never once looked into them after having filled them. That is collecting mania pure and simple. From another offensive angle what a confession of inferior taste is made in preferring the note-books of others to one's own. A little more self-respect in this matter is clearly necessary if your conversation is to be personal at all; for in all probability the references and quotations you make *without* the authority of your own collection are hackneyed. They are the reach-me-downs of every encyclopædia. Is this the reason that the vast majority of current quotations are as worn as they are; that a constant reader, forewarned of the subject about to be dealt with, is usually forearmed against the tags he will find employed in it? In any case, the advice I have just given is the corrective of this depressing phenomenon of modern writing. You have only to trade in your own note-books to be, and to give the air of being, truly original.

Browsing is a rather more advanced regimen for convalescence than the re-arrangement of books. The latter can be performed without the smallest taste for reading. It is a matter of sizing them up, and any bookseller's apprentice can do it. But browsing means dipping into the contents here and there; it is both a symptom of returning health and a means to it. In the last few days I must have nibbled in a hundred different pastures, chiefly, I think, in the pastures of books about books. De Quincey, Matthew Arnold, Bagehot,[5] Macaulay, Johnson, etc.—what meadows, what lush grass, what feed! After all, one begins to say, literature cannot be unsatisfying that fed such bulls and that so plumped their minds. It cannot be only a variety of newspaper. Thus a new link with health is established, and one becomes able to take one's books again. Here I should end, but that a last observation in the form of a question occurs to me. Is not or can not a taste for literature be acquired by the same means by which it can be re-acquired? Are not the child and the invalid similar? In that case the foregoing directions may be not altogether useless.

NOTES

[1] "Reducing to the absurd"; in debate it is accomplished by taking a parallel illustration and extending it by logic to a ridiculous conclusion, thereby implying that the entire principle involved is absurd.

[2] "Guard yourself!" The friendly warning of swordsmen before they start hacking at each other. Here a warning to pay close attention to reasoning differing from our habitual thinking.

[3] Interesting contemporary essays on this topic are "On Destroying Books" by J. C. Squire (1884–) and "Too Many Books" by Gilbert Norwood (1880–).

[4] Italian river crossed by Caesar when returning to Rome in conquest: the expression "Crossing the Rubicon" is now equivalent to "taking the decisive step" or "the die is cast."

[5] Walter Bagehot (1826–1877), English critic and essayist. The other authors mentioned here should be familiar enough.

QUESTIONS

1. What is Orage's explanation for the drugging effect of newspapers?

2. In what respects do American newspapers differ from this judgment of English papers? In what respects are they alike?

3. In what part of the newspaper is one most likely to find individual thought? In what part, the least likely to find it?

4. Years ago aspiring writers were advised to go into journalism as the best training for fluency in style; now, with the growth of the syndicates and the consequent loss of individuality of the separate units, the prevalent opinion is that journalism destroys, rather than develops, style. What authors have gained prominence through the newspaper? What American authors are now gaining prominence through the newspapers?

5. What experiences of "convalescence" have you had while poring over collections of any sort?

THE GENERAL CHARACTER OF
AMERICAN ENGLISH *

H. L. MENCKEN

HENRY LOUIS MENCKEN was born in Baltimore, Maryland, in 1880, where his father intended him to carry on the business of the family in a tobacco factory. Educated in private schools and at Baltimore Technic from which he was graduated in 1896, he entered journalism and became in 1903 City Editor on the *Baltimore Morning Herald.* After three years he transferred to the *Baltimore Sun* and two years later became the literary critic for *Smart Set.* In 1914 he became co-editor with George Jean Nathan of that magazine. Ten years later Mencken and Nathan founded the *American Mercury.* As editor, Mencken has attracted widespread attention by his vitriolic attacks upon Methodism, Puritanism, and the Republican Party. As private citizen he is beloved as a likable worker in Democratic politics in Baltimore and as second pianist in a small classical orchestra composed mostly of professors at Johns Hopkins University. *The American Language,* from which the present essay is taken, appeared in 1918.

THE characters chiefly noted in American speech by all who have discussed it, are, first, its general uniformity throughout the country, so

---

* Reprinted from *The American Language* by H. L. Mencken by permission of and special arrangement with Alfred A. Knopf, Inc., authorized publishers.

that dialects, properly speaking, are confined to recent immigrants, to the native whites of a few isolated areas, and to the negroes of the South; and, secondly, its impatient disregard of rule and precedent, and hence its large capacity (distinctly greater than that of the English of England) for taking in new words and phrases and for manufacturing new locutions out of its own materials. The first of these characters has struck every observer, native and foreign. In place of the local dialects of other countries we have a general *Volkssprache* [1] for the whole nation, and if it is conditioned at all it is only by minor differences in pronunciation and by the linguistic struggles of various groups of newcomers. "The speech of the United States," says Gilbert M. Tucker,[2] "is quite unlike that of Great Britain in the important particular that here we have no dialects." "We all," said Mr. Taft during his presidency, "speak the same language and have the same ideas." "Manners, morals and political views," said the New York *World,* commenting upon this dictum, "have all undergone a standardization which is one of the remarkable aspects of American evolution. Perhaps it is in the uniformity of language that this development has been most noteworthy. Outside of the Tennessee mountains and the back country of New England there is no true dialect." [3] "While we have or have had single countries as large as Great Britain," says another American observer, "and in some of our states

England could be lost, there is practically no difference between the American spoken in our 4,-039,000 square miles of territory, except as spoken by foreigners. We, assembled here, would be perfectly understood by delegates from Texas, Maine, Minnesota, Louisiana, or Alaska, from whatever walk of life they might come. We can go to any of the 75,000 postoffices in this country and be entirely sure we will be understood, whether we want to buy a stamp or borrow a match." "From Portland, Maine, to Portland, Oregon," agrees an English critic, "no trace of a distinct dialect is to be found. The man from Maine, even though he may be of inferior education and limited capacity, can completely understand the man from Oregon." To which add the testimony of a Scandinavian: "In the small country of Denmark it is sometimes difficult for an islander to understand a Jutlander. Every country has its own expression; every province its own dialect. In England we find not only more than 200 dialects, but also entire language groups, distinct from one another in their roots, despite the fact that the land itself is certainly not large. But in the United States one may travel over the greater part of a continent without encountering a single dialect. The language is the same from ocean to ocean."

No other country can show such linguistic solidarity, nor any approach it—not even Canada, for there a large part of the population resists learning English altogether. The Little Russian of the Ukraine is unintelligible to the citizen of Petrograd; the Northern Italian can scarcely follow a conversation in Sicilian; the Low German from Hamburg is a foreigner in Munich; the Breton flounders in Gascony. Even in the United Kingdom there are wide divergences. "When we remember," says the New International Encyclopedia, "that the dialects of the countries (*sic*) in England have marked differences—so marked, indeed, that it may be doubted whether a Lancashire miner and a Lincolnshire farmer could understand each other—we may well be proud that our vast country has, strictly speaking, only one language." This uniformity was noted by the earliest observers; Pickering [4] called attention to it in the preface to his Vocabulary and ascribed it, no doubt accurately, to the restlessness of the Americans, their inheritance of the immigrant spirit, "the frequent removals of people from one part of our country to another." It is especially marked in vocabulary and grammatical forms— the foundation stones of a living speech. There may be slight differences in pronunciation and intonation—a Southern softness, a Yankee drawl, a Western burr—but in the words they use and the way they use them all Americans, even the least tutored, follow the same line. One observes, of course, a polite speech and a common speech. But the common speech is everywhere the same, and its uniform vagaries take the place of the dia-

lectic variations of other lands. A Boston street-
car conductor could go to work in Chicago or San
Francisco without running the slightest risk of
misunderstanding his new fares. Once he had
picked up half a dozen localisms, he would be, to
all linguistic intents and purposes, fully natural-
ized.

Of the intrinsic differences that separate American from English the chief have their roots in the
obvious disparity between the environment and
traditions of the American people since the seventeenth century and those of the English. The
latter have lived under a relatively stable social
order, and it has impressed upon their souls their
characteristic respect for what is customary and
of good report. Until the Great War brought
chaos to most of their institutions, their whole
lives were regulated, perhaps more than those of
any other people save the Spaniards, by a regard
for precedent. The Americans, though partly of
the same blood, have felt no such restraint, and
acquired no such habit of conformity. On the
contrary, they have plunged to the other extreme,
for the conditions of life in their new country
have put a high value upon the precisely opposite
qualities of curiosity and daring, and so they have
acquired that character of restlessness, that impatience of forms, that disdain of the dead hand,
which now broadly marks them. From the first,
says a recent literary historian, they have been
"less phlegmatic, less conservative than the Eng-

lish. There were climatic influences, it may be; there was surely a spirit of intensity everywhere that made for short effort." Thus, in the arts, and thus in business, in politics, in daily intercourse, in habits of mind and speech. The American is not, in truth, lacking in a capacity for discipline; he has it highly developed; he submits to leadership readily, and even to tyranny. But, by a curious twist, it is not the leadership that is old and decorous that fetches him, but the leadership that is new and extravagant. He will resist dictation out of the past, but he will follow a new messiah with almost Russian willingness, and into the wildest vagaries of economics, religion, morals, and speech. A new fallacy in politics spreads faster in the United States than anywhere else on earth, and so does a new fashion in hats, or a new revelation of God, or a new means of killing time, or a new shibboleth, or metaphor, or piece of slang.

Thus the American, on his linguistic side, likes to make his language as he goes along, and not all the hard work of his grammar teachers can hold the business back. A novelty loses nothing by the fact that it is a novelty; it rather gains something, and particularly if it meets the national fancy for the terse, the vivid, and, above all, the bold and imaginative. The characteristic American habit of reducing complex concepts to the starkest abbreviations was already noticeable in colonial times, and such highly typical Americanisms as *O.K.*,

N.G., and *P.D.Q.*, have been traced back to the first days of the republic. Nor are the influences that shaped these early tendencies invisible today, for the country is still in process of growth, and no settled social order has yet descended upon it. Institution-making is yet going on, and so is language-making. In so modest an operation as that which has evolved *bunco* from *buncombe* and *bunk* from *bunco* there is evidence of a phenomenon which the philologist recognizes as belonging to the most youthful and lusty stages of speech.

But of more importance than the sheer inventions, if only because much more numerous, are the extensions of the vocabulary, both absolutely and in ready workableness, by the devices of rhetoric. The American, from the beginning, has been the most ardent of recorded rhetoricians. His politics bristles with pungent epithets; his whole history has been bedizened with tall talk; his fundamental institutions rest as much upon brilliant phrases as upon logical ideas. And in small things as in large he exercises continually an incomparable capacity for projecting hidden and often fantastic relationships into arresting parts of speech. Such a term as *rubber-neck* is almost a complete treatise on American psychology; it reveals the national habit of mind more clearly than any labored inquiry could ever reveal it. It has in it precisely the boldness and contempt for ordered forms that are so characteristically American, and it has too the grotesque humor of

the country, and the delight in devastating oppro-
briums, and the acute feeling for the succinct and
savory. The same qualities are in *rough-house,
water-wagon, near-silk, has-been, lame-duck* and
a thousand other such racy substantives, and in
all the great stock of native verbs and adjectives.
There is, indeed, but a shadowy boundary in
these new coinages between the various parts of
speech. *Corral,* borrowed from the Spanish, immediately becomes a verb and the father of an
adjective. *Bust,* carved out of *burst,* erects itself
into a noun. *Bum,* coming by way of an earlier
bummer from the German *bummler,* becomes
noun, adjective, verb and abverb. Verbs are fash-
ioned out of substantives by the simple process of
prefixing the preposition: *to engineer, to chink,
to stump, to hog.* Others grow out of an interme-
diate adjective, as *to boom.* Others are made by
torturing nouns with harsh affixes, as *to burglar-
ize* and *to itemize,* or by groping for the root, as
to resurrect and *to jell.* Yet others are changed
from intransitive to transitive: a sleeping-car
sleeps thirty passengers. So with the adjectives.
They are made of substantives unchanged: *cod-
fish, jitney.* Or by bold combinations: *down-and-
out, up-state, flat-footed.* Or by shading down
suffixes to a barbaric simplicity: *scary, classy,
tasty.* Or by working over adverbs until they
tremble on the brink between adverb and adjective: *right* and *near* are examples.

All of these processes, of course, are also to be

observed in the English of England; in the days
of its great Elizabethan growth they were in the
lustiest possible being. They are, indeed, common to all tongues; "the essence of language,"
says Dr. Jespersen,[5] "is activity." But if you will
put the English of today beside the American of
today you will see at once how much more for-
cibly they are in operation in the latter than in the
former. The standard southern dialect of English has been arrested in its growth by its purists
and grammarians. It shows no living change in
structure and syntax since the days of Anne, and
very little modification in either pronunciation or
vocabulary. Its tendency is to conserve that
which is established; to say the new thing, as
nearly as possible, in the old way; to combat all
that expansive gusto which made for its pliancy
and resilience in the days of Shakespeare. In place
of the old loose-footedness there is set up a pre-
ciosity which, in one direction, takes the form of
unyielding affectations in the spoken language,
and in another form shows itself in the heavy John-
sonese [6] of current English writing—the Jargon
denounced by Sir Arthur Quiller-Couch [7] in his
Cambridge lectures. This "infirmity of speech"
Quiller-Couch finds "in parliamentary debates
and in the newspapers"; . . . "it has become the
medium through which Boards of Government,
County Councils, Syndicates, Committees, Commercial Firms, express the processes as well as
the conclusions of their thought, and so voice the

reason of their being." Distinct from journalese, the two yet overlap, "and have a knack of assimilating each other's vices."

· American, despite the gallant efforts of the professors, has so far escaped any such suffocating formalization. We, too, of course, have our occasional practitioners of the authentic English Jargon; in the late Grover Cleveland we produced an acknowledged master of it. But in the main our faults in writing lie in precisely the opposite direction. That is to say, we incline toward a directness of statement which, at its greatest, lacks restraint and urbanity altogether, and toward a hospitality which often admits novelties for the mere sake of their novelty, and is quite uncritical of the difference between a genuine improvement in succinctness and clarity, and mere extravagant raciness. "The tendency," says one English observer, "is . . . to consider the speech of any man, as any man himself, as good as any other." "All beauty and distinction," says another, "are ruthlessly sacrificed to force." "The Americans, in a kind of artistic exuberance," says a third, "are not afraid to use words as we sometimes are in England." Moreover, this strong revolt against conventional bonds is by no means confined to the folk-speech, nor even to the loose conversational English of the upper classes; it also gets into more studied discourse, both spoken and written. I glance through the speeches of Dr. Woodrow Wilson, surely a conscientious purist and Anglomaniac if we have ever had one, and find, in a few moments, half a dozen locutions that an Englishman in like position would never dream of using, among them *we must get a move on, hog* as a verb, *gum-shoe* as an adjective with verbal overtones, *onery* in place of *ordinary*, and *that is going some*. I turn to Dr. John Dewey,[8] surely a most respectable pedagogue, and find him using *dope* for *opium*.

From the earliest days, indeed, English critics have found this gipsy tendency in our most careful writing. They denounced it in Marshall, Cooper, Mark Twain, Poe, Lossing, Lowell and Holmes, and even in Hawthorne and Thoreau; and it was no less academic a work than W. C. Brownell's "French Traits" which brought forth, in a London literary journal, the dictum that "the language most depressing to the cultured Englishman is the language of the cultured American." Even "educated American English," agrees the chief of modern English grammarians, "is now almost entirely independent of British influence, and differs from it considerably, though as yet not enough to make the two dialects—American English and British English—mutually unintelligible." Surely no Englishman of position equal to Dr. Wilson's or Dr. Dewey's would venture upon such locutions as *dope* and *to hog*. One might conceivably think of George Saintsbury doing it—but Saintsbury is a privileged iconoclast. Gilbert Murray [9] would blush to death if merely accused of it falsely. When, on August 2, 1914, Sir Edward Grey ventured modestly to speak of "pressing the button in the interest of peace," the *New Age* denounced him for indulging in vulgarism, and, as one English correspondent writes to me, various other Britons saw in the locution "a sign of the impending fall of the Empire."

American thus shows its character in a constant experimentation, a wide hospitality to novelty, a steady reaching out for new and vivid forms. No other tongue of modern times admits foreign words and phrases more readily; none is more careless of precedents; none shows a greater fecundity and originality of fancy. It is producing new words every day, by trope, by agglutination, by the shedding of inflections, by the merging of parts of speech, and by sheer brilliance of imagination. It is full of what Bret Harte called the "saber-cuts of Saxon"; it meets Montaigne's ideal of "a succulent and nervous speech, short and compact, not as much delicated and combed out as vehement and brusque, rather arbitrary than monotonous, not pedantic but soldierly, as Suetonius called Caesar's Latin." One pictures the common materials of English dumped into a pot, exotic flavoring added, and the bubblings assiduously and expectantly skimmed. What is old and respected is already in decay the moment it comes into contact with what is new and vivid. "When we Americans are through with the English language," says Mr. Dooley, "it will look as if it had been run over by a musical comedy." Let American confront a novel problem alongside English, and immediately its superior imaginativeness and resourcefulness become obvious. *Movie* is better than *cinema;* and the English begin to admit the fact by adopting the word; it is not only better American, it is better English. *Bill-board* is better than *hoarding*. *Office-holder* is more honest, more picturesque, more thoroughly Anglo-Saxon than *public-servant*. *Stem-winder,* somehow has more life in it, more fancy and vividness, than the literal *keyless-watch*. Turn to the terminology of railroading (itself, by the way, an Americanism): its creation fell upon the two peoples equally, but they tackled the job independently. The English, seeking a figure to denominate the wedge-shaped fender in front of a locomotive, called it a *plough;* the Americans, characteristically, gave it the far more pungent name of *cow-catcher*. So with the casting where two rails join. The English called it a *crossing-plate*. The Americans, more responsive to the suggestion in its shape, called it a *frog*.

This boldness of conceit, of course, makes for vulgarity. Unrestrained by any critical sense— and the critical sense of the professors counts for little, for they cry wolf too often—it flowers in such barbaric inventions as *tasty, alright, go-getter, he-man, go-ahead-ativeness, tony, semi-occasional, to fellowship* and *to doxologize*. Let it be admitted: American is not infrequently vulgar; the Americans, too, are vulgar (Bayard Taylor called them "Anglo-Saxons relapsed into semi-barbarism"); America itself is unutterably vulgar. But vulgarity, after all, means no more than a yielding to natural impulses in the face of conventional inhibitions, and that yielding to natural impulses is at the heart of all healthy language-making. The history of English, like the history of American and of every other living tongue, is a history of vulgarisms that, by their accurate meeting of real needs, have forced their way into sound usage, and even into the lifeless catalogues of the grammarians. The colonial pedants denounced *to advocate* as bitterly as they ever denounced *to compromit* or *to happify,* and all the English authorities gave them aid, but it forced itself into the American language despite them, and today it is even accepted as English and has got into the Concise Oxford Dictionary. *To donate,* so late as 1870, was dismissed by Richard Grant White as ignorant and abominable but today there is not an American dictionary that doesn't accept it, and surely no American writer would hesitate to use it.[10] *Reliable, gubernatorial, standpoint* and *scientist* have survived opposition of equal ferocity. The last-named was coined by William Whewell, an Englishman, in 1840, but was first adopted in America. Despite the fact that Fitzedward Hall and other eminent philologists used it and defended it, it aroused almost incredible opposition in England. So recently as 1890 it was denounced by the *London Daily News* as "an ignoble Americanism," and according to William Archer it was finally accepted by the Engish only "at the point of the bayonet." [11]

The purist performs a useful office in enforcing a certain logical regularity upon the process, and in our own case the omnipresent example of the greater conservatism of the English corrects our native tendency to go too fast, but the process itself is as inexorable in its workings as the procession of the equinoxes, and if we yield to it more eagerly than the English, it is only a proof, perhaps, that the future of what was once the Anglo-Saxon tongue lies on this side of the water. "The story of English grammar," says Murison, "is the story of simplification, of dispensing with grammatical forms." [12] And of the most copious and persistent enlargement of vocabulary and mutation of idiom ever recorded, perhaps, by descriptive philology. English now has the brakes on, but American continues to leap in the dark, and the prodigality of its movement is all the indication that is needed of its intrinsic health, its capacity to meet the ever-changing needs of a restless and emotional people, constantly fluent in racial composition, and disdainful of tradition. "Language," says Sayce, "is no artificial product, contained in books and dictionaries and governed by the strict rules of impersonal grammarians. It is the living expression of the mind and spirit of a people, ever changing and shifting, whose sole standard of correctness is custom and the common usage of the community. . . . The first lesson to be learned is that there is no intrinsic right or wrong in the use of language, no fixed rules such as are the delight of the teacher of Latin prose. What is right now will be wrong hereafter, what language rejected yesterday she accepts today." [13]

NOTES

[1] Folk language, or common stock.

[2] Mr. Tucker's article, *American English,* appeared in the *North American Review,* January 1883.

[3] Written October 1, 1909.

[4] John Pickering, Massachusetts lawyer, published his dictionary of Americanisms in 1816 and started a whirlwind of criticism from many philologists, including Noah Webster.

[5] Dr. Otto Jespersen's *Growth and Structure of the English Language,* Leipzig, 1919.

[6] The ponderous style of Dr. Samuel Johnson.

[7] See his lecture "On Jargon."

[8] Professor Dewey of Columbia University, leader in his chosen field of philosophy.

[9] George Saintsbury, English critic and professor (1845–   ). Gilbert Murray, English classical scholar and critic (1866–   ).

[10] It was banned by *Century Magazine* editors, The *New York Evening Post,* and The *Chicago Daily News* as late as 1908.

[11] *Humans* is presently going through the fierce battle for permission to live. *Viewpoint* seems farther along; is used at Yale but not at Harvard.

[12] From *Changes in the Language since Shakespeare's Time* in *The Cambridge History of English Literature.*

[13] *Introduction to the Science of Language,* by A. H. Sayce.

QUESTIONS

1. What function does the purist perform in the development of language?

2. In what branches of language does American excel English? *Vice versa?*

3. What is the obvious benefit derived from stability of language? What are the dangers in a fluctuating language?

4. Analyze American slang words and determine what qualities they show.

THE POSTURE OF AUTHORS *

CHARLES S. BROOKS

Born in Cleveland in 1878, educated in the Cleveland schools and at Yale University, CHARLES S. BROOKS has had a successful career in the printing business, followed by lecturing on English literature at Western Reserve University and teaching composition at the Yale Sheffield Scientific School. Of late years Mr. Brooks has been interested in the affairs of The Playhouse in Cleveland, to which he occasionally contributes plays. His *Journeys to Bagdad* in 1915 immediately won for him a reputation as a delightful and discriminating essayist, a reputation which subsequent volumes have increased. In addition to familiar essays on miscellaneous subjects, Mr. Brooks, in *Roads to the North, A Thread of English Road,* and *Round About to Canterbury,* has done as much for travel books as has E. V. Lucas in England, and may conceivably take his place alongside Robert Louis Stevenson, whose *Travels with A Donkey* and *An Inland Voyage* were milestones in the essay field.

THERE is something rather pleasantly suggestive in the fashion employed by many of the older writers of inscribing their books from their cham-

* Reprinted from *Hints to Pilgrims* by Charles S. Brooks by permission of and arrangement with the Yale University Press, publishers.

bers or lodging. It gives them at once locality and circumstance. It brings them to our common earth and understanding. Thomas Fuller,[1] for example, having finished his Church History of Britain, addressed his reader in a preface from his chambers in Sion College. "May God alone have the glory," he writes, "and the ingenuous reader the benefit, of my endeavors! which is the hearty desire of Thy servant in Jesus Christ, Thomas Fuller."

One pictures a room in the Tudor style, with oak wainscot, tall mullioned windows and leaded glass, a deep fireplace and black beams above. Outside, perhaps, is the green quadrangle of the college, cloistered within ancient buildings, with gay wall flowers against the sober stones. Bells answer from tower to belfry in agreeable dispute upon the hour. They were cast in a quieter time and refuse to bicker on a paltry minute. The sunlight is soft and yellow with old age. Such a dedication from such a place might turn the most careless reader into scholarship. In the seat of its leaded windows even the quirk of a Latin sentence might find a meaning. Here would be a room in which to meditate on the worthies of old England, or to read a chronicle of forgotten kings, queens, and protesting lovers who have faded into night.

Here we see Thomas Fuller dip his quill and make a start. "I have sometimes solitarily pleased myself," he begins, and he gazes into the dark shadows of the room, seeing, as it were, the pleasant spectres of the past. Bishops of Britain, long dead, in stole and mitre, forgetful of their solemn office, dance in the firelight on his walls. Popes move in dim review across his studies and shake a ghostly finger at his heresy. The past is not a prude. To her lover she reveals her beauty. And the scholar's lamp is her marriage torch.

Nor need it entirely cool our interest to learn that Sion College did not slope thus in country fashion to the peaceful waters of the Cam, with its fringe of trees and sunny meadow; did not possess even a Gothic tower and cloister. It was built on the site of an ancient priory, Elsing Spital, with almshouses attached, a Jesuit Library, and a college for the clergy. It was right in London, down near the Roman wall, in the heart of the tangled traffic, and street cries kept breaking in—muffins, perhaps, and hot spiced gingerbread, and broken glass. I hope, at least, that the good gentleman's rooms were up above, somewhat out of the clatter, where muffins had lost their shrillness. Gingerbread, when distance has reduced it to a pleasant tune, is not inclined to rouse a scholar from his meditation. And even broken glass is blunted on a journey to a garret. I hope that the old gentleman climbed three flights or more and that a range of chimney-pots was his outlook and speculation.[2]

It seems as if a rather richer flavor were given to a book by knowing the circumstance of its composition. Not only would we know the complexion of a man, whether he "be a black or a fair man," as Addison [3] suggests, "of a mild or choleric disposition, married or a bachelor," but also in what posture he works and what objects meet his eye when he squares his elbows and dips his pen. We are concerned whether sunlight falls upon his papers or whether he writes in shadow. Also, if an author's desk stands at a window, we are curious whether it looks on a street, or on a garden, or whether it squints blindly against a wall. A view across distant hills surely sweetens the imagination, whereas the clatter of the city gives a shrewder twist to fancy.

And household matters are of proper concern. We would like to be informed whether an author works in the swirl of the common sitting-room. If he writes within earshot of the kitchen, we should know it. There has been debate whether a steam radiator chills a poet as against an open fire, and whether a plot keeps up its giddy pace upon a sweeping day. Histories have balked before a household interruption. Novels have been checked by the rattle of a careless broom. A smoky chimney has choked the sturdiest invention.

If a plot goes slack, perhaps it is a bursted pipe. An incessant grocer's boy, unanswered on the back porch, has often foiled the wicked Earl in his attempts against the beautiful Pomona. Little did you think, my dear madam, as you read your latest novel, that on the very instant when the heroine, Mrs. Elmira Jones, deserted her babies to follow her conscience and become a movie actress—that on that very instant when she slammed the street door, the plumber (the author's plumber) came in to test the radiator. Mrs. Jones nearly took her death on the steps as she waited for the plot to deal with her. Even a Marquis, now and then, one of the older sort in wig and ruffles, has been left—when the author's ashes have needed attention—on his knees before the Lady Emily, begging her to name the happy day.

Was it not Coleridge's cow that calved while he was writing "Kubla Khan"? In burst the housemaid with the joyful news. And that man from Porlock—mentioned in his letters—who came on business? Did he not despoil the morning of its poetry? Did Wordsworth's pigs—surely he owned pigs—never get into his neighbor's garden and need quick attention? Martin Luther threw his inkpot, supposedly, at the devil. Is it not more likely that it was at Annie,[4] who came to dust? Thackeray is said to have written largely at his club, the Garrick or the Athenæum. There was a general stir of feet and voices, but it was foreign and did not plague him. A tinkle of glasses in the distance, he confessed, was soothing, like a waterfall.

Steele makes no complaint against his wife Prue, but he seems to have written chiefly in taverns. In the very first paper of the *Tatler* he gratifies our natural curiosity by naming the several coffee-houses where he intends to compose his thoughts. "Foreign and domestic news," he says, "you will have from Saint James's Coffee-House." Learning will proceed from the Grecian. But "all accounts of gallantry, pleasure and entertainment shall be under the article of White's Chocolate-House." In the month of September, 1705, he continues, a gentleman "was washing his teeth at a tavern window in Pall Mall, when a fine equipage passed by, and in it, a young lady who looked up at him; away goes the coach—" Away goes the beauty, with an alluring smile—rather an ambiguous smile, I'm afraid—across her silken shoulders. But for the continuation of this pleasant scandal (you may be sure that the pretty fellow was quite distracted from his teeth) one must turn up the yellow pages of the *Tatler*.

We may suppose that Steele called for pens and paper and a sandbox,[5] and took a table in one of White's forward windows. He wished no garden view or brick wall against the window. We may even go so far as to assume that something in the way of punch, or canary, or *negus luke, my dear*,[6] was handy at his elbow. His paragraphs are punctuated by the gay procession of the street. Here goes a great dandy in red heels, with lace at his beard and wrists. Here is a scarlet captain who has served with Marlborough and has taken a whole regiment of Frenchmen by the nose. Here is the Lady Belinda in her chariot, who is the pledge of all the wits and poets. That little pink ear of hers has been rhymed in a hundred sonnets —ear and tear and fear and near and dear. The King has been toasted from her slipper. The pretty creature has been sitting at ombre [7] for most of the night, but now at four of the afternoon she takes the morning air with her lap dog. That great hat and feather will slay another dozen hearts between shop and shop. She is attended by a female dragon, but contrives by accident to show an inch or so of charming stocking at the curb. Steele, at his window, I'm afraid, forgets for the moment his darling Prue and his promise to be home.

There is something rather pleasant in knowing where these old authors, who are now almost forgotten, wrote their books. Richardson [8] wrote "Clarissa" at Parson's Green. That ought not to interest us very much, for nobody reads "Clarissa" now. But we can picture the fat little printer reading his daily batch of tender letters from young ladies, begging him to reform the wicked Lovelace and turn the novel to a happy end. For it was issued in parts and so, of course, there was no opportunity for young ladies, however impatient, to thumb the back pages for the plot.

Richardson wrote "Pamela" at a house called the Grange, then in the open country just out of London. There was a garden at the back, and a grotto—one of the grottoes that had been the fashion for prosperous literary gentlemen since

Pope had built himself one at Twickenham. Here, it is said, Richardson used to read his story, day by day, as it was freshly composed, to a circle of his lady admirers. Hugh Thompson has drawn the picture in delightful silhouette. The ladies listen in suspense—perhaps the wicked Master is just taking Pamela on his knee—their hands are raised in protest. La! The Monster! Their noses are pitched up to a high excitement. One old lady hangs her head and blushes at the outrage. Or does she cock her ear to hear the better?

Richardson had a kind of rocking-horse in his study and he took his exercise so between chapters. We may imagine him galloping furiously on the hearth rug, then, quite refreshed, after four or five dishes of tea, hiding his villain once more under Pamela's bed. Did it never occur to that young lady to lift the valance? Half a dozen times at least he has come popping out after she has loosed her stays, once even when she has got her stockings off. Perhaps this is the dangerous moment when the old lady in the silhouette hung her head and blushed. If Pamela had gone rummaging vigorously with a poker beneath her bed she could have cooled her lover.

Goldsmith wrote his books, for the most part, in lodgings. We find him starving with the beggars in Axe Lane, advancing to Green Arbour Court—sending down to the cook-shop for a tart to make his supper—living in the Temple,[9] as his fortunes mended. Was it not at his window in the

Temple that he wrote part of his "Animated Nature"? His first chapter—four pages—is called a sketch of the universe. In four pages he cleared the beginning up to Adam. Could anything be simpler or easier? The clever fellow, no doubt, could have made the universe—actually made it out of chaos—stars and moon and fishes in the sea—in less than the allotted six days and not needed a rest upon the seventh. He could have gone, instead, in plum-colored coat—"in full fig" —to Vauxhall [10] for a frolic. Goldsmith had nothing in particular outside of his window to look at but the stone flagging, a pump and a solitary tree. Of the whole green earth this was the only living thing. For a brief season a bird or two lodged there, and you may be sure that Goldsmith put the remnant of his crumbs upon the window casement. Perhaps it was here that he sent down to the cook-shop for a tart, and he and the birds made a common banquet across the glass.

Poets, depending on their circumstance, are supposed to write either in garrets or in gardens. Browning,[11] it is true, lived at Casa Guidi, which was "yellow with sunshine from morning to evening," and here and there a prosperous Byron has a Persian carpet and mahogany desk. But, for the most part, we put our poets in garrets, as a cheap place that has the additional advantage of being nearest to the moon. From these high windows sonnets are thrown, on a windy night. Rhymes and fancies are roused by gazing on the stars.

The rumble of the lower city is potent to start a metaphor. "These fringes of lamplight," it is written, "struggling up through smoke and thousand-fold exhalation, some fathoms into the ancient reign of Night, what thinks Boötes of them, as he leads his Hunting-dogs over the Zenith in their leash of sidereal fire? That stifled hum of Midnight, when Traffic has lain down to rest . . ."

Here, under a sloping roof, the poet sits, blowing at his fingers. Hogarth [12] has drawn him—the *Distressed Poet*—cold and lean and shabby. That famous picture might have been copied from the life of any of a hundred creatures of "The Dunciad," [13] and, with a change of costume, it might serve our time as well. The poor fellow sits at a broken table in the dormer. About him lie his scattered sheets. His wife mends his breeches. Outside the door stands a woman with the unpaid milk-score. There is not a penny in the place—and for food only half a loaf and something brewing in a kettle. You may remember that when Johnson [14] was a young poet, just come to London, he lived with Mr. Cave in St. John's Gate. When there were visitors he ate his supper behind a screen because he was too shabby to show himself. I wonder what definition he gave the poet in his dictionary. If he wrote in his own experience, he put him down as a poor devil who was always hungry. But Chatterton actually died of starvation in a garret, and those other hundred poets of his time and ours got down to the bone and took to coughing. Perhaps we shall change our minds about that sonnet which we tossed lightly to the moon. The wind thrusts a cold finger through chink and rag. The stars travel on such lonely journeys. The jest loses its relish. Perhaps those merry verses to the Christmas— the sleigh bells and the roasted goose—perhaps those verses turn bitter when written on an empty stomach.

But do poets ever write in gardens? Swift, who was by way of being a poet, built himself a garden seat at Moor Park when he served Sir William Temple, but I don't know that he wrote poetry there. Rather, it was a place for reading. Pope in his prosperous days wrote at Twickenham, with the sound of his artificial waterfall in his ears, and he walked to take the air in his grotto along the Thames. But do poets really wander beneath the moon to think their verses? Do they compose "on summer eve by haunted stream"? I doubt whether Gray conceived his *Elegy* in an actual graveyard. I smell oil. One need not see the thing described upon the very moment. Shelley wrote of mountains—the awful range of Caucasus—but his eye at the time looked on sunny Italy. Ibsen wrote of the north when living in the south. When Bunyan wrote of the Delectable Mountains he was snug inside a jail. Shakespeare, doubtless, saw the giddy cliffs of Dover, the Rialto, the Scottish heath, from the vantage of a London lodging.

Where did Andrew Marvell stand or sit or walk when he wrote about gardens? Wordsworth is said to have strolled up and down a gravel path with his eyes on the ground. I wonder whether the gardener ever broke in—if he had a gardener—to complain about the drouth or how the dandelions were getting the better of him. Or perhaps the lawn-mower squeaked—if he had a lawn-mower —and threw him off. But wasn't it Wordsworth who woke up four times in one night and called to his wife for pens and paper lest an idea escape him? Surely he didn't take to the garden at that time of night in his pajamas with an inkpot. But did Wordsworth have a wife? How one forgets! Coleridge told Hazlitt that he liked to compose "walking over uneven ground, or breaking through the straggling branches of a copse-wood." But then, you recall that a calf broke into "Kubla Khan." On that particular day, at least, he was snug in his study.

No, I think that poets may like to sit in gardens and smoke their pipes and poke idly with their sticks, but when it comes actually to composing they would rather go inside. For even a little breeze scatters their papers. No poet wishes to spend his precious morning chasing a frisky sonnet across the lawn. Even a heavy epic, if lifted by a sudden squall, challenges the swiftest foot. He puts his stick on one pile and his pipe on another and he holds down loose sheets with his thumb. But it is awkward business, and it checks the mind in its loftier flight.

Nor do poets care to suck their pencils too long where someone may see them—perhaps Annie at the window rolling her pie-crust. And they can't kick off their shoes outdoors in the hot agony of composition. And also, which caps the argument, a garden is undeniably a sleepy place. The bees drone to a sleepy tune. The breeze practices a lullaby. Even the sunlight is in the common conspiracy. At the very moment when the poet is considering Little Miss Muffet and how she sat on a tuffet—doubtless in a garden, for there were spiders—even at the very moment when she sits unsuspectingly at her curds and whey, down goes the poet's head and he is fast asleep. Sleepiness is the plague of authors. You may remember that when Christian [15]—who, doubtless, was an author in his odd moments—came to the garden and the Arbour on the Hill Difficulty, "he pulled his Roll out of his bosom and read therein to his comfort . . . Thus pleasing himself awhile, he at last fell into a slumber." I have no doubt—other theories to the contrary—that "Kubla Khan" broke off suddenly because Coleridge dropped off to sleep. A cup of black coffee might have extended the poem to another stanza. Mince pie would have stretched it to a volume. Is not Shakespeare allowed his forty winks? Has it not been written that even the worthy Homer nods?

> "A pleasing land of drowsyhed it was:
> Of dreams that wave before the half-shut eye;
> And of gay castles in the clouds that pass,
> For ever flushing round a summer sky."

No, if one has a bit of writing to put out of the way, it is best to stay indoors. Choose an uncomfortable, straight-backed chair. Toss the sheets into a careless litter. And if someone will pay the milk-score and keep the window mended, a garret is not a bad place in which to write.

Novelists—unless they have need of history—can write anywhere, I suppose, at home or on a journey. In the burst of their hot imagination a knee is a desk. I have no doubt that Mr. Hugh Walpole, touring in this country, contrives to write a bit even in a Pullman. The ingenious Mr. Oppenheim surely dashes off a plot on the margin of the menu-card between meat and salad. We know that "Pickwick Papers" was written partly in hackney coaches while Dickens was jolting about the town.

An essayist, on the other hand, needs a desk and a library near at hand. Because an essay is a kind of back-stove cookery. A novel needs a hot fire, so to speak. A dozen chapters bubble in their turn above the reddest coals, while an essay simmers over a little flame. Pieces of this and that, an odd carrot, as it were, a left potato, a pithy bone, discarded trifles, are tossed in from time to time to enrich the composition. Raw paragraphs, when they have stewed all night, at last become tender to the fork. An essay, therefore, cannot be written hurriedly on the knee. Essayists, as a rule, chew their pencils. Their desks are large and are always in disorder. There is a stack of books on the clock shelf. Others are pushed under the bed. Matches, pencils, and bits of paper mark a hundred references. When an essayist goes out from his lodging he wears the kind of overcoat that holds a book in every pocket. His sagging pockets proclaim him. He is a bulging person, so stuffed, even in his dress, with the ideas of others that his own leanness is concealed. An essayist keeps a notebook, and he thumbs it for forgotten thoughts. Nobody is safe from him, for he steals from everyone he meets.

An essayist is not a mighty traveler. He does not run to grapple with a roaring lion. He desires neither typhoon nor tempest. He is content in his harbor to listen to the storm upon the rocks, if now and then, by a lucky chance, he can shelter someone from the wreck. His hands are not red with revolt against the world. He has glanced upon the thoughts of many men; and as opposite philosophies point upon the truth, he is modest with his own and tolerant toward the opinion of others. He looks at the stars and, knowing in what a dim immensity we travel, he writes of little things beyond dispute. There are enough to weep upon the shadows; he, like a dial, marks the light. The small clatter of the city beneath his window, the cry of peddlers, children chalking

their games upon the pavement, laundry dancing
on the roofs, and smoke in the winter's wind—
these are the things he weaves into the fabric of
his thoughts. Or sheep upon the hillside—if his
window is so lucky—or a sunny meadow, is a
profitable speculation. And so, while the novelist
is struggling up a dizzy mountain, straining
through the tempest to see the kingdoms of the
world, behold the essayist snug at home, content
with little sights. He is a kind of poet—a poet
whose wings are clipped. He flaps to no great
heights and sees neither the devil, the seven
oceans, nor the twelve apostles. He paints old
thoughts in shiny varnish and, as he is able, he
mends small habits here and there. And therefore,
as essayists stay at home, they are precise—almost amorous—in the posture and outlook of
their writing. Leigh Hunt wished a great library
next his study. "But for the study itself," he
writes, "give me a small snug place, almost entirely walled with books. There should be only
one window in it looking upon trees." How the
precious fellow scorns the mountains and the
ocean! He has no love, it seems, for typhoons and
roaring lions. "I entrench myself in my books,"
he continues, "equally against sorrow and the
weather. If the wind comes through a passage, I
look about to see how I can fence it off by a better
disposition of my movables." And by movables
he means his books. These were his screen against
cold and trouble. But Leigh Hunt had been in

prison for his political beliefs. He had grappled with his lion. So perhaps, after all, my argument fails.

Mr. Edmund Gosse had a different method to the same purpose. He "was so anxious to fly all outward noise" that he desired a library apart from the house. Maybe he had had some experience with Annie and her clattering broomstick. "In my sleep," he writes, " 'Where dreams are multitude,' I sometimes fancy that one day I shall have a library in a garden. The phrase seems to contain the whole felicity of man. . . . It sounds like having a castle in Spain, or a sheepwalk in Arcadia."

Montaigne's study was a tower, walled all about with books. At his table in the midst he was the general focus of their wisdom. Hazlitt wrote much at an inn at Winterslow, with Salisbury Plain around the corner of his view. Now and then, let us hope, when the London coach was due, he received in his nostrils a savory smell from the kitchen stove. I taste pepper, sometimes, and sharp sauces in his writing. Stevenson, except for ill-health and a love of the South Seas (here was the novelist showing himself), would have preferred a windy perch overlooking Edinburgh.

It does seem as if a rather richer flavor were given to a book by knowing the circumstance of its composition. Consequently, readers, as they grow older, turn more and more to biography. It is chiefly not the biographies that deal with great crises and events, but rather the biographies that are concerned with small circumstances and agreeable gossip, that attract them most. The life of Gladstone, with its hard facts of British policy, is all very well; but Mr. Lucas's [16] life of Lamb is better. Who would willingly neglect the record of a Thursday night at Inner Temple Lane? In these pages Talfourd, Procter, Hazlitt and Hunt have written their memories of these gatherings. It was to his partner at whist, as he was dealing, that Lamb once said, "If dirt was trumps, what hands you would hold!" Nights of wit and friendly banter! Who would not crowd his ears with gossip of that mirthful company?—George Dyer, who forgot his boots until half way home (the dear fellow grew forgetful as the smoking jug went round)—Charles Lamb feeling the stranger's bumps.[17] Let the Empire totter! Let Napoleon fall! Africa shall be parceled as it may. Here will we sit until the cups are empty.

Lately, in a bookshop at the foot of Cornhill, I fell in with an old scholar who told me that it was his practice to recommend four books, which, taken end on end, furnished the general history of English letters from the Restoration to a time within our own memory. These books were "Pepys' Diary," "Boswell's Johnson," the "Diary and Letters of Madame d'Arblay" and the "Diary of Crabb Robinson."

Beginning almost with the days of Cromwell here is a chain of pleasant gossip across the space of more than two hundred years. Perhaps, at the first, there were old fellows still alive who could remember Shakespeare—who still sat in chimney corners and babbled through their toothless gums of Blackfriars and the Globe. And at the end we find a reference to President Lincoln and the freeing of the slaves.

Here are a hundred authors—perhaps a thousand—tucking up their cuffs, looking out from their familiar windows, scribbling their large or trivial masterpieces.

NOTES

[1] Thomas Fuller (1608–1661), essayist and divine, about whom most critics have at one time or another written in highest praise.

[2] One of Brooks' earliest volumes was *Chimney Pot Papers*, essays on imaginary wanderings with a room high among chimney pots as the setting. *Journeys to Bagdad* is in the same vein.

[3] Joseph Addison (1672–1719), co-author with Richard Steele of *The Tatler* and *The Spectator*, most prominent of the eighteenth-century periodicals.

[4] You will encounter further references to Annie. Who is she?

[5] The eighteenth-century writer wiped his pen by sticking the quill or nib into a small box of fine sand.

[6] These are different kinds of wines.

[7] Ombre, or omber, a card game of Spanish origin, very popular in England in the eighteenth century.

[8] Samuel Richardson (1689–1761), one of the first English novelists, got his literary start by writing love letters to order for young ladies and young men who felt incapable of such literary expression. Henry Fielding's novel *Joseph Andrews* is an admirable satire on Richardson's *Pamela*, a novel in letters.

[9] The apartments of barristers attached to the Inns of Court.

[10] Vauxhall Gardens, favorite promenade of Fashion in London, closed and built over in 1859.

[11] Robert Browning (1812–1889), English poet, raided the home of the Barretts of Wimpole Street, London, and after one of the most famous courtships in literary history married Elizabeth Barrett, English poetess, and took her to Florence, Italy, where they lived in the Casa Guidi.

[12] William Hogarth (1697–1764), English satirical painter, whose cartoons and paintings are inextricably linked with the literature of his period.

[13] *The Dunciad,* by Alexander Pope (1688–1744) is a poem about *The House of Dunces* into which he put all of his enemies and some of his friends.

[14] Samuel Johnson (1709–1784), son of an obscure bookseller in Lichfield, overcame great obstacles to become the literary dictator of eighteenth-century England.

[15] The hero of John Bunyan's *Pilgrim's Progress.*

[16] E. V. Lucas, contemporary English essayist and travel writer, author of the outstanding Life of Charles Lamb.

[17] Phrenology or the study of the skull and brain formation was popularly studied in the nineteenth century.

Questions

1. Point out the elements in this essay common to the early essays of Montaigne and Bacon; those elements suggestive of the work of Lamb and Hazlitt.

2. How, according to Brooks, does the essayist differ from the novelist and the poet in his writing method?

3. How does this essay prove the essayist's method of composition?

4. Which of the literary names mentioned in this essay have become familiar to you through your reading?

ON KNOCKING AT THE GATE IN
MACBETH

Thomas De Quincey

More imaginative than Coleridge, equally fun-loving and nonsensical as Lamb, as brilliant and sound in his critical opinions as Hazlitt, as carefree of his little money as Shelley was with his larger store, shy to a degree yet loving human companionship—such was Thomas De Quincey (1785–1859). Friend of Wordsworth, Coleridge, and the other "Lake poets", he brought to that revolutionary group a philosophic mind superior to theirs. Precocious in school, he had at thirteen astounded his masters at the Bath Grammar School by his mastery of Greek, so that one of them remarked, "That boy could harangue an Athenian mob better than you or I could address an English one." At sixteen he ran away from another school because of the stupidity of the work (he was already adequately prepared for Oxford), and after roaming about the mountains of Wales, sleeping out of doors during the summer, he went to London in hope of getting together enough money to finance study at Oxford. After two years of extreme poverty and suffering among London's poorest, he succeeded in making arrangements with his family which enabled him to enter Worcester College, Oxford. Privation had begun to tell on him, causing a stomach ailment the usual cure for which was opium. He prescribed for himself and started an addiction to the drug which is immortalized in his *Confessions of an English Opium Eater,* remarkable analyses of the effect of the drug upon his dreams. On leaving Oxford in 1808 he went to the "Lake country" to live among his circle of poet friends. By 1821 after being a slave to drugs to the extent of taking 8000 drops of laudanum a day, he brought the habit into control through sheer will power and extensive physical exercise. That year he went up to London and became an editor of the *London Magazine* to which he contributed his famous *Confessions*. Five years later he started to contribute to *Blackwood's Magazine* and in 1830 moved to Edinburgh, where the magazine was published, to be near his work there. It was in this periodical that his "Murder Considered as One of the Fine Arts," appeared. Edinburgh intellectual circles immediately accepted him as the most brilliant conversationalist, holding his hearers "spell-bound by his wonderful affluence of talk, such as that of the fairy whose lips dropped rubies and diamonds". His idiosyncrasies, which remind one of Doctor Samuel Johnson, added to his individuality. He polished every shilling that came into his hands. He set something on fire almost daily, frequently his own hair, whereupon, his daughter exclaiming, "Papa, your hair is on fire," he would calmly say, "Is it, my love?", rub out the blaze with his hand, and continue working. Working feverishly on his critical papers, he would habitually cover the floor, tables, and chairs with sheets of manuscript, thrown helter-skelter, and when that room was filled, hire another somewhere else in Edinburgh; at his death in 1859 he had six such chaotic rooms. He was physically and intellectually active up to his death at the age of seventy-four, in spite of the inroads of drugs. His "On Knocking at the Gate in *Macbeth*" and "Literature of Knowledge and Literature of Power" are characteristic at once of his imaginative and critical powers.

FROM my boyish days I had always felt a great perplexity on one point in *Macbeth*. It was this: —the knocking at the gate which succeeds to the murder of Duncan produced to my feelings an effect for which I never could account. The effect was that it reflected back upon the murderer a peculiar awfulness and a depth of solemnity; yet, however obstinately I endeavoured with my understanding to comprehend this, for many years I never could see *why* it should produce such an effect.

Here I pause for one moment to exhort the reader never to pay any attention to his understanding when it stands in opposition to any other faculty of his mind. The mere understanding, however useful and indispensable, is the meanest faculty in the human mind and the most to be distrusted; and yet the great majority of people trust to nothing else,—which may do for ordinary life, but not for philosophical purposes. Of this, out of ten thousand instances that I might produce, I will cite one. Ask of any person whatsoever who is not previously prepared for the demand by a knowledge of perspective, to draw in the rudest way the commonest appearance which depends upon the laws of that science—as, for instance, to represent the effect of two walls standing at right angles to each other, or the appearance of the houses on each side of a street, as seen by a person looking down the street from one extremity. Now, in all cases, unless the person has happened to observe in pictures how it is that artists produce these effects, he will be utterly unable to make the smallest approximation to it.

Yet why? For he has actually seen the effect every day of his life. The reason is that he allows his understanding to overrule his eyes. His understanding, which includes no intuitive knowledge of the laws of vision, can furnish him with no reason why a line which is known and can be proved to be a horizontal line should not *appear* a horizontal line: a line that made any angle with the perpendicular less than a right angle would seem to him to indicate that his houses were all tumbling down together. Accordingly he makes the line of his houses a horizontal line, and fails of course to produce the effect demanded.[1] Here then is one instance out of many, in which not only the understanding is allowed to overrule the eyes, but where the understanding is positively allowed to obliterate the eyes, as it were; for not only does the man believe the evidence of his understanding in opposition to that of his eyes, but (what is monstrous) the idiot is not aware that his eyes ever gave such evidence. He does not know that he has seen (and therefore *quoad* his consciousness has *not* seen) that which he *has* seen every day of his life.

But to return from this digression. My understanding could furnish no reason why the knocking at the gate in *Macbeth* should produce any effect, direct or reflected. In fact, my understanding said positively that it could *not* produce any effect. But I knew better; I felt that it did; and I waited and clung to the problem until further knowledge should enable me to solve it. At length, in 1812, Mr. Williams [2] made his *début* on the stage of Ratcliffe Highway, and executed those unparalleled murders which have procured for him such a brilliant and undying reputation. On which murders, by the way, I must observe, that in one respect they have had an ill effect, by making the connoisseur in murder very fastidious in his taste, and dissatisfied with anything that has been since done in that line. All other murders look pale by the deep crimson of his; and, as an amateur once said to me in a querulous tone, "There has been absolutely nothing *doing* since his time, or nothing that's worth speaking of." But this is wrong, for it is unreasonable to expect all men to be great artists, and born with the genius of Mr. Williams. Now it will be remembered that in the first of these murders (that of the Marrs) the same incident (of a knocking at the door soon after the work of extermination was complete) did actually occur which the genius of Shakespeare has invented; and all good judges, and the most eminent *dilettanti*, acknowledged the felicity of Shakespeare's suggestion as soon as it was actually realized. Here, then, was a fresh proof that I had been right in relying on my own feeling in opposition to my understanding; and again I set myself to study the problem. At length I solved it to my own satisfaction; and my solution is this:—Murder, in ordinary cases, where the sympathy is wholly directed to the case of the murdered person, is an incident of coarse and vulgar horror; and for this reason,—that it flings the interest exclusively upon the natural but ignoble instinct by which we cleave to life: an instinct which, as being indispensable to the primal law of self-preservation, is the same in kind (though different in degree) amongst all living creatures. This instinct, therefore, because it annihilates all distinctions, and degrades the greatest of men to the level of "the poor beetle that we tread on," exhibits human nature in its most abject and humiliating attitude. Such an attitude would little suit the purposes of the poet. What then must he do? He must throw the interest on the murderer. Our sympathy must be with *him* (of course I mean a sympathy of comprehension, a sympathy by which we enter into his feelings, and are made to understand them—not a sympathy of pity or approbation). In the murdered person all strife of thought, all flux and reflux of passion and of purpose, are crushed by one overwhelming panic; the fear of instant death smites him "with its petrific mace." But in the murderer, such a murderer as a poet will condescend to, there must be raging some great storm of passion —jealousy, ambition, vengeance, hatred—which will create a hell within him; and into this hell we are to look.

In *Macbeth*, for the sake of gratifying his now enormous and teeming faculty of creation, Shakespeare has introduced two murderers; and, as

usual in his hands, they are remarkably discriminated: but—though in Macbeth the strife of mind
is greater than in his wife, the tiger spirit not so
awake, and his feelings caught chiefly by conta-
gion from her—yet, as both were finally involved
in the guilt of murder, the murderous mind of
necessity is finally to be presumed in both. This
was to be expressed; and on its own account, as
well as to make it a more proportionable antagonist to the unoffending nature of their victim,
"the gracious Duncan," and adequately to ex-
pound "the deep damnation of his taking off,"
this was to be expressed with peculiar energy. We
were to be made to feel that the human nature—
i.e., the divine nature of love and mercy, spread
through the hearts of all creatures, and seldom
utterly withdrawn from man—was gone, vanished, extinct, and that the fiendish nature had
taken its place. And, as this effect is marvellously
accomplished in the *dialogues* and *soliloquies*
themselves, so it is finally consummated by the
expedient under consideration; and it is to this
that I now solicit the reader's attention. If the
reader has ever witnessed a wife, daughter, or
sister, in a fainting fit, he may chance to have
observed that the most affecting moment in such
a spectacle is *that* in which a sigh and a stirring
announce the recommencement of suspended life.
Or, if the reader has ever been present in a vast
metropolis on the day when some great national
idol was carried in funeral pomp to his grave, and,

chancing to walk near the course through which it passed, has felt powerfully, in the silence and desertion of the streets and in the stagnation of ordinary business, the deep interest which at that moment was possessing the heart of man,[3]—if all at once he should hear the death-like stillness broken up by the sound of wheels rattling away from the scene, and making known that the transitory vision was dissolved, he will be aware that at no moment was his sense of the complete suspension and pause in ordinary human concerns so full and affecting as at that moment when the suspension ceases, and the goings-on of human life are suddenly resumed. All action in any direction is best expounded, measured, and made apprehensible, by reaction. Now apply this to the case in *Macbeth*. Here, as I have said, the retiring of the human heart and the entrance of the fiendish heart was to be expressed, and made sensible. Another world has stepped in; and the murderers are taken out of the region of human things, human purposes, human desires. They are transfigured: Lady Macbeth is "unsexed"; Macbeth has forgot that he was born of a woman; both are conformed to the image of devils; and the world of devils is suddenly revealed. But how shall this be conveyed and made palpable? In order that a new world may step in, this world must for a time disappear. The murderers, and the murder, must be insulated—cut off by an immeasurable gulf from the ordinary tide and

succession of human affairs—locked up and se-
questered in some deep recess; we must be made
sensible that the world of ordinary life is suddenly
arrested—laid asleep—tranced—racked into a
dread armistice; time must be annihilated, relation to things without abolished; and all must
pass self-withdrawn into a deep syncope and suspension of earthly passion. Hence it is that, when
the deed is done, when the work of darkness is
perfect, then the world of darkness passes away
like a pageantry in the clouds: the knocking at
the gate is heard, and it makes known audibly
that the reaction has commenced; the human has
made its reflux upon the fiendish; the pulses of
life are beginning to beat again; and the re-
establishment of the goings-on of the world in
which we live first makes us profoundly sensible
of the awful parenthesis that has suspended them.

O mighty poet! Thy works are not as those of
other men, simply and merely great works of art,
but are also like the phenomena of nature, like
the sun and the sea, the stars and the flowers, like
frost and snow, rain and dew, hail-storm and
thunder, which are to be studied with entire sub-
mission of our own faculties, and in the perfect
faith that in them there can be no too much or
too little, nothing useless or inert, but that, the
farther we press in our discoveries, the more we
shall see proofs of design and self-purporting
arrangement where the careless eye had seen
nothing but accident!

Notes

[1] Allowing for the optical illusion that makes a horizontal line seem to sag in the middle, the ancient Greeks raised the foundation lines of their temples in the center in order to give the effect of a horizontal line.

[2] A Shakespearean actor who enjoyed considerable vogue early in the nineteenth century.

[3] See Walt Whitman's poem "When Lilacs Last in the Dooryard Bloomed" about the passing of Abraham Lincoln's funeral cortège.

Questions

1. What effect did the knocking on the gate have upon De Quincey? What similar experience have you had?

2. Upon what does our reaction to a murder depend?

3. What is De Quincey's conception of sympathy? How may it be compared with Aristotle's? See page 631.

LITERATURE OF KNOWLEDGE AND LITERATURE OF POWER

Thomas De Quincey

What is it that we mean by *literature?* Popularly, and amongst the thoughtless, it is held to include everything that is printed in a book. Little logic is required to disturb *that* definition. The most thoughtless person is easily made aware that in the idea of *literature* one essential element is some relation to a general and common interest of man,—so that what applies only to a local, or professional, or merely personal interest, even though presenting itself in the shape of a book, will not belong to Literature. So far the definition is easily narrowed; and it is as easily expanded. For not only is much that takes a station in books not literature, but inversely, much that really *is* literature never reaches a station in books. The weekly sermons of Christendom, that vast pulpit literature [1] which acts so extensively upon the popular mind—to warn, to uphold, to renew, to comfort, to alarm—does not attain the sanctuary of libraries in the ten-thousandth part of its extent. The drama again,—as, for instance, the finest part of Shakespeare's plays in England, and all leading Athenian plays in the noontide of the Attic stage,—operated as a literature on the public mind, and were (according to the strictest letter of that term) *published* through the audiences that witnessed their representation some time before they were published as things to be read; and they were published in this scenical mode of publication with much more effect than they could have had as books during ages of costly copying or of costly printing.

Books, therefore, do not suggest an idea co-extensive and interchangeable with the idea of literature; since much literature, scenic, forensic, or didactic (as from lecturers and public orators), may never come into books, and much that does come into books may connect itself with no literary interest. But a far more important correction, applicable to the common vague idea of literature, is to be sought not so much in a better definition of literature as in a sharper distinction of the two functions which it fulfils. In that great social organ which, collectively, we call literature, there may be distinguished two separate offices, that may blend and often do so, but capable, severally, of a severe insulation, and naturally fitted for reciprocal repulsion. There is, first, the literature of *knowledge,* and secondly, the literature of *power*. The function of the first is to *teach;* the function of the second is to *move;* the first is a rudder, the second an oar or a sail. The first speaks to the mere discursive understanding; the second speaks ultimately, it may happen, to the higher understanding or reason, but always through affections of pleasure and sympathy. Remotely, it may travel towards an object seated in what Lord Bacon calls "dry light"; but proximately it does and must operate—else it ceases to be a literature of power—on and through that *humid* light which clothes itself in the mists and glittering iris of human passions, desires, and genial emotions. Men have so little reflected on the higher functions of literature as to find it a paradox if one should describe it as a mean or subordinate purpose of books to give information. But this is a paradox only in the sense which makes it honourable to be paradoxical. Whenever we talk in ordinary language of seeking information or gaining knowledge, we understand the words as connected with something of absolute novelty. But it is the grandeur of all truth which can occupy a very high place in human interests that it is never absolutely novel to the meanest of minds; it exists eternally by way of germ or latent principle in the lowest as in the highest, needing to be developed, but never to be planted. To be capable of transplantation is the immediate criterion of a truth that ranges on a lower scale. Besides which, there is a rarer thing than truth,— namely *power*, or deep sympathy with truth. What is the effect, for instance, upon society of children? By the pity, by the tenderness, and by the peculiar modes of admiration which connect

themselves with the helplessness, with the innocence, and with the simplicity of children, not
only are the primal affections strengthened and
continually renewed, but the qualities which are
dearest in the sight of heaven—the frailty, for
instance, which appeals to forbearance, the innocence which symbolizes the heavenly, and the
simplicity which is most alien from the worldly—
are kept up in perpetual remembrance, and their
ideals are continually refreshed. A purpose of the
same nature is answered by the higher literature,
viz., the literature of power. What do you learn
from *Paradise Lost?* Nothing at all. What do you
learn from a cookery-book? Something new, something that you did not know before, in every paragraph. But would you therefore put the wretched
cookery-book on a higher level of estimation than
the divine poem? What you owe to Milton is not
any knowledge, of which a million separate items
are still but a million of advancing steps on the
same earthly level; what you owe is *power,*—
that is, exercise and expansion to your own latent
capacity of sympathy with the infinite, where
every pulse and each separate influx is a step up-
wards, a step ascending as upon a Jacob's ladder
from earth to mysterious altitudes above the
earth. All the steps of knowledge, from first to
last, carry you further on the same plane, but
could never raise you one foot above your ancient
level of earth; whereas the very first step in

power is a flight—is an ascending movement into another element where earth is forgotten.

Were it not that human sensibilities are ventilated and continually called out into exercise by the great phenomena of infancy, or of real life as it moves through chance and change, or of literature as it recombines these elements in the mimicries of poetry, romance, etc., it is certain that, like any animal power or muscular energy falling into disuse, all such sensibilities would gradually droop and dwindle. It is in relation to these great *moral* capacities of man that the literature of power, as contradistinguished from that of knowledge, lives and has its field of action. It is concerned with what is highest in man; for the Scriptures themselves never condescended to deal by suggestion or coöperation with the mere discursive understanding: when speaking of man in his intellectual capacity, the Scriptures speak not of the understanding, but of "the understanding heart,"—making the heart, i.e., the great *intuitive* (or non-discursive) organ, to be the interchangeable formula for man in his highest state of capacity for the infinite. Tragedy, romance, fairy tale, or epopee,[2] all alike restore to man's mind the ideals of justice, of hope, of truth, of mercy, of retribution, which else (left to the support of daily life in its realities) would languish for want of sufficient illustration.

What is meant, for instance, by *poetic justice?* It does not mean a justice that differs by its ob-

ject from the ordinary justice of human jurispru-
dence, for then it must be confessedly a very bad
kind of justice; but it means a justice that differs
from common forensic justice by the degree in
which it attains its object,—a justice that is more
omnipotent over its own ends, as dealing, not
with the refractory elements of earthly life, but
with the elements of its own creation, and with
materials flexible to its own purest preconceptions.
It is certain that, were it not for the literature of
power, these ideals would often remain amongst
us as mere arid notional forms; whereas, by the
creative forces of man put forth in literature, they
gain a vernal life of restoration, and germinate
into vital activities. The commonest novel, by
moving in alliance with human fears and hopes,
with human instincts of wrong and right, sustains
and quickens those affections. Calling them into
action, it rescues them from torpor. And hence
the preëminency over all authors that merely
teach, of the meanest that *moves,* or that teaches
if at all, indirectly by moving. The very highest
work that has ever existed in the literature of
knowledge is but a provisional work,—a book
upon trial and sufferance, and *quamdiu bene se
gesserit.*[3] Let its teaching be even partially revised, let it be but expanded,—nay, even let its
teaching be but placed in a better order,—and
instantly it is superseded. Whereas the feeblest
works in the literature of power, surviving at all,
survive as finished and unalterable amongst men.

For instance, the *Principia* of Sir Isaac Newton [4] was a book militant on earth from the first. In all stages of its progress it would have to fight for its existence: first, as regards absolute truth; secondly, when that combat was over, as regards its form or mode of presenting the truth. And as soon as a Laplace,[5] or anybody else, builds higher upon the foundations laid by this book, effectually he throws it out of the sunshine into decay and darkness; by weapons won from this book he superannuates and destroys this book, so that soon the name of Newton remains as a mere *nominis umbra*,[6] but his book, as a living power, has transmigrated into other forms. Now, on the contrary, the *Iliad*, the *Prometheus* of Æschylus, the *Othello* or *King Lear*, the *Hamlet* or *Macbeth*, and the *Paradise Lost*, are not militant, but triumphant for ever, as long as the languages exist in which they speak or can be taught to speak. They never *can* transmigrate into new incarnations. To reproduce these in new forms, or variations, even if in some things they should be improved, would be to plagiarize. A good steam engine is properly superseded by a better. But one lovely pastoral valley is not superseded by another, nor a statue of Praxiteles by a statue of Michael Angelo. These things are separated not by imparity, but by disparity. They are not thought of as unequal under the same standard, but as different in kind, and, if otherwise equal, as equal under a different standard. Human works of immortal beauty and works of nature in one respect stand on the same footing: they never absolutely repeat each other, never approach so near as not to differ, and they differ not as better and worse, or simply by more and less,—they differ by undecipherable and incommunicable differences, that cannot be caught by mimicries, that cannot be reflected in the mirror of copies, that cannot become ponderable in the scales of vulgar comparison. . . . At this hour, five hundred years since their creation, the tales of Chaucer, never equalled on this earth for their tenderness and for life of picturesqueness, are read familiarly by many in the charming language of their natal day, and by others in the modernizations of Dryden, of Pope, and Wordsworth. At this hour, one thousand eight hundred years since their creation, the pagan tales of Ovid, never equalled on this earth for the gaiety of their movement and the capricious graces of their narrative, are read by all Christendom. This man's people and their monuments are dust, but *he* is alive; he has survived them, as he told us that he had it in his commission to do, by a thousand years, "and shall a thousand more."

All the literature of knowledge builds only ground-nests, that are swept away by floods, or confounded by the plough; but the literature of power builds nests in aerial altitudes of temples sacred from violation, or of forests inaccessible to fraud. This is a great prerogative of the *power* literature, and it is a greater which lies in the mode of its influence. The *knowledge* literature, like the fashion of this world, passeth away. An encyclopædia is its abstract; and, in this respect, it may be taken for its speaking symbol,—that before one generation has passed an encyclopædia is superannuated; for it speaks through the dead memory and unimpassioned understanding, which have not the repose of higher faculties, but are continually enlarging and varying their phylacteries. But all literature properly so called— literature Κατ' ἐξοχην [7]—for the very reason that it is so much more durable than the literature of knowledge, is (and by the very same proportion it is) more intense and electrically searching in its impressions. The directions in which the tragedy of this planet has trained our human feelings to play, and the combinations into which the poetry of this planet has thrown our human passions of love and hatred, of admiration and contempt, exercise a power for bad or good over human life that cannot be contemplated, when stretching through many generations, without a sentiment allied to awe. And of this let every one be assured—that he owes to the impassioned books which he has read many a thousand more of emotions than he can consciously trace back to them. Dim by their origination, these emotions yet rise in him, and mould him through life, like forgotten incidents of his childhood.

NOTES

[1] In the eighteenth and nineteenth centuries sermons were widely published and read.

[2] Epopee is epic poetry.

[3] "As long as it conducts itself well."

[4] Sir Isaac Newton (1642–1727) discovered fundamental laws of physics which revolutionized seventeenth-century thought and science.

[5] Pierre Simon de Laplace (1749–1827), French astronomer and mathematician.

[6] The shadow of a name.

[7] Having strength; hence, literature of power.

QUESTIONS

1. What are the differences between literature of knowledge and literature of power? Illustrate.

2. Which of your studies illustrate each of De Quincey's two divisions of literature?

TRAGIC EMOTION, AND THE HERO

DUDLEY FITTS

DUDLEY FITTS was born in Boston in 1903 and was educated at Harvard University in the Departments of Classics
and Mediævalism. Upon graduation he associated himself
with the more radical group of young poets and critics and
has since contributed to periodicals of advance-guard tendencies, both here and abroad. He is now an instructor in
English literature at The Choate School. This paper, one
of a series dealing with aspects of Aristotle's *De Arte
Poetica*, will prove useful to the student of modern drama
as well as to the student of Shakespeare. It has real value
as a critical analysis of the fascination that Tragedy has
for everyone.

IN MY last lecture, Gentlemen, I discussed certain aspects of Aristotle's famous definition of
Tragedy.[1] We concluded that Tragedy is "a compact, balanced representation of a serious course
of action, designed to excite pity and fear, and
thereby to effect an emotional purgation"; that
the Tragic is of a higher type than the Comic,
whose purpose is merely to satirize or to entertain; that "a serious course of action" does not
necessarily imply death, or even an unhappy ending (though this is the convention); that the
action should involve as little time and space as

possible; and that it should have a beginning, a middle, and an end. It remains to consider the emotional effect of Tragedy, and the type of Hero best suited to tragic representation.

I shall begin by observing that no one knows exactly what Aristotle meant when he said that Tragedy should excite pity and fear, thereby effecting an emotional purgation. He said it, as a matter of fact, even more obscurely: "through pity and fear effecting the proper purgation of these emotions". The conjectures on this phrase have been as rhapsodic and as diverse as those arising from certain Biblical texts. What is the purpose of Tragedy? Why do we go to tragedies? Is it because we take a malicious pleasure in watching the sufferings of others? Every newspaper knows that each sordid hanging has its absent thousands of avid witnesses, eager for the most intimate detail. We have even coined the phrase "morbid curiosity". Is it possible that our enjoyment of *King Lear* is only a refined expression of this curiosity? The idea is absurd. Again, there are critics who regard Tragedy as a kind of mental-healing: caught up in the surge of tragic emotion, the audience forgets its complexes and headaches, its tailor's bills and unhappy loves, and leaves the theatre "purified" and at least temporarily happy. There is unquestionably more truth in this theory; but we shall do well to remember F. L. Lucas' pungent remark: "The theatre is not a hospital". Or, there are those who

adhere to what might be called the Pulpit School
of criticism, and who find in Tragedy only a code
of ethics: Thus X, poor sin-ridden soul, happens
into a performance of *Hamlet;* there, if he survives the customary direction, performance, and
mise en scène,[2] his reflexions will be something
like this: "Poor Hamlet! He certainly came to a
melancholy end: he died, and painfully. Why?
Well, as nearly as I can make out, because he
hesitated to kill his uncle. And poor Claudius!
His end was lamentable, too. And why? Apparently because he *didn't* hesitate to kill his brother.
And poor Polonius! Just because he was a prying
old busybody—" and so on. Now it is possible
that X will leave the theatre a better man, somewhat confused as to the advisability of assassina-
tion, but convinced that Procrastination and Curiosity are moral defects to be avoided. (His own
phrase will be, "They don't pay".) It is possible,
I say, that he will go and sin no more. But if the
theatre is not a hospital, I am pretty sure that it
is not a church, either.

Let us see. A proper tragedy should excite "pity
and fear" in us. Pity and fear, acting almost like
chemical reagents, produce a "purgation". The word
that Aristotle uses is κάθαρσις (kátharsis), which
we recognize in our word *cathartic*. The tragic
emotion, then, is cathartic: that is to say, it
cleanses and purifies; and, as the result of bodily
purification is bodily well-being and exuberance,
so the result of mental purgation is emotional

well-being and exaltation. The tragic *kátharsis* is a concentration of the emotions that well up within us, that trouble us, and may even become dangerous, if they are not granted a periodic outlet; it is an evocation, a concentration, and a release of these emotions. Participants in the passions and agonies of the Hero, we expend upon him those emotional forces which otherwise might fester within ourselves; he takes upon himself, as it were, the fears, the hopes, the violences of us all; he is our Scapegoat; in him we experience the exultations and despairs that our otherwise colourless life denies us; for the time being, his virtues are our virtues, and our frailties are expiated in his downfall. This process is very weakly described by the word "enjoyment": it is really an ecstasy, a spiritual exaltation; it is not, however, a therapeutic or an ethical exercise. We do not leave the theatre "better men", in the moral sense. We go out in the mental condition accurately described by Milton:

With calm of mind, all passion spent.[3]

Such, then, is the effect that Tragedy should have upon us, if it is a tragedy of the right sort, and if we are qualified to appreciate it. We have already considered some of the elements that compose a tragedy of the right sort: the dignity of its subject-matter, the craftiness of its architecture, the beauty of its diction. But these things, though inevitable, are of secondary importance to the Symbol upon which our emotions centre, and which acts as the releasing-agent of our "pity and fear": the Tragic Hero himself. The Tragedy stands or falls by the poet's conception of this character. What kind of man is the suitable Tragic Hero?

I have used the phrase "pity and fear" without definition. However, if we are to understand the nature of our Hero, we must agree upon the meaning of these words; otherwise we shall be talking in the dark. By "pity", then, I would suggest something more than "feeling sorry" for someone, as we should vaguely "feel sorry" for an acquaintance whom we saw run down in the street. By "pity" I mean a much more active thing: I mean *participation in,* as well as *sorrow for,* the misfortune of another. Aristotle's Greek word were better translated "compassion", which, from its very derivation [*con + patior*] means "feeling with". In order truly to *feel with* a man in his adversity, it is necessary to identify oneself with that man, "to imagine" (as we say) "how he must feel". Tragic Pity, then, is the emotion which results from our sympathetic participation in the Hero's misfortune.

Tragic "fear" is less easily defined. Aristotle rather unhelpfully says that it is called forth "by the misfortune of a man like ourselves". Like "pity", then, it implies our self-identification with the Hero. Perhaps we may arrive at the idea in this way: If the spectator of a tragedy is moved powerfully enough to be able to enter into the character of the Hero in the way I have described above, he is actually in a position to experience the action on two planes. Knowing the plot of *Othello,* for instance, he is like God watching the progress of the drama of human life: that is to say, he foresees the perils and errors which threaten Othello, perils and errors of which Othello is necessarily ignorant. This heightens his appreciation of the irony of Othello's conclusions and actions, which appreciation is one of the strongest elements of the enjoyment to be derived from drama. Very well; but the spectator is at the same time *living* the action with Othello himself. Knowing what he knows, and being at the same time limited by the ignorance of the Hero, he participates all the more earnestly in Othello's tormented doubts because he is always conscious that *if Othello knew what* he *knew—* His impulse is to cry out from his seat a warning to Othello: "Look out, Othello! Not that, Othello! These are lies, lies . . ."; an impulse so strong that it has actually led to the invasion of the stage by transported members of the audience. And with this fear for the Hero (which is also a sublimated fear for himself) there may be combined another sort of fear, which might be phrased thus: "There is the Hero, a great man and a good man; yet I perceive that he has fallen into the most bitter disgrace. Why is it impossible that something of the sort might happen to me?" This seems to be what Aristotle meant by his "fear by the misfortune of a man like ourselves". In any case, it is dependent upon the spectator's participation in the vicissitudes of the Hero; and participation implies the spectator's acceptance of the Hero as a credible personage.

What, then, are the characteristics of this ideal Hero of Tragedy? He should be, says our Critic, a prosperous person of renown—a man like Œdipus, or Lear, or (in Milton's epic) [4] Lucifer. He need not be eminently good and just; but his downfall *must* be brought about, not by vice or depravity, but by some error or frailty. (Remember, Gentlemen, that Tragedy is the spectacle of a man passing from prosperity to adversity.) It would be tedious to discuss at length what Aristotle means by "vice or depravity", by "error or frailty". Let us consider for a moment the hypothetical downfalls of characters of a different composition from that of the ideal: the fall of an absolutely good man, and that of an utter villain.

We do not have to go far. Both types are made familiar to us in Tennyson's *Idylls of the King*. There we have, in Arthur, the type of the perfectly virtuous man brought, through no fault of his own, from prosperity to adversity; and, in Modred, the type of the absolute villain destroyed by his own malignancy. There is action enough, there are suffering and deaths enough, to satisfy the most bloodthirsty taste; yet I am afraid that only an unthoughtful reader, or an advanced sentimentalist has ever really pitied Arthur (as we now understand the word), or been moved to the tragic kind of fear by Modred. In the first case, Aristotle would say that we are merely shocked. There is nothing *tragic* in the suffering of a wholly blameless individual (assuming for the moment that such an individual is possible), or in calamity that is wholly external, the operation of what Coleridge called "motiveless malignity". An excellent illustration occurs in James Joyce's *Portrait of the Artist*.[5] Stephen Daedalus is discussing this very point with a friend, and cites an example:

> "A girl got into a hansom a few days ago . . . in London. She was on her way to meet her mother whom she had not seen for many years. At the corner of a street the shaft of a lorry shivered the window of the hansom in the shape of a star. A long fine needle of the shivered glass pierced her heart. She died on the instant. The reporter called it a tragic death. It is not. It is remote from terror and pity according to the terms of my definition."

Shocking, yes; but not tragic: the victim must cooperate, to however slight an extent, in his own ruin. If for no other reason, then, the downfall of Arthur (as Tennyson intended him: guiltless) is not tragic. But what of Modred? Surely he "cooperated in his own ruin"? He did, wholeheartedly. But Modred is as improbably black in his depravity as Arthur is white in his virtue. It is true, his fall satisfies our desire to see justice done; but we feel neither pity nor fear for Modred, for it is impossible for us to accept the reality of such a character as Modred. "Fear is aroused by the misfortune of a man like ourselves." "A man like ourselves"—that is the crux of the matter. As soon as the audience (or the reader) suspects that the character whose suffering is being depicted is *unreal,* an impossible idealization, then the interplay of sympathy, the very essence of the tragic emotion, ceases. None of us can excite himself about an abstraction, a never-never man, a human impossibility. We pity, we experience fear, only when we believe in the existence of the object of our pity and fear. We realize instinctively that no such men as Arthur and Modred ever lived, or ever could live. As well pity Jeff, who is mauled every day, piteously and improbably, by Mutt. As well fear for the Jabberwock, or for Humpty-Dumpty, or for Fafner, the papier-mâché dragon in *Siegfried.*[6] It is this improbability of characterization, and not the *Idylls'* birthday-album sententiousness, that is the fundamental flaw in Tennyson's poem. Arthur is too good to exist; Modred, too bad to exist; both, more than a little silly. No; the tragic Hero is neither of these.

His will be, then, a character which we shall recognize not only as humanly probable, but as nearly normal as can be. That is to say, he will be neither a Tennysonian prig, nor a cinema-thriller villain. Since mankind as a whole rather inclines to the good than to the bad (I am walking perilously here!), he will be what the world recognizes as a good man, a man of honour, a reputable member of society: an average man, in short. Accordingly, his character, though essentially good, will yet be imperfect; and it is this imperfection which will set in motion the machinery of his destruction. What the imperfection will be, rests with the dramatist; but it is obvious that the greater the disproportion between it and the resultant catastrophe, the greater the tragic force of the drama. Allow me to illustrate my meaning: Œdipus killed his father, though he was ignorant of the old man's identity. Indeed, had he known who the aged traveler was, he would have avoided him sedulously: for was he not running away from home for no other reason than to avoid killing his father,—a crime which had been foresung by the Oracle? Nevertheless, he committed patricide in an access of meaningless rage; and the horror of his crime can only diminish the pity we feel for Œdipus in his later misfortune. Here, then, we have a moral imperfection—anger—manifesting itself in a crime of magnitude. But let us take an example less extreme. King Lear was a vain old man who publicly staged a panegyric-contest, with his three daughters as eulogists and himself as the object of their praise. He knew that his daughters loved him (of course! had he not already granted to each a third of his kingdom?), but he wanted to hear them tell him so, and he wanted his assembled court to hear them, too. Consequently, when Cordelia, his favourite, refused to compete with her sisters in vocal love, and proudly refused more than a curt

> *I love your majesty*
> *According to my bond, nor more nor less,*[7]

the King's vanity was cruelly hurt. He reacted normally: though he knew quite well that Cordelia loved him, he felt, correctly enough, that she had made him ridiculous before his courtiers; therefore he banished her, and bestowed her portion upon her two more compliant sisters, who, ironically, managed later to destroy their father between them. Again we have a moral imperfection—vanity—evolving anger; but it is a slighter flaw than Œdipus', though the punishment is as heavy, and for this reason we feel more strongly the pity of Lear's subsequent misery.

You will observe, Gentlemen, that both these tragedies involve the Hero's conscious transgression of a moral law. Let us now consider a borderline case. I have said that the poignancy of our tragic response depends largely upon the disproportion between the initial error and its punishment. Now, if the initial error be no moral error at all, but merely a mistake in judgment, or an accident precipitating a series of ill-conceived actions, we shall have come as close as we can to the point where legitimate drama passes over into the Tennysonian melodrama of the punishment of the guiltless. The hero of *Othello* is, I suppose, *morally* guiltless of the murder of Desdemona: that is to say, his was a murder without malice, a justifiable act—indeed, he saw it not as a murder at all, but as a "sacrifice". Iago, with a series of more or less convincing lies and circumstantial proofs, had managed to bring him to the point of believing that Desdemona was faithless. True, the evidence was questionable: events played with an almost melodramatic patness into Iago's hands; but Othello was, in his own words, a man

> . . . *not easily jealous, but, being wrought,*
> *Perplex'd in the extreme:* [8]

he was one of those trusting, hot-headed individuals whose rage, once aroused, sweeps everything before it. He never questioned, never analysed, never weighed; and it was not until he had killed his harmless Desdemona that he realised the truth. The moral onus of the whole shocking crime falls upon Iago; but Othello, because he was rashly credulous, and because, however high-mindedly, he destroyed an innocent life, suffered, and was himself destroyed. It is possible that tragedies of this kind touch us most of all: there is no question of "vice or depravity", no question, even, of serious moral imperfection; the character's punishment seems to us disproportionate, or at best casuistically merited. The retribution is, nevertheless, merited; but the margin is so thin between this and the melodrama of the sheep led to the slaughter! Othello, Lear, Œdipus, Macbeth—each of them, and every tragic Hero, coöperates to some extent in his ruin. No man is tragically destroyed by a force entirely beyond his control. The Fatal Sisters must kindle the criminal spark in Macbeth before they can accomplish his destruction. Iago must awaken Othello's deadly rage before he can bring about the Moor's hideous fall. The theatre is not a hospital, the theatre is not a church; but neither is the theatre a mad-house. Our sense of justice is too strong to permit of any reaction but horror, confronted with the spectacle of reasonless calamity.

One more consideration, and I am done. A quality which I have not mentioned, but which we instinctively look for in our tragic heroes, is a certain magnanimity, a great-souled courage in the face of disaster, a resistance, a fighting-back against the inevitable doom. So strongly do we associate this quality with our Heroes that we have called it after them,—"heroism". You will remember that Aristotle described the Hero as being "a person of renown"; and, indeed, the Hero of classical drama, and of drama pretty generally down to the Nineteenth Century, was always a great man—a King, like Œdipus, or a General, like Othello. There is a variety of reasons for this. In the first place, everyone would know in advance the history of an Œdipus; consequently, the dramatist could count on a more intelligent comprehension on the part of his audience than would have been the case if he were expounding an entirely unfamiliar tale, and he could therefore devote himself to more relevant matters. For novelty, you see, was not yet esteemed *per se* by the unsophisticated ancients. Moreover, the theme of Tragedy is a man's downfall; and the more exalted the man, the more spectacular the downfall, just as a falling star is certainly more spectacular than a falling leaf. We realize today, thanks to the despised Romantics, that while the tragedy of a millionaire may be more spectacular than the tragedy of a clerk, it is not for that reason more significant. We have learned that the pity and terror of common life are just as moving as the pity and terror of the mighty. *Hedda Gabler* is as tragic as the *Elektra*.[9] But Aristotle was right in turning to his "person of renown" for a third reason: the necessity of heroic magnanimity. For without "fighting back", the doomed Hero is not tragic, but only pathetic. The true Hero will not accept his fate passively, will not suffer himself to be slaughtered like a beast. He will be, in Pope's fine phrase,

A brave man struggling in the storms of Fate: [10]

Macbeth, valiant to the last; Othello, with his splendid final gesture; Œdipus, denying himself the consolation of death, driving himself to wander blinded through the grim land. There is all the difference in the world between Lady Macbeth and Desdemona, between Torvald Helmer and Oswald Alving,—the difference between the tragic and the merely pathetic.

In conclusion, I would say that tragic emotion is largely dependent upon the element of "if". "If", in spite of Mr. Kipling's rather noxious doggerel, is a powerful word . . . I shall spare you the rest of this platitude; what I was about to say is this: it is not the regret for inevitable calamities that most strongly moves us, but the regret for calamities that might so easily have been averted, were human nature a bit more poised: for misfortunes resulting from misunderstanding, for miseries arising from accident. *If* Œdipus had known who the old man was . . . *If* King Lear had not indulged his sentimental vanity (and, *If* Cordelia could have swallowed her silly pride . . .) . . . *If* Othello had been more of the jurist, and less of the warrior . . . *If* Hamlet could have made up his mind . . . It could so easily have been different (though in that case, of course, there would have been no plays!) . . . The Greeks knew that a man's happiness depends upon just such threads as these, and that what they called Destiny (and we call Ironic Circumstance) most tragically destroys when it destroys most casually. . . . A dusty hot road, the bitter sweat on a young man's lips, the needless quarrel with the horsemen at the crossroads, the blind fury shaking against the sun: "O three roads," cried the darkened King, years after, "O three roads, O secret glen; O coppice and narrow way where three roads met; you that drank up the blood I spilt, the blood that was my own, my father's blood . . ." And the Chorus pronounced its unforgettable benediction:

> *Make way for Œdipus. All people said*
> *"That is a fortunate man";*
> *And now what storms are beating on his head?*
> *Call no man fortunate that is not dead.*
> *The dead are free from pain.*[11]

NOTES

[1] *De Arte Poetica:* cap. vi: "tragedy, therefore, is an imitation of an action that is serious, complete, and of a certain magnitude; in language embellished with each kind of artistic ornament, the several kinds being found in separate parts of the play; in the form of action, not of narrative; through pity and fear effecting the proper purgation of these emotions." (tr. S. H. Butcher.)

[2] *mise-en-scène:* stage-setting, décor.

[3] Milton, *Samson Agonistes.* 1755 *seq:*

> His servants he with new acquist
> Of true experience from this great event
> With peace and consolation hath dismist,
> And calm of mind all passion spent.

[4] "Milton's epic": *Paradise Lost;* see especially, Books I and II.

[5] James Joyce: One of the most significant of modern novelists. The fortunes of Stephen Daedalus (*i.e.,* an autobiographical projection of Joyce himself) are traced in *The Portrait of the Artist as a Young Man* (1916) and in *Ulysses* (1922). The latter of these books has probably

had more influence than any other single work upon contemporary artistic trends.

[6] "Siegfried": the third of Wagner's "Ring" operas, derived from the Germanic *Niebelungenlied*. Fafner is the dragon who is destroyed by the Hero, Siegfried.

[7] Shakespeare's *King Lear*, I: i.

[8] Shakespeare's *Othello*, V: ii.

[9] *Hedda Gabler:* a tragedy by the Norwegian dramatist, Henrik Ibsen. *Elektra:* a tragedy by the Greek Sophocles.

[10] In the Prologue to Addison's *Cato* (1713).

[11] "O three roads", etc. This and the concluding Chorus are a free paraphrase of the *Œdipus Rex* of Sophocles, by William Butler Yeats (*King Œdipus, a Version for the Modern Stage:* 1928).

QUESTIONS

1. What, in your own words, is Aristotle's definition of tragedy?

2. Why do we go to watch tragedies?

3. Define the "tragic hero."

4. Why is "destiny" or "ironic circumstance" inevitably associated with tragedy?

BIOGRAPHIA LITERARIA

Samuel Taylor Coleridge

It is doubtful whether the Reverend James Boyer, Headmaster of Christ's Hospital School and ardent flogger, recognized in the youth SAMUEL TAYLOR COLERIDGE (1772–1834) and Charles Lamb those qualities which were later to make them leading forces in the realms of poetry and the essay respectively. That Coleridge was outstanding was evident; for what, it remained for time to tell. One of the most precocious boys in all literary history, Coleridge had become more or less a character at the age of eight, and had already developed that intense imagination later to make him immortal. It was to feed this hungry imaginative force within him that he later took opium. One could never tell what to expect next of Coleridge. At twenty-one he ran away from Cambridge and enlisted in the Light Horse Dragoons under the name of Silas Tomkyn Comberbach, but quickly tired of this. Next he appeared as a leading member of a group striving to set up a Pantisocracy on the banks of the Susquehanna, an ideal community consisting of twelve men and twelve women freed from all restraints upon thought or action. That failing to materialize, Coleridge turned his affections to Sarah Fricker and soon entered upon a marriage in which happiness and stability proved about as permanent as Pantisocracy. Lamb said of this ill-fated match, "Coleridge ought not to have a wife or children; he should have a sort of diocesan care of the world—no parish duty." Ardent in conversation to the point of monopoly, he was easily capable of augmenting his slender income by lecturing or by preaching in scattered Unitarian chapels. Once asked by Coleridge if he had ever heard him preach, Lamb replied, "I have never heard you do anything else!" Coleridge's excellent critical sense early drew him into sympathetic contact with Southey and Wordsworth who were engaged in revolt against the old conventions in poetry, seeking to bring poetry nearer to common people and employing the simple language of simple folk. How he agreed with and differed from Wordsworth in this new Romantic Movement may be found, in part, in this selection from his *Biographia Literaria,* a history of his thought rather than of his life.

DURING the first year that Mr. Wordsworth and I were neighbours, our conversations turned frequently on the two cardinal points of poetry, the power of exciting the sympathy of the reader by a faithful adherence to the truth of nature, and the power of giving the interest of novelty by the modifying colours of imagination. The sudden charm, which accidents of light and shade, which moon-light or sunset diffused over a known and familiar landscape, appeared to represent the practicability of combining both. These are the poetry of nature. The thought suggested itself— (to which of us I do not recollect)—that a series of poems might be composed of two sorts. In the one, the incidents and agents were to be, in part at least, supernatural; and the excellence aimed at was to consist in the interesting of the affections by the dramatic truth of such emotions, as would naturally accompany such situations, supposing them real. And real in this sense they have been to every human being who, from whatever source of delusion, has at any time believed himself under supernatural agency. For the second class, subjects were to be chosen from ordinary life; the characters and incidents were to be such as will be found in every village and its vicinity, where there is a meditative and feeling mind to seek after them, or to notice them, when they present themselves.

In this idea originated the plan of the *Lyrical Ballads;* in which it was agreed, that my endeavours should be directed to persons and characters supernatural, or at least romantic; yet so as to transfer from our inward nature a human interest and a semblance of truth sufficient to procure for these shadows of imagination that willing suspension of disbelief for the moment, which constitutes poetic faith. Mr. Wordsworth, on the other hand, was to propose to himself as his object, to give the charm of novelty to things of every day, and to excite a feeling analogous to the supernatural, by awakening the mind's attention to the lethargy of custom, and directing it to the loveliness and the wonders of the world before us; an inexhaustible treasure, but for which, in consequence of the film of familiarity and selfish solicitude, we have eyes, yet see not, ears that hear not, and hearts that neither feel nor understand.

With this view I wrote *The Ancient Mariner,* and was preparing among other poems, *The*

Dark Ladie, and the *Christabel,* in which I should have more nearly realized my ideal, than I had done in my first attempt. But Mr. Wordsworth's industry had proved so much more successful, and the number of his poems so much greater, that my compositions, instead of forming a balance, appeared rather an interpolation of heterogeneous matter. Mr. Wordsworth added two or three poems written in his own character, in the impassioned, lofty, and sustained diction, which is characteristic of his genius. In this form the *Lyrical Ballads* were published; and were presented by him, as an experiment, whether subjects, which from their nature rejected the usual ornaments and extra-colloquial style of poems in general, might not be so managed in the language of ordinary life as to produce the pleasurable interest, which it is the peculiar business of poetry to impart. To the second edition he added a preface of considerable length; in which, notwithstanding some passages of apparently a contrary import, he was understood to contend for the extension of this style of poetry of all kinds, and to reject as vicious and indefensible all phrases and forms of speech that were not included in what he (unfortunately, I think, adopting an equivocal expression) called the language of real life. From this preface, prefixed to poems in which it was impossible to deny the presence of original genius, however mistaken its direction might be deemed, arose the whole long-continued controversy. For from the conjunction of perceived power with supposed heresy I explain the inveteracy and in some instances, I grieve to say, the acrimonious passions, with which the controversy has been conducted by the assailants.

Had Mr. Wordsworth's poems been the silly, the childish things, which they were for a long time described as being: had they been really distinguished from the compositions of other poets merely by meanness of language and inanity of thought; had they indeed contained nothing more than what is found in the parodies and pretended imitations of them; they must have sunk at once, a dead weight, into the slough of oblivion, and have dragged the preface along with them. But year after year increased the number of Mr. Wordsworth's admirers. They were found too not in the lower classes of the reading public, but chiefly among young men of strong sensibility and meditative minds; and their admiration (inflamed perhaps in some degree by opposition) was distinguished by its intensity, I might almost say, by its religious fervour. These facts, and the intellectual energy of the author, which was more or less consciously felt, where it was outwardly and even boisterously denied, meeting with sentiments of aversion to his opinions, and of alarm at their consequences, produced an eddy of criticism, which would of itself have borne up the poems by the violence with which it whirled them round and round. With many parts of this preface in the sense attributed to them and which the words undoubtedly seem to authorize, I never concurred; but on the contrary objected to them as erroneous in principle, and as contradictory (in appearance at least) both to other parts of the same preface, and to the author's own practice in the greater part of the poems themselves. Mr. Wordsworth in his recent collection has, I find, degraded this prefatory disquisition to the end of his second volume, to be read or not at the reader's choice. But he has not, as far as I can discover, announced any change in his poetic creed. At all events, considering it as the source of a controversy, in which I have been honoured more than I deserve by the frequent conjunction of my name with his, I think it expedient to declare once for all, in what points I coincide with the opinions supported in that preface, and in what points I altogether differ. But in order to render myself intelligible I must previously, in as few words as possible, explain my views, first, of a Poem; and secondly, of Poetry itself, in kind, and in essence.

The office of philosophical disquisition consists in just distinction; while it is the privilege of the philosopher to preserve himself constantly aware, that distinction is not division. In order to obtain adequate notions of any truth, we must intellectually separate its distinguishable parts; and this is the technical process of philosophy. But having so done, we must then restore them in our conceptions to the unity, in which they actually coexist; and this is the result of philosophy. A poem contains the same elements as a prose composition; the difference therefore must consist in a different combination of them, in consequence of a different object being proposed. According to the difference of the object will be the difference of the combination. It is possible, that the object may be merely to facilitate the recollection of any given facts or observations by artificial arrangement; and the composition will be a poem, merely because it is distinguished from prose by metre, or by rhyme, or by both conjointly. In this, the lowest sense, a man might attribute the name of a poem to the well-known enumeration of the days in the several months;

> "Thirty days hath September,
> April, June, and November," etc.

and others of the same class and purpose. And as a particular pleasure is found in anticipating the recurrence of sounds and quantities, all compositions that have this charm super-added, whatever be their contents, *may* be entitled poems.

So much for the superficial form. A difference of object and contents supplies an additional ground of distinction. The immediate purpose may be the communication of truths; either of truth absolute and demonstrable, as in works of science; or of facts experienced and recorded, as in history. Pleasure, and that of the highest and most permanent kind, may result from the attainment of the end; but it is not itself the immediate end. In other works the communication of pleasure may be the immediate purpose; and though truth, either moral or intellectual, ought to be the ultimate end, yet this will distinguish the character of the author, not the class to which the work belongs. Blest indeed is that state of society, in which the immediate purpose would be baffled by the perversion of the proper ultimate end; in which no charm of diction or imagery could exempt the *Bathyllus* even of an Anacreon, or the *Alexis* of Virgil, from disgust and aversion! [1]

But the communication of pleasure may be the immediate object of a work not metrically composed; and that object may have been in a high degree attained, as in novels and romances. Would then the mere superaddition of metre, with or without rhyme, entitle these to the name of poems? The answer is, that nothing can permanently please, which does not contain in itself the reason why it is so, and not otherwise. If metre be superadded, all other parts must be made consonant with it. They must be such, as to justify the perpetual and distinct attention to each part, which an exact correspondent recurrence of accent and sound are calculated to excite. The final definition then, so deduced, may be thus worded. A poem is that species of composition, which is opposed to works of science, by proposing for its *immediate* object pleasure, not truth; and from all other species—(having *this* object in common with it) —it is discriminated by proposing to itself such delight from the *whole,* as is compatible with a distinct gratification from each component *part.*

Controversy is not seldom excited in consequence of the disputants attaching each a different meaning to the same word; and in few instances has this been more striking, than in disputes concerning the present subject. If a man chooses to call every composition a poem, which is rhyme, or measure, or both, I must leave his opinion uncontroverted. The distinction is at least competent to characterize the writer's intention. If it were subjoined, that the whole is likewise entertaining or affecting, as a tale, or as a series of interesting reflections, I of course admit this as another fit ingredient of a poem, and an additional merit. But if the definition sought for be that of a *legitimate* poem, I answer, it must be one, the parts of which mutually support and explain each other; all in their proportion harmonizing with, and supporting the purpose and known influences of metrical arrangement. The philosophic critics of all ages coincide with the ultimate judgment of all countries, in equally denying the praises of a just poem, on the one hand, to a series of striking lines or distiches, each of which, absorbing the whole attention of the reader to itself, becomes disjoined from its context, and forms a separate whole, instead of a harmonizing part; and on the other hand, to an unsustained composition, from which the reader collects rapidly the general result unattracted by the component parts. The reader should be carried forward not merely or chiefly by the mechanical impulse of curiosity, or by a restless desire to arrive at the final solution; but by the pleasurable activity of mind excited by the attractions of the journey itself. Like the motion of a serpent, which the Egyptians made the emblem of intellectual power; or like the path of sound through the air;—at every step he pauses and half recedes, and from the retrogressive movement collects the force which again carries him onward. *Præcipitandus est liber spiritus,* says Petronius most happily.[2] The epithet, *liber,* here balances the preceding verb; and it is not easy to conceive more meaning condensed in fewer words.

But if this should be admitted as a satisfactory character of a poem, we have still to seek for a definition of poetry. The writings of Plato, and Jeremy Taylor, and Burnet's Theory of the Earth,[3] furnish undeniable proofs that poetry of the highest kind may exist without metre, and even without the contradistinguishing objects of a poem. The first chapter of Isaiah—(indeed a very large portion of the whole book)—is poetry in the most emphatic sense; yet it would be not less irrational than strange to assert, that pleasure, and not truth was the immediate object of the prophet. In short, whatever specific import we attach to the word, Poetry, there will be found involved in it, as a necessary consequence, that a poem of any length neither can be, nor ought to be, all poetry. Yet if an harmonious whole is to be produced, the remaining parts must be preserved in keeping with the poetry; and this can be no otherwise effected than by such a studied selection and artificial arrangement, as will partake of one, though not a peculiar property of poetry. And this again can be no other than the property of exciting a more continuous and equal attention than the language of prose aims at, whether colloquial or written.

My own conclusions on the nature of poetry, in the strictest use of the word, have been in part anticipated in some of the remarks on the Fancy and Imagination in the early part of this work. What is poetry?—is so nearly the same question with, what is a poet?—that the answer to the one is involved in the solution of the other. For it is a distinction resulting from the poetic genius itself, which sustains and modifies the images, thoughts, and emotions of the poet's own mind.

The poet, described in ideal perfection, brings the whole soul of man into activity, with the subordination of its faculties to each other according to their relative worth and dignity. He diffuses a tone and spirit of unity, that blends and (as it were) *fuses*, each into each, by that synthetic and magical power, to which I would exclusively appropriate the name of Imagination. This power, first put in action by the will and understanding, and retained under their irremissive, though gentle and unnoticed, control, *laxis effertur habenis*,[4] reveals itself in the balance of reconcilement of opposite or discordant qualities: of sameness, with difference; of the general with the concrete; the idea with the image; the individual with the representative; the sense of novelty and freshness with old and familiar objects; a more than usual state of emotion with more than usual order; judgment ever awake and steady self-possession with enthusiasm and feeling profound or vehement; and while it blends and harmonizes the natural and the artificial, still subordinates art to nature; the manner to the matter; and our admiration of the poet to our sympathy with the poetry. Doubtless, as Sir John Davies [5] observes of the soul—(and his words may with slight alteration be applied, and even more appropriately, to the poetic Imagination)—

> Doubtless this could not be, but that she turns
>   Bodies to *spirit* by sublimation strange,
> As fire converts to fire the things it burns,
>   As we our food into our nature change.

> From their gross matter she abstracts *their* forms,
>   And draws a kind of quintessence from things;
> Which to her proper nature she transforms
>   To bear them light on her celestial wings.

> *Thus* does she, when from *individual states*
>   She doth abstract the universal kinds;
> *Which then re-clothed in divers names and fates*
>   *Steal access through the senses to our minds.*

Finally, Good Sense is the Body of poetic genius, Fancy its Drapery, Motion its Life, and Imagination the Soul that is everywhere, and in each; and forms all into one graceful and intelligent whole.

NOTES

[1] Anacreon, Greek poet (563–478 B.C.), noted for graceful lyrics extolling love and wine.

Virgil (70–19 B.C.), Roman epic poet—less and less known every year.

[2] Petronius Arbiter, Roman satirist, friend of Emperor Nero. His *Trimalchio's Dinner* is still the world's best satire on the *nouveau riche. Præcipitandus est liber spiritus:* The free spirit must be driven headlong.

[3] Plato (427–347 B.C.), Greek philosopher, founder of the celebrated School of Athens.

Jeremy Taylor (1613–1667), English divine and writer.

Thomas Burnet (1635–1715), the English divine whose *Sacred Theory of the Earth* (1681) occasioned widespread comment on its fanciful structure of the earth.

[4] *laxis effertur habenis:* driven with loose reins.

[5] Sir John Davies (1569–1626), English poet and, in later life, fanatical prophet.

QUESTIONS

1. In what sense are Coleridge and Wordsworth complementary poets?

2. What may prose have in common with poetry, according to Coleridge?

3. How would you apply Coleridge's definition of poetry to modern poetry?

ON POETRY IN GENERAL

WILLIAM HAZLITT

When WILLIAM HAZLITT met Wordsworth, Southey, and
Coleridge, the poets then engaged in turning the tide of
English poetry away from artificial cleverness into the
expression of something essentially beautiful in terms that
common folk might understand, all of the fundamental
qualities of the man were stimulated—his independence,
his love of the solitary, his habit of analyzing abstract
questions and enjoying the battle over the conclusions. At
no better time could this lover of controversy have been
introduced into English literary circles. His essay "On
Poetry in General", here presented, and constituting the
reflections of one of the most brilliant bystanders of that
great upheaval, is one of the classics in critical writing.

THE best general notion which I can give of
poetry is, that it is the natural impression of any
object or event, by its vividness exciting an involuntary movement of imagination and passion,
and producing, by sympathy, a certain modulation of the voice, or sounds, expressing it.

In treating of poetry, I shall speak first of the
subject-matter of it, next of the forms of expression to which it gives birth, and afterwards of its
connection with harmony of sound.

Poetry is the language of the imagination and
the passions. It relates to whatever gives imme-

diate pleasure or pain to the human mind. It comes home to the bosoms and businesses of men; for nothing but what so comes home to them in the most general and intelligible shape, can be a subject for poetry. Poetry is the universal language which the heart holds with nature and itself. He who has a contempt for poetry, cannot have much respect for himself, or for any thing else. It is not a mere frivolous accomplishment, (as some persons have been led to imagine) the trifling amusement of a few idle readers or leisure hours—it has been the study and delight of mankind in all ages. Many people suppose that poetry is something to be found only in books, contained in lines of ten syllables with like endings: but wherever there is a sense of beauty, or power, or harmony, as in the motion of a wave of the sea, in the growth of a flower that "spreads its sweet leaves to the air and dedicates its beauty to the sun,"—*there* is poetry, in its birth. If history is a grave study, poetry may be said to be a graver: its materials lie deeper, and are spread wider. History treats, for the most part, of the cumbrous and unwieldy masses of things, the empty cases in which the affairs of the world are packed, under the heads of intrigue or war, in different states, and from century to century: but there is no thought or feeling that can have entered into the mind of man, which he would be eager to communicate to others, or which they would listen to with delight, that is not a fit subject for poetry.

It is not a branch of authorship: it is "the stuff of which our life is made." The rest is "mere oblivion," a dead letter: for all that is worth remembering in life, is the poetry of it. Fear is poetry, hope is poetry, love is poetry, hatred is poetry; contempt, jealousy, remorse, admiration, wonder, pity, despair, or madness, are all poetry. Poetry is that fine particle within us, that expands, rarefies, refines, raises our whole being: without it "man's life is poor as beast's." Man is a poetical animal: and those of us who do not study the principles of poetry, act upon them all our lives, like Molière's [1] *Bourgeois Gentilhomme,* who had always spoken prose without knowing it. The child is a poet in fact, when he first plays at hide-and-seek, or repeats the story of Jack the Giant-killer; the shepherd-boy is a poet, when he first crowns his mistress with a garland of flowers; the countryman, when he stops to look at the rainbow; the city-apprentice, when he gazes after the Lord-Mayor's show; the miser, when he hugs his gold; the courtier, who builds his hopes upon a smile; the savage, who paints his idol with blood; the slave, who worships a tyrant, or the tyrant, who fancies himself a god;—the vain, the ambitious, the proud, the choleric man, the hero and the coward, the beggar and the king, the rich and the poor, the young and the old, all live in a world of their own making; and the poet does no more than describe what all the others think and act. If his art is folly and madness, it is folly and madness at second hand. "There is warrant for it." Poets alone have not "such seething brains, such shaping fantasies, that apprehend more than cooler reason" can.

> The lunatic, the lover, and the poet
> Are of imagination all compact.
> One sees more devils than vast hell can hold;
> That is the madman. The lover, all as frantic,
> Sees Helen's beauty in a brow of Egypt.
> The poet's eye in a fine frenzy rolling,
> Doth glance from heav'n to earth, from earth to heav'n;
> And as imagination bodies forth
> The forms of things unknown, the poet's pen
> Turns them to shape, and gives to airy nothing
> A local habitation and a name.
> Such tricks hath strong imagination.

If poetry is a dream, the business of life is much the same. If it is a fiction, made up of what we wish things to be, and fancy that they are, because we wish them so, there is no other nor better reality. Ariosto [2] has described the loves of Angelica and Medoro: but was not Medoro, who carved the name of his mistress on the barks of trees, as much enamoured of her charms as he? Homer [3] has celebrated the anger of Achilles: but was not the hero as mad as the poet? Plato [4] banished the poets from his Commonwealth, lest their descriptions of the natural man should spoil his mathematical man, who was to be without passions and affections, who was neither to laugh nor weep, to feel sorrow nor anger, to be cast down nor elated by any thing. This was a chimera, however, which never existed but in the brain of the inventor; and Homer's poetical world has outlived Plato's philosophical Republic.

Poetry then is an imitation of nature, but the imagination and the passions are a part of man's nature. We shape things according to our wishes and fancies, without poetry; but poetry is the most emphatical language that can be found for those creations of the mind "which ecstacy is very cunning in." Neither a mere description of natural objects, nor a mere delineation of natural feelings, however distinct or forcible, constitutes the ultimate end and aim of poetry, without the imagination. The light of poetry is not only a direct but also a reflected light, that while it shows us the object, throws a sparking radiance on all around it: the flame of the passions, communicated to the imagination, reveals to us, as with a flash of lightning, the inmost recesses of thought, and penetrates our whole being. Poetry represents forms chiefly as they suggest other forms; feelings, as they suggest forms or other feelings. Poetry puts a spirit of life and motion into the universe. It describes the flowing, not the fixed. It does not define the limits of sense, or analyze the distinctions of the understanding, but signifies the excess of the imagination beyond the actual or ordinary impression of any object or feeling. The poetical impression of any object is that uneasy, exquisite sense of beauty of power that cannot be contained within itself; that is impatient of all limit; that (as flame bends to flame) strives to link itself to some other image of kindred beauty or grandeur; to enshrine itself, as it were, in the highest forms of fancy, and to relieve the aching sense of pleasure by expressing it in the boldest manner, and by the most striking examples of the same quality in other instances. Poetry, according to Lord Bacon,[5] for this reason "has something divine in it, because it raises the mind and hurries it into sublimity, by conforming the shows of things to the desires of the soul, instead of subjecting the soul to external things, as reason and history do." It is strictly the language of the imagination; and the imagination is that faculty which represents objects, not as they are in themselves, but as they are moulded by other thoughts and feelings, into an infinite variety of shapes and combinations of power. This language is not the less true to nature, because it is false in point of fact; but so much the more true and natural, if it conveys the impression which the object under the influence of passion makes on the mind. Let an object, for instance, be presented to the senses in a state of agitation or fear—and the imagination will distort or magnify the object, and convert it into the likeness of whatever is most proper to encourage the fear. "Our eyes are made the fools" of our other faculties. This is the universal law of the imagination,

That if it would but apprehend some joy,
It comprehends some bringer of that joy:
Or in the night imagining some fear,
How easy is a bush suppos'd a bear!

When Iachimo says of Imogen,[6]

The flame o' the taper
Bows toward her, and would under-peep her lids
To see the enclosed lights—

this passionate interpretation of the motion of the flame to accord with the speaker's own feelings, is true poetry. The lover, equally with the poet, speaks of the auburn tresses of his mistress as locks of shining gold, because the least tinge of yellow in the hair has, from novelty and a sense of personal beauty, a more lustrous effect to the imagination than the purest gold. We compare a man of gigantic stature to a tower: not that he is any thing like so large, but because the excess of his size beyond what we are accustomed to expect, or the usual size of things of the same class, produces by contrast a greater feeling of magnitude and ponderous strength than another object of ten times the same dimensions. The intensity of the feeling makes up for the disproportion of the objects. Things are equal to the imagination, which have the power of affecting the mind with an equal degree of terror, admiration, delight, or love. When Lear [7] calls upon the heavens to avenge his cause, "for they are old like him," there is nothing extravagant or impious in this sublime identification of his age with theirs; for there is no other image which could do justice to the agonising sense of his wrongs and his despair!

Poetry is the high-wrought enthusiasm of fancy and feelings. As in describing natural objects, it impregnates sensible impressions with the forms of fancy, so it describes the feelings of pleasure or pain, by blending them with the strongest movements of passion, and the most striking forms of nature. Tragic poetry, which is the most impassioned species of it, strives to carry on the feeling to the utmost point of sublimity or pathos, by all the force of comparison or contrast; loses the sense of present suffering in the imaginary exaggeration of it; exhausts the terror or pity by an unlimited indulgence of it; grapples with impossibilities in its desperate impatience of restraint; throws us back upon the past, forward into the future; brings every moment of our being or object of nature in startling review before us; and in the rapid whirl of events, lifts us from the depths of woe to the highest contemplations on human life. When Lear says, of Edgar, "Nothing but his unkind daughters could have brought him to this"; what a bewildered amazement, what a wrench of the imagination, that cannot be brought to conceive of any other cause of misery than that which has bowed it down, and absorbs all other sorrow in its own! His sorrow, like a flood, supplies the sources of all other sorrow. Again, when he exclaims in the mad scene, "The little dogs and all, Tray, Blanche, and Sweetheart, see, they bark at me!" it is passion lending occasion to imagination to make every creature in league against him, conjuring up ingratitude and insult in their least looked-for and most galling shapes, searching every thread and fibre of his heart, and finding out the last remaining image of respect or attachment in the bottom of his breast, only to torture and kill it! In like manner the "So I am" of Cordelia [8] gushes from her heart like a torrent of tears, relieving it of a weight of love and of supposed ingratitude, which had pressed upon it for years. What a fine return of the passion upon itself is that in Othello [9]—with what a mingled agony of regret and despair he clings to the last traces of departed happiness—when he exclaims,

> Oh now, for ever
> Farewell the tranquil mind. Farewell, content;
> Farewell the plumed troops and the big wars,
> That make ambition virtue! Oh! farewell!
> Farewell the neighing steed, and the shrill trump,
> The spirit-stirring drum, th' ear-piercing fife,
> The royal banner, and all quality,
> Pride, pomp, and circumstance of glorious war:
> And O you mortal engines, whose rude throats
> Th' immortal Jove's dread clamours counterfeit,
> Farewell! Othello's occupation's gone!

How his passion lashes itself up and swells and rages like a tide in its sounding course, when, in answer to the doubts expressed of his returning love, he says,

> Never, Iago. Like to the Pontic sea,
> Whose icy current and compulsive course
> Ne'er feels retiring ebb, but keeps due on
> To the Propontic and the Hellespont:
> Even so my bloody thoughts, with violent pace,
> Shall ne'er look back, ne'er ebb to humble love,
> Till that a capable and wide revenge
> Swallow them up.—

The climax of his expostulation afterwards with Desdemona is at that line,

> But there where I had garner'd up my heart,
> To be discarded thence!

One mode in which the dramatic exhibition of passion excites our sympathy without raising our disgust is, that in proportion as it sharpens the edge of calamity and disappointment, it strengthens the desire of good. It enhances our consciousness of the blessing, by making us sensible of the magnitude of the loss. The storm of passion lays bare and shews us the rich depths of the human soul: the whole of our existence, the sum total of our passions and pursuits, of that which we desire and that which we dread, is brought before us by contrast; the action and re-action are equal; the keenness of immediate suffering only gives us a more intense aspiration after, and a more intimate participation with the antagonist world of good;

makes us drink deeper of the cup of human life; tugs at the heart-strings; loosens the pressure about them; and calls the springs of thought and feeling into play with tenfold force.

Impassioned poetry is an emanation of the moral and intellectual part of our nature, as well as of the sensitive,—of the desire to know, the will to act, and the power to feel; and ought to appeal to these different parts of our constitution, in order to be perfect. The domestic or prose tragedy, which is thought to be the most natural, is in this sense the least so, because it appeals almost exclusively to one of these faculties, our sensibility. The tragedies of Moore and Lillo,[10] for this reason, however affecting at the time, oppress and lie like a dead weight upon the mind, a load of misery which it is unable to throw off: the tragedy of Shakespeare, which is true poetry, stirs our inmost affections; abstracts evil from itself by combining it with all the forms of imagination, and with the deepest workings of the heart, and rouses the whole man within us.

The pleasure, however, derived from tragic poetry, is not anything peculiar to it as poetry, as a fictitious and fanciful thing. It is not an anomaly of the imagination. It has its source and ground-work in the common love of strong excitement. As Mr. Burke[11] observes, people flock to see a tragedy; but if there were a public execution in the next street, the theatre would very soon be empty. It is not then the difference between fiction and reality that solves the difficulty. Children are satisfied with the stories of ghosts and witches in plain prose: nor do the hawkers of full, true, and particular accounts of murders and executions about the streets, find it necessary to have them turned into penny ballads, before they can dispose of these interesting and authentic documents. The grave politician drives a thriving trade of abuse and calumnies poured out against those whom he makes his enemies for no other end than that he may live by them. The popular preacher makes less frequent mention of heaven than of hell. Oaths and nicknames are only a more vulgar sort of poetry or rhetoric. We are as fond of indulging our violent passions as of reading a description of those of others. We are as prone to make a torment of our fears, as to luxuriate in our hopes of good. If it be asked, Why we do so? the best answer will be, Because we cannot help it. The sense of power is as strong a principle in the mind as the love of pleasure. Objects of terror and pity exercise the same despotic control over it as those of love or beauty. It is as natural to hate as to love, to despise as to admire, to express our hatred or contempt, as our love or admiration.

> Masterless passion sways us to the mood
> Of what it likes or loathes.

Not that we like what we loathe; but we like to indulge our hatred and scorn of it; to dwell

upon it, to exasperate our idea of it by every refinement of ingenuity and extravagance of illustration; to make it a bugbear to ourselves, to
point it out to others in all the splendour of deformity, to embody it to the senses, to stigmatise
it by name, to grapple with it in thought, in action,
to sharpen our intellect, to arm our will against
it, to know the worst we have to contend with,
and to contend with it to the utmost. Poetry is
only the highest eloquence of passion, the most
vivid form of expression that can be given to our
conception of any thing, whether pleasurable or
painful, mean or dignified, delightful or distressing. It is the perfect coincidence of the image and
the words with the feeling we have, and of which
we cannot get rid in any other way, that gives an
instant "satisfaction to the thought." This is
equally the origin of wit and fancy, of comedy
and tragedy, of the sublime and pathetic. When
Pope [12] says of the Lord Mayor's show,—

Now night descending, the proud scene is o'er,
But lives in Settle's numbers one day more!

when Collins [13] makes Danger, with "limbs of
giant mould,"

Throw him on the steep
Of some loose hanging rock asleep:

when Lear calls out in extreme anguish,

Ingratitude, thou marble-hearted fiend,
How much more hideous shew'st in a child
Than the sea-monster!

—the passion of contempt in the one case, of terror in the other, and of indignation in the last, is perfectly satisfied. We see the thing ourselves, and shew it to others as we feel it to exist, and as, in spite of ourselves, we are compelled to think of it. The imagination, by thus embodying and turning them to shape, gives an obvious relief to the indistinct and importunate cravings of the will.— We do not wish the thing to do so; but we wish it to appear such as it is. For knowledge is conscious power; and the mind is no longer, in this case, the dupe, though it may be the victim of vice or folly.

Poetry is in all its shapes the language of the imagination and the passions, of fancy and will. Nothing, therefore, can be more absurd than the outcry which has been sometimes raised by frigid and pedantic critics, for reducing the language of poetry to the standard of common sense and reason: for the end and use of poetry, "both at the first and now, was and *is* to hold the mirror up to nature," seen through the medium of passion and imagination, not divested of that medium by means of literal truth or abstract reason. The painter of history might as well be required to represent the face of a person who has just trod upon a serpent with the still-life expression of a common portrait, as the poet to describe the most striking and vivid impressions which things can be supposed to make upon the mind, in the language of common conversation. Let who will strip nature of the colours and the shapes of fancy, the poet is not bound to do so; the impressions of common sense and strong imagination, that is, of passion and indifference, cannot be the same, and they must have a separate language to do justice to either. Objects must strike differently upon the mind, independently of what they are in themselves, as long as we have a different interest in them, as we see them in a different point of view, nearer or at a greater distance (morally or physically speaking) from novelty, from old acquaintance, from our ignorance of them, from our fear of their consequences, from contrast, from unexpected likeness. We can no more take away the faculty of the imagination, than we can see all objects without light or shade. Some things must dazzle us by their preternatural light; others must hold us in suspense, and tempt our curiosity to explore their obscurity. Those who would dispel these various illusions, to give us their drab-coloured creation in their stead, are not very wise. Let the naturalist, if he will, catch the glow-worm, carry it home with him in a box, and find it next morning nothing but a little grey worm; let the poet or the lover of poetry visit it at evening, when beneath the scented hawthorn and the crescent moon it has built itself a palace of emerald light. This is also one part of nature, one appearance which the glow-worm presents, and that not the least interesting; so poetry is one part of the history of the human mind, though it is neither science nor philosophy. It cannot be concealed, however, that the progress of knowledge and refinement has a tendency to circumscribe the limits of the imagination, and to clip the wings of poetry. The province of the imagination is principally visionary, the unknown and undefined: the understanding restores things to their natural boundaries, and strips them of their fanciful pretensions. Hence the history of religious and poetical enthusiasm is much the same; and both have received a sensible shock from the progress of experimental philosophy. It is the undefined and uncommon that gives birth and scope to the imagination: we can only fancy what we do not know. As in looking into the mazes of a tangled wood we fill them with what shapes we please, with ravenous beasts, with caverns vast, and drear enchantments, so, in our ignorance of the world about us, we make gods or devils of the first object we see, and set no bounds to the wilful suggestions of our hopes and fears.

> And visions, as poetic eyes avow,
> Hang on each leaf and cling to every bough.

There can never be another Jacob's dream.[14] Since that time, the heavens have gone farther

off, and grown astronomical. They have become
averse to the imagination, nor will they return to
us on the squares of the distances, or on Doctor
Chalmers's Discourses.[15] Rembrandt's [16] picture
brings the matter nearer to us.— It is not only the
progress of mechanical knowledge, but the necessary advances of civilization that are unfavour-
able to the spirit of poetry. We not only stand in
less awe of the preternatural world, but we can
calculate more surely, and look with more indifference, upon the regular routine of this. The
heroes of the fabulous ages rid the world of mon-
sters and giants. At present we are less exposed
to the vicissitudes of good or evil, to the incur-
sions of wild beasts or "bandit fierce," or to the
unmitigated fury of the elements. The time has
been that "our fell of hair would at a dismal
treatise rouse and stir as life were in it." But the
police spoils all; and we now hardly so much as
dream of a midnight murder. *Macbeth* is only
tolerated in this country for the sake of the music;
and in the United States of America, where the
philosophical principles of government are carried still farther in theory and practice, we find
that the *Beggar's Opera* [17] is hooted from the
stage. Society, by degrees, is constructed into a
machine that carries us safely and insipidly from
one end of life to the other, in a very comfortable
prose style.

> Obscurity her curtain round them drew,
> And siren Sloth a full quietus sung.

The remarks which have been here made, would, in some measure, lead to a solution of the question of the comparative merits of painting and poetry. I do not mean to give any preference, but it should seem that the argument which has been some-times set up, that painting must affect the imagi-nation more strongly, because it represents the image more distinctly, is not well founded. We may assume without much temerity, that poetry is more poetical than painting. When artists or connoisseurs talk on stilts about the poetry of painting, they shew that they know little about poetry, and have little love for the art. Painting gives the object itself; poetry what it implies. Painting embodies what a thing contains in itself: poetry suggests what exists out of it, in any man-ner connected with it. But this last is the proper province of the imagination. Again, as it relates to passion, painting gives the event, poetry the progress of events: but it is during the progress, in the interval of expectation and suspense, while our hopes and fears are strained to the highest pitch of breathless agony, that the pinch of the interest lies

> Between the acting of a dreadful thing
> And the first motion, all the interim is
> Like a phantasma or a hideous dream.
> The mortal instruments are then in council;
> And the state of man, like to a little kingdom,
> Suffers then the nature of an insurrection.

But by the time that the picture is painted, all is over. Faces are the best part of a picture; but even faces are not what we chiefly remember in what interests us most.— But it may be asked then, Is there any thing better than Claude Lorrain's landscapes, than Titian's portraits, than Raphael's cartoons,[18] or the Greek statues? Of the two first I shall say nothing, as they are evidently picturesque, rather than imaginative. Raphael's cartoons are certainly the finest comments that ever were made on the Scriptures. Would their effect be the same if we were not acquainted with the text? But the New Testament existed before the cartoons. There is one subject of which there is no cartoon, Christ washing the feet of the disciples the night before his death. But that chapter does not need a commentary! It is for want of some such resting-place for the imagination that the Greek statues are little else than specious forms. They are marble to the touch and to the heart. They have not an informing principle within them. In their faultless excellence they appear sufficient to themselves. By their beauty they are raised above the frailties of passion or suffering. By their beauty they are deified. But they are not objects of religious faith to us, and their forms are a reproach to common humanity. They seem to have no sympathy with us, and not to want our admiration.

Poetry in its matter and form is natural imagery or feeling, combined with passion and fancy. In its mode of conveyance, it combines the ordinary use of language, with musical expression. There is a question of long standing in what the essence of poetry consists; or what it is that determines why one set of ideas should be expressed in prose, another in verse. Milton [19] has told us his idea of poetry in a single line—

> Thoughts that voluntary move
> Harmonious numbers.

As there are certain sounds that excite certain movements, and the song and dance go together, so there are, no doubt, certain thoughts that lead to certain tones of voice, or modulations of sound, and change "the words of Mercury into the songs of Apollo". There is a striking instance of this adaptation of the movement of sound and rhythm to the subject, in Spenser's description of the Satyrs accompanying Una to the cave of Sylvanus.

> So from the ground she fearless doth arise
>   And walketh forth without suspect of crime.
> They, all as glad as birds of joyous prime,
>   Thence lead her forth, about her dancing round,
> Shouting and singing all a shepherd's rhyme;
>   And with green branches strewing all the ground,
> Do worship her as queen with olive garland crown'd.
>
> And all the way their merry pipes they sound,
>   That all the woods with doubled echo ring;
> And with their horned feet do wear the ground,
>   Leaping like wanton kids in pleasant spring;
> So towards old Sylvanus they her bring,
>   Who, with the noise awaked, cometh out.
>
>   Faery Queen, book i. canto vi.

On the contrary, there is nothing either musical or natural in the ordinary construction of language. It is a thing altogether arbitrary and conventional. Neither in the sounds themselves, which are the voluntary signs of certain ideas, nor in their grammatical arrangements in common speech, is there any principle of natural imitation, or correspondence to the individual ideas, or to the tone of feeling with which they are conveyed to others. The jerks, the breaks, the inequalities, and harshnesses of prose are fatal to the flow of poetical imagination, as a jolting road or a stumbling horse disturbs the reverie of an absent man. But poetry makes these odds all even. It is the music of language, answering to the music of the mind, untying as it were "the secret soul of harmony." Wherever any object takes such a hold of the mind as to make us dwell upon it, and brood over it, melting the heart in tenderness, or kindling it to a sentiment of enthusiasm;—wherever a movement of imagination or passion is impressed on the mind, by which it seeks to prolong and repeat the emotion, to bring all other objects into accord with it, and to give the same movement of harmony, sustained and continuous, or gradually varied according to the occasion, to the sounds that express it—this is poetry. The musical in sound is the sustained and continuous; the musical in thought is the sustained and continuous also. There is a near connection between music and deep-rooted passion.

Mad people sing. As often as articulation passes naturally into intonation, there poetry begins. Where one idea gives a tone and colour to others, where one feeling melts others into it, there can be no reason why the same principle should not be extended to the sounds by which the voice utters these emotions of the soul, and blends syllables and lines into each other. It is to supply the inherent defect of harmony in the customary mechanism of language, to make the sound an echo to the sense, when the sense becomes a sort of echo to itself—to mingle the tide of verse, "the golden cadences of poetry," with the tide of feeling, flowing and murmuring as it flows—in short, to take the language of the imagination from off the ground, and enable it to spread its wings where it may indulge its own impulses—

> Sailing with supreme dominion
> Through the azure deep of air—

without being stopped, or fretted, or diverted with the abruptnesses and petty obstacles, and discordant flats and sharps of prose, that poetry was invented. It is to common language, what springs are to a carriage, or wings to feet. In ordinary speech we arrive at a certain harmony by the modulations of voice: in poetry the same thing is done systematically by a regular collocation of syllables. It has been well observed, that every one who declaims warmly, or grows intent upon a subject, rises into a sort of blank verse or measured prose. The merchant, as described in Chaucer,[20] went on his way "sounding always the increase of his winning." Every prose-writer has more or less of rhythmical adaptation, except poets, who, when deprived of the regular mechanism of verse, seem to have no principle of modulation left in their writings.

An excuse might be made for rhyme in the same manner. It is but fair that the ear should linger on the sounds that delight it, or avail itself of the same brilliant coincidence and unexpected recurrence of syllables, that have been displayed in the invention and collocation of images. It is allowed that rhyme assists the memory; and a man of wit and shrewdness has been heard to say, that the only four good lines of poetry are the well-known ones which tell the number of days in the months of the year.

Thirty days hath September, etc.

But if the jingle of names assists the memory, may it not also quicken the fancy? and there are other things worth having at our fingers' ends, besides the contents of the almanac.— Pope's versification is tiresome, from its excessive sweetness and uniformity. Shakespeare's blank verse is the perfection of dramatic dialogue.

All is not poetry that passes for such: nor does verse make the whole difference between poetry and prose. The Iliad does not cease to be poetry in a literal translation; and Addison's [21] *Campaign* has been very properly denominated a Gazette in rhyme. Common prose differs from poetry, as treating for the most part either of such trite, familiar, and irksome matters of fact, as convey no extraordinary impulse to the imagination, or else of such difficult and laborious processes of the understanding, as do not admit of the wayward or violent movements either of the imagination or the passions.

I will mention three works which come as near to poetry as possible without absolutely being so, namely, the *Pilgrim's Progress, Robinson Crusoe,* and the *Tales of Boccaccio.* Chaucer and Dryden [22] have translated some of the last into English rhyme, but the essence and the power of poetry was there before. That which lifts the spirit above the earth, which draws the soul out of itself with indescribable longings, is poetry in kind, and generally fit to become so in name, by being "married to immortal verse." If it is of the essence of poetry to strike and fix the imagination, whether we will or no, to make the eye of childhood glisten with the starting tear, to be never thought of afterwards with indifference, John Bunyan and Daniel Defoe may be permitted to pass for poets in their way. The mixture of fancy and reality in the *Pilgrim's Progress* was never equalled in any allegory. His pilgrims walk above the earth, and yet are on it. What zeal, what beauty, what truth of fiction! What deep feeling in the description of Christian's swimming across the water at last, and in the picture of the Shining Ones within the gates, with wings at their backs and garlands on their heads, who are to wipe all tears from his eyes! The writer's genius, though not "dipped in dews of Castalie," was baptised with the Holy Spirit and with fire. The prints in this book are no small part of it. If the confinement of Philoctetes in the island of Lemnos was a subject for the most beautiful of all the Greek tragedies, what shall we say to Robinson Crusoe in his? Take the speech of the Greek hero on leaving his cave, beautiful as it is, and compare it with the reflections of the English adventurer in his solitary place of confinement. The thoughts of home, and of all from which he is for ever cut off, swell and press against his bosom, as the heaving ocean rolls its ceaseless tide against the rocky shore, and the very beatings of his heart become audible in the eternal silence that surrounds him. Thus he says,

As I walked about, either in my hunting, or for viewing the country, the anguish of my soul at my condition would break out upon me on a sudden, and my very heart would die within me to think of the woods, the mountains, the deserts I was in; and how I was a prisoner, locked up with the eternal bars and bolts of the ocean, in an uninhabited wilderness, without redemption. In the midst of the greatest composures of my mind, this would break out upon me like a storm, and make me wring my hands, and weep like a child. Sometimes it would take me in the middle of my work, and I would immediately sit down and sigh, and look upon the ground for an hour or two together, and this was still worse to me, for if I could burst out into tears, or vent myself in words, it would go off, and the grief having exhausted itself would abate.

The story of his adventures would not make a poem like the Odyssey, it is true; but the relator had the true genius of a poet. It has been made a question whether Richardson's [23] romances are poetry; and the answer perhaps is, that they are not poetry, because they are not romances. The interest is worked up to an inconceivable height; but it is by an infinite number of little things, by incessant labour and calls upon the attention, by a repetition of blows that have no rebound in them. The sympathy excited is not a voluntary contribution, but a tax. Nothing is unforced and spontaneous. There is a want of elasticity and motion. The story does not "give an echo to the seat where love is throned." The heart does not answer of itself like a chord in music. The fancy does not run on before the writer with breathless expectation, but is dragged along with an infinite number of pins and wheels, like those with which the Lilliputians dragged Gulliver [24] pinioned to the royal palace.— Sir Charles Grandison is a coxcomb. What sort of figure would he cut translated into an epic poem, by the side of Achilles? Clarissa, the divine Clarissa, [25] is too interesting by half. She is interesting in her ruffles, in her gloves, her samplers, her aunts and uncles—she is interesting in all that is uninteresting. Such things, however intensely they may be brought home to us, are not conductors to the imagination. There is infinite truth and feeling in Richardson; but it is extracted from a *caput mortuum*[26] of circumstances: it does not evaporate of itself. His poetical genius is like Ariel[27] confined in a pine-tree, and requires an artificial process to let it out. Shakespeare says—

> Our posey is as a gum
> Which issues whence 'tis nourished, our gentle flame
> Provokes itself, and like the current flies
> Each bound it chafes.

I shall conclude this general account with some remarks on four of the principal works of poetry in the world, at different periods of history—Homer, the Bible, Dante,[28] and let me add, Ossian.[29] In Homer, the principle of action or life is predominant; in the Bible, the principle of faith and the idea of Providence; Dante is a personification of blind will; and in Ossian we see the decay of life, and the lag end of the world. Homer's poetry is the heroic: it is full of life and action: it is bright as the day, strong as a river. In the vigour of his intellect, he grapples with all the objects of nature, and enters into all the relations of social life. He saw many countries, and the manners of many men; and he has brought them all together in his poem. He describes his heroes going to battle with a prodigality of life, arising from an exuberance of animal spirits: we see them before us, their number, and their order of battle, poured out upon the plain, "all plumed like ostriches, like eagles newly bathed, wanton as goats, wild as young bulls, youthful as May, and gorgeous as the sun at midsummer," covered with glittering armour, with dust and blood; while the Gods quaff their nectar in golden cups, or mingle in the fray; and the old men assembled on the walls of Troy rise up with reverence as Helen passes by them. The multitude of things in Homer is wonderful; their splendour, their truth, their force, and variety. His poetry is, like his religion, the poetry of number and form: he describes the bodies as well as the souls of men.

The poetry of the Bible is that of imagination and of faith: it is abstract and disembodied: it is not the poetry of form, but of power; not of multitude, but of immensity. It does not divide into many, but aggrandizes into one. Its ideas of nature are like its ideas of God. It is not the poetry of social life, but of solitude: each man seems alone in the world with the original forms of nature, the rocks, the earth, and the sky. It is not the poetry of action or heroic enterprise, but of faith in a supreme Providence, and resignation to the power that governs the universe. As the idea of God was removed farther from humanity, and a scattered polytheism, it became more profound

and intense as it became more universal, for the
Infinite is present to every thing: "If we fly into
the uttermost parts of the earth, it is there also;
if we turn to the east or the west, we cannot escape from it." Man is thus aggrandized in the
image of his Maker. The history of the patriarchs
is of this kind; they are founders of the chosen
race of people, the inheritors of the earth; they
exist in the generations which are to come after
them. Their poetry, like their religious creed, is
vast, unformed, obscure, and infinite; a vision is
upon it—an invisible hand is suspended over it.
The spirit of the Christian religion consists in the
glory hereafter to be revealed; but in the Hebrew
dispensation, Providence took an immediate share
in the affairs of this life, Jacob's dream arose out
of this intimate communion between heaven and
earth: it was this that let down, in the sight of
the youthful patriarch, a golden ladder from the
sky to the earth, with angels ascending and descending upon it, and shed a light upon the lonely
place, which can never pass away. The story of
Ruth,[30] again, is as if all the depth of natural
affection in the human race was involved in her
breast. There are descriptions in the book of Job
more prodigal of imagery, more intense in passion,
than anything in Homer, as that of the state of
his prosperity, and of the vision that came upon
him by night. The metaphors in the Old Testament are more boldly figurative. Things were col-

lected more into masses, and gave a greater momentum to the imagination.

Dante was the father of modern poetry, and he may therefore claim a place in this connection. His poem is the first great step from Gothic darkness and barbarism; and the struggle of thought in it to burst the thraldom in which the human mind had been so long held, is felt in every page. He stood bewildered, not appalled, on that dark shore which separates the ancient and the modern world; and saw the glories of antiquity dawning through the abyss of time, while revelation opened its passage to the other world. He was lost in wonder at what had been done before him, and he dared to emulate it. Dante seems to have been indebted to the Bible for the gloomy tone of his mind, as well as for the prophetic fury which exalts and kindles his poetry; but he is utterly unlike Homer. His genius is not a sparking flame, but the sullen heat of a furnace. He is power, passion, self-will personified. In all that relates to the descriptive or fanciful part of poetry, he bears no comparison to many who had gone before, or who have come after him; but there is a gloomy abstraction in his conceptions, which lies like a dead weight upon the mind; a benumbing stupor, a breathless awe, from the intensity of the impression; a terrible obscurity, like that which oppresses us in dreams; an identity of interest, which moulds every object to its own purposes, and clothes all things with the passions and imagi-

nations of the human soul,—that make amends
for all other deficiencies. The immediate objects
he presents to the mind are not much in themselves, they want grandeur, beauty, and order;
but they become every thing by the force of the
character he impresses upon them. His mind lends
its own power to the objects which it contemplates, instead of borrowing it from them. He
takes advantage even of the nakedness and
dreary vacuity of his subject. His imagination
peoples the shades of death, and broods over the
silent air. He is the severest of all writers, the
most hard and impenetrable, the most opposite to
the flowery and glittering; who relies most on
his own power, and the sense of it in others, and
who leaves most room to the imagination of his
readers. Dante's only endeavour is to interest;
and he interests by exciting our sympathy with
the emotion by which he is himself possessed. He
does not place before us the objects by which that
emotion has been created; but he seizes on the
attention, by shewing us the effect they produce
on his feelings; and his poetry accordingly gives
the same thrilling and overwhelming sensation,
which is caught by gazing on the face of a person
who has seen some object of horror. The improbability of the events, the abruptness and
monotony in the Inferno, are excessive: but the
interest never flags, from the continued earnestness of the author's mind. Dante's great power is
in combining internal feelings with external ob-

jects. Thus the gate of hell, on which that withering inscription is written, seems to be endowed with speech and consciousness, and to utter its dread warning, not without a sense of mortal woes. This author habitually unites the absolutely local and individual with the greatest wildness and mysticism. In the midst of the obscure and shadowy regions of the lower world, a tomb suddenly rises up with the inscription, "I am the tomb of Pope Anastasius the Sixth": and half the personages whom he has crowded into the Inferno are his own acquaintance. All this, perhaps, tends to heighten the effect by the bold intermixture of realities, and by an appeal, as it were, to the individual knowledge and experience of the reader. He affords few subjects for picture. There is, indeed, one gigantic one, that of Count Ugolino, of which Michael Angelo made a bas-relief, and which Sir Joshua Reynolds [31] ought not to have painted.

Another writer whom I shall mention last, and whom I cannot persuade myself to think a mere modern in the groundwork, is Ossian. He is a feeling and a name that can never be destroyed in the minds of his readers. As Homer is the first vigour and lustihead, Ossian is the decay and old age of poetry. He lives only in the recollection and regret of the past. There is one impression which he conveys more entirely than all other poets, namely, the sense of privation, the loss of all things, of friends, of good name, of country—

Irish poet and essayist who later became a dean in the Church.

²⁵ In *Clarissa Harlowe* by Samuel Richardson, written in letter form.

²⁶ *Caput Mortuum* is a dead head.

²⁷ Ariel was the spiritlike character in Shakespeare's *The Tempest*.

²⁸ Dante Alighieri (1265–1321), Italian poet, author of the *Divine Comedy*.

²⁹ Ossian, or Oisin, was the supposed author of a body of third-century Celtic poetry. Macpherson, eighteenth-century writer, built up a convincing "Life" of Ossian which Doctor Johnson denounced.

³⁰ The Book of Ruth in the Bible, an allegory against forced divorce, is one of the world's best short stories.

³¹ Michael Angelo Buonarroti (1475–1564), one of the great masters of the Italian Renaissance, painter, sculptor, architect.

Sir Joshua Reynolds (1723–1792), English portrait painter, head of the Royal Academy, and member of Doctor Samuel Johnson's literary club.

QUESTIONS

1. How does poetry, through its very nature, come close to the hearts of people? How does it differ from mathematics in this respect? From history?

2. How does Hazlitt's comment on the poetry of the Bible compare with De Quincey's analysis of literature of knowledge and literature of power?

3. Compare Hazlitt's paragraph on tragic poetry with Aristotle's definition of tragedy.

4. What definitions of poetry can you derive from this essay of Hazlitt's?